DEAREST CHILD

Letters between Queen Victoria and the Princess Royal

1858-1861

The Princess Royal, after a painting by Winterhalter

DEAREST CHILD

*Letters between Queen Victoria
and the Princess Royal*

1858-1861

Edited by

ROGER FULFORD

HOLT, RINEHART AND WINSTON

NEW YORK   CHICAGO   SAN FRANCISCO

Library of Congress Catalog Card Number: 65-14228

Grateful acknowledgment for the use of photographs in
this book is due Prince Wolfgang of Hesse, Radio Times
Holton Picture Library, and the Royal Archives at
Windsor by gracious permission of Her Majesty
The Queen.

First published in the United States, March, 1965

82959-0115
Printed in the United States of America

CONTENTS

ILLUSTRATIONS

PREFACE

I should like to express my particular obligation to Mr. David Duff. Whilst engaged at Friedrichshof on research for his biography of Princess Beatrice, *The Shy Princess*, he did preliminary work on this correspondence. He saw that the early letters of Queen Victoria to her eldest daughter would make a very interesting book and arranged with the Princes of Hesse that certain volumes of the letters should be sent to this country. He has generously allowed me to build on these foundations. For this I express my deep gratitude.

Prince Philip, Landgrave of Hesse, who is the owner of Queen Victoria's letters to the Empress Frederick, allowed me to work on the bound volumes of the letters in this country. I thank him most sincerely for entrusting them to me and for giving me permission to edit and publish them. He and his brothers, Prince Wolfgang and Prince Richard, have generously entertained me at Kronberg and given me every possible encouragement. They have helped me to unravel countless abstruse passages and steered me away from many insular prejudices about their forbears and about the Royal Family of Prussia. I wish to acknowledge my great debt to them with respectful gratitude.

By gracious permission of Her Majesty the Queen I have been able to consult and use the letters of the Empress in reply to those of Queen Victoria; these letters are in the Royal Archives at Windsor. Her Majesty, as owner of the copyright of Queen Victoria's letters, has in addition given gracious permission for their publication in this book.

At every turn and in all difficulties I have availed myself of the ungrudging help and guidance given to me by the Queen's Librarian, Mr. Mackworth-Young. I am truly grateful to him, and to Miss Price-Hill and Miss Langton of the Royal Archives.

I should like to thank Miss Paddon, who was the assistant Director of Education for Westmorland, and helped me with some of the German passages, and also Mr. D. E. W. Morgan, who came over from Giggleswick School to translate other passages. Mr. Laurence Irving put his exceptional knowledge of the Victorian stage at my service, and Mr. Martin Cooper gave me valuable guidance over nineteenth-century musicians and operas. I used the valuable Enthoven Collection at the Victoria and Albert Museum to verify some particulars about the theatre. Mr. Robert Cecil saved me from several bad mistakes over the Berlin palaces and the Prussian Royal Family. Lady Longford read the typescript and gave me much helpful material for the notes.

The staff of the London Library and the Librarian, Mr. Stanley Gillam, have spared no trouble to find books and information for me and have, as always, made me undyingly grateful for my membership of the London Library. Miss Kay Hallett typed impeccably what proved to be a complicated and difficult manuscript.

I am well aware of the long-suffering patience shown by my publishers, to whom I express my thanks. Miss Audrey White, of Evans Brothers, has worked on the text with care and devotion.

August 1963   ROGER FULFORD

INTRODUCTION

"Nobody writes letters nowadays." "The art of letter-writing is dead." How used we have grown to such lamentations in the twentieth century! A hundred years ago the habit or the art (as the reader cares to regard it) flourished magnificently. For our well-to-do forbears used the pen, as a means of communication, almost as much as the mouth. In London, notes flew between the houses of Mayfair and Belgravia: in the country, mornings were given up to letter-writing, while in the background statesmen, professional men and city merchants wrote letters on all topics of their lives—trifling or portentous. The letters of leading men and women of the time have been treasured by posterity, but it is difficult to say how much correspondence of ordinary people has survived the awful hazard of an executor's bonfire. Possibly not very much: certainly very little complete correspondence with letters and answers intact. In consequence searchers have to look rather closely at the shelves of any library before they can draw out a collection of letters which reveals domestic life in the nineteenth century—habits, manners and feelings with the fidelity of, say, the letters written by Dorothy Osborne to Sir William Temple in the seventeenth century. The overriding interest of the correspondence in this book is that it reveals those feelings and carries the reader back to the very heart of Victorian life.

This book consists of the unpublished letters written by Queen Victoria to her eldest daughter, the Princess Royal, afterwards German Empress and mother of the Kaiser. It also includes a number of the Princess's letters in reply to those from her mother. The Queen wrote at least twice a week, and her daughter almost as frequently. They kept up this stream of letters for forty years. All of them have survived. The Princess wrote to her mother that she had never had a correspondence which she enjoyed so much because "it is so natural and like thinking aloud". While it would have been possible to make a book of the outstanding letters on both sides or of the letters dealing with the famous episodes of those four decades, I decided against this. I thought it would be of greater interest to readers (and of greater value to students) to give a much narrower selection from the correspondence over a very few years so that attention can be concentrated on the interests and occupations of the Queen. The reader can follow her daily life with that almost affectionate attention to detail which distinguished Gulliver's observations on the Emperor of Lilliput. A selection from a correspondence which jumps the reader from decade to decade is inevitably distracting. This selection from the letters therefore begins in January 1858: it ends in December 1861, with the death of the Prince Consort.

The history of the correspondence is somewhat curious. At irregular intervals the Princess had the letters from both her parents mounted and bound in half leather, and kept them at Berlin, moving them after the Emperor Frederick's death to Friedrichshof, the house which she built as a memorial to him at Kronberg in the Taunus mountains, north of Frankfurt. Her letters to her father and mother were bound in full morocco and kept at Windsor. When the official biography of the Prince Consort was being written she sent to the author, Sir Theodore Martin, the letters from her father. They were written in German, and translations of many of them will be found in that biography. The originals were then returned to her. Some time before her death the Empress must have asked Queen Victoria to lend her the bound volumes of her own letters, and these were sent out to her at Friedrichshof from Windsor. She no doubt refreshed her memory with them, and realised that there was a great deal in them to distress and pain the Kaiser. When the Empress was dying, King Edward came to see her at Friedrichshof and brought Sir Frederick

Ponsonby with him as his private secretary. Ponsonby seems to have gained the impression that the Empress wanted these letters taken back to Windsor after her death. The circumstances in which he achieved this are described, with dramatic exaggeration, in his book—*Letters of the Empress Frederick*, published in 1928. His decision to publish these letters—though it led to a valuable book—was indeed strange and distressed the ex-Kaiser, who was then living in exile at Doorn. The decision to publish was also ill-received by members of the English Royal Family. The Kaiser himself wrote an introduction to the German edition of the book. Only one letter—the excellent one describing the King of Prussia's death—was used by Sir Frederick from the years covered by this book. Although it will be found there I have decided to include it.

At her death the Empress made her youngest daughter, the Landgravine of Hesse, who inherited Friedrichshof and its contents, her literary executor. Queen Victoria's letters remained there in her custody. They were not apparently seen, and certainly not used, by the editors of Queen Victoria's letters—possibly because they were regarded as too personal. The only letters which they used are the ones describing the King of Prussia's death, which the Queen had had copied at the time, and the one describing the coronation of King William I.

Although the letters were in the custody of the Landgravine, the copyright, as is the case with all Queen Victoria's writings, remained with the English Sovereign. At the close of the war in 1945, the Landgravine was turned out of her home by the Americans in a somewhat unfeeling fashion. King George VI sent out his librarian, Sir Owen Morshead, who, with the consent of the Landgravine, brought the letters back to Windsor for safe custody. The Landgravine had always felt that the character of her mother, overpainted in sombre colours, had never been fairly drawn, and after some years she asked that the letters might be sent back for the use of Count Corti who wrote the Empress's life. Some short passages from the letters of 1858–1861, amounting to rather less than 200 lines, will be found in Count Corti's book and rather more in the original version in German. The book was published in Germany under the title *Wenn*, and in England in 1957 by Messrs. Cassell as *The English Empress*.

I should like to explain the methods I have used in selecting and editing the letters for the years I have chosen. It was impossible to consider publishing the letters in full, even for this brief period. There are more than 300,000 words in the Queen's letters alone. I have in consequence had to exclude two-thirds of them. I have accordingly left out almost all the Balmoral letters, accounts of the weather, repetitions, things which seemed of purely transitory interest and those personal matters about which any mother would be expected to write to her young, married daughter. I have left out the beginning and ending of almost all the letters. The Queen began with either "My Beloved Child" or "My Dearest Child" and ended with "Ever your devoted Mama V.R." I have left in most of the Queen's references to political matters, though these are meagre because such things were covered by the correspondence between the Princess and her father. I have tried to retain the heart of the correspondence, revealing the life of the Queen, her interests and preoccupations.

I was tempted to leave in the characteristic nineteenth-century underlinings of the Queen, but the expense of doing this was considerable and the effect of a page constantly broken up by italics is not attractive. Readers will accept the fact that the Queen, as ever, underlined freely and indiscriminately. The Queen's handwriting is extremely difficult to decipher. I cannot hope that I have got every word right, but I can at least claim that I have spent a long time puzzling over every word and phrase which seemed dubious. The Queen fairly frequently used a French word or phrase which I have left. She sometimes used German. Where she merely uses a German phrase or word to repeat or emphasise what she has said in English I have sometimes (though not always) left it out. Where the German word or phrase conveys a new idea I have translated it—though without indicating that it was German. Gemütlich, meaning comfortable, and unberufen, meaning touch wood, are favourite words of the Queen which I have left as written. I have not always followed the Queen's use of capitals: I have sometimes altered her punctuation: I have practically never followed her use of abbreviations. She never, for example, wrote "and" in full. In all these matters I have been governed by a single consideration—the convenience of the reader.

The annotation of the letters was a more difficult problem. I have decided against a linking narrative between the letters chiefly because it interrupts the flow of the book, but partly because I personally find that by the time I come to a difficult passage I have completely forgotten what was said in the narrative. I have accordingly left the whole of the text of the book to the letters, preferring to explain them at the instant of ambiguity by a foot-note. Readers who are repelled by the sight of foot-notes can ignore them: those who glance at the notes will, in my judgment, find their appreciation of the letters enhanced.

Many readers will doubtless find the notes excessive, others will lament that there were not many more. To all those I can only apologise. I have simply used the notes where, in my opinion, the average reader would miss the point of what is being said. I hope that I have nowhere slipped into the mistake of seeming to nudge the reader and say: "This is a fine passage: for goodness sake do not miss it."

The fussiness of an editor can be maddening. But in one particular I am very conscious that I have been guilty of fussiness—that is over the innumerable princes and princesses who, not always gracefully, flit in and out of the letters. I sympathise with the courtier, Lord Hervey, who was furious when he had to listen to a lecture from his royal master, King George II, on the connexions of the Count Palatine of Sulzbach. Many readers will no doubt say with Lord Rosebery: "Why should we bother about these people: they led lives as dull as those of the carp in their own stewponds." But we must strive to rise above the prejudices of our ancient aristocracy, for Queen Victoria was greatly concerned by these matters. Had she not to find brides and bridegrooms for eight other royal children? I think the reader will be surprised by the astonishing knowledge of all these minor continental potentates shown by the island queen. Again I felt that the reader, especially in the later part when the choice of a bride for the Prince of Wales is under discussion, would miss much of the force of the correspondence without some guidance from the editor over these personages.

In the index but not in the notes I have briefly identified people to be found in any standard English book of reference. For this and the notes I have used the standard books of reference, and particularly the *Dictionary of National Biography* and the royal lineage in *Burke's Peerage*—and possibly it would not be unfair to say that both works are accustomed to usage rather than an expression of gratitude. For reasons of space I have given at the beginning a list of the Christian or familiar names used by the Queen and Princess so as to save constantly identifying them by foot-notes. In the foot-notes I always refer to the Princess as the Princess Royal and to her husband as Prince Frederick William. I felt it essential to refer to each of them specifically so as to avoid confusing the reader with the multitude of princes and princesses ("legions of Fritz's" the Prince Consort called them) and particularly the Prince and Princess of Prussia—Prince Frederick William's parents.

I have used some of the Princess Royal's letters in the text, placing them in their chronological order with those of the Queen. Some more I have used in the notes to explain a passage in letters from the Queen. They give meaning to the letters of the Queen. I have also used one or two letters from the Princess to her father to illustrate the relationship between father and daughter. How often when we read the collected letters of a notability we long for the answers, to know the effect of what is being said. There is a children's song which describes the joys of being able to hollow down an empty water-butt. Reading a selection of letters without the answers is not dissimilar from that innocent, childish pastime: we hear exactly what is being said but the force of it vanishes in a strange, hollow echo. The inclusion of the Princess Royal's answers to her mother's letters brings the correspondence to reality and life, for we are able to share the feelings of the recipient and to know that, when the letters were written, they went on their way with something more to them than a meaningless echo.

On both sides the correspondence is massive. In the period covered by this book, that is to say from January 1858, when the Princess married, to December 1861, when her father died, there are eight bound volumes of her letters to the Queen. (She also wrote to her father with regularity and there are four volumes of her letters to him.) On her side the Queen wrote to her daughter twice a week and for the same period there are thirteen bound volumes of her letters. She wrote on four-sided writing paper—always uniform in size—7 in. by $4\frac{1}{2}$ in. The first sheet often had an attractive lithograph of the place from which she was writing, Balmoral, Windsor, Osborne, Aldershot—though never Buckingham Palace. The subsequent sheets were plain, though sometimes she used a cipher of her initials entwined with those of the Prince Consort. She seldom used less than three of these four-sided sheets of paper and sometimes as many as five or six. It is a mighty and impressive testimony to the energy of the Queen and to her devotion to her daughter. While it is true that Queen Victoria never had to waste a second in the house doing anything for herself (even the doors were opened for her and she went straight to her writing table knowing that everything would be perfectly ready for her to dip her quill-pen in the ink) her output of words is astonishing, remembering that she was writing regularly to her uncle in Brussels, that she wrote up her journal at length and that she was burdened by a pressing official correspondence and all the exacting official functions of the Sovereign.

Her hand-writing could be called vehement, but in all thirteen volumes she hardly makes a slip of the pen. The present writer would be surprised if there are ten times when she leaves a word out by mistake, and the times when she makes a spelling mistake are less even than that. She was quick to pounce on such things in her daughter's letters: "I must tell you that you have mis-spelt some words several times, which you must attend to, for if others saw it, it might make them think you did not attend to orthography and had not been taught well. You wrote in 2 letters—appeal and appreciate each with one p."[1] The Queen's punctuation is uncertain: she puts down her thoughts with rapidity, in the fashion that most of us speak—qualifying or expanding what she has said with additions inside brackets or parentheses. And like all who talk freely the Queen seems at times carried away in the rush of volubility saying more than she intended and often more than she would have said on reflection. This spontaneity—tinged with indiscretion—is one of the secrets of Queen Victoria's charm as a letter writer.

She wrote in the knowledge that her letters might be read in the continental post-offices, and she therefore distinguishes between a letter going by messenger and one going by post. She used a device with silver paper to make it difficult for the envelope to be opened and unstuck by censorious fingers. It is clear that the contents of private letters were often gratefully received, through post-office spies, in foreign royal palaces. Consequently the Queen's letters through the post refer cryptically to individuals, often she uses merely an initial.

The Queen's letters from Balmoral and Osborne are written with noticeably less haste: they are perhaps less interesting, for she dwells much on topographical details and particulars of the lives of her younger children. At Windsor and Buckingham Palace the Queen seems in the mid-stream of business, society and official life—and the sparkle of the stream is fully reflected in the letters. Almost one half of the Queen's letters is written on paper edged with black. We can picture the servant changing the plain paper for the black-edged, and then the Queen coming in, settling down at the table and starting, almost triumphantly, to write to her daughter: "Here we are again in

---

[1] March 31, 1858.

mourning for a dear relation." But grief was conquered by anniversaries and when writing a birthday letter to her daughter the Queen invariably left off the mourning paper. After the dark shadow of December '61 such niceties of feeling were no longer possible for the Queen.

In these letters the Queen is completely herself, revealing her inner feelings with confidence and without restraint. The moment her daughter married, childhood and the discipline of family life fell away. The Queen felt that in the married girl of 17 she had at once a confidante to whom she could pour out not only everything that happened but her private feelings about the family, even about the Prince Consort, and those physical details of existence which most nineteenth-century parents could only discuss with their children with repugnance. Marriage transformed everything: it was the grand equaliser. We notice it at once. The Princess had only known the Duchess of Kent as the tender mother of the Queen, the respected but over-indulgent grandmother at Frogmore or Clarence House. Writing a few weeks after her daughter's marriage the Queen reveals how miserably different her relations had once been with the Duchess. She had obviously never given her children the slightest inkling of this: she can hardly wait for her daughter's comments and she writes a few days later, evidently longing to hear what the Princess has to say: "Now do enter into this in your letters."

The interest of the letters is enhanced and fortified by the clear picture which they give of family life in Buckingham Palace, Windsor Castle and Berlin and by the sudden irruption into their decorous flow of political struggles and sounds of war. But the reader's attention will be drawn to the feelings of the woman and the girl—so clearly revealed in the letters of each—reminding us of the morality, the prejudices and the dignity of Victorian life and perhaps correcting some myths about it on which we have been nurtured. For Queen Victoria in particular has the power, undiminished by time, of compelling the reader to share her feelings. As we read her letters we are convinced by her that all babies are hideous, that foreigners need never be ill if only they would take aperients, that German princesses are always restless, that no mother in history was ever so ill-used as she was in not being allowed to go to Berlin for the birth of her first grandchild, and that the quickest road to the grave is a hot room. The effect of her eloquence may wear off, but while we are under its spell, who dare raise an eyebrow?

When Queen Victoria married she withdrew into the citadel of family life which consisted of the Prince, her children and, by degrees, her mother. Members of the court, in their turn, were admitted to this private existence and, long before the Prince Consort died, she was critical and resentful of those outside—even of other members of the Royal Family. This explains her strictures on her aunt, the Duchess of Cambridge, and her two daughters, the Cambridge princesses Augusta and Mary. They stood for those worldly frivolities which the Queen had once enjoyed with them, but from which she had been rescued by her husband. She was fond of her Cambridge relations (especially Princess Mary) but they stood for a less high-minded, less respectable way of life than that which prevailed in Buckingham Palace and Windsor Castle. She looked on them with the cold, unfeeling glance of the rector as he passes the bright glitter of the "Ring o' Bells". One consequence of this withdrawal was important. The Queen longed for a comfortable friendship with people of her own sex. Apart from one or two courtiers like the Duchess of Sutherland, whom she had known from her earliest days—and there were obvious difficulties about being too much with them when they were out of waiting—the Queen was lonely except for the family within the citadel. Her feelings for friendship with her own sex have been captured by Winterhalter in "The Cousins" where she is depicted with the Duchess of Nemours who, unfortunately for the Queen, died young. It is clear from this correspondence that the Prince Consort, greatly preoccupied with politics, the family and the court was less of a companion to the Queen, when they were at London or at Windsor, than is often imagined. There was a void in the Queen's life which was filled, at the instant of her marriage, by the young Princess. The letter-writing, which many people would regard as a burden, became at once to the Queen "our dear correspondence".

The reader will therefore see in this true perspective the observations which the Queen makes about her other children. As her letters were clearly not seen by the Prince Consort it is not absolutely certain that she intended all of them to be read by the Princess's husband. She prefaces something she has to say about the Prince of Wales— "Don't mention this to a human being" (March 8, '58). Many people might reasonably feel that these family judgments, intended to be private, should be still excluded from public notice. But they are now known from many other sources: they explain the Queen's intense anxiety about the choice of a wife for the Prince of Wales which fills much of the later part of this correspondence; and they show in the clearest way how the Queen trusted her daughter and used this correspondence as an outlet for all her most private feelings. "It is such proof of my confidence when I speak to you so openly about your brothers." And it is fair to add that one of the reasons why she felt so strongly on these family matters was lest, through her children, those things of which she and the Prince Consort intensely disapproved should find their way to the citadel of the royal family life.

There was, of course, an element of iron in the Queen's character: she never appears to put herself in her daughter's place and think what might be the effect of some of the things she has to say on the young girl a thousand miles from home. But that impatience, that indignation with what she can not understand is the flaw in the Queen's nature which the critics will censure but others will understand. As a skilled biographer of old has advised: "Nay, scars and blemishes, as well as beauties ought to be expressed; otherwise, it is but an outline filled up with lilies and roses."

To the gifts of the partner in this royal correspondence history has scarcely done justice. Queen Victoria's eldest daughter, the Princess Royal, was the most remarkable English princess of modern history—certainly since the Hanoverian dynasty arrived in England. She had the political acumen of her father with all the impetuosity of her mother: moreover the Princess had an understanding of literature and the Arts which alone made her conspicuous among the princesses of her day.

The present writer was privileged to see the library of English books formed by the Empress Frederick. It is an interesting collection. In it are to be found the influential books on politics and economics of the middle decades of the nineteenth century, preserved in all their cloth magnificence from sun and dust—but read. They include Jowett's *Dialogues of Plato*, Walter Bagehot's *Literary Studies*, Mill's works, the *Essays of the Cobden Club*, Dilke's *Problems of Greater Britain*, together with all the standard books of political history and biography. She possessed almost all Thackeray's first editions, collected before marriage, the Aldis Wright Shakespeare and Dean Plumptre's *Dante*, with its dedication sonnet to her, in which she was placed with the goodly band of those who read and understand Dante. She also had a remarkable library of mid-nineteenth-century books on the Arts. We are hardly surprised to know that she was the only royal person to show an interest in Karl Marx during his life-time. There was something moving about this great storehouse of learning, a don's library alive with all the optimism of the Victorians, entombed in the gloom of a Berlin schloss. We can picture the Empress reading her books to herself and occasionally to her husband. Who else, in that distant city, cared? She was the cleverest member of the English Royal Family since the days of her distant ancestress, Queen Caroline, whom in many particulars she resembled. But the Queen was lucky. She found in her adopted country (though not in her husband King George II) a circle of wits and intellectuals who genuinely admired and encouraged her. Her descendant lacked that consolation and stimulus. When we realise the gifts of her mind we sense the reality of her sorrows.

Her powers will not of course be judged by the letters in this book—for she is immature, a school-girl passing along the road to maternity. But some of her comments will touch sensitive readers and arrest their attention. Sometimes her views may strike readers as sententious and even priggish, but these are explained by her youth, and by her feeling that she was an emissary from the citadel of Queen Victoria's family to convert others to the high principles which flourished there. "You are a star of light and hope in the midst of darkness," wrote her mother some weeks after her marriage.

Married to a prince who was gentle, intelligent, well-educated and humane she seemed destined for a commanding rôle in the history of central Europe. But for this Prince and Princess was reserved the harshest of fates. They were perpetual apprentices to power. For thirty years they occupied the second place, unable to obstruct policies which they detested. When at last they moved to the first place as German Emperor and Empress, the Emperor Frederick was doomed to die from cancer of the throat within three months of his accession. All the grandeur and the high hopes of 1858 died fruitless in 1888. "The tragedy for my poor child is too ghastly"—wrote Queen Victoria—"much worse even than mine in 1861." By the last few words she meant that the influence, the work, the position and indeed the usefulness of the Empress died with her husband. Her son—the Kaiser—relentlessly pushed her into the shadows.

Moreover she had two essential elements for tragedy—the power to feel acutely and the sense to see what was happening. If her fate had befallen her mother-in-law, the Empress Augusta, the wife of the Emperor William I, we should have felt moved but comforted by knowing that she would have found consolation in religion and in an endless round of social engagements. If her fate had befallen her daughter-in-law, the wife of Kaiser William II, "poor little insignificant Princess"—the words are Queen Victoria's—we should have felt for her the compassion which we feel for any helpless victim of spitefulness and cruelty. But it was just because the Empress Frederick scorned the easy delights of Berlin social life and the frivolities of German ladies of her generation that her sorrows left her in a solitude which was conspicuous and is affecting.

In order to explain the Princess Royal's position in Prussia, readers may be glad of a short, historical preamble.

The marriage of Queen Victoria's eldest daughter, the Princess Royal, to Prince Frederick William of Prussia took place in the Chapel Royal at St. James's Palace on January 25, 1858. The bride was just 17: the bridegroom 26. The title Princess Royal was introduced to the English Royal Family by King George II, and it marked the holder among a large family of sisters as pre-eminent, in the same way as the title of Prince of Wales distinguished the eldest son of the sovereign from his brothers. Although at this time the bridegroom had no distinctive title other than Prince he was inevitably heir to the throne of Prussia. In fact only two lives, those of his uncle and father (and they were both sexagenarians), stood between him and the kingdom. From the point of dignity and rank the marriage was a fine one, a great occasion.

The marriage was celebrated "with amazing éclat"; these are the words of the diarist Charles Greville, who could recollect the shabbier, more furtive nuptials of the princesses of George III's family. Londoners saw an astonishing concentration of royalty: kings, princes, royal and serene highnesses with thirteen members of the English Royal Family crowded into their capital: from Brussels, Berlin, Coburg and Naples they were carried by steam— that wonderful invention which broke down the isolation of royalty. A bridal ball was held at Buckingham Palace— gay, exclusive, enjoyable without too many English people crowding the rooms. Disraeli, who was present, thought that there were as many princes as at the Congress of Vienna. But if the ball was limited the enthusiasm of the general public for the child Princess was unbounded. Lord Shaftesbury—the philanthropist—told the Queen that there was nothing in history like the feeling shown for her daughter. The cockneys were supposed to have shouted to the bridegroom, "if you don't treat her well, we will have her back".

Of ill-treatment by the bridegroom there was never the slightest danger: but the twist of history, the narrowness of German conservatism and the antagonism to her of a section of the Prussian Royal Family were to turn the young Princess into one of the saddest personalities in nineteenth-century history. How did it happen that what started so prosperously and famously was to end in anguish and tribulation? The letters in this book cover only the first three and a half years of the Princess's married life, and it would be an exaggeration to say that they give the answer to that question. But they do very clearly reveal the beginning of those difficulties which were to crush the happiness of this gifted and lively girl. A rather more detailed background to the marriage than can be derived from the letters may help the reader to sense the dangers which lay ahead.

There have been in English history, excluding mediaeval times, only three important dynastic alliances made by daughters of English sovereigns—the one with which this book is concerned, the marriage of King James I's daughter to the Elector Palatine, and the marriage of King James II's daughter to the Prince of Orange. If the seizure of the crown off a father's head be accounted misery, we should be justified in saying that all three marriages were disasters. The happiness of all three was shattered by politics. Of the Princess Royal's marriage this was peculiarly true.

At the moment of her arrival in Berlin she was faced by difficulties of two kinds—political and personal.

First there was the political situation in Prussia. In 1848 Berlin had witnessed some disorders, several casualties, and humiliations to the Royal Family in the great wave of revolution which came rolling across Europe from Paris. For some months Prussia had a Liberal government and a not ineffective constitution, but in November 1848 a Conservative government was formed. The internal history of the country throughout the 1850's is of a gradual paring away of those constitutional safeguards which had been hardly won in the year of revolution by the Liberals. As the reaction from the liberal ideals progressed, increasing power was won by the aristocracy and Prussian Junker class. The political party which they composed was known, after their newspaper, as the Kreuzzeitung Party. Prussian internal politics, guided by foolish and degraded reactionaries, drifted far from the hopes of a handful of enlightened men and women within, and liberal well-wishers without. At the same time the opportunities for Prussia were immense: the whole of Germany was seething with national ambitions and new ideas, turning away from the old (Austria) and looking hopefully to the new—to Prussia, that distracted but formidable power resting on the strength of its military tradition. The Crimean War, which had come to an end a few months before the Princess's arrival, had offered both Austria and Prussia an opportunity to take a German lead against the reactionary power of Russia. But Prussia, with the Junkers looking hopefully to the East and with its Royal Family tied by marriage to the Czar, preferred an ineffective and shameful neutrality. To a member of the Prussian Royal Family the Prince Consort wrote: "I do not believe that there is another example of such behaviour in all history."

So far as the Prussian Royal Family was concerned these political complications were bedevilled by personal ones. The King, Frederick William IV, was a curious character —liberal by fits and starts, incurably romantic, talented but with the fatal gift in any German leader of a passion for impromptu speeches. His political manœuvres were reminiscent of someone attempting the hesitation waltz. He was regarded at the time as a frothy idealist and can be found in the pages of *Punch* as King Clicquot. Queen Victoria was very fond of him, and he was godfather to King Edward VII. He was son of the renowned Queen Louise, who was first cousin to Queen Victoria's father. He was brother to the Empress of Russia, and was married to a Bavarian princess who was childless, strongly pro-Russian and anti-English. When the correspondence begins the King was in his middle sixties and was afflicted by an arterial disorder which affected his reason. The melancholy addition to his misfortune was that although he could not play a king's part he still had the feelings of a king.

The King's next brother, William, was the Princess's father-in-law. A successful soldier, he lacked the idealism of the King, but he was prepared to make some cautious concessions to liberal opinions. He kept up a large correspondence with the Prince Consort and was to an extent influenced by him. His wife, Augusta, was a princess of Saxe Weimar; with the liberal and enlightened views of her house and an echo of the great days of Goethe, she combined a leaning towards Catholicism. Relations between husband and wife were not good, and the Princess's attempts to exert political influence led to stormy scenes.

Although the Prince's appearance was splendid—he seemed in physique an appropriate master for the Iron Chancellor—he was in reality a rather weak character. The English Foreign Secretary, Lord Clarendon, a shrewd observer, noticed in talking to the Prince how often the French words "mais" and "pourtant" were on his lips. He was known as The Prince of Prussia at the time of the Princess's marriage, becoming Regent in October 1858 and King in January 1861. Soon after he assumed the Regency he dismissed the reactionary government and appointed a Liberal government under the Prince of Hohenzollern-Sigmaringen. But in spite of this, the political struggles of 1860 and 1861 turned on the Regent's attempt, in defiance of liberal opinion, to strengthen the Prussian Army and to lengthen the term of service.

The Regent had two younger brothers living—Prince Charles and Prince Albrecht. A modern writer on Germany quotes a remark of Frederick William IV which well describes the four brothers: "If we had been born as sons of a petty official I should have become an architect, William an N.C.O., Charles would have gone to prison, and Albrecht would have become a drunkard." These elderly and difficult brethren, with their families, were the background to the life of the child Princess. In the winter they all huddled in their Berlin palaces, and then with the better weather stretched themselves in their Potsdam palaces. From the Princess's letters they seem to have led a species of communal life, meeting for dinner and tittle-tattle. How could the lofty principles from the citadel of the English monarchy flourish in a setting which was a mixture of high Tory club and regimental barracks?

Queen Victoria and the Prince Consort had had their

warning. When the engagement first became known *The Times* published a leading article which was described as "a dagger aimed at the heart of the Queen". Yet the article only said—possibly in rather too forceful words—what was felt by many thoughtful Englishmen in 1856. The Prussian Royal Family was said to be associated in the minds of the Prussian people with "national degradation". "The days of these paltry German dynasties are numbered," was another wounding sentence, and the writer closed with a lurid picture of the Princess as a refugee in the home of her fathers, while her bridegroom was held captive by the Muscovite court. Though readers of these letters will notice and sympathise with Queen Victoria's anxiety for her daughter, some criticism must fall on her and the Prince Consort for encouraging such a marriage and for attempting to control the girl Princess far away in surroundings which they did not fully understand.

The Prince Consort's brother—a shrewd if disagreeable prince—offered this explanation which is probably correct. He saw that his brother had formed the highest opinion of the intelligence and capacity of the Princess—indeed so much is clear from many references in this book. He wished her to occupy a position of power and influence which the Prussian Prince clearly offered. Moreover the young people were much attracted to one another. But the Prince Consort over-estimated what could be achieved by an enlightened prince—or a pliable prince with an enlightened wife—in the dangerous rapids of Prussian political life.

"If the Princess can leave the Englishwoman at home and become a Prussian, then she may be a blessing to the country." The remark of Bismarck was sensible. Probably it was not in the nature of the Princess to comply with Bismarck's hope, but this correspondence shows that it was impossible. The recurring theme of her mother's letters is that she must never forget what she owes to her home, to England and to her parents. The attentive reader will not overlook, in the very first letter from Queen Victoria, the direction how her daughter was to sign her name. "V. Princess Royal and Princess F.W. of Prussia." This was in her mother's visitors' book, and no doubt in Prussia the order was reversed. But the point is that the Princess invariably signed with both titles until she became German Empress. Her father reiterated the same theme: "You will not give up anything which you owe to your husband or your mother." Both parents told her repeatedly in conversation and in their letters that she was to carry with her that conception of constitutional monarchy which she had learned from them—from the citadel of English constitutional monarchy.

> "Can we to men benighted
> The lamp of life deny?"

They trained and encouraged her to be their missionary, looking to them for direction, guidance and advice as the faithful devotees looked back from darkest Africa to the comforting and sustaining counsels of the Society for the Propagation of the Gospel. But Berlin alas! was darker than any Africa.

Nor was her position in Berlin made easier by her attachment to certain fixed progressive principles—an attachment made the stronger because of her devotion to her father who shared them. This was clearly seen by her uncle, the Prince Consort's brother, who was the reigning Duke of Saxe-Coburg-Gotha. In his memoirs he writes:

"She had, in the true sense, ripened in a masculine school . . . she not only always remained the favourite, but, in many things, the image of her father. What peculiarly distinguished her in early youth, from those of her own age, was her strict adherence to fixed principles, a peculiarity which my brother himself possessed, and which he succeeded in conferring upon his favourite daughter."

Although the writer's standards of morality were not remarkable he does not of course mean that adherence to principle was peculiar: his meaning, blurred in translation, is that both the Prince Consort and his daughter believed in certain fixed principles in government from which nothing would make them deviate.

Walburga, Lady Paget, who was maid-of-honour to the Princess, emphasises this point when she writes in her memoirs: "the very approach of a Tory or a reactionary seemed to freeze her up".

If the reader feels that the parents were to an extent unwise, criticism is silenced by the anguish each so plainly felt and by the depth of their love for the child. For her part she looked back from Berlin to England and her home as a golden land where learning, good taste and advanced opinions could happily thrive. "Home" she always called it. "My country," she wrote to her mother, "which I shall love so passionately to my dying day, and be too proud to have belonged to ever to let myself forget."

THE PRUSSIAN PALACES

I felt that it would be a convenience for the reader to have this brief account of the Prussian palaces so as to identify the place from which the Princess Royal is writing or to which she alludes. The name of each palace is set out in italic type so that if readers wish to verify one of them from the text this can be readily done.

The home of the Prussian Monarchy was the Royal Palace of Berlin or the *Schloss*, the greater part of which was built in the baroque style by Andreas Schlüter at the end of the seventeenth century, though parts were older. The Schloss was vast and formed the setting for many of those evening dinners of all the Royal Family which the Princess Royal disliked. It stood at the end of the Unter den Linden. Prince Frederick William's palace, which was separated from the Schloss by an arm of the Spree, had been the Berlin home of his grandfather, Frederick William III; it had to be completely renovated and it was not ready by the time of his marriage, so that the young couple started their life in the Schloss.

One of the Princess Royal's German maids-of-honour has left this account of the Schloss as it seemed to her when the Princess went to live there immediately after her marriage:

"Endless, dark corridors connected huge, mysterious rooms, hung with large pictures of long-forgotten Royal personages: the wind whistled down through the large chimneys, and the unspoken terror of the Weisse Dame[1]

---

[1] The ghost of a long-dead member of the Royal Family. This is a slip; the ghost was called "die weisse frau".

brooded over all. Between the Princess's boudoir and library was the room in which Frederick William III had died. This was kept by his sons as 'the death room'."[1]

The Berlin Schloss was damaged in the last war and demolished after it.

Prince Frederick William and the Princess Royal moved into their own palace on November 20, 1858. They always lived here till Prince Frederick William's death in 1888, and thereafter it was the Princess Royal's Berlin home. Walburga, Lady Paget called it "an ugly house: not perhaps improved by being furnished in the style of Osborne."[1] It was known as *Kronprinzenpalais*. A seventeenth-century building, it perhaps hardly deserved Lady Paget's strictures. The Opera House divided the home of the young Princess from the home of her parents-in-law, which was on the Unter den Linden, by the statue of Frederick the Great. Prince Frederick William's father lived on the ground floor and his mother on the first floor. They never moved to the Schloss but lived in this house as King and Queen, and Emperor and Empress.

The Palace of *Charlottenburg* is some three miles westward from the Berlin Palace through the Brandenburg Gate. This palace was built for George I's sister, Sophia Charlotte, the wife of Frederick I. It was built at the end of the seventeenth century. Frederick William III, and the Princess Royal's parents-in-law, the Emperor William and Empress Augusta, are buried here. Queen Louise is buried in the garden.

As the eighteenth century developed, the Prussian Royal Family moved further west from Charlottenburg into the country to Potsdam, which was the favoured home of Frederick the Great. It was in the *Palace* (the *Stadtschloss*), in the small town of Potsdam, that he spent the winter; this building was totally destroyed in the war.

Outside the town of Potsdam he built the palace of *Sanssouci*—his private home. King Frederick William IV

[1] *Scenes and Memories*, by Walburga, Lady Paget.

— 22 —

lived here, in seclusion, at the time of the Princess Royal's marriage.

At a dire moment in his fortunes Frederick the Great decided to impress his enemies by building the *Neue Palais* at Potsdam—a vast, impressive and not unsuccessful eighteenth-century building of 200 rooms. It was here that the Princess Royal spent the summer, and it was perhaps the only one of the palaces which she liked. Here her husband died. He had re-named it Friedrichskron—in allusion to the crown supported by the Three Graces which was superimposed above it. At the time it was being built people liked to think that the Three Graces represented the three enemies of the King—Madame de Pompadour, Maria Theresa and the Empress Catherine. After the Emperor Frederick's death the building reverted to its original name. The Neue Palais was built between 1705 and 1709. Inside it is largely rococo. The Prince Consort, on his first visit to his daughter, suggested that she and her husband should make this their home.

Frederick the Great's successor, Frederick William II, built the *Marmorpalais* and laid out the Neue Garten in Potsdam, but the real builder of the family was Frederick William IV—his grandson. He was given a farm by his father near Potsdam—Charlottenhof—and here he built a house for himself designed in the style of a Roman villa. He added other romantic buildings in Potsdam—the Neue Orangerie, the Pfingstberg, the Römische Bad and the Friedenskirche. Here King Frederick William IV and his Queen are buried, and the Princess Royal and her husband are buried immediately outside.

Prince Frederick William's father built *Babelsberg* at Potsdam as a summer palace for himself, and spent the summers here from 1835 until his death. Queen Victoria called it "a Gothic bijou, full of furniture".

His brother, Prince Charles, built *Klein-Glienicke*, also as a summer home, on the road from Potsdam to Berlin.

The Palace of *Bellevue*, where King Frederick William IV lived in seclusion when he was in the capital, was in the Tiergarten.

FAMILIAR NAMES USED IN THE CORRESPONDENCE

ABBAT. Prince Albrecht of Prussia, brother to Princess Alexandrine and nephew to the King.

ADALBERT. First cousin to the King of Prussia. His sister was Princess Charles of Hesse.

ADDIE or ADDY. Princess Alexandrine (see later).

AFFIE. Prince Alfred, Queen Victoria's second son.

AUNT ALEXANDRINE. Duchess of Saxe-Coburg-Gotha, the wife of the Prince Consort's elder brother.

PRINCESS ALEXANDRINE. Daughter of Prince Albrecht of Prussia, sister to Abbat and niece to the King.

ALICE. Princess Alice—Queen Victoria's second daughter.

ALIX. Alexandra, later Princess of Wales.

ANNA. Daughter of Prince Charles of Hesse, brother to the Grand-Duke of Hesse, and sister to Prince Louis who married the Queen's second daughter.

ARTHUR. Prince Arthur, Queen Victoria's third son.

AUGUSTA B. Lady Augusta Bruce.

AUGUSTA or AUGUSTA M. Grand Duchess of Mecklenburg-Strelitz, elder daughter of the Duchess of Cambridge.

BARON, The Young. Ernest Stockmar, the Princess Royal's secretary.

MADAME BAUER. German governess to the English Royal Family.

BEATRICE or BABY. Princess Beatrice.

BERTIE. The Prince of Wales.

LADY CAROLINE. Lady Caroline Barrington.

PRINCE CHARLES. Brother to the King of Prussia.

CHARLOTTE. Archduchess Maximilian, and daughter of King Leopold I.

PRINCESS CHARLOTTE. George IV's daughter.

THE COUNTESS or THE DEAR COUNTESS or OUR DEAR
COUNTESS. Countess Blücher.

THE DEAN. Dean of Windsor.

EDWARD W. Prince Edward of Saxe-Weimar.

EDWARD or EDWARD L. Prince Edward of Leiningen,
younger son of Queen Victoria's half-brother.

UNCLE ERNEST or UNCLE E. Duke of Saxe-Coburg-Gotha,
brother of the Prince Consort.

ERNEST or ERNEST L. Prince Ernest of Leiningen, elder
son of the Queen's half-brother.

AUNT FEO or FEODORE. Princess of Hohenlohe-Langenburg,
Queen Victoria's half-sister.

FEO. Aunt Feo's daughter, wife of the Duke of Saxe-
Meiningen.

FRITZ. Prince Frederick William of Prussia, afterwards
Crown Prince, King of Prussia, and German Emperor,
the Queen's son-in-law.

FRITZ CARL or F.C. Prince Frederick Charles of Prussia,
nephew of the King, and son of Prince Charles.

FRITZ OF B. Prince Frederick of Baden, Grand-Duke (1856–
1907): he had married Prince Frederick William of
Prussia's sister.

FRITZ HOLSTEIN. Hereditary Prince of Schleswig-Holstein,
married to the daughter of Queen Victoria's half-sister.

UNCLE GEORGE or GEORGE C. Duke of Cambridge.

GRANDMAMA. The Duchess of Kent. According to context
occasionally the Prince Consort's step-mother the Dowager Duchess of Saxe-Coburg-Gotha.

HEINRICH. Prince Henry of Hesse, younger brother of
Prince Louis.

HELENE. Duchess of Orleans.

PRINCE HOHENZOLLERN or HOHENZOLLERN or MY FRIEND
HOHENZOLLERN. Prince Anton of Hohenzollern-Sigmaringen; Prime Minister of Prussia, 1858–62.

SIR JAMES or GOOD SIR JAMES. Sir James Clark.

JANE C. Lady Churchill.

THE KING or THE POOR KING. King Frederick William IV
of Prussia.

LENCHEN. Princess Helena, the Queen's third daughter.

UNCLE LEOPOLD. Leopold I, King of the Belgians.

LEOPOLD or LEOPOLD B. Duc de Brabant, elder son of King Leopold of the Belgians, afterwards Leopold II.

LEOPOLD. Prince Leopold, the Queen's youngest son.

LOUIS or LOUIS OF H. Prince Louis of Hesse, afterwards Grand Duke and later husband of Princess Alice.

LOUISE. In the context Princess Louise, fourth daughter of Queen Victoria, or more usually Louise Grand-Duchess of Baden, sister of Prince Frederick William.

LOUISE OF B. Always the latter.

MARIANNE. Princess of Anhalt, wife of Prince Frederick Charles of Prussia.

MARIE or MARIE B. Wife of Duc de Brabant.

MARIE or MARIE L. Wife of Ernest, Prince of Leiningen.

MAROUSSY. Princess Marie of Leuchtenberg, great niece of the King of Prussia.

MARY or POOR MARY or COUSIN MARY. Princess Mary of Cambridge.

PEDRO. King Pedro V of Portugal.

PHILIPPE or PHILIP. Count of Flanders, the younger son of the King of the Belgians.

THE PRINCE. Prince William of Prussia, afterwards King of Prussia and German Emperor, father-in-law of the Princess Royal.

THE PRINCESS or THE DEAR PRINCESS. Wife of above.

THE QUEEN. Queen Elizabeth of Prussia, wife of Frederick William IV.

THE DEAR QUEEN or THE POOR QUEEN or THE GOOD OLD QUEEN. Queen Amélie, widow of Louis Philippe.

SAUNDERS. Sir Edwin, the Royal dentist.

STEPHANIE. Daughter of Prince Hohenzollern-Sigmaringen, married King Pedro of Portugal.

VALERIE. Valerie, Countess Hohenthal.

VICTOR. Son of Prince Ernest of Hohenlohe-Langenburg who had married the Queen's half-sister.

WALLY. Walburga, Countess Hohenthal, afterwards Lady Paget.

WEGNER. The Prussian court doctor.

1858

The Princess was married in the Chapel Royal, St. James's Palace
at noon on January 25, 1858. In the afternoon she and her
husband left for Windsor Castle where the honeymoon was spent.
On February 2 they sailed in the Royal Yacht from Gravesend
for Antwerp, travelling from there to Berlin by train.

BUCKINGHAM PALACE, JANUARY 25, 1858

My own darling Child,

Your dear little note reached me just as we were sitting
down to dinner, and gave us both the greatest pleasure. We
missed you much. The object for which so much had been
going on had disappeared, the object of our tenderest solicitude for 17 years is now in other but truly safe and loving
hands.

This has been a very trying day for you, my dearest
child—and you behaved excessively well so that you have
only added to the love and affection so many bear to you. It
is a very solemn act, the most important and solemn in
every one's life, but much more so in a woman's than in a
man's. I have ever looked on the blessed day which united
me to your beloved and perfect Papa—as the cause not only
of my own happiness (a happiness few if any enjoy) but as
the one which brought happiness and blessings on this
country! You have also the blessing of a dear, kind, excellent
husband who loves you tenderly devotedly. Let it be your
study and your object to make his life and his home a peaceful and happy one and to be of use to him and be a comfort
to him in every possible way. Holy and intimate is this
union of man and wife as no other can be, and you can never
give your parents more happiness and comfort than when
they know and see that you are a truly devoted, loving and
useful wife to your dear husband.

Your going away gave us all a great pang. Dearest Papa
sends you many many blessings and kisses.

Ever your truly devoted and loving Mama.

V.R.

Our kindest love and blessing also to dear Fritz, our son. God bless you!

My first occupation on this sad, sad day—is to write to you.[1] An hour is already past since you left—and I trust that you are recovering a little, but then will come that awful separation from dearest Papa! How I wish that was over for you, my beloved child! I struggle purposely against my feelings not to be too much overcome by them, as it is our duty to do, but I feel very sick when I think all, all is past, all that seemed so distant, all the excitement, every thing—and nothing here but a sad, sad blank! Yes it is cruel, very cruel—very trying for parents to give up their beloved children, and to see them go away from the happy peaceful home—where you used all to be around us! That is broken in, and you, though always our own dear child, and always able to be at home in your parents' house, are no longer one of the many, merry children who used to gather so fondly round us!

But we have such reason to be thankful, very very thankful, and this will carry us over the first bitter moments of separation, which are bitter indeed, and the knowledge of your having such a very dear, kind, excellent, tender-hearted husband on whose bosom you can pour out every grief, whom we love and trust as our own son (indeed more than a son, for the husband of one's own daughter stands to a mother, after her daughter, the nearest of anyone) is a comfort and a satisfaction and a relief which we do most truly realise and appreciate, and which will soothe our sorrow and our anxiety and enable us very soon to look with peace and pleasure (unmixed with the grief we now experience) which filled our hearts with such unbounded joy, when we saw you at Windsor—and since. Those days at

---

[1] The Prince and Princess left Buckingham Palace on the morning of February 2, in an open carriage, through a snow-storm, to the Bricklayers Arms which was then the London terminus for Gravesend. They were accompanied by the Princess's father and two elder brothers.

Windsor, so full of joyful recollections to you both, will ever remain most bright and happy ones to us!

It is snowing away and everything is white and dreary! I could not go out—and shall see if I can this afternoon.

Poor dear Alice,[1] whose sobs must have gone to your heart—is sitting near me writing to you.

One thing has been forgot which I am very unhappy about, as I purposely delayed it, till today—wrote down not to forget and told Mary[2] to remind me of—and just now discovered had been forgotten! viz: your writing your names in my book! It is most vexatious—but I will cut a leaf out and send it you to Berlin by the messenger—and you and Fritz must write in it and date it—today B. Palace, so that it will be the same. You will write V., Princess Royal, Princess F. W. of Prussia.

Dearest, dearest child, may every blessing attend you both. Continue as you have begun in private and public, and you will be happy and succeed in all you undertake!

5 o'clock

Dearest Papa came back at 4 very sad and gave me the touching details of the parting which I dreaded for you, my darling child, very much. He told me also how gratifying the reception you met with and the sympathy shown by all was. It is very, very gratifying and will I am sure make dear Fritz love our dear old England still more and make him wish to come back very often, and I hope for longer than his visits (two in a year) used to be! I am already planning how we shall go to Germany.

Your brothers are much affected, in particular dear Affie.[3]

---

[1] Princess Alice (1843–78), afterwards Grand-Duchess of Hesse and the Rhine, the Queen's second daughter.
[2] Mary Bulteel, Maid of Honour to the Queen, married Sir Henry Ponsonby in 1861.
[3] The Prince of Wales afterwards King Edward VII (1841–1910) and Prince Alfred afterwards Duke of Edinburgh and Reigning Duke of Saxe-Coburg-Gotha (1841–1910). On this occasion both wept; their behaviour was described by the *Annual Register* as "very unsophisticated". The faults of the Prince of Wales were redeemed by a warm

From the Princess Royal

H.M. YACHT VICTORIA AND ALBERT, FEBRUARY 2, 1858

Once more before this dreadful day ends, let your child thank you for all your kindness—for all your love. Once more let me repeat that dreadful word good-bye, which twice today had well-nigh broke my heart.

Nobody knows what I suffered today as we went down the staircase at dear Buckingham Palace with an aching head and a far more aching heart—and hardest of all almost the last farewell here on board.

BUCKINGHAM PALACE, FEBRUARY 4, 1858

I am better today, but my first thoughts on waking were very sad—and the tears are ever coming to my eyes and ready to flow again but I am feeling much better today. But the idea of not seeing you for so long seems unbearable. Every thing I do—or see makes me think of you, makes me long to tell you all about it. Buckstone[1] in The Rivals which we saw together last Friday, and which we saw the last act of yesterday evening made me think so sadly of you, my dearest child. Today we have been to the British Museum (this afternoon) and have seen the splendid new Reading Room and as we looked at the antiques—I kept thinking how our dear Vicky would have admired their beauties! Everything recalls you to our mind, and in every room we shall have your picture!

Parliament meets today and Lord John[2] means to be troublesome. I hope you have ordered English newspapers

---

heart, and the reader will notice throughout this correspondence the Queen's affectionate devotion to Prince Alfred. Of the Queen's four sons Prince Alfred was undoubtedly the most accomplished. His long service abroad in the Royal Navy and his ultimate assumption of the sovereignty of Saxe-Coburg-Gotha made him less familiar at home than were his brothers. These facts, coupled with a certain taciturnity, which developed as he grew older, have tended in English eyes to obscure both his talents and his fine qualities.

[1] J. B. Buckstone (1802–79), comedian. Manager of the Haymarket.

[2] Lord John Russell (1792–1878), statesman. He was out of office at this time—the too candid friend of Palmerston, the Prime Minister.

to be taken in and sent to you—The Baron[1] might always call your attention to whatever events of importance are going on in Parliament so that you might be kept au fait of all that is going on here, which it is of importance you should know.

From the Princess Royal

ON BOARD H.M.Y. VICTORIA & ALBERT ON THE SCHELDT

My Beloved Papa

The pain of parting from you yesterday was greater than I can describe; I thought my heart was going to break when you shut the cabin door and were gone—that cruel moment which I had been dreading even to think of for 2 years and a-half were past,—it was more painful than I had ever pictured it to myself.

Yesterday evening I felt weighed down by grief, today though very melancholy I am able to think with more composure of all that has passed—and of all that is to come.

I miss you so dreadfully dear Papa, more than I can say; your dear picture stood near me all night, it was a comfort to me to think that I had even that near me. I meant to have said so much yesterday, but my heart was too full for words. I should have liked to have thanked you for all that you have done for me, for all your kindness. All your love, etc. I shall most earnestly endeavour to deserve. To you, dear Papa, I owe most in this world. I shall never forget the advice it has been my privilege to hear from you at different times, I treasure your words up in my heart, they will have with God's help an influence on the whole of my life. You know, dear Papa, how entirely you possess the deep confidence, reverence and affection of your child, who is proud to call herself such; and I may say of my husband too; and we feel

---

[1] Ernest Alfred Christian Stockmar (1823–66), the Princess's secretary. He was son of Christian, the celebrated Baron Stockmar. The Queen generally calls him "the young Baron", and his father "the old Baron". He edited his father's memoirs in 1872, and the Queen described his doing this as "a dreadful breach of confidence in using what was not his to use".

secure and happy in the thought that you will never refuse us
your precious advice, in anxious moments.

I feel that writing to you does me good, dear Papa, I feel
that I am speaking to you, and though the feeling that I
cannot see you or hear your dear voice in return makes the
tears rise to my eyes, yet I am thankful that this is left to me.

Goodbye, dearest Papa—I must end;
Your most dutiful and affectionate daughter

Victoria

BUCKINGHAM PALACE, FEBRUARY 5, 1858

Many, many thanks for your two dear letters from
Brussels! And you wrote dearest Papa such a beautiful
letter, it made me cry so much, as indeed every thing does.
I don't find I get any better. Even looking at your fine large
photograph which I have mounted standing on a small easel
before me—upsets me!

God bless you for your dear warm affectionate heart and
for your love to your adored father. That will bring blessings on you both! How he deserves your worship—your confidence. What is he not? What a pride to be his child as it is
for me to be his wife!

BUCKINGHAM PALACE, FEBRUARY 6, 1858

Don't trouble yourself with descriptions of great things,
leave that to Jane C.[1] and Lord Sydney[2] and the papers, but
give me your feelings—and your impressions about people
and things, and little interior details.

.   1st What dress and bonnet did you wear on landing?
And what bonnet the 2 next days?

2d What sort of rooms had you at Cologne and Magdeburg?

3d Did you dine with your people at Cologne and did
you sup at Magdeburg at 12?

---

[1] Jane, daughter of 2nd Marquess Conyngham, married 2nd Lord
Churchill. Lady of the Bedchamber to the Queen. Died 1900.
[2] Third Viscount and first Earl (1805–90), Groom of the Bedchamber.
Lady Churchill and Lord Sydney accompanied the Princess to Germany.

4 What cloak did you wear on the road, and have you been drawing?

5 How do you like the German diet?—and how do your poor maids bear this hurry scurry?

In one of the Belgian papers they say that you are like me "avec des traits moins réguliers mai plus délicats que la Reine" and in another about Fritz "beau et robuste Cavalier"!

The feeling here is the warmest and heartiest and such pretty things were said in both Houses by Lords Granville and Derby—Lord Palmerston and Mr. Disraeli last night. Every one last night and every one I see, inquires so anxiously after you. Grandmama[1] is in the lowest of spirits of us all. I am much better in every way today.

We receive the Addresses of the two Houses on the throne today and on Tuesday—the City—two Universities etc. Think of Papa having to congratulate me![2] Quel supplice pour moi!

No one tells us what weather you have; pray do so by telegraph. Now I am thinking so much of your arrival at Potsdam, and am so thankful to think you will have soon reached your journey's end. If we could only be in the crowd—to see you, dearest precious child, arrive!

6 o'clock. We heard more than an hour ago of your safe arrival at Potsdam which I thank God for!, only I fear you must be very tired. How have you slept on the journey?— Sir G. Grey cries whenever he speaks of you and Lord Clarendon is quite enthusiastic about you. In short I must not say all people write and say as it would make you vain.

Say every thing most kind and affectionate to your dear parents-in-law[3]—Fritz I embrace and pray thank Abbat[4] for his very kind letter and say I am delighted he was

---

[1] The Duchess of Kent (1786–1861).
[2] As Chancellor of the University of Cambridge.
[3] William, Prince of Prussia afterwards King and German Emperor (1797–1888); his wife Augusta, (1811–90), daughter of the Grand-Duke of Saxe-Weimar. She was unpopular in Berlin, and was frequently absent in her old home, where she was much liked.
[4] Prince Albrecht (1837–1906) nephew of the King of Prussia.

pleased with our dear Osborne. To Fritz Carl,[1] and Prince Adalbert[2] also say civil things and most particularly to my kind friend Hohenzollern[3] and to the dear future Queen.[4] Now may God bless and protect you and dear Fritz.

BUCKINGHAM PALACE, FEBRUARY 7, 1858

We have just come back from the chapel where last Sunday we were still together,—and the Dean[5] preached such a beautiful sermon about you, my dearest child. His text was from Ruth "Thy people shall be my people and my God thy God". I shall ask him to print it and send it you. I think so much of you and long to know what you are doing —but alas! I cannot tell! I had hoped to get a telegraph but have had none, and no one has told me what your toilette was to be these next days! Oh! this terrible separation, till one hears and knows all—it makes one so terribly fidgety and impatient.

Do only let Lady Churchill describe all your rooms at the palace at Berlin and you must tell me exactly how your hours are—what you do—when you dress and undress and breakfast, etc., for you know all what we do to a minute but unfortunately we know nothing and that makes the separation so much more trying. Do therefore do what you can to let me see l'intérieur du cher ménage and leave the descriptions of fêtes etc. to the others.

---

[1] Prince Frederick Charles (1828–85), nephew of the King of Prussia. The "Red Prince"—so called after his favourite Hussar uniform.

[2] Prince Adalbert (1811–73), first cousin of the King of Prussia.

[3] Prince Hohenzollern-Sigmaringen (1811–85), Prussian General and statesman. Father of first King of Rumania. He succeeded as reigning prince in 1848, but resigned his dominions, which were in South Germany, to Prussia in 1849. He was Prime Minister of Prussia (1858–62). His views were liberal and enlightened. He was very much admired by Queen Victoria.

[4] Stephanie (1837–59), daughter of above, married Pedro V of Portugal. She was the grand-daughter of Stephanie Beauharnais— cousin of the Empress Josephine. "She will bring views of life with her which will not be those of the other old Catholic Houses. New blood and German culture, with Prussian and the North to lean upon, will strike you at once as being the advantages of the selection." The Prince Consort, writing to his brother.

[5] Gerald Valerian Wellesley (1809–92), Dean of Windsor.

I went to the Olympic last night and saw Robson[1] in the extravaganza of "The Doge of Duralto",[2] in which he was very good. The Princess Capricia, who cries pearls, was very amusing.

Now that you are established at your new home, you must try and answer my questions and enter into some of the subjects I mention else we can never replace conversation. You remember how vexed you always were when you did not get answers to your letters.

8th. By the letters of Count Perponcher[3] and Jane C. we hear how well every thing has gone off, a regular *triumphzug* and that you pleased every body, which is of course an immense happiness and pride to your affectionate and devoted parents; but I can't tell you how trying, how almost unbearable it is to know so little of real details which alas! no one will tell us.

Get Jane C. to tell me all about your rooms—the railway carriages etc. Has the railway carriage got a small room to it? And (you will think me as bad as Leopold B.)[4] were your rooms on the journey and at Potsdam arranged according to English fashion? Then I see by the papers you wore a green dress at the Cologne concert. Was that the one with black lace?—You must not be impatient about all these details which I am so anxious to know, for I am anxious to know how all my toilettes succeeded? The pink ball dress at Brussels was so much admired. How I do long to hear all about the King[5] and Queen[6] and family. What did you think of

---

[1] Thomas Frederick Robson (1822–64), at this time joint manager of the Olympic. One of the greatest comic actors of his day.

[2] Written by Robert Brough (1828–60).

[3] Count Perponcher-Sedlintsky, Chamberlain to Prince Frederick William. When the Princess Royal married, Count and Countess Perponcher were placed at the head of her household.

[4] Leopold of Brabant (1835–1909), afterwards King Leopold II of the Belgians. His inquisitiveness—especially on domestic trifles—irritated the Queen. She is, of course, asking about the arrangements for retiring on the journey.

[5] King Frederick William IV (1795–1861). He was, at this time, only partially in control of his faculties.

[6] Elizabeth (1801–73), daughter of King Maximilian I of Bavaria. She was somewhat anti-English and decidedly pro-Russian. She was a Protestant convert from Catholicism.

the Duke of Brunswick?[1] We went to the Kensington Museum this morning. Lady Winchester had a son on Saturday morning and is doing well, and all Lord Suffolk's stolen pictures have been recovered to their great joy.[2]

Pray, dearest, always give the dates of my letters when you acknowledge them.

From the Princess Royal

BERLIN, FEBRUARY 8, 1858

Dearest, dearest Mama,

At Bellevue we saw the King and Queen. If I had not known that the King had been ill I should certainly never have guessed it. He was down at the foot of the stairs and almost screamed with delight as he spoke.[3] He was extremely kind—and seemed so pleased to see us; he asked after Papa immediately and after you, dearest Mama. I did not perceive any hesitation in his speech or any words that he could not find. He went upstairs with a firm step. The Queen stood at the top of the staircase, and it is impossible to be kinder than she was. Both left us immediately today; the King returned to Charlottenburg—the Queen went on to Berlin where she was to receive us—She gave me a magnificent pearl brooch with some very large and fine pearls in it which I am to wear tomorrow.

BUCKINGHAM PALACE, FEBRUARY 9, 1858

Every one says how well you behave—how good, quiet, civil and dignified your manner is! How thankful and happy do we feel! How right your sometimes not very patiently and kindly listened to Mama was, when she told you, you

---

[1] William (1806–84). The last of the Brunswick family which was closely related to the English Royal Family. He had been suggested as a possible husband for Queen Victoria. He spoke English perfectly and much resembled the sons of George III. His father was killed at Quatre Bras.

[2] Ten old master paintings were stolen by Lord Suffolk's former valet from Charlton Park, Wiltshire.

[3] His voice was always pitched high.

could do every thing, if you would but take pains, control yourself and conquer all little difficulties—as you had such great qualities, such a heart of gold! And so it is, my beloved child, ever since the 15 of January: you have had a great deal to go through,—and you have gone through the greatest trials and emotions which a young girl has to go through —and how well, how modestly, calmly, naturally! All your great and good qualities of heart and head have been brought out in a way which I am sure will be of everlasting use to you. The very agonies of grief at parting with and tearing yourself from all you loved best from your birth, will have helped to strengthen your character; the tender love, affection and tenderness of your dear husband—the knowledge that you can make him happy—can be of real and great use to him and to others, all this will do you the greatest good—will help you over, and cheer in the midst ot trials and difficulties, while your loving parents will watch and bless you from afar off! If only we could meet just sometimes to talk over what has passed—what a comfort and happiness that would be! But we must not complain—all, thank God, goes off so well, that we have every reason to be thankful and happy! Tomorrow you will think much of us—and understand more now, than before even, what a day it is to us![1]

We had 6 Congratulatory Addresses today—all very kind—and Papa had to receive 3 also. It was very droll to hear Papa speaking to me of "all the virtues of H.R.H. the Princess Royal".

BUCKINGHAM PALACE, FEBRUARY 10, 1858

I was quite unhappy when this morning—while I was dressing for breakfast—and Fritz's and the dear Princess's letters came, and none arrived from you;—how delighted was I—when dear, good Alice gave me your dear, warmhearted affectionate words—when she and the others greeted us before breakfast! Your kind telegraphic message greeted us just as we got up.

---

[1] The eighteenth anniversary of the Queen's wedding day.

Naughty Affie took no notice whatever of the day till I telegraphed to him to ask if he remembered what day it was! !—The band played under the windows at 7 this morning:—and I began to cry when I thought of you so far away, no longer one of the happy, merry children but belonging to another, engrossed with foreign things—and almost a feeling of a little anger towards Fritz who has carried you away—rose in my mind! But it was only for a short while and it is but a passing thought of pain at the separation and at your not shining here instead of there amongst strangers—which is speedily followed by gratitude to God for having given you so kind and loving a husband—and for having supported and carried you through all your trials and fatigues and difficulties. In time I shall accustom myself to all this, but it will require time.

Do you feel more and more at ease in your married life, do you feel as peaceful and happy as you did—when we met at Windsor? Do you feel that (apart from the pain of being separated from us and your home) you are quite contented and happy? Is it all as right as it was then? I trust to hear it is! Don't worry yourself to write long letters while you are so busy and so worried, only let me have an affectionate little line—but by and by let me hear how every thing is and what your feelings and impressions are. I am particularly vexed at hearing nothing about your dresses. Let your German ladies[1] give me an account of them and of your

---

[1] In addition to Countess Perponcher (see note on page 35) there were two younger German ladies attached to the Princess. One was Walburga, Countess Hohenthal, who appears in the correspondence as Wally. She was the daughter of a Saxon count and the grand-daughter, through her mother, of Field Marshal Gneisenau. She was born in 1839 and both her parents died when she was a girl. She married the English diplomat Sir Augustus Paget in 1860 and was succeeded in her position with the Princess by her younger sister, Valerie, Countess Hohenthal. The other lady was Marie, Countess Lynar. She was born in 1835 and married Charles, Count von der Goltz in 1860. Of herself and these two countesses the Princess Royal has written, "we three suited so well and were so happy, like three friends only can be who love each other truly". When the Queen first met Countess Hohenthal, which was at the time of the

Prince Frederick William of Prussia, 1858

The Marriage of the Princess Royal at the Chapel Royal, St. James's, 25 January, 1858, from the painting by J. Phillip, R.A.

parures. Pray do—and let J. Churchill tell me when you get up and dress and breakfast etc.

There have been more attempts to encourage an arrangement for a future marriage of one of your younger sisters with the Prince of Denmark's[1] son (the mother is sister to Prince Fred. of Hesse) but we won't hear of it and have thrown cold water upon it. It never would do. Whatever you hear or find out—about any things of this kind— pray be sure to tell us.

So you have got the order of St. Catherine.[2] You can wear it with the others if you like.

BUCKINGHAM PALACE, FEBRUARY 11, 1858

The Duchess of Cambridge[3] has heard such very flattering accounts from her sister Princess Louise[4] and from Augusta;[5] you had given such satisfaction at Hanover by speaking to every body and smiling and being très aimable. How I do long to hear your impressions of all your new acquaintances—I can hardly wait patiently.

---

wedding, she said—laughing, "The Princess is 17, the Maid of Honour, 18. What a respectable court that will make."

Countess Blücher (see note on page 40) was a close personal friend of the Queen's. She belonged to the household of the Princess of Prussia, not to that of the Princess Royal.

[1] Christian (1818–1906), Prince, and afterwards King Christian IX, of Denmark. His wife was Princess Louise (1817–96), daughter of the Landgrave of Hesse-Cassel who was grandson of Princess Mary of Great Britain, daughter of George II. The Queen objected to any marriage into this family because of the difficult political relations between Prussia and Denmark, though eventually she agreed to the marriage of the Prince of Wales with Princess Alexandra—"the Danish beauty" as the Queen called her, who was Prince Christian's daughter.

[2] The Russian imperial order for ladies. When the Princess Royal married, the wearing of orders was a matter for her husband's family so that permission from the Queen (not very gracefully given) was not strictly necessary.

[3] Augusta Wilhelmine Louise (1797–1889), daughter of the Landgrave of Hesse-Cassel, married Adolphus, Duke of Cambridge, son of George III, died 1850.

[4] Louise, sister of above, married Count von der Decken.

[5] Augusta (1822–1916), daughter of Adolphus, Duke of Cambridge. Married Frederick, Grand Duke of Mecklenburg-Strelitz (1819–1904). Their little duchy was close to Berlin.

You cannot think what a delight for us it was to receive your dear, long, affectionate and interesting letter of the 8th, 9th and 10th, this morning. It is far the best way to write a little every day and then send it off on the 2d, 3d or 4th day. But pray don't write on that enormous paper—for it will go into no box or book.

How glad I am that you are comfortably established but how are the rooms placed—and are there passages or must you (as in the greater part of those old palaces) go through all the rooms to get to the others?

I am so glad you are so pleased with Stephanie, and others. More of this by the messenger.

How do you like the houses and the diet? Lady Churchill says the rooms at night are so awfully hot. But yours, Countess Blücher[1] writes to me, have got nice fireplaces and though I daresay the cold is very trying still I am sure it enables you to bear up through all these great fatigues.

How glad we are that the poor king was so well, the day you saw him. I am curious how he will be, when you see him again.

Dear Mrs. Wellesley[2] and dear Mary Biddulph[3] talked so much about you on Wednesday. We went to the Photographic Exhibition today which is very good. Tonight the three younger ones go with Lady Caroline[4] to the Haymarket to see the pantomime and I take Bertie and Alice to the Adelphi, and dear Papa joins us there after attending one of Faraday's lectures. Many thanks for all the bills of fare etc.—some dinner lists I should like to have had.

---

[1] Countess Blücher was an Englishwoman, Madeline Dallas, daughter of a High Court judge. Her husband Count Gustavus Blücher was the grandson of Prince Blücher.
[2] Magdalen, wife of the Dean of Windsor.
[3] Mary Fredericka, daughter of Frederick Seymour, married Colonel (afterwards Sir Thomas) Biddulph, Master of the Queen's Household.
[4] Lady Caroline Barrington, daughter of 2nd Lord Grey. Her husband was a naval officer; she was a widow, and one of the Women of the Bedchamber to the Queen.

BUCKINGHAM PALACE, FEBRUARY 13, 1858

Again today I have had such delightful letters from the dear Princess, Augusta, who is very kind about you and praises you so much and Jane C., Lord Sydney—that it makes us very happy, thankful and easy. I have now had such minute details that if I could only just see where you live I could follow everything. Perhaps there are some old prints of the rooms etc.—by which I could judge?

Tell Fritz that I find that after all he managed to escamoter a Fackeltanz for it seems with the exception of the torches and your dress, this Polonaisien Bal was just the same.[1]

How did you manage at the Princess's and other balls about the dancing and valtzing?

I think upon reflection that it would decidedly be best if Lady Churchill had a few quiet days to rest herself after the great festivities are at an end, before she undertakes the journey back and I should be glad also for her to be able to see things quietly, so as to give me an account of your general life—which is naturally what we care about most —I have written to her about it today. She complains dreadfully of the heat in the rooms at night. Surely that could be prevented.

Lölein who returned on Tuesday, has told us a great deal and explained all about your rooms etc. Garwood is going to be made State Page and Sprague is to come in his place.[2]

---

[1] A Fackeltanz was a dance or procession with torches in which only those of the highest rank could take part. In Prussia the wedding of a member of the King's family was celebrated by a Fackeltanz, the Ministers of the Crown carrying the torches. The Queen disliked this— probably because it brought the celebration of the wedding too much to Berlin. Escamoter means "slip in".

[2] Lölein was the Prince's valet. Joseph Garwood left the Royal Service after the Prince's death. Gilbert Sprague died in 1873, and was one of the earliest recipients of Queen Victoria's Faithful Service Medal.

From the Princess Royal

BERLIN, FEBRUARY 12, 1858

*Princess Anna¹ is very pretty, the most splendid figure
you ever saw, but I do not like her style quite, her gowns are
a good deal fuller than the Empress's² and so low, I cannot
bear that; and I do not like to see the Princesses dancing
about with everybody, but of course I keep all these observations to myself. Louise the Landgravine is very insignificant,
poor thing. I like Marianne best of them, but she is so cowed
by her husband and yet it is very unwise of her to complain
as she does of not being allowed to move off her chair etc.; she
is very pretty, the Princess thinks her heavy. She does not
make that impression upon me. Fritz Carl was in excellent
humour and is very civil to me. The Grand Duchess of
Mecklenburg-Schwerin, the sister of the King, is his living
image, she is very good natured to me, as they all are, but
she is not very distingué. Princess Charles is very strange, I
don't know what to make of her and can only feel sorry that
she is the Princess's sister.³ Her husband has got (perhaps I
ought not to say so) a wicked expression and from what I
hear now, and what I heard before, it must be his character
also. The Grand Duke of Weimar is particularly kind to me,
he always talks English and really is extremely good
natured. All the family receive me very kindly and it makes
it doubly painful to me to see them all together with only the
mere outward appearance of mutual affection; it is very sad
to see husbands and wives and parents and children unable to*

---

¹ This is a description of the family of Prince Charles (1801–83), the
brother of the King of Prussia. Princess Anna was his second daughter
married five years earlier to Prince Frederick of Hesse-Cassel. Princess
Louise was the eldest daughter, and had married four years earlier the
Landgrave of Hesse Philippsthal. Marianne was his daughter-in-law,
married to his only son Prince Fritz Carl. In *Scenes and Memories*
Walburga, Lady Paget, writes "Prince and Princess Charles held a
brilliant court surrounded by dandies and sportsmen and ladies, who
were pretty, lively and fashionable. The Princess went to the famous
ballet *Flick and Flock* 123 times consecutively."
² Eugénie, Empress of the French.
³ They were both daughters of the Grand Duke of Saxe-Weimar.

respect one another as they ought. The Court here is certainly very grand and brilliant and I may say dignified. I take great pains to remember names and faces and to talk to people and remember their place. Count and Countess Perponcher are of the greatest assistance to me; every evening some gentlemen and ladies are presented to me, he presents the gentlemen and she the ladies and certainly people are so kind that I find it very easy to talk to them, and dear Fritz takes such pains with me, and helps me much.

We always breakfast at nine or a quarter past just the same as at home then I sit down to write, speak to Doctor Wegner,[1] then to the Baron, and usually Heinz[2] has some question to ask about the dinner or about presentations. At twelve every day we have received deputations and addresses and presents from different towns, it becomes very tiresome at last; they all make long speeches, and poor Fritz has always to answer them which he does quite wonderfully. He has such a command of the language. I have never heard him hesitate once. As soon as the business is over we dine out of the town and then walk in the places where we are least tormented by being run after. Our usual dinner hour is five, as I never take anything between breakfast and dinner, and then nothing afterwards. And I find that very pleasant; the gentlemen and ladies sit or stand and talk a little after dinner, and then we usually go back to our room and go to bed about half past ten or eleven when there are no balls or opera or parties, but that is a rare case.

BUCKINGHAM PALACE, FEBRUARY 15, 1858

Your dear long letter of the 12th and 13th arrived safely this morning, with heaps of other letters and newspapers so that I could hardly get through them but yours are always so well written, so well expressed that independent of the happiness of hearing from you, they are a real pleasure to receive. I am happy to think you have a little leisure, for

---

[1] Personal doctor to Prince Frederick William and the Princess Royal. Later he became the leading army doctor.
[2] Chamberlain of Prince Frederick William's household.

that cutting up of your day is very bad for every thing, for the mind as well as the body. The cold I am sure, dear, helps to keep you so well and brisk—quite as much as the hours (which I can't bear to think of, though I wish particularly to follow them when we visit you)—for you will recollect how you used to shiver when it was damp and mild—and how you used to wrap up then and catch cold—whereas the bright, dry frosty, cold always did you good, warmed you and made you less chilly. I think it hardly safe to go from $9\frac{1}{4}$ till 5 without any thing? I would advise never to do it if you felt faint or hungry—but take a biscuit or dry crust. You take, I suppose, a cup of tea at night?

Only remember that the better you become acquainted with the family and court the more you must watch yourself and keep yourself under restraint. No familiarity—no loud laughing. You know, dearest, how necessary it is to have self control, tiresome as it may be. Kindness, friendliness and civility but no familiarity except with your parents (in-law).

I fear that a good many minor arrangements are still wanting to make you comfortable. I will write fully by the messenger upon other points.

That you are so happy is a great happiness and great comfort to us and yet it gives me a pang, as I said once before to see and feel my own child so much happier than she ever was before, with another. But it must be so, for it is so different a happiness—the support and comfort and intimacy is so completely different to what was great happiness before; there is great happiness and great blessedness in devoting oneself to another who is worthy of one's affection; still men are very selfish and the woman's devotion is always one of submission which makes our poor sex so very unenviable. This you will feel hereafter—I know; though it cannot be otherwise as God has willed it so.

I love to hear your simple warm expressions of happiness and praise—for how could you bear being where you are—away from all your nearest and dearest were it not for your kind, affectionate husband—who writes so proudly and kindly of you?

You know, my dearest, that I never admit any other wife can be as happy as I am—so I can admit no comparison for I maintain Papa is unlike anyone who lives or ever lived and will live.

Never mind about my sheet of the autograph album. I prefer waiting till we meet—which will be in the course of the year—and then D.V. for my birthday next year and for the Season you will be with us. The first time you ought to come to England and London—as people are so anxious to see you and asking now when you come back, and would be much disappointed if you came to Scotland and at the dead time of the year. Besides that would be such a long time to wait. The next year after then, you can come for dear Papa's birthday and for Scotland. It is so nice to think of all this.

Only think the telegram which I sent you yesterday asking you what you were doing, left here at $\frac{1}{4}$ past 7 yesterday evening and I got the answer at 11 last night—less than 3 hours![1] Delightful! How glad I was to think you spent the evening nicely together alone! I long to hear of your leading a quiet life and reading together.

I must now end—my beloved child, your confidence makes us truly happy. May God bless and preserve you both many, many years!

From the Princess Royal

BERLIN, FEBRUARY 15, 1858

Dear Mama, I did not think you would miss me as you do, I was often such a plague to you; but sweet is the thought that one is missed by those whom one loves so passionately so intensely as I love Papa and you, and the dear children and the whole of England. It pains me that you should still be sad. If you knew how much nearer I feel drawn to you, my beloved parents; instead of feeling myself cut off from you, I feel that I am serving you both and proving my deep gratitude to you, in doing my duty here and in imitating your great and glorious example. I may I hope be of real use to you. How happy that would make me.

[1] A slip for four.

There are such thousands of things I would like to hear Papa's opinion about. Whatever I hear or see I always think what would Papa say what would he think. Dear Papa always has been my oracle.

BUCKINGHAM PALACE, FEBRUARY 17, 1858

I shall confine this letter principally to answer any questions which I do not wish to confide to the post. In your first dear, long letter of the 8, 9 and 10th you speak of Augusta's great kindness and affection and of Papa's "altering his opinion of her"; Papa says that was an imprudent remark to go by the post; not for you to write to me—for the more you do tell me of your feelings and impressions—the better, but you should not have said it by the post. I tell you this, my love, as you wished me to tell you, whether you had committed any imprudence.

Now as regards dear Augusta's kindness and affection which the dear Princess also mentions to me in each letter, no one can be more pleased than we are about it; but still I would caution you even here as to too great intimacy in the intérieur or in details of your ménage or dress—in which no one should be let into except the dear Princess and dear Aunt Feodore[1] who you know is discretion itself and is like your own Mama;—and for this reason: Augusta writes every little trifling detail to her mother who repeats it; for instance she wrote to her mother, who told it Grandmama, that Sophie H.[2] had complained to her, that she never knew before hand here what you were going to put on! Now this has alarmed us—for Sophie ought never to venture such a remark to any one and ought not to have come in contact with Augusta. It is these little misères which lead to gossip and mischief which should be most carefully avoided. Sophie ought to be cautioned; perhaps if you or Fritz don't like doing it, the Baron would.

---

[1] Feodore (1807–72) Princess of Hohenlohe-Langenburg, daughter of the Duchess of Kent, and half-sister of Queen Victoria.
[2] Probably the Princess Royal's dresser.

I reminded you in my day before yesterday's letter of watching yourself very much—when you get more at your ease with people—your court, relations etc. never to let yourself go—or forget what you owe to your own self. You know, dearest child, how often we have talked on this topic and therefore you will at once I am sure bear this in mind. Also, always to be tidy—in your own intérieur—for one owes one's husband so much more in fact than every one else.

We hear of your going to Weimar;[1] if you do, only be sure not to forget your visit to Gotha to your Grandmama[2] and uncle[3] and aunt.[4] I know how anxious Grandmama is to see you.

Dear Papa is gone today to the White Lodge[5] to see how it will do for Bertie later,—all the arrangements for Affie's going to sea are made, he will go on board the *Euryalus* commanded by Capt. Tarleton whom you saw at Osborne. Tomorrow my first levée—Friday another congratulatory address—from the Convocation. On Monday we all go to dear Osborne, how you will long to go there too—and how painfully we shall miss you!—I do not know what you are doing today or did yesterday, so I have telegraphed. You must not be impatient at Mama's curiosity but you must remember how hard it is for me not to know what you are doing.

Do you see dear Stephanie often? And have you spoken about Pedro[6] together? Tell her how impatient I am to make her acquaintance.

Dear Papa was much pleased with the White Lodge and

---

[1] Prince Frederick William's uncle was the Grand-Duke of Saxe-Weimar.

[2] Step-grandmother. The Prince Consort's father, Ernest I of Saxe-Coburg, married secondly this lady who was Princess Mary of Württemberg and his own niece.

[3] Ernest II, Duke of Saxe-Coburg-Gotha, elder brother of the Prince Consort.

[4] Alexandrine, wife of above, daughter of Grand-Duke of Baden.

[5] In Richmond Park; built by King George I. The Duchess of Gloucester, George III's last surviving child, had lived there till her death in 1857.

[6] King Pedro V of Portugal (1837–61), whom she was about to marry.

thinks it will besides do for us very nicely to go down there sometimes for a night from London in the summer.

I shall be very curious to hear by and by from you of the different relationships in the family[1] of which we have often talked, as you judge quickly and rightly. I shall ever be happy to kiss dearest beloved Papa's hand for you; I should like often and often to fall at his feet—for I feel how unworthy I must be of one so great and perfect as he is! Your great worship of him makes me only too happy; it can only be a blessing to you as it has been to me! You are, my dearest child, like him in many things, which is a great happiness to me; I wish you were one and all his image. Alas! some are not!

I send you today 2 of the "Honey Couple", 3 of the photographs of your pretty rooms at Windsor coloured and the embroidered cyphers from the bed. Sad that they must be removed! The dear Princess who speaks of you so affectionately and maternally—says you have been riding in the Riding House; where, and with whom and on what horse? I meant to do so today, but these horrid neuralgic pains flow a little about my face today.

Now I must end, else I could go on for hours. Love to your dear lord.

BUCKINGHAM PALACE, FEBRUARY 18, 1858

Yes, my dearest child, we do miss you sadly, and though no doubt you did give us occasionally trouble—you ever possessed those great qualities of heart and head which have made you the object of such interest and love and affection and the last 3 weeks you were all the fondest mother could wish.

I was distressed to hear of your having a cold—and a little cough though I am not surprised with the cold weather —and at night the fearfully hot, oppressive rooms which Lady Churchill says are dreadful. You fortunately do not suffer from them, as I and most people do, but still you know how very unwholesome they are. I hope you keep

---

[1] Prussian Royal Family.

your's not over-poweringly hot and air them and use my little thermometer?

We had a levée today and 169 Addresses presented (not bad) all in honour of your marriage! I wore a dark crimson velvet train trimmed with grebe.

Tonight the Maharajah,[1] Lord Panmure, Lord and Lady Emlyn, etc. dine here. The poor Maharajah is not very well; he is going abroad to the Isle of Sardinia to shoot; Sir John Login[2] is no longer with him; he is to take some one else with him. He inquired very much after you. I hear from all sides how much your dresses and toilettes are admired, so I take a good deal for myself as I took such great pains with your dresses.

There is another thing which I tell nobody, but which you will remember my telling you to be sure to do—and which has produced the greatest effect: viz: your trying to kiss the King's hand. Don't you remember me telling you to be sure to do this?

Only think that Bernstorff[3] singled out Ash Wednesday (yesterday) to give a dinner ("le grand dîner en l'honneur de la signature du contrat de mariage") 3 weeks after the marriage, and invited the Archbishop and Bishop of London who declined on account of its being Ash Wednesday!!! Poor dear Princess how glad I am you can quiet her—and how I do rejoice for you, at dearest Aunt Feodore's being near you. It must indeed be like a bit of home. Good, amiable Countess Blücher is also a great comfort—and I hope she will soon write to me again.

The Dean is so kindly anxious about you. I feel sure I have not said half of what I ought to you, but I must end. Bertie goes to dearest Papa again at 6 now.[4]

---

[1] Dhuleep Singh (1837–93), Maharajah of Lahore and a particular favourite of the Queen. He had been deposed in 1849, and had lived in England, becoming a Christian.

[2] Guardian of the Maharajah, 1849–58: formerly surgeon at the British Residency, Lucknow. Sir John had interested the Maharajah in Christian missionary work.

[3] Albrecht Bernstorff, Prussian Ambassador in London (1854–61 and again from 1862 to 1873).

[4] As the Queen's children grew up they were given the opportunity of these evening discussions with their father.

The Duchess of Orleans[1] kindly sent me a letter with an extract from a letter from the Grand Duchess Alexandrine of Mecklenburg-Schwerin[2] about you which is very amiable and kind. It was naturally not written for us to see, so don't pray let her perceive any thing. Only one thing I can't understand she says: "She is very small" which considering that you are a good deal taller than me, and I am not a dwarf, is rather hard.

From the Princess Royal

BERLIN, FEBRUARY 20, 1858

It has been a great trial to me to be prevented from writing to you for so many days—but really I was quite unable, my cough had pulled me down so much and my headache tormented me, so that I was unable to do anything. But I feel well again now, and am so glad to resume writing which I missed not a little these last few days.

But now, dear Mama, to thank you a thousand times for your dear letter of the 17th full of such precious advice. Oh if I could tell you how I value a word of advice now, and how anxious I am to follow it, and how I take every remark you make as a more especial proof of your love; for my reform is complete I hope. I know you would not find me the same as I used to be, I trust.

It was indeed most imprudent of me to have written as I did by the post—and it gave me a great deal of uneasiness after my letter was gone, but I hope you will forgive that piece of folly. You may make yourself easy dear Mama, on this point of my talking with Augusta; I am perfectly well aware that she would write every thing home, (besides she is the daughter of her mother) so she gets no details whatever of my "intérieur" from me, because I have made it a rule, never to speak with anyone, except the Princess and you and

[1] Hélène, daughter of Grand Duke of Mecklenburg-Schwerin, widow of Louis Philippe's eldest son, the Duke of Orleans.
[2] The Grand Duchess was daughter of King Frederick William III of Prussia.

*Papa about my intérieur. I am aware that a new "ménage"
is a subject of interest and curiosity, particularly to ladies,
and as Augusta can get nothing out of me, I think it quite
natural she should try to hear from other people. She was
unwell and I sent her some medicine for her cold through
Sophie, and I suppose Augusta profited of this opportunity to
ask questions, which the other who is rather talkative will
have answered, but she has been cautioned, and has promised
never to mention my name when she talks to any one, and say
nothing whatever either about me or Fritz. (Countess Blücher,
who does not know Augusta well, said she hoped I did not
make a confidente of her, as she did not appear to be the
person. I told Countess B. that I never made confidentes of
any body—that between my husband and me there were no
secrets, that my parents and my mother-in-law were the only
ones to whom I was completely unreserved.)*

*I cannot be too careful here, where the Royal Family is
the perpetual topic of stories and criticisms, alas often too
true, but still exaggerated sometimes. An unguarded word is
repeated and of course distorted, and hence stories of which
no one knows the origin. For instance the ménage of Fritz
Carl, is so much talked about. All the stories are more or less
inventions but still neither he nor Marianne do anything to
prove that they are false remarks, or once for all by their
words—and appearance in public put to silence all the nonsense that goes about. Alas there is no sort of respect for the
family here—and there cannot be! It pains me deeply—I am
accustomed to something so different.*

*Each of these princes have in their household a person
who is a sort of spy—and repeats all over the town what the
princes or princesses say or do—for instance Marianne's and
Prince Charles's.*

*You do not know how guarded I try to be when I speak
with my cousins and aunts and uncles. Thank God all the
people placed about me are carefully chosen, but that does not
put me off my guard. There are 2 topics on which I have
firmly resolved never to open my lips—those are my husband
—and my parents-in-law.*

I trust and hope that in this way and with God's help and

*your advice I shall keep out of scrapes and live with a quiet
conscience and a good reputation, without which I could not
be happy, nor be able to do the good I would wish. But please,
Mama and Papa, never cease to remark to me anything
that strikes you as not right or anything you hear, it can never
do harm and may—often—do good. We shall always be
deeply grateful—we are young and inexperienced in a difficult position, you have made for yourselves a reputation, and
a happiness—such as no other—you will not deny your children your help—we know that all you say to us is only in our
interest, and we wish to imitate your example. This is a
serious letter and I meant to have said much more on a subject so important but I still feel rather unwell and unable to
collect my woolgathering thoughts.*

*I must confess that I cried bitterly last night at the
thought of your going to dear Osborne, and without me. My
pretty rooms that I loved so much, the dear view out of the
windows—the darling Swiss cottage, my garden, the tree I
planted the day we left—and all those objects to which I am
attached, you will see them all again the day after tomorrow
and I can only dream and think of them, and look at the
photographs and cry. Sometimes I cannot believe that I am
so far away from you all, because I am so constantly thinking
of you! Thank you a thousand times, dear beloved Mama, for
the cyphers from Windsor, we have put them up in our room
for the present, and they remind us of dear Windsor and the
happy days we spent there, and we think with double gratitude of the far greater happiness we are enjoying now, for
every day brings us new joys.*

*How silly of Bernstorff to choose Ash Wednesday for his
dinner party, but I suppose he had printed on his cards,
instead of "Frock Dress" "Sackcloth and Ashes"—the party
must have had a most peculiar aspect in that unusual costume.*

*I am indeed delighted that poor Marie's[1] troubles and
trials are safely over, but did not the event take place sooner*

---

[1] Marie. Archduchess of Austria, married to Leopold, afterwards
Leopold II of the Belgians, in 1854. The birth of this child, a daughter,
after four years of marriage was a disappointment.

than she expected it? I cannot fancy Leopold a papa! What a disappointment that it is a little girl!

I fear I must end, dear Mama, not having thanked you half enough for your dear letters and for the charming coloured photographs of our rooms at Windsor.

Ever your most devoted, grateful, respectful daughter,
Victoria

P.S. I have just received your dear kind letter of the 18th how very very kind it is, God bless you, dearest Mama, for your words, you make your child very happy—and make her feel still more how unworthy she is of so much love.

Thank you for the photographs of the "Honey couple". The Prince of Prussia was so delighted with your letter.

We never dreamt of going to Weimar, at the earliest before April, and that was the time we meant also to go to Gotha. May I beg to be remembered to all my friends and to Colonels Biddulph and Phipps and General Grey.

BUCKINGHAM PALACE, FEBRUARY 20, 1858

I have not much time to write and know you will feel grieved to think that we are threatened with a ministerial crisis, indeed not threatened but in for it. Lord Palmerston has just been here and says that the Cabinet were unanimous in the opinion that they must offer their resignation which I must accept! I have just sent for Lord Derby—and shall have the happiness of going through what you remember taking place at this very time of year in 51—again 52 and again in 55! It is very disagreeable as the state of affairs is so very uncomfortable. It was most unexpected as Lord Derby had spoken in such very strong and good terms about this very bill[1]—I think while you were still here. (How I wish that were the case now!)

---

[1] An attempt had been made to murder the Emperor and Empress of the French; the conspirators had concocted their plans in England where their bombs had been made. The outcry in France against England was vociferous. Palmerston's Government introduced a bill to change the crime of conspiring to murder from a misdemeanour to a felony. In spite of Lord Derby's lead, the Conservative Party and the country as a whole disliked the appearance of truckling to France, "acting from compulsion", and brought the Government down.

But the Emperor has been so very unwise in all that he has done in France and the insulting language held in France towards this country has so irritated and exasperated the people here, that they would not hear of what they call acting from compulsion, which is not true. The bill itself is merely an improvement of our law and nothing to restrain the liberties of any one—but here we are in a pretty way! Never to go above two or three years with a Government is terrible. I am not in a very fit state for all this with my nervous pains—but I am thankful to say I am a great deal better today but could only go out once, as the air this morning brought it on a little again. I had an excellent night.

We had put off our journey to Osborne to Tuesday—but I fear it may again be delayed on account of this unfortunate crisis. I am happy to hear you are better; but your answers yesterday and today by telegram are not quite satisfactory and you don't say whether your cold is better or not, but merely: "I am still unwell" and—"I am pretty well". Were you feverishly unwell with it or not? Your staying at home as Countess Perponcher wrote—for two days was I am sure right, but another time please—if it is ever so slight—do desire Doctor Wegner to write as soon as you have a cold, for accustomed as I was to know everything about you from hour to hour, I get terribly fidgeted at not knowing what really is the matter.

We have a great dinner tonight—with the Cambridges, Nemours,[1] Manchesters, Clarendons (these are very pleasant) it is rather a trial tonight. Uncle George[2] has got the gout.

BUCKINGHAM PALACE, FEBRUARY 22, 1858

Your delightful long letter of the 20th arrived this morning and gave me the greatest pleasure. It is full of

---

[1] Duc de Nemours, the second son of Louis Philippe. His wife, Princess Victoire of Saxe-Coburg-Gotha, was a favourite cousin of the Queen's and had died in 1857.
[2] George, Duke of Cambridge (1819–1904).

Above: The Princess Royal in her wedding gown with the Queen and Prince Consort and (right) the Royal bridesmaids

Right: The Royal Wedding cake

Below: Sketches of the Princess Royal at her marriage drawn by Queen Victoria from memory

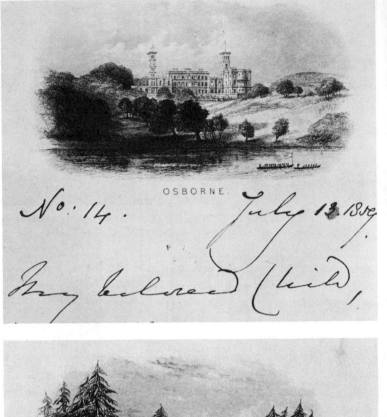

OSBORNE.

No: 14. *July 13 1859.*

My beloved Child,

THE SHEEL OF ALLT NA GIUTHASACH.

No: 40 *Spt: 26. 1859.*

Queen Victoria's writing-paper bore engravings showing the place from which her letters were written

what is right and good and shows on what a firm basis your happiness rests! That you should have longings and yearnings for your own dear home and your parents and brothers and sisters is not only natural but it is right; if it were not so, we should be surprised and grieved.

Now I must tell you that you numbered the pages of your letter wrong, and then I must scold you a little bit for not answering some questions; but above all for not telling me what you do. My good dear child never liked matter of fact things—but Mama does, and when Lady Churchill leaves you I shall know nothing of what is going on which makes me sad. I tell you all that is going on, so that you may follow everything, daily, and I wish you for the future to adopt the plan of beginning your letters with the following sort of headings.

Yesterday—or day before we did so and so; dined here or there and then where you spent the evening. If once you omit, for days, what you do—I shall be quite at sea—and it makes me sad, and feel the separation painfully. You must promise me, my dearest. Then let your Ladies tell me any future toilettes—regularly in fact which your maids may be unable to do. I hear you had a dress made by the tailor. Lastly, I should wish very much your Ladies to write me down a full list of all the public presents you have received —as well as of the private ones from relations.

Now pray, my dearest child, don't forget these things— as they do make such a difference to me. They won't give you trouble. You ought I think to have a capuchon made (like you had at Osborne for the dear corridor—only stiff) to put on at night. People think you didn't dress warm enough, which considering this fearful heat of the rooms (as dear Fritz himself calls it) at night, may be the case. You should take care,—for it would be bad if you got into the way of catching cold.

Pray do answer my questions, my dearest child, else you will be as bad as Bertie used to be, and it keeps me in such a fidget.

I asked you several questions on a separate paper about your health, cold sponging—temperature of your rooms etc. and you have not answered one! You should just simply and shortly answer them one by one and then there could be no mistake about them. My good dear child is a little unmethodical and unpunctual still. Fritz always answers all questions. Just write them down on a bit of paper—when you have time—and put them into your letter; never mind if they are old—only pray do answer them.

But now to speak of all our troubles and plagues. We saw Lord Derby on Saturday and when I charged him to form a Government begged I would consider it till next day, which we did, but felt there was no other course; so I sent to him yesterday morning and saw him again yesterday evening but cannot report any progress yet as he waits to see whether he can't get the Duke of Newcastle to join him. He was to see the Duke this evening and ascertain what he will do. There was a great assembly of people in Hyde Park yesterday—some 30,000 and they pelted some people who they thought were French. How vexatious and unfortunate all this is. Of course we must delay our visit to Osborne,— for a few days.

My poor face is still not well. Though free from real pain (there is great tenderness) through the day. It has come on each day just for dinner though perhaps less severely than yesterday; the nights are good—but it pulls me, and I can only get out for a short time with double veils and much wrapped as the wind is so cold. I fear it may be long in going off.

Edward W.[1] and his brother Gustave, the kind Duchess of Sutherland[2] and Sir G. C. Lewis dined here yesterday. Today we dine at home. Bertie and Alice almost always dine with us when we dine alone which will make you jealous. The Duchess of Argyll had a little girl this morning and on the 19th Lady James Murray had a 3d girl!—Marie's[3] con-

---

[1] Prince Edward of Saxe-Weimar, nephew of Queen Adelaide, lived in England and served in the British Army. He married morganatically Lady Augusta Gordon-Lennox, daughter of the Duke of Richmond.
[2] Wife of the 2nd Duke of Sutherland, and daughter of the 6th Lord Carlisle. The Queen's closest personal friend.
[3] See note on p. 52.

finement was expected about this time. Uncle Leopold and both the young people are much disappointed. The child is called Louise. I will give all your kind messages and I have given the others. There are still some people I want to hear about; the Princess Liegnitz[1] (whom we wished to be remembered to) the Princess of Hohenlohe-Ingelfingen; have you seen her? That is Uncle Hohenlohe's sister. And then you have not answered my question if you have talked to Stephanie about Pedro?

I will answer the other part of your dear letter by the messenger.

You may be sure, my beloved child, that I shall ever tell you plainly what I think can be of use to you both. Are you even happier than at Windsor? I thought that you could not be. Bertie is shocked at your liking every thing so much. But I have no fear of old England and home suffering by that. It is in one's own power to be happy—and to be contented. And with a husband whom one loves, as you do, one is sure to see every thing en couleur de rose and so one ought.

BUCKINGHAM PALACE, FEBRUARY 24, 1858

I fully expected that you would be very homesick when the excitement was over, and a cold like the one you have had always reduces and makes one very low, and you must recollect that you have been from the 15th of January till now living a life of the greatest excitement both moral and physical which I wonder you could bear. Therefore it is not only the cold you have been suffering from, but the reaction of such a very unnatural life. I repeat it again, my dearest, think often that, D.V., we shall certainly meet again in a few months—and next year here, for my birthday but you never enter into these observations which you should, my

---

[1] Daughter of Count of Harrach and widow (morganatic) of King Frederick William III of Prussia. King Frederick William's will was published and, among the blessings of his life he emphasised "the signal and unexpected providence of God, which gave to me in my fifth decennium a consort, whom I feel in duty bound thus publicly to mention as a pattern of constancy and delicate attachment".

dearest. Think as you used to do—about Fritz when he was absent—that every week brings our meeting nearer. Doesn't it? Only don't hide your feelings from your husband or from your dear, kind mother-in-law who feels so completely and deeply for you.

I was sure you would be dreadfully annoyed at the resignation of the Government. The new one is formed, but cannot last, I should think. The list is in today's *Times*. The household is also partially settled. Lord Exeter to be Lord Steward, Lord de la Warr to be Lord Chamberlain (he was this under Sir R. Peel) and the Duchess of Manchester, Mistress of the Robes![1] A German Mistress of the Robes! What will Fritz say to this? You see we are not exclusive here, though this is the first time such a thing happened!

All the others you shall hear later, and Lord Colville will have his old place—and Lord Raglan is to be one of the Lords-in-waiting. I hope and trust that matters will be settled with France; Lord Derby has seen Mons. de Persigny[2]—and he hopes every thing will be settled satisfactorily, by answering the despatch of Count Walewski[3] (the not doing which caused the misfortune on Friday) then Count W. will answer this satisfactorily and after that, the Conspiracy Bill will pass. You may tell this to the dear Princess who is very anxious, but in confidence.

How do you find the relationship between the Prince and Princess?[4] All you say in your letter of the 20th—by the

---

[1] Daughter of the Hanoverian Count of Alten. She subsequently married the 8th Duke of Devonshire, and was known as the double Duchess.

[2] The French Ambassador in London.

[3] Natural son of Napoleon I. At this time he was the French Minister of Foreign Affairs.

[4] It was extremely bad, and formed one of the aggravations in the Princess Royal's early life in Prussia. The Princess Royal's mother-in-law spent much time away from Berlin—in Coblentz and Baden-Baden. It is curious that although later the paths of the Princess and her mother-in-law diverged, they were on the same side politically—each being Liberal. When King Frederick William IV died his sister—the reactionary Grand Duchess of Mecklenburg-Schwerin—flung herself into the arms of his successor (the Princess Royal's father-in-law) and implored him not to trust his wife because "she is an intriguer who will

messenger—about Augusta,—and the family[1]—your tone
with them,—the line of discretion you pursue of never talking about your husband or parents-in-law is just what I
expected and what I could wish. Pursue that course always
and never pour out your troubles or trials to any ears but
our's. What a sad family it must be! How melancholy! You
have never told me how you like the Princess Liegnitz?
She is an excellent person.

I send you by this messenger 4 copies of the Dean's
pretty sermon—which I hope you will read to Fritz, and the
Bishops of Chester's, Oxford's and London's sermons.[2]

BUCKINGHAM PALACE, FEBRUARY 25, 1858

Describing her farewell to the Ministers and courtiers of the old
Government the Queen says:

I also saw the dear Duchess of Sutherland today and
took leave of her. She is a terrible loss for she is one of our
dearest, kindest, truest friends. I gave her a bracelet. She
has had your print framed charmingly—with the orange-
flowers at the top under blown glass.

It was the ball and dining-room which Lady Churchill
meant were so hot—and so oppressive and much worse than
elsewhere from the stoves and gas light, not the living
rooms. Pray don't forget putting on something warm whenever you go out into the passages and don't think you are
here; have a wadded cloak or thick shawl always by you
for that.

Tonight we go to the Haymarket to see "Much Ado
about Nothing" in which a new and very pretty and good
actress[3] they say, performs: Miss Swanborough[4] also acts
and I shall think of my beloved child, whom I wish was

---

try to meddle with affairs of state". *The Duchess of Dino* by Philip
Ziegler 1962.
[1] The Prussian Royal Family.
[2] On the Princess Royal's marriage.
[3] Miss Amy Sedgwick (1830–97) played the part of Beatrice. Some of the
critics thought her acting in this part a little artificial.
[4] Probably Ada Swanborough, later famous on the comedy stage.

here! Oh! if I only knew what you were doing. You must tell me all about your day—and where you breakfast etc. What a pity it is you have no garden to walk in just to get a little daily exercise. The poor despised garden here would be a great blessing to you now.

What is your wardrobe maid called? I asked this before, my love. Tomorrow is the dreadful Council for the new Government.

From the Princess Royal

BERLIN, FEBRUARY 26, 1858

You say I do not enter into the subject of seeing you! Dear Mama, that this should strike you I am indeed sorry for. Your visit I dream and think and talk of every day, and feel as I used to do before my marriage, that every day brings the longed for hour nearer. There is not a feeling or a thought I conceal from my husband, and although you do not allow that anyone can be as happy as you are, dear Mama, I often think to myself that there is no-one blessed as I am, your child and Fritz's wife. What a lot! I sometimes fear that there are some great trials or sorrows awaiting me, or I should not be allowed to enjoy happiness such as this. You say, dear Mama, you do not think it can be greater than it was at Windsor; I thought so too then, but I find I made a mistake—it is greater, and becomes so from day to day. I can more fully realise it now. But I must not try your patience so hard, dear Mama. I used to do I fear, and my feelings are so deep on that subject that if I was to put them on paper they would sound unnatural, exaggerated or sentimental and I have not the slightest wish to be any of them.

The thing which pains me most of all is to see the Prince and Princess, two noble souls bound together by the ties of marriage—and both unhappy! I am so fond of them both, they overwhelm me with kindness—what would I give to see them really happy. I have been witness to a great many little scenes which are painful. The dear, dear Princess told me once not to think ill of her if I saw her lose her command over herself, and she said that she was all day reproaching herself

— 60 —

and it made her very unhappy. I told my dear mother-in-law that I could never think otherwise of her than I ever had done, and that I could see she had many things to try her, that I could understand how painful it must be to her to know and feel herself in the right when nobody else will acknowledge it. But she never sets the right way about it and she gets so impatient with the Prince and Fritz sometimes, with me I do not care because as I happen usually to think the same way as she does I can often pacify her. But the Princess gets so fidgety and so worried that it isn't always easy. It makes me sad when I think of you and then of myself, who are so happy—the least word I say listened to with patience and kindness, it makes everything easy; I feel as I could not do a single thing small or great without asking my husband's advice, and he takes such pains to explain everything to me; the moments when we are left alone together are the happiest of the day. I do not like to think what that noble heart must have suffered all her life. All and everything I can do to be of comfort to her I will try to do.

BUCKINGHAM PALACE, FEBRUARY 27, 1858

I am glad you go often to the play—but regret Juliet not being well personified—and the costumes being so incorrect. Could that not be rectified? We came too late to see more but the end of "Much Ado about Nothing" so we are going again tonight. Miss Swanborough looked so pretty as Hero in a bridal dress.

The Baron[1] must be a great treasure; the accounts of his father are much better.

All your arrangements seem very good; I hope you will draw a little whenever you can. Papa and I used formerly always to draw of an evening when we were read to—and you should do the same; it is much better than working. What book do you read out of to Fritz? Does he ever read aloud to you in English? Last night I received your telegram also the one you sent this morning—poor Marianne how very unfortunate to have a third girl and how angry

---

[1] Baron Ernest Stockmar.

Fritz Carl will be; still you must wish him and her joy in both our names, and inquire after her in my name. What will they call this poor little unwelcome thing? I can fancy his indignation!

Your dinners must be very nice; Lord Sydney says they are very good. You say that all your ladies and gentlemen dine always with you. Does that include Stockmar? The cold must indeed be tremendous and I am sure I should find it too much—for I have felt the cold e. wind here these last 10 days very unpleasant,—and you know, though I like bright, brisk frosty weather and dislike heat—particularly oppressive heat, and feel ill by it—I feel the cold more quickly than you do, and generally have had twice as warm things on as you, in cold weather—don't you remember? I am so glad you find the sealskin comfortable; it is a nice warm thing; I hope when it is a little less severe you will find the mole skin useful too.

Good Sir James[1] is much pleased at your kind mention of him, and is quite satisfied at all he hears of you.

Since I began this I have seen the Duchess of Manchester who was very smart and looked very pretty in a pink terry velvet mantelet or cloak trimmed with ermine, a pink bonnet and black velvet gown. She inquired much after you and says her only brother who is at Berlin in the Prussian service, wrote to her how well everything went off. Only think that the Duke of Wellington has made the poor dear Duchess resign because she is not made Mistress of the Robes, and because I believe he wished to remain in office.[2] I am so grieved. She goes with us to Osborne and remains till Jane Churchill arrives, as I have accidently no other available lady! Yesterday was a long day and a painful one; I enclose a list of all that took place. It lasted from a $\frac{1}{4}$ past 2 to $\frac{1}{2}$ past 4. I saw all the out-going ministers sep-

---

[1] Sir James Clark (1788–1870), the Queen's doctor.

[2] The 2nd Duke; he had been Master of the Horse since 1853—an office which then changed with the Government. The Duchess, a personal friend of the Queen and not too kindly treated by the Duke, had been Lady of the Bedchamber since 1843. A Lady of the Bedchamber could hold her position irrespective of the fall of Governments.

arately. Lord Granville, Lord Clarendon, Sir G. Grey very much upset, and even Lord Panmure was; poor dear Lord Breadalbane was so grieved to leave us. Both he and Lord Clarendon hope to go to Berlin in the course of the summer to see you. People are so kind about you! You must feel very grateful for such extraordinary loyalty and affection. Lord Shaftesbury (who, as well as the Van de Weyers,[1] Uncle George and Victor[2] dined here last night) said, there was nothing in history like the feeling shown on this occasion— and the great affection, not for us only—but for you personally. That he had (as you know) so many opportunities of going amongst all classes, and that it was the same with all—exactly as if it was their own child!, the old women in the workhouse saying on the day you went away (that horrid day,) "a bad day for our young people to go away". Tell this to Fritz for you know (and he ought to know) that such a feeling in England is worth a great deal—as it is the real feeling of the people, not merely a sense of respect— which can be put on, for you cannot force people here to be enthusiastic if they don't choose. Lord S. added, that it showed how the people here valued and loved a moral court and a happy domestic home, like, thank God our's has been and is! May your's my dearest, ever be the same! Try and make me a scribble of the tournure and sort of toilette of the various young princesses. I mean to finish "Violet"[3] in remembrance of my dearest, absent child, but it gave me such a turn when I opened it, that I fear I shall cry over it.

---

[1] Sylvain Van de Weyer, the Belgian Minister in London.
[2] Prince Victor of Hohenlohe-Langenburg, a younger son of the Queen's half sister. After a successful career in the Royal Navy he achieved some distinction as a sculptor. He married morganatically the youngest daughter of Admiral Sir George Seymour and they were known as Count and Countess Gleichen.
[3] This is probably "Violet" or "The Danseuse" an old novel of the 1830's.

BERLIN, FEBRUARY 27, 1858

Dearest Papa

I am so unhappy at having only a moment to answer your dear and kind letter in, for which I thank you a thousand times.

What you say about my position is so right and is often a matter for reflection with me. If I was to lose sight of my English title and dignity I should do myself and my husband much harm, besides be forgetting my duty to you and England.

I am aware that there are people who would be too happy if they could forget who I am, and I am also aware that if I was to forget it I should be taking the tools out of my hands for doing good. As you say, dearest Papa, my position like everybody else's has its difficulties which require to be considered. I must take up my ground in this large family and then remain there; it must be completely neutral, if one can say so, and my extreme youth makes this only natural. I avoid carefully talking on politics with anybody except the Princess, as I might be saying many things from ignorance which I might be sorry for afterwards. Altogether it is better never to talk with strangers about things one knows nothing about; one may wish to appear learned or wise, and in consequence make the most stupid bévues which are not so quickly forgotten, particularly in a family like this.

But this does not prevent my having my own ideas about politics, although I do not think it is my place to make it my usual subject of conversation.

I have not in vain heard you speak, and from the newspapers, and the conversation of clever people, one may have one's own notions and opinions.

I think that a Princess (or any woman) who pretends to know nothing of what is going on, or takes no interest in public affairs or no pains to form her own opinions upon them, must be just as much a bore to her husband and useless to the world, as one who is always mixing herself up in those matters, and for them neglecting her other duties.

Oh how difficult it is to find the golden "mean", to keep oneself from being run away with by one's feelings or prejudices and without being in a calm state of mind it is impossible for one's reason to be in a fit state to work and keep its judgment.

I read the English papers most steadily, and of German ones the Kölnische Zeitung[1] *and* Allgemeine Zeitung *have been recommended to me. Lord Sydney and Lady Churchill are leaving us on Tuesday I think you are quite right to wish it, although I do not think people look upon their stay in the light you seem to fear, as yet. They might do so if their stay was prolonged.[2]*

They were begged to stop till this ball at Potsdam was over, my being unwell put it off, and that is the reason for their departure being put off.

Matters in England seem in a great mess surely this Government cannot last, what will Lord Derby do with all these difficult questions he who is not the most prudent and calm of men.

Is it true that Lord Clarendon means to support the new Government? They have it so here. Poor Lord Palmerston I am sorry that his long troublesome ministry should end for him with unpopularity, but people were so shocked at Lord Clanricarde's[3] appointment.

I fear, dear Papa, that I must end here. I have not a moment's time, I have written to Grandmama, but shall not be able to send it now. I saw a photograph in a shop which I send, thinking you may like it, I am always looking out for some when I drive, which I think you might fancy.

Ever your most dutiful and affectionate, grateful daughter
Victoria

I have had such a kind letter from the Empress Eugénie to enquire after the Prince of P.

---

[1] Said by Bismarck to be as valuable as an army corps on the Rhine.
[2] i.e. that they were watching her on behalf of the Queen.
[3] The first Marquis of Clanricarde, who had married Canning's daughter, was appointed Lord Privy Seal by Palmerston. His private character had been damaged by an action in the Irish Courts.

From the Princess Royal

BERLIN, MARCH 1, 1858

There was a very pretty ball in the Casino in the evening —presentations without end—I have got quite used to them now; fancy, dear Mama, some 30 or 40 ladies being brought up and named, without a word being said of who they are or what they are, and a great chance if one could catch the name, the music playing very loud all the while and the lady who presents them so shy that she whispers. And then I have to speak with every one of these ladies, all standing so close together that what I say to one the whole of them hears, and one dares not repeat the same thing; I don't know what nonsense I said at last.

Yesterday we had our first family-dinner the whole of the family except the Prince and Princess. We sat down 20 to dinner. I sat between Prince Albrecht and Prince Charles; on needles and pins the whole time for fear either of these worthy uncles should make ill-timed, improper jokes, or quarrel with some of the rest, which they are always inclined to do particularly when they think themselves under no restraint. Oh the things that happen here sometimes—if you knew. I do not like to write all the foolish, mischievous things that are said and done. I wish Papa could just be here for a little, he would see the whole thing in a moment. The only way in which I can keep my ground is in ignoring the happy state of sixes and sevens they're all in,—listening to no stories —and being completely neutral, which is easy at present as they are all extremely kind to me and being new and in a high position there is still a sort of restraint between them and me, which I shall do everything possible to keep up—as it is the only way in which I can keep myself from being mixed up in all their frivolous talk. Aunt Feodore is my comfort— to her I can talk more unreservedly than to anyone on that subject—she knows everything better than anyone else, and can tell you that I have not always an easy task of it. However all goes on well at present, heaven grant it may remain so. Yesterday all went off very well indeed. They were all in the best humour, Prince Charles only joked about his grand-

— 66 —

daughters whom he called the Three Graces. Princess Lieg-
nitz I am much attached to, she is so kind—so unaffected,
keeps her position so well, and is the one of all the Princesses
the most respected here. Fritz C. is perpetually talking of you,
and of England and said to me the other night he hoped he
had been civil to you. Abbat raves about Osborne and the
pictures there, as he does about my two large ones by
Mr. Corbould[1] here.

The Baron always dines with us,—he always appears
with my Court. I made a point of that. I read my English
newspapers to Fritz, sometimes out of Shakespeare, and once
or twice out of a very pretty novel Miss H.[2] gave me—
"Adam Graeme".[3] He reads German to me, not English.

OSBORNE, MARCH 1, 1858

Your dear letter of the 26th–27th by messenger with
the pumpernickel and tower-shaped cake (which is delicious)
reached us just before we left B. Palace. Such a day like
when you left—only much colder and much more wind;
fortunately however off shore, so with the exception of a
few rolls in coming out—we got a quiet passage.

Here all is white and the wind sets so strongly on the
windows that we can't get the rooms above 50–52 and so
on, and it is bitterly cold—but I think it will soon get better.
How strange and lost we all seem without you—how looking
for you at every step! Oh! it is very sad when a daughter is
torn away and carried off to another home! Hard indeed for
the poor parents and brothers and sisters. One great drawback you all (our daughters I mean) will have, which I have
not viz: the being exiled from your native land. This is a
sad necessity. One great advantage however you all have
over me, and that is that you are not in the anomalous

---

[1] E. H. Corbould, the water-colour painter: he instructed Queen
Victoria's children in painting.

[2] Miss Hildyard, daughter of a clergyman; governess to the Royal Family.
A fine, unselfish character. She retired in 1865, and became a sister of
St. Katherine's, dying in 1889.

[3] *Adam Graeme of Mossgay*—published by Mrs. Oliphant in 1852.

position in which I am,—as Queen Regnant. Though dear Papa, God knows, does everything—it is a reversal of the right order of things which distresses me much and which no one, but such a perfection, such an angel as he is— could bear and carry through.

You should write a longer letter to dear Papa by next messenger[1]—as I know he wishes it and expects it and wishes you to enter into his letters fully—and therefore you should write a little whenever you have time, quietly and at leisure and then send it off by the messenger, not attempting to answer it by the messenger who goes next day. Try and do that, my darling, your letters are delightful— without flattery—and I read them over and over again. I must end here, with every blessing for my dearest child.

OSBORNE, MARCH 2, 1858

This letter is to go by tomorrow's messenger, and there- fore I begin it this evening—not to be hurried by the $\frac{1}{2}$ past 1 o'clock messenger.

What a strange person the Queen must be! Cold and unfriendly—and then suddenly—receiving Lady Churchill and Lord Sydney being very gracious and civil and speaking kindly of you. I know that you will not mind her ways— though of course it is always pleasanter if people are kind and civil; always be respectful and kind and attentive, with- out otherwise letting her conduct interfere with yours. This I know you will do.

The poor dear King! How I do pity him! This illness is a loss to you, for he would have been so kind to you. I am sure, made quite a pet of you. I wish the Queen would not prevent your seeing him; it can surely do him no harm, and nothing seems to do him real good. When you see him again, try and say something affectionate and kind from us to him. What you say of Stephanie is so delightful; how I long to see her and know her. I told you, I think, that I copied out what you said of her and Pedro—and sent it him.

---

[1] The Princess Royal's letter of February 27 had evidently not arrived.

— *68* —

Poor Princess Alexandrine[1] is very much to be pitied and it is quite right to be kind to the poor girl, but I would be cautious even there, for the poor thing has had a bad education—been neglected and has seen and heard much she ought not—therefore I would caution against intimacy; but I really only tell you this as I tell you all that I think strikes me, for in your long letter by the messenger of the week before—you told me, that you knew exactly on what terms of intimacy you ought to be with all your relations. I am not surprised at your finding Prince F. of Hesse very disagreeable;[2] we saw him several times in England, and always thought him so; even the Duchess of Cambridge (whose nephew he is) and certainly Cousin Mary, disliked him. And yet some years ago the Duchess told me she thought he would be a good husband for you!! *Qu'en dites vous?*

What you say about your dear excellent parents-in-law is indeed very sad, but just what we always thought; but think, dearest, what a happy privilege it is for you to be a comfort to the poor dear Princess which I can see you are, and also to the poor dear Prince, who is very fond of his daughter-in-law. Yes, you can be of the greatest use. You feel and appreciate the inestimable blessing of a perfectly united marriage—where there is perfect confidence—love and affection. It is the greatest blessing which mortals are allowed to enjoy and surely a foretaste of future life! You said in your long letter of the 24th–25th that the happiest time for you—was when you were alone with Fritz; you will now understand why I often grudged you children being always there, when I longed to be alone with dearest Papa! Those are always my happiest moments!

OSBORNE, MARCH 5, 1858

You long for Osborne and for running after dear Papa —and ask me to think of you sometimes when I look at

---

[1] Daughter of Prince Albrecht of Prussia, younger brother of the King. He had married a daughter of the King of the Netherlands. They were divorced. Princess Alexandrine was 16.

[2] He was the eldest son of the Landgrave of Hesse, and had married the daughter of Prince Charles of Prussia.

Winterhalter's picture[1] and at those in Papa's room. My dearest child—I can assure you, that there is not an hour in the day, not a picture or an object of any kind which I look at—when I do not think of you! Every event—both familiar and new ones recalls our absent child—much more than you can be thinking of us—as we miss you out of our daily circle and I constantly wish to tell you all that passes.

Still I see by your letters (and really they are such charming letters, so like yourself) to us both how you long to talk to us—to tell us and show us every thing—and we rejoice at that—and are sure of it. Distance, thank God, can never separate love—and thoughts and feelings.

I go on today. My intention for the future would be to write regularly to you on Mondays (by post) Wednesdays (by messenger) and Saturdays (by post)—I mean to send them off on those days. Any additional letter would be besides of course.

Papa is afraid you will overtire yourself by writing so many letters—but I think it is a relief to you to pour out your feelings to us. Dear Miss Hildyard is so delighted with your letter. No one except ourselves, can, naturally watch with such anxiety for every account of you—than she does —to whom you owe so much.

I shall be ready and happy to send some of the trimmings of your train for Fritz C. and poor Marianne. Papa has written to Fritz C. We think that perhaps "Mrs. Arthur" may be one of those little girls![2] Say every thing kind and civil from me to Fritz C.—and Abbat and say "que j'ai gardé un bien bon souvenir d'eux" and that we shall always be happy to see them here. Capt. de Ros[3] has been talking a good deal about F.C., and says he took such interest in every thing he saw—even as to how the living rooms were

---

[1] The famous family group painted in 1849.
[2] The Queen means that Prince Arthur, afterwards Duke of Connaught. might marry one of Prince Frederick Charles's daughters. He did.
[3] Equerry to the Prince Consort, afterwards 24th Lord de Ros. An enthusiastic photographer; a lot of the earliest photographs of the Royal Family were taken by him.

arranged as in England. I am so glad Abbat liked our dear Paradise here.

Do you think Fritz C. and M. would like if I sent the two girls a pretty frock each? What sort of frocks would you recommend—and are they big children of their age? What is the poor little swaddled-up baby to be called? Can't you send me some photographs of the little girls—and of the Princes whom I know—I mean Fritz C.—Abbat, Prince Adalbert, Prince Hohenzollern etc. for my album?

I read yesterday in "Heartsease"[1] (not "Violet") and it made me think so much of you. Bertie had a sick head-ache yesterday from imprudence.

From the Princess Royal

BERLIN, MARCH 4, 1858

Referring to the alterations in Prince Fritz's palace, which was at the eastern extremity of Unter den Linden and divided from his parents' house by the Opera House, the Princess wrote:

People here are much duller and slower of comprehension in these matters it seems to me. They go on dreadfully slowly with the house, they answer everything with eternal, most commonplace excuses.

Professor Schellbach[2] is coming tomorrow at 12—we are going to hear a lecture on electricity. He is to come twice a week. Professor Raumer[3] is going to give us lectures on the German history of the middle ages, and someone else whose name I have forgotten on literature.

Count Perponcher comes and puts Fritz au fait of all that is going on in the political world, and I am always present; he is very clever, and has an agreeable way of explaining. With him and the Baron besides the newspapers, we are able to hear all that goes on. I have had a most interesting lesson from Professor Schellbach in chemistry. Will you tell Dr. Becker[4] I found that I had forgotten but little of what he taught us.

---

[1] Charlotte M. Yonge's novel published in 1854. Lord Raglan read it in the Crimea—the last book he ever read.
[2] Formerly tutor in mathematics to Prince Fritz.
[3] The historian, Frederick von Raumer (1781–1873).
[4] German secretary to the Prince Consort.

We had your two brothers and Alice to dinner, à 5, and then when they were gone I began reading to Papa out of "Jane Eyre" which is very interesting, and then we played as usual. It is given much in Germany as "The Orphan of Lowood".[1]

By the by I have not heard you mention the English Church? Have you not been there yet? You remember I deprecated your going there too often as you ought to go to the others usually—but you should go to the English Church some time also, to show the English that you do not forget the Church in which you have been brought up; moreover the poor King was very kind about this chapel and gave it to the English residents.

Since you have told me all your hours and arrangements and since I have seen Jane C. I am much happier in that respect. Could you not just scribble on a little bit of paper—how your table stands etc. in your sitting-room—how the toilet table—and bed etc. I could then try to picture it to myself. I mean a sort of plan.

MARCH 9—I will go on with my letter today and just mention first what I send you by this messenger 1 the writing paper, 2 A little bit of orange flowers and myrtle for your train; 3 some real Osborne ivy which keeps well and which makes very pretty wreaths for the hair, and I am sure you will like to wear some of your own dear native ivy—from the woods here. I wore a wreath of it with some red ribbon on Monday night, also some years ago I put diamonds amid the leaves. 4 a little sketch I did from my window only with the brush,—and another scribble in ink which you will remember I did some time ago, and which I thought you might like to have.

All you say about the family[2] reminds me so much of what I was always used to as a child. Always on pins and needles, with the whole family hardly on speaking terms. I (a mere child) between two fires—trying to be civil and

[1] *Jane Eyre* had been published ten years earlier.
[2] The Prussian Royal Family.

— 72 —

then scolded at home! Oh! it was dreadful, and that has given me such a horror of Windsor, which I can't get over; you will perhaps understand now what I mean. Then after I married, they behaved shockingly to dearest Papa—that I was always in a state of feud about it—I could write many stories but I will keep them till we meet, as pendants to yours. Be very civil but keep your position just as you say— and a certain distance—then you will not be exposed to improper remarks or jokes etc. You speak most sensibly about it all.

The dear Princess writes so touched at your affection and kindness towards her—and says the Prince is so fond of you too. All this, my love, is delightful for us to hear. God bless you for all that is right and good, my precious child.

I hope and trust matters are coming straight with France again thanks to Lord Cowley's[1] indefatigable exertions but it has been most "touch and go" work. Most delicate ground—and the Emperor very wilful and high which with the people here—never would have done for a moment. I have got a charming successor to the dear Duchess of Wellington (who is a great loss) in Lady Caledon; youngest sister to Lady Clarendon;—a young widow.

Affie is going on admirably;[2] he comes to luncheon to-day (which is a real, brilliant Osborne day) and oh! when I see him and Arthur and look at . . .! (You know what I mean!) I am in utter despair! The systematic idleness, laziness—disregard of everything is enough to break one's heart, and fills me with indignation. Alice behaved so admirably about it—and has much influence with him— but, to you I own, I am wretched about it. But don't mention this to a human being!

---

[1] British Ambassador in Paris.
[2] He was being prepared for the Royal Navy at Alverbank, near Gosport, by the Reverend W. R. Jolley.

BERLIN, MARCH 5, 1858

My dearest Papa,

We are at last getting a little more into rest and order, and I am trying to follow your advice by pursuing regular occupations. You can understand that this was not possible before. I had not got accustomed to the hours and new ways and felt quite at sea, but now we are trying to arrange our day so that we may have time for ourselves in which to come to our senses and gain information. I confess I could not live as the rest do here, in busy idleness, without rest, without work, doing no good, and at the end of the day—knocked up and tired—the next morning a headache! Often it makes me melancholy to see health and strength thrown away and existence wasted, in joyless frivolity when there is so much to be done! It frightens me. I am always dreading being, without my knowledge, drawn into the current but luckily there are those about me that would warn me in time.

There is another thing which causes me much anxiety. We look upon the great enthusiasm demonstrated on the occasion of our marriage and our entry here as the expression of the feelings of the people which are at present those of hope. They think now that they have a chance of seeing Russian sympathies, the source of so much harm, lessened and of seeing those hopes realised which were raised to such a pitch when the present King under such good auspices with so many good promises and patriotic liberal expressions ascended the throne; those hopes were blighted; and I fear that it is too clear there is a want of confidence, of reciprocal confidence, between people and sovereign, and it is not strange! Besides this the people cannot help feeling that the life led by most members of the Royal Family is not such as could be respected or held out as an example. This must be a grief to the nation. They look at England, at Mama's court then at the bright character which I am thankful to hear my husband bears and expect good results of this alliance.

Now the moment of excitement is over a lull comes and all eyes will be fixed upon us. I fear a reaction, that where ex-

pectations are so raised, they must be disappointed and I deeply feel the responsibility we are under. We must do all we can to surround ourselves with good and useful people,— who are known to be free from party prejudice, from them to gain knowledge and whose character and ideas are such that the people may rest secure. We hear nothing but the truth and have no illiberal ideas instilled into us. This is also another reason why it is necessary for me to keep up my English title and what belongs to it, so that in hearing the name people may be reminded of the alliance.

I am sure, dear Papa, I have expressed myself most unclearly. I feel so ashamed of myself when I begin to put things on paper but it is the only way of improving the arrangement of my thoughts and ideas, if they all remain in my confused head there is no means of criticising them; and I am not afraid of you, dear Papa. You know I always said everything I thought to you rather than to anyone else because you are always so patient and so just.

I often tremble when I think of all the awful scrapes I might get not only myself but my husband and mother-in-law into, if I had not your advice, dearest Papa, and if I had not heard what things were like here. I might have found them out too late—in the family for instance. If I were to write the many little trifling things which are said which might lead one into a snare if one was not always on the watch—it would really seem utter gossip, and if there is a thing which I despise and detest it is that; and if I was constantly living with ladies I should fall a victim to it. I cannot tell you, dear Papa, since I am married, how scales have fallen from my eyes on so many subjects. Life is no joke; and those who like to consider it as such are much to be pitied. How so much frivolity can exist in the world I cannot understand! It is too sad! And how so many people can make themselves so unhappy when they might make themselves and others so happy. I keep a store of things to talk to you about when you come here which I earnestly hope will be before long.

In my own home I feel myself daily happier; when we are together all seems peace and joy; it is so delightful to feel that one belongs to a being to whom one can say anything and everything and be always listened to with patience as I am; may I ever be worthy of love and confidence as Mama is.

How I wish, dear Papa, we could once have Bertie here quietly to ourselves, when there is no Court here, which is the case now as the King is ill; there is much here which might benefit Bertie and which would interest him, and I am so anxious he should look upon Fritz with confidence and as a friend; I know Bertie is fond of him, and I know you would trust Fritz as a useful friend to him; some day if this could be done it would be such a good thing! But I fear for two or three years there is no chance.

Goodbye dearest, dearest Papa I should like to sit and write to you for ever, and thank you over and over again for all your goodness and kindness.

From the Princess Royal

BERLIN, MARCH 15, 1858

The Queen had rebuked her for not writing.

I am sorry you should have been so long without letters from me. I wrote to you three times last week, twice by post, and once by messenger and I thought they would arrive all right. I have such a horror of their being opened by Manteuffel[1] that I told the Baron to give the post letters to my banker here who sends them to Rothschild in London. Perhaps this may be the cause of the delay that you find so disagreeable.

Don't be angry, dear Mama, I mind that more from a distance even than nearby. It is very painful to think I have annoyed you or displeased you. These lines will go by messenger tomorrow.

---

[1] Prussian Conservative. In 1858 he was Prime Minister and Foreign Secretary.

After complaining of the exceptional heat the Queen describes a visit
to Aldershot:

Aldershot was really rather too hot a pleasure. Hazy—
not a particle of wind and such a sickening sun—we all
agreed it was not hotter in August. I have paid for it,
though I did not ride and held a large parasol over my nose,
by a scorched really sore red face, but I hope powder will
prevent my being too great a figure at the levée. Militia
and very raw recruits are a sad change from what we saw
last summer, though not from what we first saw in 55.
They played our two marches—not 95 or Monymusk—but
the Crimean one and "Bella Napoli", both of which we
listened to at Holyrood—and it nearly made me cry when
it began—to think of you so far away!

That you should feel shy sometimes I can easily understand. I do so very often to this hour. But being married
gives one one's position which nothing else can. Think however what it was for me, a girl of 18 all alone, not brought
up at court as you were—but very humbly at Kensington
Palace—with trials and difficulties, to receive[1] and to be
everywhere the first! No, no one knows what a life of difficulties mine was—and is! How thankful I am that none of
you, please God! ever will have that anomalous and trying
position. Now do enter into this in your letters, you so
seldom do that, except to answer a question.

Now to reply to your observation that you find a married
woman has much more liberty than an unmarried one; in
one sense of the word she has,—but what I meant was—
in a physical point of view—and if you have hereafter (as
I had constantly for the first 2 years of my marriage)—aches
—and sufferings and miseries and plagues—which you must
struggle against—and enjoyments etc. to give up—constant
precautions to take, you will feel the yoke of a married
woman! Without that—certainly it is unbounded happiness
—if one has a husband one worships! It is a foretaste of

---

[1] i.e. To receive people or "company".

heaven. And you have a husband who adores you, and is, I perceive, ready to meet every wish and desire of your's. I had 9 times for 8 months to bear with those above-named enemies and real misery (besides many duties) and I own it tried me sorely; one feels so pinned down—one's wings clipped—in fact, at the best (and few were or are better than I was[1]) only half oneself—particularly the first and second time. This I call the "shadow side" as much as being torn away from one's loved home, parents and brothers and sisters. And therefore—I think our sex a most unenviable one.

Your saying you thought a young girl was not in an enviable position comes I think a little from that proud, high spirit, which you will remember we did all we could to check and which it would have been so wrong in us to have tolerated. I am sure you feel now my dear child— how right and wise we were. But you were trying. Alice, I don't think feels a young girl's life trying—she is really very good, so aimable, so gentle, so obliging and so humble.

All you say about your dear mother-in-law is very nice, and right and kind. In every letter she speaks with the greatest love and affection of you and wishes I should tell you how much she feels your affection. All you say about F. C.[2] pleases and interests us. And I hope he will often come to England.

We expect Prince George of Saxony[3] soon; he will come to Windsor on the 5th for 4 nights—on his way to Lisbon. We wish we knew when the Hohenzollerns with their dear daughter[4] and son were coming here as it keeps us in a state of uncertainty as to what we are to do. I fear dear Pedro is rather slow in deciding and this leads to delay.

I am shocked at what you say about Countess Oriola[5]

---

[1] The Queen is saying that she suffered less than most women.
[2] Fritz Carl.
[3] Second son of the King of Saxony: he was on his way to Lisbon to see the King of Portugal's sister with a view to marriage.
[4] i.e. Stephanie who was about to marry the King of Portugal.
[5] Lady-in-waiting to the Princess of Prussia. On March 15 the Princess had written to the Queen that "Countess Blücher does what no one else does, or can do—keeps Countess Oriola in order".

Queen Victoria and the Prince Consort, 1860

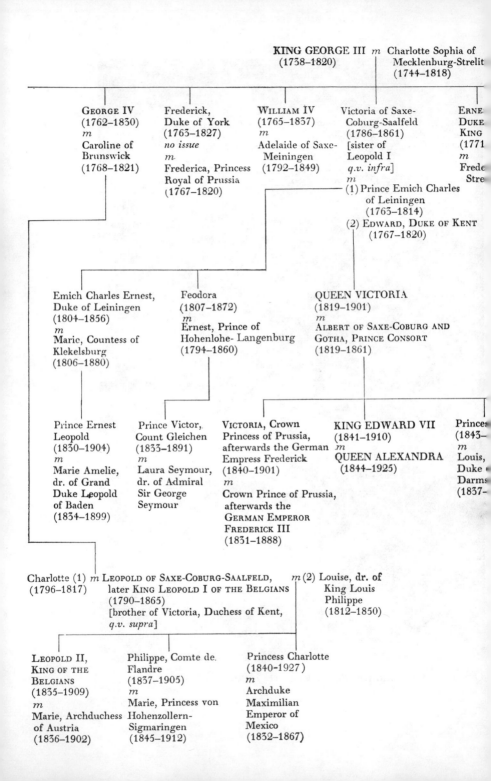

KING GEORGE III *m* Charlotte Sophia of
(1738–1820) Mecklenburg-Strelit
(1744–1818)

GEORGE IV
(1762–1850)
m
Caroline of
Brunswick
(1768–1821)

Frederick,
Duke of York
(1763–1827)
no issue
m.
Frederica, Princess
Royal of Prussia
(1767–1820)

WILLIAM IV
(1765–1837)
m
Adelaide of Saxe-
Meiningen
(1792–1849)

Victoria of Saxe-
Coburg-Saalfeld
(1786–1861)
[sister of
Leopold I
q.v. infra]
m
(1) Prince Emich Charles
of Leiningen
(1763–1814)
(2) EDWARD, DUKE OF KENT
(1767–1820)

ERNE
DUKE
KING
(1771
m
Frede
Stre

Emich Charles Ernest,
Duke of Leiningen
(1804–1856)
m
Marie, Countess of
Klekelsburg
(1806–1880)

Feodora
(1807–1872)
m
Ernest, Prince of
Hohenlohe- Langenburg
(1794–1860)

QUEEN VICTORIA
(1819–1901)
m
ALBERT OF SAXE-COBURG AND
GOTHA, PRINCE CONSORT
(1819–1861)

Prince Ernest
Leopold
(1830–1904)
m
Marie Amelie,
dr. of Grand
Duke Leopold
of Baden
(1834–1899)

Prince Victor,
Count Gleichen
(1833–1891)
m
Laura Seymour,
dr. of Admiral
Sir George
Seymour

VICTORIA, Crown
Princess of Prussia,
afterwards the German
Empress Frederick
(1840–1901)
m
Crown Prince of Prussia,
afterwards the
GERMAN EMPEROR
FREDERICK III
(1831–1888)

KING EDWARD VII
(1841–1910)
m
QUEEN ALEXANDRA
(1844–1925)

Princes
(1843–
m
Louis,
Duke
Darms
(1837–

Charlotte (1) *m* LEOPOLD OF SAXE-COBURG-SAALFELD,
(1796–1817) later KING LEOPOLD I OF THE BELGIANS
(1790–1865)
[brother of Victoria, Duchess of Kent,
q.v. supra]

m (2) Louise, dr. of
King Louis
Philippe
(1812–1850)

LEOPOLD II,
KING OF THE
BELGIANS
(1835–1909)
m
Marie, Archduchess
of Austria
(1836–1902)

Philippe, Comte de.
Flandre
(1837–1905)
m
Marie, Princess von
Hohenzollern-
Sigmaringen
(1845–1912)

Princess Charlotte
(1840–1927)
m
Archduke
Maximilian
Emperor of
Mexico
(1832–1867)

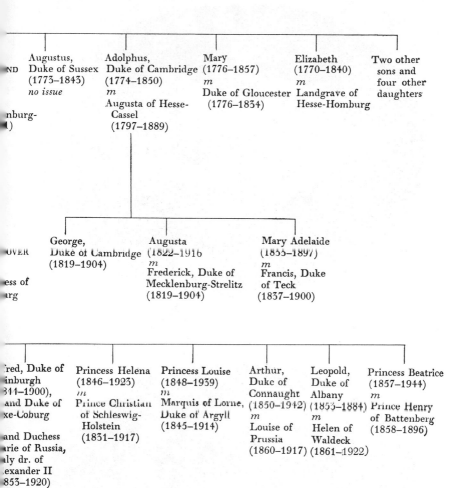

ND
Augustus,
Duke of Sussex
(1773–1843)
no issue

nburg-
⊣)

Adolphus,
Duke of Cambridge
(1774–1850)
m
Augusta of Hesse-
Cassel
(1797–1889)

Mary
(1776–1857)
m
Duke of Gloucester
(1776–1834)

Elizabeth
(1770–1840)
m
Landgrave of
Hesse-Homburg

Two other
sons and
four other
daughters

OVER

ess of
arg

George,
Duke of Cambridge
(1819–1904)

Augusta (1822–1916
m
Frederick, Duke of
Mecklenburg-Strelitz
(1819–1904)

Mary Adelaide
(1833–1897)
m
Francis, Duke
of Teck
(1837–1900)

red, Duke of
inburg
844–1900),
and Duke of
xe-Coburg

and Duchess
rie of Russia,
ly dr. of
exander II
853–1920)

Princess Helena
(1846–1923)
m
Prince Christian
of Schleswig-
Holstein
(1831–1917)

Princess Louise
(1848–1939)
m
Marquis of Lorne,
Duke of Argyll
(1845–1914)

Arthur,
Duke of
Connaught
(1850–1942)
m
Louise of
Prussia
(1860–1917)

Leopold,
Duke of
Albany
(1853–1884)
m
Helen of
Waldeck
(1861–1922)

Princess Beatrice
(1857–1944)
m
Prince Henry
of Battenberg
(1858–1896)

THE ROYAL FAMILY-TREE

Prince Alfred, 1858

Prince Leopold, 1858

but she is I fear a traitor in the camp, at least so we have heard. Have you heard it or do you think it is so?

You have never told me what Marianne's baby is to be called?

I am delighted to hear that people stare at seeing husband and wife together! Fritz is not the man to be ashamed of it, I am sure, and poor Persigny's observation to me that I had "popularisé les bons ménages", will I am sure become true in your dear case and a blessing it will be; I am rather glad to hear you don't become a "living Army list" as some of the princesses there, I believe are. One can admire them[1] quite well without all that.

Lord Granville (also Lord Stafford) inquired so much after you and wished me to offer his respectful thanks for your kind message through Lord Sydney. He, and I believe the Clarendons, and also Breadalbanes will I think very likely go and see you in the course of the summer, I encourage them all to do so—as I am sure it would give you such pleasure.

It is completely a hot summer's day—quite incredible and really very trying. It has lasted now—nearly a fortnight (no, about 12 days) but not as hot near as these 2 last which are quite June and hotter than June often is!

Bertie reads with me of a morning—Arnold's Sermons; I try to make a good and deep impression. À propos of him, would you (which you could do quite without any appearance of arrière pensée) question Countess Perponcher and him too—as closely and fully as you can—about the young Princess Anna of Hesse who is the daughter of Prince and Princess Charles of Hesse. She is Alice's age, and you know the Perponchers were for some time at Darmstadt,—and also inquire about the sons.[2]

I send you a photograph of Windsor which I think you

---

[1] i.e. the soldiers.

[2] Prince Charles of Hesse was brother and heir to the Grand Duke of Hesse-Darmstadt. Princess Charles was Princess Elizabeth of Prussia, first cousin to the King. Their eldest son, Louis, married Princess Alice of Great Britain. Their only daughter Princess Anna, 1843–65, married the Grand Duke of Mecklenburg-Schwerin.

have not, also a little box from Affie—and a very interesting little diary by Mrs. now Lady Inglis—who is the present Chancellor's[1] daughter, which he himself thought would interest you. Only think that after all her dreadful sufferings and trials—she was wrecked on her way to England and lost all she had! It is terrible. She is daily expected. Pray read it to Fritz.

From the Princess Royal

BERLIN, MARCH 29, 1858

We are going to have a very nice dinner just as I like it today—only our entourage and Curtius (Fritz's former tutor, a very clever man)[2] and Brandis[3] (the same who was in England and who taught Bertie) M. Droysen[4] (the same who wrote that pamphlet which you will remember reading and which I also helped in translating) and Professor Werder[5] who wrote a very fine thing called "Columbus" (does Papa know it?) and who is an unbounded and enthusiastic admirer of Shakespeare, which pleases me greatly.

These are all clever and interesting people from whom one can learn and above all they are truly patriotic because they know the truth and are clear sighted which is not the fashion nowadays here.

WINDSOR CASTLE, MARCH 31, 1858

I write today one of my long, confidential letters. I was just interrupted by receiving your dear, delightful and very satisfactory letter of the 29th. It only wanted more pasting

---

[1] Lord Chelmsford.
[2] Ernest Curtius, the classical scholar. He directed the German excavations at Olympia.
[3] Christian August Brandis, the German classical philologist.
[4] J. G. Droysen, the Prussian historian. Before her marriage the Princess Royal had translated one of his pamphlets into English. This pamphlet was written for the Goethe and Schiller Festival at Weimar, and advocated a liberal policy for Germany.
[5] Karl Werder, 1806–93. He was professor of philosophy in Berlin. He also lectured on Hamlet and Macbeth. *Columbus* was a tragedy in five acts.

—but seemed quite safe; the silver paper ought to be so pasted that it tears off—like mine, and like some which the Baron made so very safe. Most certainly I shall give your message to poor Bertie. Alas! I feel very sad and anxious about him: he is so idle and so weak! But God grant that he may take things more to heart and more seriously for the future, and get more power. The heart is good, warm and affectionate—if there were but reflection and power, and self-control. Still there is a Power above who will watch over him and yet help us all. Dearest child, when we think of you—when we receive your dear, clever sensible letters— so full of all that is excellent and good and right, then we thank God for such a blessing as such a dear, distinguished and loving child is—and feel easy and comforted in the midst of the bitter separation and rewarded for all the anxiety and trouble we had about you. Yes, the tears are in my eyes when I write this. I see how every account of your anxiety to improve yourself, and to become wiser daily—and more fit for your difficult position—delights your dearest Papa and how dear Miss Hildyard's eyes fill with tears, when I show these accounts to her! God bless and protect you, dearest child! You are right in saying that with such perfect confidence, separation becomes as nothing.

Really you should protest against Prince Charles's jokes; I would not go there if he was so *inconvenant*, or at least not speak to him, if he gets on such abominable subjects, but be very stiff and reserved.[1] I am glad your journey is settled, and hope the visit to Weimar will go off well. You must be

---

[1] See the Princess Royal's letter of March 1, and on March 29 she had written to her mother: "Yesterday there was a Familiendinner at Prince Charles's which (was) most disagreeable, he made such disagreeable jokes—one does not know where to look sometimes. The only way is not to laugh; and to take it with the greatest indifference, as if one did not understand it; and not to look all the contempt one feels. But it is difficult for ladies not to colour sometimes."
Lady Paget in *Embassies of Other Days* has described these German royal dinners. "Dinner at German Courts was a movable feast and varied between 2 and 5, but always in full dress, and at 8 o'clock there was tea and supper. Being young and strong I bore up gallantly against

very respectful and think much of les formes, and speak very loud to the old Grand Duchess.[1]

Papa has just received F. C's letter;[2] it is really very aimable of him to ask us to be sponsors.

You don't tell me enough about the people you see; you had to dinner the other day—Countess Blankensee[3] who is a very old friend of mine and whom I knew so well when I was a child; she was Aunt Feodore's bridesmaid, and a great friend of dear Papa's poor mother.[4] I am sure she talked to you about me;—say every thing kind from me to her, and tell her, I hope so much to see her some day again. Now don't forget this. And pray don't forget inquiring about the young Princess of Hesse. We must look out for princesses for Bertie—as his wife ought not to be above a year or 2 younger than him, therefore 14 or 15 now, pretty, quiet and clever and sensible. Oh! if you would find us one!

We are delighted at the sensible and reasonable way in which you occupy your time:—it is very wise. And then we are delighted at your seeing these sensible, patriotic people; it will do so much good to you both, and to Prussia generally. How do you like Curtius?

Be sure and tell me what you think of the confirmation —the sacrament and the christening and describe the dresses of the principal people. Say something kind and civil to Alexandrine[5] and to Abbat.

You translated Droysen's pamphlet—you are too modest. I read it too with great interest. How do you like him?

---

these ghastly hours and modes of feeding. . . . The afternoons were passed by the victims of these barbarous customs in a state of coma."
[1] Of Saxe-Weimar. She was the mother of the Princess (grandmother of Prince Frederick William) and daughter of the Emperor Paul I of Russia. Her father-in-law was the friend of Goethe.
[2] Fritz Carl.
[3] Princess Amelia Carolath, a cousin of Queen Adelaide, married the Count of Blankensee.
[4] The Prince Consort's mother, Louise, Duchess of Saxe-Coburg-Gotha. She was divorced.
[5] She was about to be confirmed.

Just a few words to say how well every thing has gone off. Yesterday Bertie was examined for a hour by the Dean before the Archbishop[1]—longer than you were—in his own room, and he answered very well, going through the first part of the catechism bringing him all through the Belief which he had to explain—to the sacraments and confirmation. The afternoon was damp: Bertie drove and walked with us. In the evening he remained quietly alone—away from the others—Affie is (with great difficulty) kept away from him—so that the right atmosphere shall not be disturbed.

This morning he came up to wish me good morning. He was quiet and gentle and seemed properly impressed. The others all looked for eggs. We assembled in the closet (at yours we did in Uncle Leopold's (the King's) rooms) and proceeded to the Chapel where all was just the same. I wore a blue moiré antique made thus [sketch] the body trimmed with blue ribbon, white silk with guipure lace over it. The lace is off the Empress's dressing-gown.[2] The same hymns were sung;—the Archbishop made a very good and impressive charge, pointing out the duties of a Christian. Bertie stood the whole time (as did I—and Cousin Mary[3]—and which I think you ought to have done.) We sitting. He wore his Windsor uniform; Alice in blue silk—light and dark stripes, Lenchen[4] (with her hair turned back) and Louise in blue silk small stripes—trimmed with black velvet. Alfred and Arthur in Highland dress. I wore the brooch of you as a little angel. After the service was over we all went into the Green Drawing Room where we talked to the company and then went to the King's room—where were Bertie's presents and where I gave your message to him, your very handsome gift; our's a vase by Veité—silver repoussé, really very fine and other more trifling but pretty gifts which the

---

[1] J. B. Sumner, Archbishop of Canterbury, 1848–62.
[2] Presumably a dressing-gown given to the Queen by the Empress Eugénie.
[3] Meaning when she and Princess Mary were confirmed.
[4] Princess Helena—the Queen's third daughter.

others will I doubt not describe to you. We lunched *en famille* at ½ past 1. Leopold[1] and darling Beatrice[2] came at the end of it. The latter for the first time today in short clothes with darling little stockings and shoes; a little silk stocking and pink satin shoes—really too darling. It was the dress she wore at your wedding only shortened.

And now having described every thing let me add—how anxious and fervent were my prayers that this day may make a lasting impression on Bertie, may give him strength to exert and control himself and that he may ever be able to look back on today and tomorrow with real satisfaction and thankfulness. We have done and shall do all to make today a really impressive one. I wrote him a letter this morning; your's was perfect and gave him great pleasure. He will dine alone with us tonight and tomorrow. We take the sacrament as usual at 9.

I have made good Mr. Gibbs[3] a Civil Companion of the Bath today, and Mr. Tarver[4]—a Chaplain.

May God protect dear Bertie—and work out in him all that is good and pure in his young heart! But a boy and a young man after some few years, can no longer be protected by his parents. He must fight the battle alone, and himself —and does require constant vigilance not to fall.

WINDSOR CASTLE, APRIL 5, 1858

I can easily understand how much affected and gripped you must have been by that touching ceremony;[5] Yes how I envy your being present at those beautiful ceremonies with their emotional sway and which I miss here so sadly. However I hope now some day to be able to witness and take part in such solemn ceremonies! We won't say any

---

[1] Prince Leopold—the Queen's youngest son.
[2] Princess Beatrice—the Queen's youngest child.
[3] Frederick Waymouth Gibbs, a Fellow of Trinity, Cambridge and member of the Bar. He was tutor to the Prince of Wales 1851–60. See *The Cornhill*, Spring 1951, for some interesting facts about him.
[4] C. F. Tarver, Fellow of King's. Classical Tutor to the Prince. The Queen means chaplain to herself.
[5] Princess Alexandrine's confirmation.

thing now about Alice's confirmation—but there is no harm in indulging in the hope, even if it can't be carried out. It would interest and please Fritz I am sure to witness, and I think great family events should be witnessed by the whole family. In Germany the Princes and Princesses fly about for every sort of often useless event—and therefore crossing the sea need make no difference. April and May would do as well as May and June. However these are only speculations.

It must have been so very touching under the peculiar circumstances and with the poor King near you—whose state remains a very sad one. I am not surprised at your headache. Easter—and every thing must be most touching and moving in Germany.

Your little sketches are quite charming. I can't sketch Bertie; a boy—and such a thin one is so unpicturesque. However he is to be photographed as a pendant to you, and you shall have it as soon as it is ready.

WINDSOR CASTLE, APRIL 7, 1858

I am again much vexed at the non-arrival of any telegraph;—I telegraphed last night to Weimar and again this morning. You must answer for I assure you we never dream of leaving telegrams unanswered; I told you this several times, for it is positively uncivil not to do it—and yet on Monday when I telegraphed our message to Fritz C.—you did not answer till I sent a second message to ask if the first was received. This is very wrong and very bad mannered, my good child.

We have perfectly horrid weather which is so provoking, as I hoped to ride so much here. By the by, look what unpleasant nonsense they put into the papers about you and Louise of Baden.[1]

All you say about your happiness—and about the impossibility of it's being perfect in this world—is most true, my dearest child. We must ever be truly grateful for the happiness we are permitted to enjoy and take with meek-

---

[1] i.e. That they were *enceinte*.

ness the dark shadow sides which there must be to it! May you ever be as happy with your good husband as you are now! Never think that I ever mention any remark of yours, like those about Curtius, to the dear Princess. I never repeat any thing except when it is this praise of herself— or expressions of love and affection and sympathy towards her— and also in general that all you write and say shows how entirely you understand the position in the family and how well-intentioned you are. Does Droysen know that you translated his pamphlet? Poor Fräulein's[1] time of departure is approaching—on Monday Mdlle. Bauer[2] will meet us in London—she will remain a week to teach her her duties, and then a week longer, at her particular request to arrange her own affairs—but I own I dread it, as she is in such a state of excitement—worked up. This morning she spoke with great irritation of never having been presented to the Princess! That even Thurston and May[3] had been spoken to—and not she! and that the Princess must find it strange as she had begged you to do it. Is this so? I can't think that in 51, 53 and 56 the Princess never spoke to her! However promise me (and answer this please) to set this right now— and to speak of Fräulein as having taught you entirely in German—at least perfected you in it: only—do write a line to Fräulein, if it is but one from Gotha, so as to soothe her, for really she is in such a state of excitement that I often am alarmed by it.

Prince George of S.[4] is here since Monday. I like him very much, he is pleasant, gemütlich, accomplished— passionately fond of "good" music and even of old tiresome music, and plays very nicely with all the children. He spoke much of the poor King of Prussia whose state he says his mother knew from the Queen had been of much longer standing than was generally known. Poor Princess Alexandrine how much I feel for her! You can I am sure give her

---

[1] The Princess Royal's German governess, afterwards Madame Müller, who was not entirely satisfactory, and was leaving.
[2] German governess to the Royal Family for many years.
[3] The Queen's personal servants. Thurston was nurse to Princess Beatrice.
[4] Saxony.

good advice. I have heard that that horrid Uncle[1] would wish to corrupt her mind—and to raise the worst feelings in her young, and it is to be hoped, still innocent heart: I am very glad the Queen has taken her to live with her. That is her best chance. I am so glad the Queen was kind; I was sure she would for she can be very kind, and sensible, and she is much to be pitied.

WINDSOR CASTLE, APRIL 10, 1858

Prince George of S. left at a little after 8 yesterday morning for Southampton and sailed at 2 for Lisbon, where I really hope that he may be successful, as I think in every way it would be desirable—it relates our family to the royal Saxon line—she is clever—unbigoted—amiable, strong and healthy and may do a great deal of good—in every way.[2] He is a nice young man, only excessively absent, like his father, but he has the most beautiful talent for music which is his passion;—he plays most beautifully and everything at first sight; he likewise sings charmingly—all sorts of German songs, with a very fine voice and great taste. He played your favourite "Harmonious Blacksmith" which he is so fond of—and some of your favourite old English tunes out of Alice's book—you would have been delighted; I was very grateful for two hours of loveliness. It is like a great artiste not like an amateur, and all good music!

Pray when you see the Queen say something civil and kind about her nephew whom she is very fond of.[3] He is very fond of children and played with your brothers big and little—very nicely. The family as Fritz will know, is

---

[1] This may be Prince Frederick of the Netherlands. He was closely linked with Prussia, having been born in Berlin and having married a daughter of King Frederick William III. His only sister was the mother of Princess Alexandrine. The reference could, of course, be to Prince Charles.

[2] Daughter of the Queen of Portugal. The Queen's husband was a Saxe-Coburg.

[3] Prince George's mother and the Queen of Prussia were daughters of Maximilian, King of Bavaria.

extremely united, and accustomed to a very simple family life; so was the good late King.[1]

The excellent news from India; viz.:—that Lucknow is all but in our hands will have pleased you much. God grant this sad war may be soon at an end!—dear old Sir Colin[2] has done so admirably.

Uncle George was here for one night on Wednesday and asked as he always does—most particularly after you. Lady Derby and Lady Emma (who is a nice girl) also asked so much after you. Now pray send me a word of acknowledgment to all who ask after you. On Monday we return to Town. This evening come the Aumales,[3] and the Princess[4] also the Hardwickes and Lady Elizabeth Yorke—and Mr. Disraeli.

Dear Mrs. Wellesley is in great beauty. You will have heard from Lady Caroline and from Mary Barrington that she (M.) is going to be married which is a great thing, though it is a poor and not brilliant marriage—still it is a very good thing.[5]

I forgot to answer your questions about poor Leopold and his bruises. He bruises as much as ever but unberufen 1000 times—is free from any at present; but he holds himself still as badly as ever and is very ugly, I think uglier even than he was, but it is a great pity he holds himself so ill for he has a fine figure with very fine limbs and chest— like Alfred. He is a very clever, amusing but very absurd child. He is dictating a letter to Thurston[6] for you.

Lord and Lady Raglan are going today to Hanover and mean to go on to Berlin. Be sure to show them some civility, as he belongs to me and then on account of his poor father;[7]

---

[1] King Frederick-Augustus. He died in 1854. He had stayed with Queen Victoria in 1844; she was very fond of him.

[2] Sir Colin Campbell, afterwards Lord Clyde. He saved the British Empire in India. Lucknow was relieved on March 19. The Queen was warmly attached to him.

[3] Henri, 4th son of Louis-Philippe, duc d'Aumale.

[4] Probably Duchess of Orleans, widow of Louis-Philippe's eldest son.

[5] She married Sir Algernon West.

[6] The Queen's dresser.

[7] Lord Raglan was a Lord-in-waiting: he was married to a daughter of Lord Beauchamp. His father was the Crimean general.

—we like him very much—and I told him how you admired
her, which pleased him very much. So take plenty of notice
of them.

And now I must again come with a little scold; you have
not written me one single word, for more than a week!!
I am vexed, for you could easily have managed—if you
would but be a little more expert—to say: "I am well—
had a good journey and am delighted with it etc." And
this could have been done in 1 minute, and would have
given me pleasure, and this you did even on your fatiguing
journey from England every day! You seem to think that
if you can't write to me a long letter you are not to write at
all. And yet I (and also Papa) wrote volumes from Osborne
to say I only wished to hear regularly (I have, from the
ladies) and yet here—you again relapse into the same fault.
I only want one word—one sign of life to cheer up the long
waiting—and when you wrote to Papa from Gotha, you
forgetful child (whom I see by all this is still unchanged
in some respects) never sent me a word! Now promise me
—you won't do this again,—only one word I want—even
don't direct it, if you haven't time, but just to say "I am
well, I'm happy—I have no time to describe anything today,
but will from Berlin"; I should have been perfectly satisfied.
I know I should certainly have done it for you.

Now let this not happen again promise me and answer
this.[1]

When do the Badens[2] come? If Louise and Fritz William
talk of a certain subject[3]—be sure and tell me all. You know

---

[1] In reply to this the Princess wrote:
"I promise never to let such a long time pass again without writing,
but will you, dearest Mama, tell me that you have forgiven me, because
it makes me quite wretched to think you are vexed and angry with me,
and I not there to be able to clear myself!"
[2] Grand-Duke Frederick of Baden. He had married the only daughter
of the Prince and Princess of Prussia—Louise.
[3] i.e. A princess to marry the Prince of Wales.

what I think and feel, though I don't breathe it. You have not answered me about the little Princess of Hesse—though I asked you nearly 3 weeks ago—and repeated it—now don't forget—also tell me all about the Weimar children, but they are much too young; whoever has the happiness of marrying B must be nearly his age; this we all feel and Mr. Tarver said it to me the other day. I must own I feel greatly relieved at his absence; he is so insupportable with the younger ones. It is most odious but they have spread a report that you and I are both in what I call an unhappy condition! It is odious and though it is naturally denied by me and all who are well informed—Lady Caroline told me—as regards me, people say they know it is so! Really too bad. Good Sir James and all who love you—hope that you will be spared this trial for a year yet, as you are so very young and I know you would feel all the homesickness—and every other little trial so much more if you were ailing and in a state of constant malaise. If I had had a year of happy enjoyment with dear Papa, to myself—how thankful I should have been! But I was 3 years and a ½ older; and therefore I was in for it at once—and furious I was. I really hope you are not getting fat again? Do avoid eating soft, pappy things or drinking much—you know how that fattens.

I have been interrupted by the levée; it was a small one but there were 6 officers from India all badly wounded one with only his fore-finger and thumb of his right hand left! Major Alison (son of the historian) secretary to dear old Sir Colin, with his left arm off at the shoulder. We are now going to the Kensington Museum to open 3 rooms which are full of fine old china. This evening we have a large dinner—Brunow[1](!) Azeglio,[2] Lavradio[3]—Duke of Terceira,[4] Clarendons and Constance, Hardinges, Pakingtons,

[1] Baron Brunow, Russian Ambassador in London, hence the Queen's exclamation mark.
[2] Sardinian Minister in London.
[3] Count Lavradio, Portuguese Minister in London.
[4] Duke of Terceira, formerly Count Villaflor, Portuguese constitutional leader against Dom Miguel in the 1820s.

Lord Sefton, Newports etc. Yesterday evening we went to the Opera where we had really a treat for they gave "The Huguenots"[1] every note of which we both are so fond of, and were so glad to hear again, extremely well—the orchestra was extremely good, new dresses and decorations and Valentine beautifully sung by a new actress a Mademoiselle Tietjens[2] an Austrian, who is a very fine actress and singer with a fine and graceful figure but not a pretty face. Giuglini sang very well as Raoul but has not enough voice— and Beletti was good as St. Bris.[3] I mean to go again to-morrow.

Dear Papa has told you of a project of his—which I know will make you jump with joy—and believe me, my dearest child, that the greatest proof of my love and affection for you is, that I have encouraged him in it—though you know how miserable and (from my isolated position) lost I am without my master; but I rejoice to think of the happiness and comfort it will be to him and you—and the joy for both to see Coburg.

BUCKINGHAM PALACE, APRIL 17, 1858

But you can't imagine the letters Aunt Alexandrine and grandmama have written. Really as if there was no body in the world like you. Aunt Alexandrine calls you an angel! Are you become one now? It is quite touching to read your dear Grandmama's letters—she is so touched and delighted.

---

[1] *The Huguenots* was the opera written by Giacomo Meyerbeer (1791–1865). He was Jewish and came of wealthy, Berlin banking stock. After training in Italy, he had a spectacular success in Paris with *Robert le Diable* (1831) followed by *Les Huguenots* (1836). King Frederick William IV observed: "Catholics and Protestants cut each others' throats and a Jew sets the proceedings to music." Raoul is the Protestant hero, Valentine de St. Bris the Catholic heroine and St. Bris the wicked Catholic nobleman, who is shown as largely responsible for the massacre of St. Bartholomew. (This occupies the last two of five very long acts.)
[2] Therese Tietgiens or Tietjens (1831–77) was born at Hamburg of Hungarian parents. She was the most famous "Valentine" and this performance was her debut in England where she settled thereafter. She died at her home in the Finchley Road.
[3] Antonio Giuglini was a popular tenor; he died insane in 1865. Giovanni Battista Beletti (1813–90) sang a great deal with Jenny Lind.

You must manage to visit her every year—I am only afraid your young head will get turned with so much praise! I say this however in fun—for I have no apprehension that it will. That is really the case—I have great confidence in your steadiness. What you say about Weimar is just what we expected; but how terribly disagreeable to be lodged in that way: nobody would dream in England such a thing! The vast machine I well remember.[1]

Yesterday Pelissier[2] had his audience; he is not near so fat as I thought—but very little, not taller certainly than the Emperor and quite unused to Courts etc. He did not know Papa who was standing near me and when Papa bowed to him he said "Comment c'est vous?" and was much shocked at his non-recognition of Papa. Tonight he dines with us and I have invited General Simpson, Sir Wm. Codrington and Uncle George to meet him. I saw on Thursday Lady Inglis (whose journal I sent you and for which I hope you will send a message). She is not 25—and looks so quiet and well, one could not think she had gone through so much.

BUCKINGHAM PALACE, APRIL 19, 1858

Does Fritz really go on going so often for his drilling? I think it a pity.

I think Fritz has not seen Prince G. of S.[3] for a long time—and would like him now. His absence is very great—but I thought him wonderfully ready to talk about all his relations. Then what I liked besides his being agreeable and such a wonderful musician—is his being so simple and good humoured and à son aise with the children—and his being

---

[1] In her letter describing her visit to Weimar, the Princess Royal had told her mother that she and Prince Frederick William were lodged on different floors, and were only able to approach each other's rooms through a scullery. She had said of her visit to Gotha "I must tell you they gave us the same *vaste machine* which is called in England a bed-bath which was made for you and has never been used since." The Queen had stayed there in 1845.
[2] Afterwards Duke of Malakoff. Supreme commander in the Crimea, and just appointed French Ambassador in London.
[3] George of Saxony.

much attached to his family and a very correct young man. He will probably become one of our family.[1]

Marshal Pélissier asked after you; I think you would like him—he is very amusing and wonderfully blunt, and naïf and has no idea of "les usages du monde"—but sensible and clever in his remarks.

From the Princess Royal

But do pray do not give up the thought of coming here. I want you to see my dear home and all the people I come daily in contact with, and hear your opinion about all; if you mean to wait for a certain event to happen to poor me you may wait an eternity. It is too bad to spread reports about Louise and me, but I can't stir a little finger here without some meaning being put upon it; it is such a plague. Not that I should be sorry, dear Mama, if such a thing were to happen. I should on the contrary be very happy and think it a great blessing, but I am thankful to be spared it now. I am too young for it. You know me well enough, dearest Mama, to know what I think about such things. I would take them just as they come, never go into sentimental ecstasies as is sometimes the case, which you and I, dear Mama, have often thought tiresome, foolish and ridiculous, but be thankful for everything God in his mercy sends us.

BUCKINGHAM PALACE, APRIL 21, 1858

We have just returned from a horticultural show in St. James's Hall, a very fine music room decorated by Owen Jones and lately opened. Dearest child—do try now that the days are so long and the weather is so fine to get out more—if even it only be once walking let it be twice driving in the open carriage. You never minded driving out in the open carriage when it was very cold and wrapped yourself up much less than me! Now pray do try and get out more; that constant driving about of an evening and to public places is anything but wholesome. I can not tell you how

[1] The Portuguese princess whom he married was daughter of Queen Maria and King-Consort Ferdinand—a Saxe-Coburg prince.

happy I am that you are not in an unenviable position. I never can rejoice by hearing that a poor young thing is pulled down by this trial.

Though I quite admit the comfort and blessing good and amiable children are—though they are also an awful plague and anxiety for which they show one so little gratitude very often! What made me so miserable was—to have the two first years of my married life utterly spoilt by this occupation! I could enjoy nothing—not travel about or go about with dear Papa and if I had waited a year, as I hope you will, it would have been very different.

You must tell me, dear, what you thought of the Weimar boy[1] I must repeat again that Bertie's wife must be very near his own age as every one who has had anything to do with him, thinks on that depends his whole future life! I wish I could see and hear more about the young Princess of Hesse. Her age would be just the thing. Do tell me a great deal about dear Louise whom I rejoice to think you will see so much of; till now, you have had no relation living in the same house with you and that makes the whole difference. There are several other things I wish you to tell me, dearest child, which you have not. First what was your impression of Grandmama, did you think her looking so old? Then to this hour though I have sent messages to her—and you never will answer them or ever tell me about Amelia Carolath[2] who as I told you is such an old friend of mine. Poor Uncle Nemours who came here with the Queen[3] (who is wonderfully well) the day before yesterday will send you the dear hands,[4] and also a little arm and foot of poor little Blanche.[5]

We went on Friday to the New Watercolour Exhibition,

---

[1] Duke Charles Augustus, nephew of the Princess of Prussia, born 1844 and evidently considered as a possible husband for one of the Queen's daughters.
[2] See letter of March 31, 1858.
[3] Louis-Philippe's widow.
[4] Of the Duchesse de Nemours who had died in 1857. They were reproduced in marble.
[5] The youngest child of the Duc de Nemours. The Duchess died at her birth.

which it made me quite melancholy to do without you, dearest child. Mr. Corbould was there; he has one pretty picture and some more little trifles. As usual he has had no end of mishaps. I send you the catalogue. On Monday evening we went to see "King Lear"; I send you here a newspaper account and have desired Mary Bulteel to write a little account of it for you. It is very fine, but it is a dreadfully painful play to see though enormously great. Kean[1] acts admirably—and Kate Terry[2] is a most charming, touching graceful Cordelia. The last scene is too sad when he carries her in—dead in his arms, the way in which her head fell back and her long fair hair flowed—reminded us painfully of the last and never to be forgotten sight of dearest Aunt Victoire.[3] And now I must end, my beloved child, the separation from whom I can not accustom myself to—and at times get quite angry about it. I think it quite wrong you should have been carried off.

From the Princess Royal

BERLIN, APRIL 24, 1858

She explains to the Queen that although she has taken to riding she can not go out for walks.

If I did not secure the morning to myself, I should pass my whole time in doing nothing at all—and that is too great a sin. Forgive this long explanation dearest Mama, but no one who has not been here can understand the busy idleness, the active waste of time that goes on. Ask Fritz and Louise of Baden, ask the Princess—or Wegner or the Baron, they will tell you the same; besides Mama, I do not like going out when Fritz is not with me unless I know he cannot come home in time, which happens now and then. I agree quite to all you say about our trials in married life but not having experienced them, I had hoped they were not quite so bad.

---

[1] Charles John Kean (1811–68), at this time lessee of the Princess's Theatre, played King Lear.
[2] The Queen was writing on Kate Terry's fourteenth birthday. She was the elder sister of Ellen Terry, and at the age of eight had played Arthur in King John before the Queen at Windsor. She was afterwards Mrs. Arthur Lewis.
[3] The Duchesse de Nemours. Queen Victoria and the Prince Consort saw

Let me first tell you that I forgive you over and over again for the 10 days' silence and would not have said so much had I not been anxious to prevent its recurrence for the future, and being very desirous that you should understand that the tiny fewest words would satisfy me; never pray fatigue yourself in writing to me—pray don't; I dare not tell Papa that I did scold you, for he always fears you exhaust yourself by writing to me.

Let me now tell you how thankful and happy I am to see how truly happy with Fritz you are. Believe me, dearest, we always knew how good and kind he was, and I therefore was often so alarmed when I saw your temper so uneven— so (I must say) very unpleasant and unamiable towards those you lived with and to whom you owed respect, obedience as I feared for his happiness. His great kindness, gentleness no doubt disarms all irritation—added to which my good child likes to be her own mistress and to be able to do as she likes. I am sure that by the habit of governing and controlling yourself—by feeling your own responsibility you have got over your few faults—which we always hoped you would—I can assure you that from all sides we hear your praise—from Vienna—from Dresden—everywhere! And we are very proud and very happy and very thankful.

At $\frac{1}{4}$ to 11 we started for the usual spot[1]—the Long Valley—then rode down the line (Papa's horse misbehaved and set off Sunset and I did not I fear manage her as I ought but it all came right in a minute). This morning a fearful wind though a soft one but I could not therefore ride; we saw some very curious experiments with the lasso and then some beautiful artillery practice firing with shot and shells at a target.

---

her after death. The Prince described her as "pale and rigid, but like an angel of beauty, her glorious hair falling in waves over her bosom".
[1] The Queen had gone to Aldershot for a review of the soldiers there.

How I rejoice to think you will be so soon at Babelsberg and in the country! Promise me then, dear, to be out as much as you can, sit out and write and read out and be really living for air and health of body a little, without which the health of mind is nothing. Remember that, dear.

You are already married 3 months! I can't believe it! And I can't reconcile myself to it! The great difficulties are the great distance between us—and the life at Berlin, which everyone who knows it, dislikes.

We were much pleased to hear yesterday from your Uncle Ferdinand of Portugal—that the marriage of Marie with Prince George of S. is settled and I send you a copy of his letter to me which you may keep and which will much interest you both I am sure—as well as the Princess. It is so like your betrothal it quite moved me in reading it. I think it—in every way an excellent marriage—and hope you will in this way see your dear cousin sometimes. I am glad Louise of B. finds Prince G. so improved. I think that reservedness comes much from his absence.

Pray tell the Queen how much pleased we are to have her nephew as our nephew. Tonight to give Alice a birthday treat—as it fell on a Sunday—we are going to King Lear— which I own I don't much like as it is such a very horrid play to see.

What sort of looking boy is the Weimar one? Cousin Augusta wrote that he was a dwarf and frightful.

I did not say sufficiently how right we do think you are to be so anxious to occupy yourself and your mind, for really that life at Berlin seems too dreadful and senseless. Sir James says that 2 hours' good air and exercise regularly daily would insure your health till you can get into the country—when of course you will live a little more for health and exercise than at Berlin. Everybody, the Princess and your ladies— say it is so hot now and you complain of its not being hot enough—which shows you have not enough circulation;— now pray don't get a worse cold.

That ride must have been very delightful. But now do tell me about your horses, you won't answer that—their colour—their names and their sex? Lenchen will ride so well.

Dear good Alice was so pleased with your kind hearty letter. She is so good and improves so much—is become so quiet and posée, is so unselfish and useful—and will be very pretty. What will be her fate? It often worries me. She must wait at any rate till a reasonable age—but she must not also be so completely exiled as you, my poor child. I could not bear that with all our girls.

I am delighted that our christening gifts pleased Marianne; what a shame to leave her so alone! That is inexcusable! I always think one of their little girls would do for one of your younger brothers. You must watch over their education a little.

Yesterday morning we went to the Old Watercolour Exhibition[1] which is full of the most beautiful things—Carl Haag was there and has 11 charming things—then Branwhite, Richardson, Collingwood Smith and quite a new artist by name Newton and a very young man have the most beautiful landscapes—I send you the catalogue.

The acquittal of Bernard[2] is a dreadful thing.

Now I must tell you a secret which perhaps Louise may have mentioned to you—but which must not be talked of, for it can't be for some years. Ernest L.[3] has seen Marie of B.[4] at Carlsruhe and again at Gotha—it seems they are engaged. I fear he has gone rather too far, for prudence, but on the other hand he says she is perfection and he could not bear to lose such a treasure, as he is sure she is le beau idéal of what he ever could wish for!! Poor Ernest, he deserves to be happy—but he must wait some time.

---

[1] There were two societies at this time for the exhibition of water colours—the Old and the New. Their exhibitions were held at the same time as that of the Royal Academy.

[2] Simon Bernard, a Frenchman living in Bayswater, was tried for the attempted assassination of the French Emperor. He was acquitted amid enormous exultation in Court.

[3] Prince Ernest Leiningen, eldest son of the Queen's half-brother.

[4] Sister of the Grand-Duke of Baden. They were married in the following September.

Sir H. Bentinck[1] talked so kindly and sensibly about you—says you are so beloved—all the shopkeepers and people calling you "that dear, charming young princess"—that you are very sensible about all the little désagréments of your position, are homesick (which I am glad of, though I pity you)—and was so delighted with you and your remembering everyone so kindly. He said you might have had such a charming palace in the Wilhelmstrasse with a nice garden, which would have been everything to you in Fritz's absence, and so much better than the crowded old Palace.

BUCKINGHAM PALACE, MAY 3, 1858

Countess de Perponcher has written me such a charming long account of the marriage and fêtes and all seemed charmed with Stephanie. How touching it must all have been. How I should have liked to have seen it—and yet how strange to be married without one's husband! I send you Ernest L.'s very happy letter. Please send it back. I think people really marry far too much; it is such a lottery after all, and for a poor woman a very doubtful happiness.

BUCKINGHAM PALACE, MAY 5, 1858

My poor, dear darling child!

How dreadfully vexed worried and fidgety I am at this untoward sprain I can't tell you! How could you do it? I am sure you had too high-heeled boots! I am haunted with your lying in a stuffy room in that dreadful old Schloss—without fresh air and alas! naturally without exercise and am beside myself. Only do take care and let some fresh air into your room and do get yourself carried out at least to get air! This happening just when you were rejoicing to get into the country and get plenty of air and exercise is quite dreadful—and distresses us both very much. This first indisposition of yours away from us is a great trial and distress and

---

[1] Major-General Sir Henry Bentinck was Groom-in-waiting to the Queen, and had evidently been visiting Berlin.

anxiety and I am afraid they will keep you in too long. You might so easily be carried down and driven out—but you must be very careful about your foot—being heavy as you are it will require great care—I can't say how vexed I am.

We have had a drawing room today—a very full one— and so many brides presented—Lady Francis Conyngham amongst others. She was in great beauty. Cecilia Molyneux[1] looked very nice,—and on Monday night at the concert Katie[2] looked so well. The concert was extremely good. Dear Papa had chosen such charming things and the people sang so well.

Dear Fritz will I am sure be a very kind, attentive nurse, and carry you as Papa does me!—but I feel very miserable to be away from you; only let me hear enough—it is terrible to be so far at such moments—but there is nothing for it, but patience, and that I know my poor child has whenever there is anything serious—like the burn and other trials.[3] And we must none of us complain when one has such cause for thankfulness as we all have—and think of the sufferings and miseries of others—those poor ladies at Lucknow[4] and elsewhere and so many now who have lost sons and husbands and brothers and so many dreadfully wounded! There is a poor young man—of the name of Bankes[5]—who has been cut almost to pieces—he fell and was surrounded by a set of fanatics who cut at him, his thigh was nearly severed from his body—and so was his arm! besides 6 other desperate wounds! he has had his right leg and his right arm amputated—and yet they hope he will live. He is, they

---

[1] Lady Cecilia Molyneux.

[2] Lady Katherine Hamilton. They had both been the Princess Royal's bridesmaids. Lady Francis Conyngham was daughter to Lord Tredegar.

[3] In the summer of 1856 the Princess was sealing a letter when her muslin dress caught on fire, and her arm was very badly burned. The accident is described by the Prince Consort—see Theodore Martin, vol. III, pp. 494–5.

[4] News of the occupation of Lucknow by British forces had been received in London in the middle of April.

[5] William George Hawtrey Bankes, V.C., who died at Lucknow from wounds received in action on April 6, and was dead when the Queen wrote.

say, the pattern of patience, resignation and Christian fortitude! Tell this dear Fritz, his military heart will take interest in such miseries. One armless, badly wounded Col. of the 93d. dines with us tonight;—also the Raglans, and Bertie. I send you the catalogue of the Royal Academy[1] with the paintings marked and described which we liked and admired.

From the Princess Royal

BERLIN, MAY 6, 1858

I have just returned from the railway where, with a heavy heart, I took leave of the beloved Princess who is indeed a second mother to me. I cannot tell you how I miss her, she is so inexpressibly dear to me, and I am able better than many to understand her feelings and her views. How great and truly noble she is—and how disinterested, unselfish and forgiving she is. She has had much to bear in her past life and has much to bear now. God knows how happy I should be if I could take the load off her mind and heart, but she is so conscientious and has had such sad experience, besides being gifted with a nature which feels quickly and ardently—and she sees a great many things going on in a sad way. Her kindness to me, I need not describe to you; but besides feeling the respect I owe to her, I felt for her in all she has to go through and felt that she really was my friend. It was such a pleasure for me when I could go and see her or try to cheer her harassed mind. She has so little gratitude shown her! I should like to show her all I can and at least make her feel that her children and children-in-law know what sacrifices she bears and in how noble a way!

---

[1] The Academy opened on May 1; the outstanding picture that year was Frith's "Derby Day".

Now to come to our dearest Queen![1] What a sweet, dear child! Yesterday evening she went through that terrible ordeal of having endless ladies and all the principal gentlemen of both parties presented to her and she went through it beautifully, saying a word to everyone—and with a grace —and quiet and innocence which must make everyone love her. There is a look of goodness and purity in those lovely eyes—which go to one's heart and could bring tears to my eyes. She is lovely, and has such a beautiful figure. People were enchanted with her yesterday—admired her so—and thought her so charming. Lord Hardwicke thought her "beautiful". Lord Clarendon was delighted with her. She looked very pretty—in a pink dress with fine lace and diadems and diamond necklace, and Pedro's portrait. She has no idea of dress, and her poor mother not being there— the Prince consults me. I am a sort of mama. Dear love, what would I not do for her—and then it makes me think of you! Of course I always make her go before me as "Majesty" and she blushes and gives me such a dear look. Poor Pedro, what a treasure he gets. He is now all impatience. Uncle Leopold is quite charmed with her. Tomorrow we take her to Claremont,[2] where I am sure they will be equally charmed. We received her in full state. She had a pompiere silk, paletot and bonnet to match—all went into '44 room[3]—then presentations of courts took place— then to her rooms. In the evening only officers of State— Lords Derby and Malmesbury—the Bernstorffs and Lavradios! Yesterday afternoon only a drive—in evening the dinner of 84 in Great Supper Room. How I thought of our great dinners in January! Also for a great marriage. This morning we have been for two hours and a half at the Crystal Palace—and I am rather stupid and sleepy in con-

---

[1] Stephanie, wife of Pedro V of Portugal. She had come over with her father, Prince Hohenzollern, after her marriage by proxy in Berlin en route for Portugal. Her mother was an invalid.

[2] Louis Philippe's widow and family were living here at this time.

[3] The 1844 Room at Buckingham Palace, so named in honour of the Emperor Nicholas I who stayed there in that year.

sequence. We went by rail, nice, quick! This afternoon we take her to Houses of Parliament (she saw the Corps Diplomatique at 3) and this evening to the Opera—tomorrow a dinner—Monday State Ball. Stephanie loves you so much! She is so fond of art—of pictures and good ones. The garden at Sydenham with two hundred thousand tulips in bloom was beautiful.

The dear Princess wrote dear Papa a charming letter about you and that good, excellent Prince Hohenzollern told us a great deal which makes us very very happy. So does Countess Blücher. They all say you do such good in the family—have made many unhappy ones happy and are a star of light and hope in the midst of darkness. God bless you dear child, go on as you have begun—you will be a blessing and will be blessed yourself. The dearest Princess is one in a thousand and I felt sure from the first that she would be a mother to you; and you ought to know what a comfort you are to her! It is a great happiness to us—to hear this. Do tell me, by and by—as you promised a little about the Catholic marriage at Berlin.[1] Don't forget —as you said you would making me some little sketches. Stephanie is great friends with Alice. The separation from her poor mother at five in the morning was dreadful.

BUCKINGHAM PALACE, MAY 10, 1858

I fear I can't write much today—as my time is much taken up with dearest Stephanie who is too lovely—too dear—too sweet and whom I am so grieved to part with tomorrow. Poor dear child, what an undertaking—do think to go alone to a husband she don't know—without a mother —or mother-in-law she knows!! Think of all this and all you know and feel must be gone through and no mother at hand! You may imagine what I feel for the dear sweet child! And she is so affectionate to me, shows me such confidence. Yesterday we went down to Claremont at 3 in four carriages. The visit was formidable but went off extremely

---

[1] i.e. Princess Stephanie's marriage by proxy.

well. The country looks quite beautiful with chestnuts and lilacs in blossom—a very hot sun and a very sharp, cold east wind but everything was beautifully green. Stephanie received all the Portuguese after Mass at Lavradio's yesterday. This morning we took her to the Royal Academy and National Gallery, and then came all the French Royal Family to see her and she was so shy—dear child. We shall drive this afternoon and then tonight is the ball.

BUCKINGHAM PALACE, MAY 12, 1858

The Queen's mind is still much occupied with Princess Stephanie.

I felt so sad to part from her. You never said half enough of her beauty; she is so lovely—such a dear little face, such eyes with a heavenly expression, and such a very lovely figure, and such an expression of confiding innocence. She was quite like a daughter to me and for the few happy days we had her, she was (like you were in January) the object of our constant solicitude, our constant thought, and it seems so sad she should be gone—and gone all alone, at least without parents, to a husband she has never seen! But while this is a great difficulty and the distance and out-of-the-wayness of Portugal another great drawback—she has advantages which you have not, and these are the being the first—and having no family—but the younger brothers and sisters of her husband who is the head of all and supreme—to interfere with her. This is an immense facility. She was so much admired at the ball, and looked so lovely in a white tulle dress spangled with gold and trimmed with pink roses and a wreath of the same on her head. When she blushes such a beautiful colour comes over her dear cheeks—and she has such a dear, dear expression. I was so proud of showing her. Then her manners—her way of moving—all are so perfect. Such a contrast to poor Cousin Mary valzing about with all the young gentlemen and in a very dirty Gown!! I assure you I think it is time to get her married. Edward's brother Gustave,[1] was willing and ready to marry

---

[1] Of Saxe-Weimar. He was 31 at this time, and made a morganatic marriage many years later.

her but the Duchess (instead of jumping at anything) set her half against it—and it dropped! I spoke about it to Prince Hohenzollern who said, as we feel, that Abbat (whom they wish for[1]) is too young and would not be happy with her—but he mentioned another person who he said was in search of a wife with money and I must say I think it would be a very good thing; viz. Prince Augustus of Württemberg whom you must know—he is 45, a handsome man, brother to Prince Fredrick of Württemberg (whose son will probably be King as the Crown Prince has no children) is nephew to the King and is of an age to suit Mary who herself has told me that she would rather marry an older man, which, from her size and her free manner would be much more appropriate than a young man. Prince H. made the suggestion, and if Fritz could indirectly find anything out—or suggest Mary it would be indeed a blessing. Prince H. says he is not clever, but a good and very fine looking man which goes a great way with the Duchess and also with Mary. You know how anxious we are—so many are about poor Mary, George constantly asking me if there is no-one, that I can't say the relief it would be to me if we could marry her—only decently. Now do see what you and dear Fritz can do.[2]

Yesterday reminded me so of your dreadful going away. The band—guard of honour—all the court in the hall—all the children, etc. We took dearest Stephanie to the Great Western Station and saw her off at half past ten—the crowd cheering as the carriage went—and have heard she sailed at 3 this morning we expect the good Prince back at 6 this evening. What an excellent, good, sensible clever man he is! I am sure you must have been delighted to speak to him.

[1] i.e. The Cambridge family.
[2] In replying to this letter the Princess Royal alluded to the importance of getting Princess Mary away from the influence and example of her mother. She went on "The Duchess (of Cambridge) is incurable but Mary is not—immensely gifted as she is, with a noble, generous, unselfish heart". The Queen would not have disagreed with this. The Princess Royal wrote that "the Prince of Württemberg is in no respect to be recommended for her in my humble opinion or that of Fritz".

Promise me faithfully dear not to keep your rooms too hot—or let the fire catch your face, and also to get fresh air as much as you can. I know that you are quite aware of the necessity of it, but you are lazy, my good child, often, and may neglect looking at thermometers and to open windows, though at Windsor you were so particular. Promise me, my dearest, solemnly—that when you are able to move again, you will live for your health, and get out really a great deal, for you know since your marriage you have not had healthy exercise regularly and very little fresh air. Now don't forget to answer this, for I assure you your future health, your looks, your nerves and your power of usefulness depend upon it. I am delighted at the arrangement of your hours—which is excellent. Lady Bloomfield[1] is come, was at the Drawing Room and dined here tonight. She has made herself a little too busy in writing about you, I am sure from the best intentions, first about your being so sadly alone, and again about your sprain—saying you would not take care and that Lord Bloomfield wished you would see another doctor and so forth—which I am not quite pleased at—unlike dear, excellent Countess Blücher whose letters are so admirable, so sensible, so straightforward and always so comforting to me.

Your account of the marriage is so very like Papa's of Charlotte's.[2] However here it was better because there was no real Mass. But our marriage ceremony (with the exception of two passages which might be left out)[3] is so simple, so fine and solemn.

My darling child, I can only repeat that I hear nothing

---

[1] She had been Maid of Honour to the Queen. She was Georgiana Liddell before her marriage to the British Minister in Berlin.

[2] Princess Charlotte, daughter of King Leopold I of the Belgians, married July 27, 1857 to Maximilian, Archduke of Austria and late Emperor of Mexico. The Prince Consort described the Roman Catholic ceremony at this marriage as "perfectly ludicrous". By "here" the Queen means in the case of Queen Stephanie.

[3] No doubt the Queen here has in mind the second of the two causes for which matrimony was ordained and the allusion to men's carnal lusts.

but what is a great happiness to us—about you. Are you not very fond of Prince Hohenzollern? I quite love him, he is so good, so kind, so sensible, so clever and straightforward. He came back on Wednesday evening very low and would hardly speak of his child! Alas! how well could we feel for him and sympathise with him. It was also in the cabin that at half past eight in the evening he took leave of his dear child; and it was dreadful—she clung to him so fast that he had to tear himself away from her.

BUCKINGHAM PALACE, MAY 19, 1858

After a long account of the death of the Duchess of Orleans,[1] which took place on May 18, the Queen goes on.

Dear Hélène loved Fritz so much, and always from the first told me she was sure he would make you happy, and be a kind and good husband—though she knew your life and position at Berlin with the family and the frivolous artificial existence there would be difficult and distasteful. She loved to tell me all the praise she heard of you. I have unfortunately very little time left to answer your letters but some of the points I will.

1. Stillfried,[2] no doubt, a very well-informed, clever man, but so full of prétention, so completely the type of that sort of courtier, so pincé and artificial as to be quite insupportable. How I pity you to have to live with so many of these people!

2. Regarding the Prince of Württemberg;—the Prince Hohenzollern did not recommend him but merely said when I observed that there was no-one whatever left that there was this Prince. You must remember, dear, that characters are not much minded either by Mary or her mother. The greatest roués are generally in favour, and I know that if

---

[1] Hélène, a princess of Mecklenburg-Schwerin, related to the Princess of Prussia.

[2] Count Stillfried, appointed Master of Ceremonies at the Prussian Court in 1853. He had come over with Queen Stephanie. The Princess Royal called him "a capital Sir Edward Cust". Cust was the Queen's Master of the Ceremonies and Queen Victoria would not seem to have relished the comparison.

Abbat's father was not married[1] Mary would marry him at once! Then you say that neither you nor Fritz need be so very particular—quite the contrary!—besides she is now desperate and bitter.

OSBORNE, MAY 22, 1858

The Queen had paid a visit to Claremont to see the family of the Duke and Duchess of Orleans.

While we were there then the Duchess of Cambridge and Mary arrived—and imagine poor Mary on such an occasion, with a small wide-awake—and pheasant's feather cocked over one ear!!

OSBORNE, MAY 26, 1858

On the afternoon of my birthday (which was a wet one) I received your dear letter of the 22nd with such dear, warm, hearty expressions of love and affection for which 1000 thanks. I have no doubt dearest child that you can now much better appreciate Mama's love and affection and understand how all what you grumbled and struggled and kicked against was for your good, and meant in love!—your love and affection you know, dearest child, I never doubted, I only was often grieved and hurt at your manner, your temper. The horrid news contained in Fritz's letter to Papa upset us dreadfully.[2] The more so as I feel certain almost it will all end in nothing.

Describing her birthday festivities the Queen says—

After luncheon the children played

1. Arthur and Alice a little duet.
2. Louise a little piece alone, fairly, but not in time.
3. Alice and Lenchen a duet beautifully.
4. Alice and Affie on the violin a little composition of his own—very pretty and of which he is not a little proud.

---

[1] Prince Albrecht made a morganatic marriage 4 weeks later. He was divorced in 1849, and the Queen is no doubt referring to his divorced wife.
[2] i.e. That the Princess Royal was to have a child.

5. Alice a long—beautiful and very difficult Sonata by Beethoven. Arthur recited a German poem, and Lenchen and Louise have something to say—which however has not yet been said.

The only one of all the children, who neither drew, wrote, played or did anything whatever to show his affection —beyond buying for me a table in Ireland—was Bertie. Oh! Bertie alas! alas! That is too sad a subject to enter on.

I hope you won't become one of the regular soldier-princesses (Fritz would call this treason) if you go out constantly to watch manœuvres. I have no fear of that however.

OSBORNE, MAY 29, 1858

Owing to the Princess Royal being in the early stages of pregnancy she was unable to go to Coburg to meet her father, who had gone there on 27 May, so he was going to Berlin to see her.

Only don't let Papa be plagued with visits. I feel of course the absence of my life and light—very much—but I am so determined not to give way—hear so constantly by telegraph and am so busy—that I feel it less than in '54 even, and decidedly less than in '44; at least I can keep up. I assure you dear that in Town and at Windsor I see very little of dear Papa very often, and often much less alone than you do Fritz—from the children etc. But I am so unhappy about you! It is well Fritz is not in sight just now or he would not be graciously received. Tell him that if he leaves you quite alone for a fortnight (he promised me never to do so without you were with his mother or sister or us) I shall not call him my son any more as I shall consider he has forfeited the claim! There is a threat! We tell everyone your foot is the cause of your not going to Coburg—and that the lying up has weakened you. I hope you do the same—and Fritz don't allow his own people and relations to enter into such subjects; it is so indelicate; Papa never allowed it and I should have been frantic. Be very careful with Augusta.

Only think we heard from India today that that gallant hero, Sir William Peel,[1] the pride of the navy—the idol and comfort of his poor widowed mother, died on 27th April at Cawnpore of smallpox! So so sad!—and I fear seven more officers are killed whose names we don't know. How many hearts will ache!

I think I shall sail a little this afternoon, and tomorrow morning we mean to steam across to Alverbank[2] for breakfast. Yesterday there was a grand tea at the Swiss Cottage[3]— and imagine good Affie by way of amusement exhibiting his air pump and steam engine (puffing and blowing all the time—in the tool house) to Grandmama, the others and the little Greys[4]—and pumping over himself and Arthur! Can't you see him? He dined with us last night and sat next to me. He is a dear, good, clever promising child—whom God may bless!

BUCKINGHAM PALACE, JUNE 6, 1858

About the mourning.[5] I wish to say a word, as I feel strongly upon the subject; and as my daughter and Princess Royal you always remain, you must not separate yourself from us. You should explain to Fritz that there is a difference here between court mourning and private mourning. Court mournings are short and worn here for all Crown Heads and Sovereigns etc. who are no relations—but private mourning we wear as long as we like; and this private mourning no earthly being can prevent you from wearing in your own home and when you do not appear at Fêtes. When you do then you can take it off. I must ask that you should respect our customs and feelings in this respect—and no one can prevent it, dear. Poor Aunt Hélène was not a near relation of yours—but a fortnight you ought to have

---

[1] Son of the statesman.
[2] The cottage near Gosport where Prince Alfred was living with his tutor.
[3] Built on the estate at Osborne.
[4] Children of General Grey, at this time private secretary to the Prince Consort.
[5] For the Duchess of Orleans who had died on 18 May.

The Prince of Wales, 1861

Frederick William I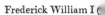

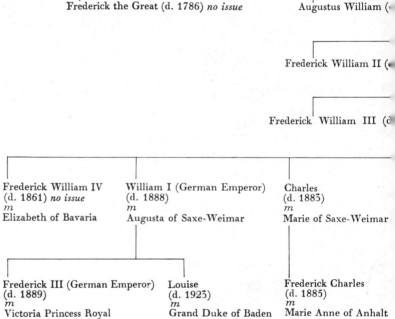

Frederick the Great (d. 1786) *no issue*   Augustus William (

Frederick William II (

Frederick William III (d

Frederick William IV   William I (German Emperor)   Charles
(d. 1861) *no issue*   (d. 1888)   (d. 1883)
m   *m*   *m*
Elizabeth of Bavaria   Augusta of Saxe-Weimar   Marie of Saxe-Weimar

Frederick III (German Emperor)   Louise   Frederick Charles
(d. 1889)   (d. 1923)   (d. 1885)
m   *m*   *m*
Victoria Princess Royal   Grand Duke of Baden   Marie Anne of Anhalt

phia Dorothea (daughter of George I
f Great Britain)

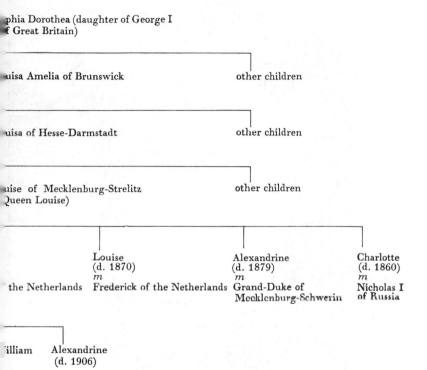

uisa Amelia of Brunswick   other children

uisa of Hesse-Darmstadt   other children

uise of Mecklenburg-Strelitz   other children
Queen Louise)

	Louise	Alexandrine	Charlotte
	(d. 1870)	(d. 1879)	(d. 1860)
	m	*m*	*m*
the Netherlands	Frederick of the Netherlands	Grand-Duke of	Nicholas I
		Mecklenburg-Schwerin	of Russia

illiam   Alexandrine
              (d. 1906)

THE ROYAL HOUSE OF HOHENZOLLERN

Queen Victoria and the Princess Royal, as a child, from a sketch by Sir Edwin Landseer

worn it. Here we wear it a month on account of respect for her memory and relationship to Papa—and our very near and numerous relationships with the Orleans family who are in this country. You cannot ignore your relations (on our side) and therefore you ought to mourn (in a less degree as you are not living with us than we do—as you are a degree further off) for your own relations—in private as you would naturally do, leaving if off at Fêtes if it is wished —and you should explain this fully and openly to the Prince as a very strong feeling of mine—and I am sure he would not object. For those who are not yours but Fritz' and the Prussian families relations that is another thing, you would naturally mourn as they do. This is a long story but I wish it to be set right.

BUCKINGHAM PALACE, JUNE 9, 1858

I mean to try and write you a long letter, and to pour out all my feelings of joy and thankfulness. Dearest Papa's return is of course the sunshine of which you said you had a gleam. And I feel as if it were hardly possible to be true— so great and irrepressible is the happiness. But I am so glad, so thankful he made this journey; I am sure it has done him so much good, refreshed and cheered him—as he is so plagued and fagged with work and I think he looks so well— so much better than when he went! And then it gave him such pleasure, it gave you such pleasure, and it was I'm sure of great use in many ways—to you and to Fritz and lastly it is almost as if I have seen you myself—so much do I feel I see through his eyes! All he told and tells me pleases me much though I am grieved at some discomforts you have for instance your bedroom being in this dreadful heat over the kitchen is awful! Can't that be altered? I must also repeat that what you say about your feelings to-wards your husband are only those which I have ever felt and shall ever feel! But I cannot ever think or admit that anyone can be as blessed as I am with such a husband and such a perfection as a husband; for Papa has been and is everything to me. I had led a very unhappy life as a child—

had no scope for my very violent feelings of affection—
had no brothers and sisters to live with—never had had a
father—from my unfortunate circumstances was not on a
comfortable or at all intimate or confidential footing with
my mother (so different from you to me)—much as I love
her now—and did not know what a happy domestic life
was! All this is the complete contrast to your happy childhood and home. Consequently I owe everything to dearest
Papa. He was my father, my protector, my guide and adviser in all and everything, my mother (I might almost say)
as well as my husband. I suppose no-one ever was so completely altered and changed in every way as I was by dearest
Papa's blessed influence. Papa's position towards me is
therefore of a very peculiar character and when he is away
I feel quite paralysed. I did my best during his absence—
and he was much pleased with my "stewardship". Dear
Papa praised Fritz very much—and said he was so kind and
good and anxious to do everything to please us—and was
devoted to you. And this is a great great comfort to us both
so far away as we are.

BUCKINGHAM PALACE, JUNE 11, 1858

The Princess was alone, Prince Frederick William being away:

Then, dear, you must be sure to have one of your
people sleeping on the sofa in the next room; I never do
otherwise, and it would be very bad for you (who have never
in your life slept alone and who are, as I am, very nervous
at night and sure to be more so now) to be without anyone
near; any noise or even suspicion of fright, might be very
hurtful for you now—and you might want anything in the
night and not be able to get it. You must be sure to do that,
dear. Wherever I go—my maid always sleeps next door—
even if Papa is with me—and I know when one is quite
alone—how every noise makes one start. I can't tell you,
dear, how constantly I am occupied with you.

I hear that Chauvening[1] is not at Babelsberg and that

---

[1] Presumably the Princess Royal's hairdresser.

your maids coiffé you—and that you don't find they do it well. Why don't you have him to do your hair in the middle of the day? Why can't he live nearby—if he can't be lodged in the house—and come daily to do your hair? You might have it early in the morning just twisted as I have—and then made later, for when one is unwell—to have one's hair pulled about is dreadful. I am terrified to hear you have such fearfully full sleeves—for God's sake take care or you will set yourself on fire, and now that might be the death of you; they are so horridly uncomfortable and ugly too.

BUCKINGHAM PALACE, JUNE 14, 1858

Be sure and read the account in Saturday's *Times* of that meeting about St. Barnabas.[1] It will shock you.

STONELEIGH ABBEY, KENILWORTH, JUNE 15, 1858

Broiled and exhausted and done up as I am by a worse heat than Paris[2] I must write to you as I fear I shall not have much time tomorrow.[3] Imagine a railway journey

---

[1] The extreme ritualistic church in Pimlico. The Queen strongly disapproved of high church practices.

The article was headed "The Confessional in Belgravia". It stated that the meeting was advertised by placards throughout the West End, and that a warning was included—"in consequence of the disclosures which will be made gentlemen only are expected to attend."

In the course of the meeting the Hon. and Rev. F. Baring made a series of revelations against the Rev. Alfred Poole, curate of St. Barnabas. Among them was the testimony of Susan B——. "I am 26. Mr. Poole asked me if I had ever robbed anyone. If I had ever pilfered trifling things from my mother, such as sugar and halfpence. How many young men I had had before I was married. Whether I had ever been to a priest." There followed questions so grossly indecent as to be unfit for publication; they created a great sensation in the meeting.

Mr. Baring was son of the first Lord Ashburton, and rector of Itchen Stoke, Hampshire. Though there is more to be said in favour of Mr. Poole than appears in the article, his licence as curate had been withdrawn by the Bishop of London before the meeting was held.

[2] She means the heat in Paris when she paid a state visit to the Emperor in 1855.

[3] The Queen had gone to open Aston Hall and grounds which had been acquired for the Corporation of Birmingham by the subscriptions of Birmingham people. The Queen was staying with Lord and Lady Leigh.

with heat and dust (for we had to have both windows open) flying in, and sun shining like a pine house! But today think to be out from 11 to 5 exposed to the most fearful sun (like Paris) driving about in the streets of Birmingham with seven hundred thousand people out—and then receiving addresses in a stifling town hall—and then finding the air so heated as to be unable, coming home, to open the windows and I think you would have a sick headache! Really it is Paris over again only with the thickness and heaviness of English atmosphere! But a finer reception I never saw; exceeding Manchester, and the decorations so beautiful—such quantities of wreaths and flags and guidons all through the streets, such order kept, no walking crowd, and such very kind and loyal inscriptions, you and Fritz not forgotten. Many Prussian flags and you and Fritz on a sort of transparency. But you must read the account, dear child, for it is really quite an event, and the Park and Aston Hall very curious. And they are so fond of dearest Papa here. This was formerly one of the most radical towns in England! I was there and at Aston Hall 28 years ago! I was a year older than Louise. Yesterday it was deliciously cool on driving and arriving here—but today even the cool river, the Avon flowing under our windows—and the splendid woods (I never saw finer timber) does no good and I dread the night. This is a beautiful place—an old seat—and everything so well arranged and kept. The old Abbey part is very old indeed; as old as Queen Elizabeth. We have charming rooms only sadly hot this evening.

15TH. So far I got before dinner, and can hardly hold my pen for the awful steaming heat this morning after a heavy thunderstorm and violent rain during the night which was too fearfully hot! Still I think it will get better as soon as the steaming is over—so many people ask kindly after you and say I must so feel the separation which God knows I do. It is so nice to see all these married daughters of Lady Westminster's[1] here together, such charming people —all so happily and so richly married and all together. It is

---

[1] Lady Leigh's mother was the wife of the 2nd Marquis of Westminster.

what I hope often to see.[1] These are Lord and Lady Macclesfield (the second daughter) Lord and Lady Wenlock (the third) Lord and Lady Leigh themselves (she the fourth daughter) Sir M. and Lady Octavia Shaw Stewart; and Lady Agnes (the sixth) and her bridegroom Sir Archibald Campbell (also a rich Scotch Baronet) are also here. Lady Leigh has charming children. There are two married and one unmarried not here.[2] The old entrance was illuminated both nights as well as the front door—and we took a walk to refresh ourselves, the band playing. I send you a Birmingham newspaper. Tuesday at one we go to Warwick Castle where we lunch and we ordered our train at five in order not to travel at the very hottest time.

What you say of the pride of giving life to an immortal soul is very fine, dear, but I own I cannot enter into that; I think much more of our being like a cow or a dog at such moments; when our poor nature becomes so very animal and unecstatic—but for you, dear, if you are sensible and reasonable not in ecstasy nor spending your day with nurses and wet nurses, which is the ruin of many a refined and intellectual young lady, without adding to her real maternal duties, a child will be a great resource. Above all, dear, do remember never to lose the modesty of a young girl towards others (without being prude); though you are married don't become a matron at once to whom everything can be said, and who minds saying nothing herself—I remained particular to a degree (indeed feel so now) and often feel shocked at the confidences of other married ladies. I fear abroad they are very indelicate about these things. Think of me who at that first time, very unreasonable, and perfectly furious as I was to be caught, having to have drawing rooms and levées and made to sit down—and be stared at and take every sort of precaution.

---

[1] Meaning her own daughters.
[2] i.e. Daughters of Lady Westminster.

Don't give way to melancholy, dear. I found the best way when Papa was away—and a feeling of loneliness and sorrow came over me to say to myself—it must not be, it must be conquered and I must control it from a sense of duty and unselfishness, and I always did—particularly by occupying myself and trying to do and see as much as I could.

But now to return to our journey. The heat on Wednesday was really quite dreadful—so thick and steamy. We went at one from Stoneleigh, then through the celebrated bathing-place of Leamington—also very tastefully decorated —to Warwick castle which is quite beautiful. The position above the town surrounded by the moat and beautiful old trees is romantic and beautiful in the extreme; then it is a really old castle and yet habitable, and was so deliciously cool; full of very fine Van Dykes and all sorts of fine and curious things many of which you saw at Manchester.[1] Poor Lady Warwick is very delicate since her marriage and the birth of her three little boys and can't stand above a minute; her mother I believe was just the same. She is a pretty, nice person, sister to Lord Elcho. People enquire so anxiously and kindly after you. We lunched here and walked about the grounds—and at near five we left and drove through the curious picturesque old town of Warwick. How I kept thinking of you whenever I saw or see anything pretty and fine and ancient wishing you could be there!

When the Queen got back to Buckingham Palace the Belgian Royal Family were visiting her and she goes on:

Charlotte they say has grown so fat that it quite spoils her! She was in Vienna for some time—part of it without Max[2] who had to go to Venice and now that Max is returned to Vienna she goes to Venice and he remains at Vienna— which I do not approve.

---

[1] In the previous year the Princess Royal had gone with her parents to the Art Treasures Exhibition in Manchester.

[2] Her husband, Archduke Maximilian, later Emperor of Mexico.

From the Princess Royal

BABELSBERG, JUNE 19, 1858

As for my being foolish and unreasonable as some ladies are, in spending their day in a manner little likely to raise or improve their minds you need not be afraid. You know me, dear Mama, too well for that; you know what I think of such people, and what I consider the duties of a lady and a princess to be. There is a juste milieu in all things.

BUCKINGHAM PALACE, JUNE 22, 1858

Augusta has told me a good deal about the dressing and undressing etc. but I don't see much of her and she is always full of your and her position, etc. I think not a safe adviser still she is very kind about you and sensible. But what I cannot understand is her intense worldliness! She goes out every night, in this heat when really one can hardly bear to go to a theatre even—to balls and dinners and concerts—and went out the very first night she arrived! I can't understand it, then all day long she has morning visits! How can people enjoy that!

Marie is looking very pretty and is I think very sensible about herself and her child—but she is becoming very reserved and though I think there is no real affection or love between them—she never allows a word to be said against Leopold who in revanche is much kinder to her than he was, and certainly always praises her now. He praises and admires things here much more than he used to do but still he is very odd—and so fond of saying disagreeable things to people. Good Philip[1] is always kind and amiable and clever.

Yesterday evening we had a dinner—the Lavradio's, Salisburys,—Lord Aberdeen, Sir G. Couper[2] and his son who came back from Lucknow and is really grown quite handsome. He is very short—but he has quite an Italian face.

---

[1] The Count of Flanders, King Leopold's younger son.
[2] Comptroller of the Household to the Duchess of Kent. His son, the 2nd baronet here referred to, was a distinguished administrator in India.

We all like Mademoiselle Bauer poor Fräulein's successor; her pronounciation is very Hessian which is not pretty —but that don't signify. At any rate it is not Hanoverian. Do you know that you've got into a habit of writing so many words with a capital letter at the beginning? With nouns that would not signify so much, but you do it with verbs and adjectives, which is very incorrect, dear, and would shock other people if you wrote to them so. In your last to me for instance you wrote "I feel Low" and "women have not much to Live for", both of which are quite wrong. You must try to break yourself of what might get a habit at last and would be wrong in any language.

You say I know you "too well" to think you would spend your day in a way unworthy of a lady and a princess—so I do, dear child, still I know your rather too great passion for very little babies, and I wish to guard you against overdoing the thing or letting the child become your slave,[1] so that you should forget your duties to your husband, your station and indeed your relations.

BUCKINGHAM PALACE, JUNE 29, 1858

We went by land to Deptford yesterday got into boats and rowed along to the Leviathan[2] which is lying there and went on board her; but they can't proceed for want of funds! Mr. Yates,[3] who also showed her to you, is so disstressed that you could not go on board her—and I said I hoped you would next year. How nice that will be! But we were half poisoned by the dreadful smell of the Thames— which is such that I felt quite sick when I came home, and people cannot live in their houses; the House of Commons can hardly sit—and the session will close soon in consequence—not a bad result.[4]

Yesterday evening after dinner—the Choral Society of

---

[1] The Queen probably means becoming a slave to the child.
[2] Originally the *Great Eastern*; this was easily the largest steam-vessel then designed—23,000 tons. Various mishaps had attended her launching in the previous year.
[3] John Yates, Secretary of the Great Eastern Steam Navigation Company.
[4] This was in part due to the exceptional heat of the summer.

Bradford sang in the Great Ballroom two hundred in number and beautifully,—and we had a small party of about seventy people and many enquiries after you—Lord Chelmsford, Lord Sydney, the Granvilles, Lord Cowley (who asked if reports were true and I got out of it by expressing ignorance and doubts) Lady Stafford, etc. In short people are very kind Lady Stafford has always been particularly so.

But now I must give you a grand scold! You write to wish me joy of the 25th!! and write also to Bertie about my accession day! How could you make such an extraordinary mistake? It was the 20th, Sunday week, I was surprised at your saying nothing then and now understand why.[1] Yesterday was my Coronation Day.

Promise me one thing, dear; don't stoop when you sit and write, it is very bad for you now, and later it will make you ill; remember how straight I always sit, which enables me to write without fatigue at all times. I always was distressed to see you bend so in drawing and writing, and now it is very, very bad for you, dear. I hope Fritz will remind you. It is a mere bad habit. Now pray don't do it.

BUCKINGHAM PALACE, JUNE 30, 1858

I also send you some soothing tincture (which Mr. Saunders[2] prescribed) which will do you great good; put a teaspoonful of it into water, and hold it in your mouth, when you have pain and it will allay it. I suffered also this way. Mr. Saunders is going to Germany and is most anxious to see you, and he is so sensible and clever and always managed your teeth so well—(and the German dentists are not famous and the German teeth are so bad) you ought to see him, for teeth suffer much from your condition, some people lose one every child they have, and you will require to have them carefully looked at. He could go to the Rhine and then see them again when you come here next year.

---

[1] This is typical of the Queen's sense of humour—a kind of shocked incredulity. As the Princess did not see it in that light the Queen wrote later "it was really only a subject of fun".

[2] Afterwards Sir Edwin Saunders—the Queen's dentist.

You know how important it is to keep one's teeth in good order and how few people have good teeth abroad (and he knows your teeth so well). Marie B. has such an opinion of Saunders that she never lets anyone else touch her poor teeth. Leopold also saw him—and indeed everyone goes to him. It is these times one must be so careful with one's teeth, and I know you will be reasonable about it.

I delight in the idea of being a grandmama; to be that at 39 (D.V.) and to look and feel young is great fun, only I wish I could go through it for you, dear, and save you all the annoyance. But that can't be helped. I think of my next birthday being spent with my children and a grandchild. It will be a treat! Of course you will never allow your "young German individual" to be treated in the horrid way you describe and draw.[1] You can do much good in setting a good example and introducing rational habits as you have already. In France even they give that up. Marie has got a nice English nurse for her baby—who is treated quite sensibly and quantities of English nurses are now in request for Germany and Russia. They are the best for babies and little children until they are five to six.

The remark made by you about Leopold's saying strange things, is one made frequently by others, and one can not tell why he does it. I asked good Philip, who is so much the contrary and he said "Je ne sais pas,—mais je crois pour avoir l'air d'être mauvais sujet qu'il n'est pas." Most paradoxical certainly—but I think he can stop it, by telling him it is a very wrong kit[2] and bad for dear Marie.

The ceremony of the Knights of St. John is indeed strange: were it not for the person of the Grand Master it would be rather fine.[3]

---

[1] In her letter of June 26 the Princess Royal wrote "The poor dear little wretched things are sewn up in cushions. Is it not horrid?"
[2] Sarcasm.
[3] The Princess Royal in the letter to which the Queen is here replying had written "Tomorrow is the horrid ceremony at Berlin, when Prince Charles, dressed in a long, black cloak confers the order of knighthood of St. John: if I were a man I should consider it a disgrace to be knighted by such a man: one who is so very opposite to chivalry".

From the Princess Royal

How delighted I am to hear of Mr. Saunders coming here, I shall be so thankful to see him; the very idea of losing a tooth is too dreadful, but thank heaven they are all sound as yet, and it is not one that aches but several on one side. I will not let a German dentist look at my teeth, unless it be really necessary and no one else at hand. Of us I have little to relate, except that we try to see clever and distinguished people whenever we can, and that we read and occupy ourselves together when we are left in peace.

From the Princess Royal

BABELSBERG, JULY 9, 1858

Come here, you really hardly can.[1] *I should be wretched if you were to come to the capital of this country for the first time incognito! There ought to be a magnificent reception whenever you do come. And then the poor King in this condition and altogether such an unfortunate moment! I had been thinking so often what a good effect it would have at home if you were brilliantly received here, and what good it would do here and how it would annoy the Russians, and many other desirable and useful effects.*

BUCKINGHAM PALACE, JULY 3, 1858

On Thursday we went to the New Opera[2] to see Martha,[3] which was very pretty, only they gave the one man's part, which Formes[4] sang so beautifully—to Graziani[5] who has not one bass note!

---

[1] The Queen and Prince Consort were planning a summer visit to their daughter. The Princess means that she regrets their not coming in state to Berlin but privately to Babelsberg.

[2] The Covent Garden Theatre had been opened in the previous May, and known, to distinguish it from the opera at Her Majesty's Theatre, as the New Opera House.

[3] By Flotow. Included in this opera is "The Last Rose of Summer".

[4] Karl Johann Formes (1815–89)—the German baritone.

[5] Francesco Graziani, born 1829, Italian baritone. A great favourite in London from 1855 to 1865.

Yesterday evening we had a dinner and a dance (only about 30 people after dinner) in the Saloon, just as the one we had, when you, dearest child, were still here, and there had not been one since that 30th of January. You may imagine how much I thought of you. I hardly liked valzing thinking of you. There was poor Lady Abercorn (who is going to be confined for the 14th time) chaperoning Tiny[1] and Katie who looked so pretty, quite in white—tulle with white lilies. Katie (Lady Abercorn confided to me) has just refused young Lord Listowel, which I am sorry for as he is a good young man, but she thought him unrefined, and I suspect—had little; poor Tiny's various hopes seem not promising, which is quite provoking for she is so nice.

OSBORNE, JULY 14, 1858

Then I send you the sermons by the Bishop of Oxford, when Archdeacon Wilberforce—which you wish to have, and lastly a very useful book by Mr. Combe[2] which I think everyone ought to read. It contains such sensible, wise views—which if followed would, I am sure prolong life— and strengthen our race. Dear Papa is very fond of it. It is a book to be read slowly and frequently referred to.

OSBORNE, JULY 20. I had such a bad headache yesterday that I could not write, and I have only time to write a line today, and thank you very much for your dear letter of the 17th, which I shall answer properly tomorrow. Upon my word, the nearer the time for our going to Germany approaches— the more unlikely it seems to be realised as again yesterday I met with so grievous a disappointment about our journey as to discourage and disgust me with it altogether. Don't feel too certain till we actually are on the other side of the water. The going to Babelsberg is certainly a great drawback, as I should have so much liked to see that beautiful

---

[1] Lady Louisa Jane Hamilton, daughter of Lady Abercorn. Her sister, Katie, was one of the Princess Royal's bridesmaids.
[2] George Combe, a phrenologist, to whose unorthdox opinions the Prince Consort and the Queen attached importance. The book is probably his *Moral Philosophy*.

Rhine again. I shall now see nothing but a very flat, ugly country I fear. Were it not for you, dear child, nothing would make me undertake this long, and I fear very fatiguing journey. However I shall write tomorrow fully—and I hope more cheerfully—today I'm so vexed and upset by what has occurred that I cannot write as I should wish to do.

Osborne is really too lovely. Charming and romantic and wild as Balmoral is—there is not that peaceful enjoyment that one has here of dear Osborne—the deep blue sea, myriads of brilliant flowers—the perfume of orange blossoms, magnolias, honeysuckles—roses etc. of all descriptions on the terrace, the quiet and retirement all make it a perfect paradise—which I always deeply grieve to leave.

OSBORNE, JULY 21, 1858

I write you again today—and in better sorts than yesterday, though I still feel the effects of the bitter disappointment which Miss Hildyard's opposition (in her most particularly dry and unpleasant way, which she can put on) to our taking Alice and Lenchen with us—as a surprise for you and them, caused me.[1] In short I yesterday was so put out and so provoked, at finding opposition and resistance, where I expected only to find joy and delight that I was almost inclined to throw up the whole journey! But that would have been very foolish, and I should have punished you and myself by doing so. I trust therefore that if we are not drowned or blown up at Cherbourg[2] we shall be, God willing, in your arms on the 12th and mean to stay till the 28th. A nice long time! This indeed is a great, great happiness, and perhaps it is better that we should come alone. Papa says that I should be fidgeting myself about your sisters all the time which would be very unpleasant as it would take off my mind from you. However the worst is—

---

[1] It is fairly clear that the Prince Consort was the instigator of Miss Hildyard's opposition.

[2] The Queen and Prince Consort were about to visit the Emporer of the French.

that it will be no better in the winter, for Papa, who is very hard-hearted and a great tyrant on all such occasions—won't hear of any one then, so that if you want to see them you have nothing for it but to come to your own loved home. This I am almost glad of. All Papa says to you of the reasons why Miss Hildyard, from a real sense of duty, represented to him why she did not wish your sisters to go this year, I must admit are sound and good, and one must do what is right; but I can't get over the way in which what I thought would give such delight was met. It was too much. But the experience of your over-premature marriage and the consequences of it, have made me very anxious to keep your sisters back as long as possible.

From the Princess Royal

BABELSBERG, JULY 24, 1858

The Princess is commenting on the Queen's disappointment at not being able to bring any of the younger children to Germany.

I do not speak of my own disappointment, although I feel it; the joy of seeing you makes me feel too grateful. Perhaps it is better so; Papa is an oracle and what he decides must be right. One thing I can not show you, and that I miss more than I can say, there are no flowers here, or none to speak of, at home at dear Osborne it is one perfumed carpet but here neither wild nor cultivated flourish.

I am indeed astonished that you wear a cage,[1]—what a comfort they are, so cool and light and take no room.

OSBORNE, JULY 28, 1858

In your letter of the 16th you allude to your love for me, and your fearing you had not shown it always well, formerly, and your hope that I never doubted your affection for me. Doubt your real affection and your love, I did not, dearest child—but you did all you could to make me doubt it; for a more insubordinate and unequal-tempered child and girl I think I never saw! I must say so, honestly, now, dear. The tone you used to me, you know, shocked all who

---

[1] The fashionable support for skirts.

heard you, and if we had not made you feel that—you might have been very unhappy and made your husband very unhappy. The trouble you gave us all—was indeed very great. Comparatively speaking, we have none whatever with the others. You and Bertie (in very different ways) were indeed great difficulties. But life—life with its bright and its dark sides,'its joys and its trials, as you learn it now, has done and will do what I believe nothing else could or would. And so it always is! I am very curious to know whether I shall find still some of the old tricks of former times in you? The standing on one leg, the violent laughing—the cramming in eating, the waddling in walking. As for your "favourite names",[1] Papa was as horrified as I was, as they are two of the ugliest "housemaids" names I ever knew. With your good taste and poetical, romantic mind how can you be so unecstatic! You have all got such lovely names, and you have no particular reason to like these two frights—except for Cousin Charlotte's sake. If ever I am to be godmother to any child of yours it must be on the condition (unless some wonderful law in Prussia obliges ancestral names to be adhered to, which explains the cause) that my godchild is to have decent, pretty names. In the case of Linfield's child, however, there is no earthly reason for Elizabeth Charlotte. They are not ours or yours or your sisters—or hers or Cowley's names; now Frederica is a pretty name and tells its story; the Wilhelmina, we will leave out, and only call it Frederica which may be shortened into Freddie. They are so ugly and after no one in the world related to you! Why not Frederica Wilhelmina? or Frederica Alice or in short something with a meaning in them.

I send you Hatton's[2] music to King Lear. There is not much in it however as there is but little occasion for music.

---

[1] In a previous letter the Queen had written: "By the by, dear, how could you give Linfield's child two such frightful and unnecessary names as Elizabeth Charlotte? Pray change them." Linfield was presumably a royal servant for on July 16 the Princess Royal wrote "I am glad Linfield is so well; I sent her word that I would name her little girl".

[2] J. L. Hatton, the Victorian composer. He was conductor of music at the Princess's Theatre under Charles Kean.

OSBORNE, JULY 31, 1858

I have not been drawing a great deal as I have so much to write (including letters to you) and so many important things to write and do, but I constantly do a little and Mr. C. Haag[1] kindly came down and gave me two lessons and has left me a lovely little sketch-book.

There has been a great deal of photographing going on —Captain De Ros has done some lovely things and so has Mr. Lake Price[2] (who is come here on his own accord)—I shall bring you a good many. He is such an odd man and tried to photograph your little brothers for two hours but it was terrible work—at last he asked Captain De Ros "if the young princes were always so mercurial". Fräulein Bauer is a dear, clever, sensible-seeming little person, 24 years old, —most unassuming, adored by the children with whom she is very firm and strict, and much liked by the ladies; she speaks very Hessian German like Dr. Becker only broader. She plays on the piano but I think does not draw; but she is very well informed. She is extremely short.

OSBORNE, AUGUST 2, 1858

Your dear letter of the 29th arrived in the middle of our Fête, which was favoured by a most splendid day only almost too hot—but it did not even get cool when the sun went down. We thought much of you. Alice looked so tall and élancée! Captain De Ros's little girl was there and is a great darling. The games were as usual. General Peel came with the other Ministers for the Council and stayed till today. We liked him very much; as he is so sensible and straight-forward and does remind me so much of his poor brother—really it almost startles to hear the voice and see the same manner which for eight years we have not known and which recalls so many bygone times to our recollection!

---

[1] A naturalised Englishman who is remembered for his pictures of Balmoral and of the Royal Family there.

[2] William Lake Price, a former water-colour painter. See *Queen Victoria*, by H. and A. Gernsheim.

I am so vexed that poor Marianne is sent away all alone; I wished so much to see her too; I hope I shall at Hanover. How stupid they are abroad in never letting children have change of air! Here you know it is considered essential to life and health and their little girls would I am sure be much the better for it. Fritz C. is strange.

OSBORNE, AUGUST 4, 1858

We are just starting for Cherbourg (in an hour) and therefore I can only write a very hurried scrawl. I too am looking forward anxiously to the very happy time we shall spend together, but I dislike much leaving the others for so long, but I much prefer not taking your two sisters with us to be stared at by everyone! This was not Miss H.'s objection but we felt it all along—and I am much relieved I own not to have to watch them all the time. I am glad you found out all about these princes and princesses but I shall take good care to have no more children's marriages like yours, dear. May your health only not suffer for it that's all I pray for!

OSBORNE, AUGUST 7, 1858

Here we are safely returned from our very interesting expedition to Cherbourg. It would be impossible for me to give you a long and detailed description of all that passed, so I have asked Mary Bulteel to do it. First of all therefore as regards the passage going; it had blown so much the day before that there was motion though not a great deal, but however enough to make me go and lie down quietly in my nice cool cabin, and good Mr. Minter[1] gave me a chloroform draught which took all discomfort and headache away.

After describing a visit on shore the Queen goes on:

We got home[2] near five—and poor Papa had to compose and arrange a French speech in answer to one the Emperor was going to make—which made us both so nervous! At seven we went to dine on board La Bretagne, a four decker

---

[1] John Minter—surgeon on the Royal Yacht.
[2] i.e. Back on board the Royal Yacht.

forty guns—dressed as you are in Germany for early dinners; I changed my bonnet for a coiffure on board. At the end of the dinner the Emperor made an admirable speech to which poor Papa answered, extremely well but was so nervous—and as for me—I was ready to die of it and never wish to hear him speak again. Papa got a migraine from it yesterday.

ON BOARD THE VICTORIA AND ALBERT, AUGUST 31, 1858

The visit to the Princess Royal was over.

I am so glad you were spared seeing any more of that dreadful Grand Duchess[1] for I think you ought to be very little in the society of so worthless a woman. I must use this expression for I believe that were she not a Princess she would not be received anywhere, and really she ought not to be. Marie B. (who with Leopold and Philip accompanied us from Verviers to Antwerp and went on board with us) told us dreadful stories of her conduct and language at Ostend. I am so glad Fritz and you did not go to the family dinner at Glienicke[2] and I hope that you will gradually make it understood that you are not obliged to go to these family dinners every time. It is very important you should not—and I am sure it will be easily effected—as they are no longer at the King's.

OSBORNE, SEPTEMBER 3, 1858

Mr. Saunders will be at Berlin on Wednesday next. He comes at his own expense, so just give him a little souvenir which will please and flatter him.

OSBORNE, SEPTEMBER 4, 1858

I received such a kind affectionate letter from the dear Prince of Prussia. Pray thank him very much in my name,

---

[1] Grand-Duchess of Mecklenburg-Schwerin, sister of the King of Prussia.
[2] Klein-Glienicke was a palace near Potsdam built by Prince Charles who, as this correspondence makes plain, was indeed a wicked uncle.

and tell him that when I feel most I never can express myself; and really I have the greatest possible affection, regard
and friendship for him. This has been the case since '44
when I first made his acquaintance.[1] Pray tell him all this—
as you know I can't say "Que je l'aime" as somebody we
know does![2]

WOODLEY HOUSE,[3] SEPTEMBER 7, 1858

I was sure you would be delighted with Robert le
Diable—the music is so magnificent—so dramatic. Do you
understand now—the similitude between somebody you
have living near you and Bertram?[4] By the by do keep
Affie from that somebody's society as much as Bertie. You
ask me what I should like to have for Xmas? I should like to
have a few of those bronze soldiers as we wish to place them
at Aldershot, and I won't give up the two which I bought
for myself. They are not very expensive. Then something
in amber I should also like.

BALMORAL CASTLE, SEPTEMBER 13, 1858

Mr. Phillip[5] will arrive soon; Fritz and Countess Blücher
can explain to him that your figure is somewhat different to

---

[1] In August 1844, when he stayed at Windsor.
[2] Probably an allusion to the Princess Royal.
[3] The Queen was staying at Leeds in the Mayor's house, which he had
lent to the Royal Family, for the opening of the Town Hall. The first
Leeds Musical Festival was held in the Town Hall on the evening of the
opening—September 6. Writing to the Princess Royal the Queen said
"Such a picturesque Mayor—he looked like a Doge painted by Titian.
Miss Hildyard is in ecsta ies with him."
[4] Meyerbeer's Opera—see also note on page 91. Robert is the son of the
arch-fiend by a human woman. Robert's father, known as Bertram, is
his evil genius, persuading him to gamble and eventually to lose his
knightly honour. Robert is saved by his love for the pure Alice, who
prevents him from signing a pact with Bertram. This was the first opera
to cater for the new middle-class public in Paris, who wanted spectacular
pageants and exciting plots with music as only of secondary importance.
   The Queen is evidently comparing Bertram with Prince Charles.
[5] John Phillip (1817–67), artist. He painted the very successful picture
of the Crown Princess's wedding; he had gone to Berlin to put some
finishing touches to the picture.

then, and that your face and neck are thicker and the latter shorter (from causes) than usual; your dress can be put on a lay figure but the wreath and veil you can put on; and please give him every assistance you can for the other sittings of the princes. You will be much pleased with the picture; except Mr. Winterhalter I know none (certainly no English artist) who paints with such fresh colours.

By the by I spoke to Papa about the prayers which Count Dohna[1] wanted to have already put up for you—and we both think it would be much better, more decent, to delay it till the last month before, when you need not be present yourself; besides the extreme awkwardness and indelicacy—of having it read with your name in your presence—it has the bad effect of making people expect it long before it can be, if it is publicly announced nearly five months before! It never was done for me, and time progresses in delicacy I hope! I am sure the Prince would understand this and do whatever you liked.

I hope you are very patient with poor Anne, and with all your servants.

BALMORAL CASTLE, SEPTEMBER 16, 1858

We are provoked at Affie's aquatic propensities even at Babelsberg; you should not have let him go on the water so often as we wished him to see all the palaces etc. and not to be making a fool of himself as I fear he has done, by playing the sailor on the Havel.[2]

SEPTEMBER 17. Bertie is so amiable, so quiet and pleasant,—it is such an improvement. He is very amiably anxious about you. Major Teesdale[3] (who will accompany him to Berlin) is a very distinguished young man, and so handsome. We have been so fortunate as to get Sir G. Grey's son[4] (just returned from India) as Bertie's third gentleman.

---

[1] The Queen of Prussia's Grand Maître.
[2] The lakes of the River Havel at Babelsberg.
[3] Distinguished himself in the fighting in the Crimea; afterwards Sir Christopher Teesdale.
[4] George, father of the Liberal statesman Lord Grey of Fallodon.

Many thanks, dear, for your letter of the 18th which I received with heaps of letters on getting up. Papa says you write too much—he is sure you make yourself ill by it, and constantly declares (which I own offends me much) that your writing to me at such length is the cause of your often not writing fully to him. I wish you would not always write to me such long letters by the messenger—but merely a few words and then (if there is no secret) write it by the post; or write a day or two before, and let it wait for the messenger. As my excellent child is very unmethodical, I am sure you don't divide your time well.

Good Affie, he is a good, dear, clever, odd boy, and I am so amused at all you say about him and Princess Charles. How do you find the King? I fear the poor Prince will not do the right thing about the regency and the Government.[1] I am shocked to hear you speak of being here[2] next year! I don't want that at all. I want you to come to England for my birthday and for the season, for Osborne and Windsor. Altogether I don't like being here this year at all. I enjoy the scenery and being out very much but I hate the life here, of which the 11 o'clock messenger is an instance. It is horrid. So dispel all notions of coming here next autumn please. I won't have you then; God knows if we shall be here then![3]

---

[1] The mental disturbance of the King had increased and the Prince was about to assume the Regency indefinitely. He was thought to be reactionary and hostile to the constitution, hence the Queen's fears. On November 5 he dismissed the Government of Manteuffel and summoned Queen Victoria's friend Prince Hohenzollern to form a Government.

[2] Balmoral.

[3] This passing annoyance is explained by the Queen's sense of ill-usage that Prince Alfred was about to be sent away to sea by the Prince Consort when she thought him too young.

From the Princess Royal

The Grand Duchess Olga[1] was here two days. She was very cold and uncivil to me, almost rude; when I went to see her she never asked me to sit down but sat at the table with her back turned to me, and condescended to ask me when I went away, whether I was sixteen. She is so shockingly dressed, her things so crumpled and soiled and she herself, oh so fannée and worn; no remains of good looks, the Grand Duchess Marie[2] must have been much prettier. Poor Grand Duchess Olga, I pity her, she looks so melancholy and sick of everything. (I don't very much wonder that she is of her own husband.) Of course I kept my reflections to myself and only tell you and Papa on paper what I think.

BALMORAL CASTLE, SEPTEMBER 27, 1858

With respect to Mary I can never promote a Catholic marriage; if ever one could have been possible, it would have been the King of Sardinia—at that moment from his conduct during the war, and his toleration in religion and stand against the Pope. That Mary herself refused, on the ground of religion, and I then told her, you can after that marry no other.[3] Papa can tell you the difficulties attending any Catholic marriage. The Duke of Brunswick is the match for her—and I wish we could bring it about.

What could the Princess Royal of Württemberg mean by being so rude to you? You ought not to keep your feelings to yourself, for you owe it to your own position—to the country you come from, not to allow yourself to be treated with rudeness. You will remember that I said to you, you must always make a great difference between your conduct to the Queen and the Princesses of your husband's family to

---

[1] The daughter of the Emperor Nicholas I of Russia: her mother was the sister of the King of Prussia. The Grand-Duchess had married the son of the King of Württemberg.

[2] Her elder sister.

[3] Roman Catholic.

whom you belong—and the Russian family who have never been considered as better or as high as our family. What moreover I cannot comprehend and think ought not to be tolerated is that people—(even your own ladies in writing to me) call the Princess Royal of Württemberg the Grand Duchess Olga—and you Princess Frederick William. She is the second daughter of the Emperor of Russia, married to the son and Heir-Prince of Württemberg consequently less in rank than her husband; you are the eldest daughter of the Queen of England, with a title and rights of your own, fifth in succession and married to a nephew of the King, therefore decidedly higher in rank than your husband; yet you—they call Princess Frederick William and make difficulties in adding even your name after the other! Now I don't at all consider it advisable or necessary that the wife should (excepting in her own country where she has her own alloted place) take her name instead of her husband's; but then it should be the same with all princesses. I don't understand what that means, when I am answered that the Princess Royal of Württemberg always has been called Grand Duchess Olga, why the Princess Royal of Great Britain should not also always be called Princess Royal! I think this distinction is one which cannot be accepted by anyone; our princes never admitted the Grand Dukes of Russia having precedence over them; Romanoffs are not to be compared to the houses of Brunswick, Saxony and Hohenzollern. Therefore there must be one rule for all, and one system. Moreover the Princess Royal of Württemberg is always called so at Stuttgart. These are things which may appear trifles, but which the honour and dignity of one's country do not allow to be overlooked.

Now, my dearest child,—I fear you exaggerate as you so often used to do, little momentary feelings of suffering and discomfort, which others who do not know your disposition put down as real suffering and indisposition and then think you are really ill—which you are not; now let me entreat you seriously not to do this, not to let your feelings (very natural and usual ones) of momentary irritation and discomfort be seen by others; don't (as you so often did and do) let every little feeling be read in your face and seen in your manner, pray don't give way to irritability before your ladies. All this I say with the love and affection I bear you— as I know what you have to contend with and struggle against.

Letter continued on October 1.

The Ball (Ghillie's Ball) went off extremely well, was very full and very gay; and darling Arthur was quite delightful dancing the perpetual jig and not letting himself be cut out. He was universally applauded, and the people were so delighted with him. He is a great darling but alas! he too approaches the time when he will be taken away from my care, though I shall take good care, that he is not treated as Affie was—but remaining with us—as long as he possibly can.

I have been shamefully deceived about Affie; it was promised me that the last year before he went to sea, he should be with us, instead of which he was taken away and I saw but very little of him, and now he is to go away for many months and I shall not see him God knows! when, and Papa is most cruel upon the subject. I assure you, it is much better to have no children than to have them only to give them up! It is too wretched.

Of course I am much occupied with our visit to you, D.V. at Easter, and wish to know whether (if we could not arrive the day before Palm Sunday) would it signify if we arrived at Berlin during the Passion Week, naturally quite quietly? And would our presence during Passion Week be any inconvenience to you? I hope not. I mention this because Parliament is only prorogued during Passion Week and Easter Week. I hope that the Prince and Fritz will take all means of ascertaining how the christening (D.V.) can be best put off. I believe for the Empress of Russia—years ago, it was once; and as Russian precedents are gospel at the Prussian Court, I suppose for the Queen of England a similar dispensation could be procured.

BALMORAL CASTLE, OCTOBER 4, 1858

OCT 5. I could not go on further yesterday, but take up
my letter now and thank you much for yours of the 3rd,
received this morning by which I am sorry to see you are so
hurried. But don't worry yourself ever in writing long to me
when you have no time; but let the young Baron (who you
know possesses entirely your and my confidence) answer
any questions or any observations which I may make and
which require an answer. Only don't worry yourself. I
only want to know and hear, but not that (when you are
overcome with cares) you should hurry and worry yourself.
I like to know if things arrive and if you get my letters etc.
but let E. Stockmar acknowledge them with two words, if
you have no time. Write when you have time and let the
lottor go whon tho mossengor gocs—without minding its
being old. If you knew how Papa scolds me for (as he says)
making you write! And he goes further, he says that I
write far too often to you, and that it would be much better
if I wrote only once a week! Therefore it is indeed a hard
case and I know not what to say! I think however Papa is
wrong and you do like to hear from home often. When you
do write to Papa again just tell him what you feel and wish
on that subject for I assure you—Papa has snubbed me
several times very sharply on the subject and when one
writes in spite of fatigues and trouble to be told it bores the
person to whom you write, it is rather too much!

I am surprised at the Princess Royal of Württemberg
not standing up for Winterhalter—as I know that the
Russians all worship him. Perhaps she knows he thought
her fausse. At Berlin they are jealous of him, that is all.
All real connoisseurs admire him as they must and ought
and time will show how unrivalled he is!

On Sunday we had a beautiful sermon from Dr.
Macleod[1] and in his beautiful prayer he brought in a most
touching allusion to you (which I shall get copied and send
you). He said "May she never forget the early lessons she
has received!" And that I trust and believe you never will!

[1] Norman Macleod, Scottish Divine, Chaplain to the Queen.

— 135 —

May you ever feel the gratitude you owe to your country which has shown you an affection and interest which I think is unparalleled for a young Princess, a child. Never, dear child, forget what you owe your country—never forget those duties which you owe to it as well as to your new one! And happily there is nothing in these two-fold affections and duties which need ever clash; the interests are so much the same, and will in time get more and more united.

Of all the wonderful German notions that one of a lady in your condition being unable to stand godmother is the most extraordinary I ever heard! Is a woman really bewitched or possessed to be considered unlucky? I think that must be only a Prussian notion (perhaps Russian?) because I have heard of so many christenings abroad where people have been in that condition and stand as godmothers. I hope that you will break through that; but above all promise me never to do so improper and indecorous a thing as to be lying in a dressing gown on a sofa at a christening! It would shock people here very much, and as my daughter and an English Princess I expect you will not do it. Conform to all what is reasonable, right—and essential, but in what is absurd and affected set a good example. In former times ladies received visits in their beds; Queen Charlotte also lay on a bed, at her children's christenings!! Let German ladies do what they like but the English Princess must not.[1]

---

[1] This letter has an important bearing on the extent of the Queen's interference with the Princess. Lord Clarendon, who was out of office, happened to be staying in Berlin at the beginning of October. The events are unfolded in Charles Greville's *Diary* (1938 edition, Volume VII, page 387 and following pages): "Stockmar [that is the old Baron] came to him (Clarendon) and said 'I want to talk to you on a very important matter and to invoke your aid. It relates to "this poor child here". Her mother is behaving abominably to her; and unless a stop can be put to her conduct I know not what may be the consequences, for she is not in good health, and she is worried and frightened to death. The Queen wishes to exercise the same authority and control over her that she did before her marriage: and she writes her constant letters full of anger and reproaches, desiring all sorts of things to be done that it is neither right nor desirable that she should do.' Stockmar then asked Clarendon, when he got back to England, to see the Prince Consort on this subject." Greville follows this with a long account of Clarendon's

From the Princess Royal

BABELSBERG, OCTOBER 9, 1858

I think I am not likely to forget the early lessons I have received at home, at least I hope to give proofs of this, and I should think myself very ungrateful if I could forget them or the duties I owe to my country which I shall love so passionately till my dying day, and be too proud to have belonged to ever to let myself forget. But my first duties are here now, and in fulfilling them to the utmost I can only be doing what my own country would wish and expect; how often have allusions been made at home to my following your example here, which I could not do if I gave offence by not observing the customs of the country. Therefore as to the possibility of being like the other princesses here, on a sofa at the event of a christening, I can give no promise against; ask dear Papa whether he does not think I am right. It would seem strange if a German princess married in England and insisted on having a christening there with the same customs observed as in her home. I fear I should make myself justly disliked if I showed a contempt for a custom which is after all an innocent one—of sitting on an armchair or chaise lounge and, as the ladies do here, is natural when their children are christened at three weeks of age as they always are here. I cannot say that I see anything indecent in the custom, no more would you if you saw it, dear Mama, but from far it does sound most extraordinary. I remember last year I was horrified when I heard of Louise of Baden lying on a sofa to receive her congratulations but now that I have seen, there is really nothing indecorous in it; the Princess of Prussia sat in an armchair.

---

talk with the Prince which is rather off the particular point, as it bears on the Queen's treatment of her children in general.

On November 14 the old Baron wrote to the Prince Consort a letter beginning "Dear and Esteemed Prince . . . For months I have been seeking to disentangle the state of confusion which has arisen, and to make from unhealthy circumstances healthier ones. . . . The great distance which separates the participants, together with the fact that their only means of reaching an understanding is through correspondence, the most incomplete and at the same time the most dangerous means of all—these are to blame.

"I had come to the conclusion," he goes on, "that the new relation-

From the Princess Royal

Yesterday was the poor King's birthday. We went to church in the morning, in the afternoon we had a family dinner here, one of those delightful ones during which one sits on hot coals all the time, because Prince Charles makes one improper joke and remark after the other at which it is wrong to laugh; but he has the talent of making what he says so ridiculous, that it really almost chokes one with the struggle not to laugh. What a dreadful man he is, I feel miserable when I sit next to him.

---

ship had been *wrongly conceived over there,* [i.e. in England] that they were proceeding much too actively from *over there* that they wanted to control matters *over here* much too much in accordance with their opinions and feelings, and that they were meddling far too much with trivialities. Accordingly I attempted, in the most sacred interests of all, to give counsel, and I urged somewhat more consideration, moderation, calm and passivity." The Prince told Clarendon that because of this letter the Queen was "in a towering passion with the Baron".

No doubt Stockmar was absolutely right, but it is unfair to put all the blame on the Queen because if she was "meddling with trivialities" the Prince was attempting to guide the young couple on political matters. Indeed the whole episode illustrates the tangle which can only too easily choke the private relationships of royal persons. The young Baron, the old Baron, Countess Blücher, Clarendon were all shaking their heads over what was happening till informed gossip was hinting that the Queen might display the hereditary malady of her grandfather George III, and Greville could write that the Queen "was never really fond of the Princess Royal". Readers, to an extent, will excuse the Queen because they realise how she blamed herself for agreeing to "the child-marriage", how anxious she was over the child's pregnancy and how distraught she was at being prevented from going to Berlin for the birth. Her characteristic was to give vent to these anxieties by fidgeting (to use her own favourite word), to broadcast criticism and rebukes. But the Princess was perfectly capable of standing her ground. We can only admire the writer of the letter of October 9—a girl of 17. In acknowledging it the Queen called it "your dear letter" and begged the Princess to ask the young Baron to write on any topics which she did not feel up to writing about herself.

I and the girls lunched while Papa was after the stag—and good J. Brown was so attentive to us and so careful—he is now my special servant; and there can't be a nicer, better or handier one. Really there is nothing like these High-landers for handiness; poor MacDonald[1] never having been able to go out at all, Brown has had everything to do for me, indeed had charge of me and all, on all those expeditions, and therefore I settled that he should be specially appointed to attend on me (without any other title) and have a full dress suit. (You know he is since two or three years per-manent servant here having charge of all the ponies.) He was so much pleased when I told him you had asked after him. But you will laugh when I tell you what happened to Lenchen; she told Brown that it was Fritz's birthday, and he misunderstood her and said "Aye! Has she got a girl or a boy?"—which startled Lenchen amazingly as she suspects nothing.

In a reference to the Princess's condition the Queen says:

Affie knows nothing, but he is wonderful in want of tact; there is no end of instances of that. Alas I look forward with horror to the separation from him this day week. Two children in one year! It is horrible. Altogether I feel so sad, as you know and feel for me, at the bitter thought of going from this blessed place—leaving these hills—this enchant-ing life of liberty—these dear people—and returning to tame, dull, formal England and the prison life of Windsor! But I must be and I am thankful for what I have enjoyed.

WINDSOR CASTLE, OCTOBER 21, 1858

Oh! I think I never felt going away from Balmoral more painful than this time, I know not why—and if even the moment itself is not more painful I feel the regret more vividly than I did last year. But then I was solely occupied with you, felt for you, and forgot myself more. This is cer-

---

[1] The ghillie at Balmoral.

tainly to a great extent also the feeling I feel about Affie, and in leaving dear Balmoral and all its wild, simple and peculiar charms, I felt so much must happen before (if God spares me) we are to go there again!

The Queen continues about Affie:

Hard it is, very hard to have to part with him so young —to know him so far—and with the certainty of not seeing him till August at the very earliest! All this makes me very melancholy and I long and pine for the hills,

> "My heart's in the Highlands, my heart is not here;
> Wherever I wander wherever I rove,
> The hills of the Highlands for ever I'll love."

Yes that is my feeling and I must fight and struggle against it. Unfortunately, Papa though loving them and the people perhaps (I don't think quite) as much as I do, can at once accustom himself to the life here—which is also to me a far greater change than to him, and is annoyed at my living in the recollections of the past! But this I can't help, and the heartache I suffer each year, on leaving Balmoral and coming here is most distressing. Then besides you know I have no feeling for Windsor—I admire it, I think it a grand, splendid place—but without a particle of anything which causes me to love it—none, I feel no interest in anything as if it were not my own; and that of course lessens all the enjoyment of one's existence.

WINDSOR CASTLE, OCTOBER 27, 1858

Dearest Affie is gone; and it will be 10 months probably before we shall see his dear face which shed sunshine over the whole house, from his amiable, happy, merry temper; again he was much upset at leaving and sobbed bitterly, and I fear the separation from dear Papa will have been equally trying. Still, sad as it is to part from dear Affie, it is nothing to parting with a daughter; she is gone, as your own child, for ever; she belongs to another, and that is so dreadful a feeling for a mother who has watched over every little trifle as well as every serious moment of the life of her daughter, and has with one small act to abdicate all her rights to another, and to a man! The sons will always remain the same. Their position after the first 9 or 10 years are past being so different to a daughter's.

I hope Fritz is duly shocked at your sufferings, for those very selfish men would not bear for a minute what we poor slaves have to endure. But don't dread the dénouement; there is no need of it; and don't talk to ladies about it, as they will only alarm you, particularly abroad, where so much more fuss is made of a very natural and usual thing. I shall see Mrs. Lilley[1] next week, and then Mrs. Innocent;[2] and then Mrs. Hobbs.[3]

I like the appearance of Miss Bennett:[4] she is 30; tall, respectable and sedate-looking—and is said to dress hair and make dresses extremely well—is accustomed to travel, and has always been liked in the houses where she was living before.

I could not tell such a child as Lenchen about you; those things are not proper to be told to children, as it initiates them into things which they ought not to know of, till they are older. Affie knows nothing either. The mistake of good J. Brown I am sure would amuse you. How you can call Windsor "dear" I cannot understand. It is prison-like, so large and gloomy—and for me so dull after Balmoral too, it is like jumping from day into night—fine as it is!

Say everything kind to my dear friend Prince Hohenzollern; there are few people I am so fond of as him.

---

[1] She was the Queen's monthly nurse.

[2] Mrs. Innocent was going out to Berlin as the Princess Royal's monthly nurse.

[3] Mrs. Hobbs went out to Germany with the Princess as a maid. She was to be nurse to the baby. She was called Hobbsy, and the Kaiser is said to have learned English from her.

[4] A personal maid engaged by the Queen for the Princess.

Then we gave Bertie in Papa's room his uniform (a colonel unattached in the Army—with a cocked hat) which he was as eager about as Arthur would have been at a bear-skin and sword. I had a shocking nervous headache—which was not very pleasant.[1] The Princes went out shooting. In the afternoon Bertie put on his uniform and reported himself to Uncle George who lectured him on obedience. He looked small—but not at all amiss. Less favourable—as he is very knock-kneed—were the shorts in the evening: but still they were not strikingly unbecoming. He was in a good mood. The usual large dinner—Alice dined, as she does generally once or twice a week. After dinner a gay dance and two merry reels! Marie[2] looked lovely and is so ladylike and gentle and quiet, and such a contrast to poor Mary, who is so big now again—much worse than she was—and whose manners and I grieve to say conversation too, now—are not refined. Fancy (your favourite word) her asking *Papa*—if you had been very sick!!! A thing I now should not ask hardly any gentleman!! and then very doubtful talk about wet nurses. I fear there is no hope for a husband. All this with her figure is too much. Her manners shocked our sweet, modest rose—Marie. Poor child she is afraid of Papa—and won't hardly speak when he is there, so that he thinks she has nothing in her, which is far from being the case. She is a delightful companion for Alice. Today is her first separation from Ernest—who is gone till Saturday to Portsmouth.

Poor Mr. Gibbs leaves tomorrow. He has failed completely the last year and a half with Bertie—and Bertie did what he liked! No-one can understand the cause and it makes it more difficult for us now. However I have great confidence in Colonel Bruce.[3]

[1] November 9, the Prince of Wales's seventeenth birthday.
[2] Sister of the Grand Duke of Baden. She had married Ernest, Prince of Leiningen in the previous September.
[3] Colonel Robert Bruce, brother of the 8th Lord Elgin and of Lady Augusta, the friend of the Duchess of Kent and the Queen. Though Colonel Bruce had something of the sternness of his race he was successful in winning the confidence of the young prince and of his parents.

WINDSOR CASTLE, NOVEMBER 13, 1858

We had the Bernstorffs and the good Maharajah (who
stayed till this morning) since Thursday. He looks so handsome and well—and is talkative and agreeable. Those eyes
and those teeth are too beautiful. He is going very shortly
to Turkey to shoot. Count Bernstorff has got a beard!

I have never felt Windsor more dull and tiresome—or
the Castle, stiffer and gloomier than this year! I long for our
cheerful and unpalace-like rooms at Osborne and Balmoral!

On the 10th in the evening I took leave of poor Mr.
Gibbs; he was affected and low—and it upset me a good deal.
We always got on extremely well together. Bertie was
much affected too, at parting from him.

WINDSOR CASTLE, NOVEMBER 17, 1858

After referring to a watch which the Queen was sending the Princess
as a present she writes:

All other commissions and questions the Baron will
answer for—as (don't be offended with the truth) my excellent darling child is not a very punctual man of business.

Miss Bennett is coming here next week. Let me advise
you dear, not to complain any more of poor Anne G.[1]—she
is going and the less said about it the better for you and for
her. She is not the first maid who has failed: I could give a
long list of my failures, and it does no-one any good to complain of all her "forgets", which moreover are no worse
than many I could tell of others, as it will soon be over. So
pray let this subject be dropped.

I know that the little being will be a great reward for
all your trouble and suffering—but I know you will not
forget, dear, your promise not to indulge in "baby worship",
or to neglect your other greater duties in becoming a nurse.
You know how manifold your duties are, and as my dear
child is a little disorderly in regulating her time, I fear you
might lose a great deal of it, if you overdid the passion for

[1] The Princess Royal's personal maid. See also note on p. 166.

— 143 —

the nursery. No lady, and still less a Princess, is fit for her husband or her position, if she does that. I know, dear, that you will feel and guard against this, but I only just wish to remind you and warn you, as with your great passion for little children (which are mere little plants for the first six months) it would be very natural for you to be carried away by your pleasure at having a child.

I can not bear to think Bertie is going to you and I can't —and when I look at the baby things, and feel I shall not be, where every other mother is—and I ought to be and can't —it makes me sick and almost frantic. Why in the world did you manage to choose a time when we could not be with you? In Nov: Dec: or the beginning of January we could have done it so easily.

Well, it is no use complaining. Let us hope on another similar occasion to be more fortunate.

Poor Bertie! He vexes us much. There is not a particle of reflection, or even attention to anything but dress! Not the slightest desire to learn, on the contrary, il se bouche les oreilles, the moment anything of interest is being talked of! I only hope he will meet with some severe lesson to shame him out of his ignorance and dullness. Colonel Bruce is most anxious you should speak very openly to him about Bertie, and I told him I was sure you would. He is a very superior and a very charming person. Poor Mr. Gibbs certainly failed during the last 2 years entirely, incredibly—and did Bertie no good.

From the Princess Royal

Tonight the dear Princess arrives, how I long to see her—! but I tremble when I think of all she will have to go through here, her life here is as disagreeable as it can be, and it does not improve her health. If only there are no more scenes; it is so painful to witness, and the Prince must really not be worried now.[1] Between Fritz and his mother I am confident all will go smooth as they are on the best footing possible, and

---

[1] i.e. When he had assumed the Regency.

as for me I have in her my best friend here and always find it so easy to get on with her, if I could only do anything to smooth and comfort her when she is so teased. I am sure I would gladly bear some of her troubles for her.

NOVEMBER 21

Writing on her first birthday away from home the Princess Royal says:

I can but repeat it, that I am happier far than I ever expected to be, that never for one single moment have I regretted the hard and bitter sacrifice of leaving my dear, dear parents and country. It always sounds like ingratitude but you know how it is meant.

WINDSOR CASTLE, NOVEMBER 20, 1858

I had hoped to write a longer letter today than I fear I can, as I have been walking and riding besides going to breakfast at Frogmore in honour of dear Marie's birthday. She is so dear; quite clever enough, very sensible, and so good and unselfish—gentle and unspoilt quite a pattern wife!

There is a terrible deal of illness here. That horrid fever continues and is really most distressing and in some cases fatal. So many of our poor servants' families are so ill. It is strange with this dry cold weather, but they say it all comes from the want of rain, the drains being all uncovered. There is illness everywhere.

You need not I think be alarmed about the scenes between the Prince and Princess—for she is so delighted at all he has done, and says now that he has got the right people she has nothing more to say.

WINDSOR CASTLE, NOVEMBER 24, 1858

Dearest child, it is hard and it is bitter on such days[1] to be parted, but as the good Dean in an excellent sermon (which I shall ask him to send you) said in his text "absent

---

[1] i.e. On the Princess Royal's birthday.

in body but present in spirit". So it is in this life—and so will it be for ever in another and a better world.

Truly, dear child, do I believe that you can now feel (and how much more still when you have a child of your own!) all that parents go through for their children and how it must try and often pain them if their children are naughty and difficult to manage—and the latter my good child always was.

As for Leopold he still bruises as much as ever, but has (unberufen) not had accidents of late. He is tall, but holds himself worse than ever, and is a very common looking child, very plain in face, clever but an oddity—and not an engaging child though amusing. I hope the new governess will be able to make him more like other children. He has not the least forgotten you. Arthur is a precious love. Really the best child I ever saw. Louise very naughty and backward, though improved and very pretty, and affectionate.

And pray do look my letter of the 17th well over so as to answer any observations in it by next messenger. I told you twice of poor McDonald's illness at Balmoral and a whole long story of Johnny Brown's being now appointed always to attend me in consequence! I begin to think you are getting like Grandmama and don't read always your letters.

The Aumales left us this morning—also the Chancellor and Lady Chelmsford—and Lady Inglis. Lady Chelmsford (Lady Thesiger) enquired much after you. Lady Inglis is a charming, admirable woman; she returns to India with her husband on the 4th—and goes to Cawnpore and is to be confined there in March!! but don't dread the journey. But she has to part with her three little boys—as it would be bad for them to go with her! She is so unselfish. I told her I wish to be sponsor to her child.

This dreadful fever continues here. Poor Hautching, the footman died this morning.

Ernest and Marie are gone to their little humble home,[1]

---

[1] Presumably a small house in the vicinity of Osborne.

and seem perfectly happy and contented. I never saw a nicer couple.

Discussing the number of children which the Princess Royal might have, the Queen writes:

but I hope you will have no chance of two for some time, and not of three for a long time. Bertie and I both suffered (and the former will ever suffer) from coming so soon after you.

We are glad to hear so good an account of poor Bertie; I have no doubt his visit to you—and the mild but firm influence of Colonel Bruce will do him much good. But we always found that he appeared for the first week—much improved, then (as is always the case with him in everything) he gradually went down hill; not paying attention to what is said or read or what he sees is the real misfortune. His natural turn and taste is very trifling, and I think him a very dull companion. But he has been quite altered, for the last few months (in short since he lived at the White Lodge) as to manner, and he is no longer difficile à vivre. Handsome I cannot think him, with that painfully small and narrow head, those immense features and total want of chin.

This note will be given you by Bennett who leaves tomorrow and who I can really recommend highly to you. She is exceptionally quiet and of a very peaceable, unassuming disposition, handy and quick in dressing—dresses hair well and evidently is a thoroughly experienced lady's maid. My dressers like her and say she is most anxious to do well and to live at peace. I have (tiresome as it is) had her every day into my room to see and help, and she has dressed me every day. All this, dear, I have done with pleasure for you, but I do, dear, expect you to be very patient and indulgent and not irritable and impatient, which your present state often causes one to be.

From the Princess Royal

We found Bertie so much improved, Fritz never lets him be with his uncle[1] alone for a moment. Prince Charles and Prince Albrecht wanted to take him for four days to Todenrode[2] for a chase where the Duke of Brunswick is and you could imagine what company, what a tone and what conversation. Fritz said he could not go, but yesterday evening they attacked me about it, saying it would amuse him so much; I said that we had been separated for nearly a year and would be so again, and that he was come to see me for three weeks, and tried every argument I could. I am glad we prevented it, I knew you never would nor could allow it so there was an end to the matter.

WINDSOR CASTLE, DECEMBER 1, 1858

After repeating more or less what she had said about Bertie in her last letter, the Queen goes on:

You can imagine the sorrow, and bitter disappointment and the awful anxiety for the future which this causes us! I dare not attempt to think of that! But all we can do to eradicate other evils and bring out his good, kind qualities we all must do. Pray have some private conversation with Colonel Bruce before he goes, and tell him everything you observe. Colonel B. seems to have judged his character (which is full of anomalies) very well. Alice is very like him in many things—but has a sweet temper and is industrious and conquers all her difficulties; she is such a good girl and has made such progress lately. She now takes lessons of an evening with Papa and reminds me so of former times, when she comes in at six—and often waits in despair for "dear Papa". Do you recollect? Papa says she is very attentive, whereas Bertie was stupid and inattentive and quite incapable of taking in or even willing to take in anything.

You were indeed quite right to stop that shooting excur-

---

[1] i.e. Prince Charles.
[2] In the Harz Mountains—a small hunting-lodge belonging to the Dukes of Brunswick.

sion for Bertie. For the future you may always say that we wished him to remain with you and pay no visits. The dear Princess speaks so kindly of you and seems so happy. Does this not show to all who considered her meddling and ambitious—that her sole anxiety was to see her husband properly surrounded and taking the lead in Germany in all that is up to date and really national? What does the King and still more the Queen say to all these changes? At Hanover they seem to think the world come to an end!

Pray continue to paste your letters for I assure you elsewhere[1] they may be opened and yours of the 29th arrived without even a half sheet to cover the writing.

WINDSOR CASTLE, DECEMBER 4, 1858

I am so glad that Bertie is amiable and companionable towards you, and occupies himself, as I am sure it will do him good. I own I think him very dull; his three other brothers are all so amusing and communicative. I am glad he is shocked at the conduct of certain people.

I long to hear of Bennett's safe arrival and your liking her; only be very patient and indulgent at first. Papa has all the ennuis of breaking in his new valet, a young German, Kohler by name, who has never been in service and seems an intelligent young man.

The fever is very bad here still and Windsor and Eton are so full of illness that the boys (of whom 300 were ill) have been sent away. I am quite glad to get away—as Windsor seems more awfully gloomy than ever and I am sure very unwholesome now. We go on Monday for a fortnight to Osborne—and Mama will probably also come there on account of the sickness here.

Papa desires me to say that it would be impossible for Bertie to visit you on his way back from Italy—and that therefore he hopes you won't make his mouth water on the subject. But even were this not the case, I would give you the answer which of late has been given me so frequently by you viz, "it is better to make no plans so long beforehand".

---

[1] i.e. In countries other than Prussia.

From Alfred we have heard from Gibraltar; he arrived there on the 27th and had had very bad weather. He is quite well, but his letters of which he has given us only three specimens are too shockingly and disgracefully written. Strange that both the boys should write so ill—and that all the girls (at least you three) so well. But Affie's is very much worse than Bertie's. I am so glad that Bertie was shocked at the improper conduct of the Princes; it will do him good, to see such things in their true light. We are all much shocked at the untimely end of poor Clementine Villiers![1] Such a beautiful, talented girl to die thus early (thirty-four without having married though I don't consider this such a misfortune for I think unmarried people are very often very happy—certainly more so than married people who don't live happily together of which there are so many instances) in fact her poor worldly ambitious mother dragged her about everywhere, thinking nothing good enough for her—till she blighted her prospects and ruined her health! We are both so grieved, for she was so old an acquaintance, clever and agreeable—and an exemplary daughter to those poor old parents whose idol she was. Poor Clemmy, she often came to see me, with her beautiful sister Sarah Esterhazy, who died of consumption a few years ago—when we were children! Such beautiful children. It has shocked us both so much.

In the first part of the letter the Queen gives certain directions to the Princess to avoid any clashes between the monthly nurse and her dressers and she goes on:

Some little further memoranda I will send you by the messenger. Mrs. Innocent has likewise copies of all the notes I put down afterwards of all I did—during my confinements—as I know you will like to know—and this will

---

[1] Daughter of 5th Lord Jersey and Lady Jersey, the celebrated leader of London Society who owned the principal part of Child's Bank.

Prince Frederick William and the infant Prince William, 1859

King Frederick William IV of Prussia

be a guide. All this I have been particularly anxious about—as my two first confinements—for want of order—and from disputes and squabbles (chiefly owing to my poor old governess[1] who would meddle) were far from comfortable or convenient and the doctors too had not found out quite how to treat me. I am therefore particularly anxious that you should profit by my experience (which resulted in my last five confinements being as quiet and comfortable as possible) and be spared as much (as possible) all the inconveniences arising from want of experience etc. which are natural in a first confinement. So you see, dear, that though alas far away (which I shall never console myself for)—I watch over you as if I were there.

Dear Countess Blücher came (as I told you) on Wednesday morning and stayed till Thursday after lunch, and she knows everything. In order to tell you all, we had very long and nice conversations with this truly invaluable friend—who is indeed the greatest of blessings. I feel that she will represent me, and do what providence has (I think so cruelly!) denied me.

There is a most touching and beautiful little brochure which you should read some day by Guizot called 'L'Amour dans Le Mariage' which is merely the history of Lady Rachel Russell, and anything more beautiful and touching than her letters cannot be described. Then there is a very amusing book called "Barchester Towers" by A. Trollope.[2]

OSBORNE, DECEMBER 18, 1858

He [Bertie] arrived at 5 yesterday afternoon looking particularly well and full of all he has seen—and of the very, very happy time he spent with you both—and truly

---

[1] Baroness Lehzen. When the Queen visited the Princess Royal in the summer of this year their train passed Bückeburg where Lehzen lived in retirement after 1842. She was on the platform waving her handkerchief: the train did not stop.

[2] Replying to this the Princess Royal said "I like Barchester Towers very much, it makes one laugh till one cries, it is so very true; but I think it very mischievous and rather wicked, everyone is bad in it almost, and it is illustrated to make one dislike everyone."

attached to Fritz. Let me say again how very, very thankful we are to your good husband for his great kindness—and to the care he took of Bertie. Colonel Bruce (and Lord Bloomfield also) say nothing could exceed it, and we are much and deeply touched by it. Fritz's example can only be of the greatest use to Bertie and his observations upon that are all that can be wished. I am sure his recollection of his first visit to Berlin will be an everlasting one.

Mr. Theed has just finished a beautiful bust of dear Papa—the best done yet; and his beautiful little ear was cast.

WINDSOR CASTLE, DECEMBER 22, 1858

Dear Papa is still not quite well—he went yesterday evening with Bertie (who understood not a word of it) to see the Westminster boys act one of their (very improper) Latin plays.

Bertie talks constantly of Berlin and all he has seen—but particularly of the people, parties, theatres what people said etc. Of the fine works of art etc., he says nothing—unless asked.

I sent you today a bottle of camphor lozenges which I always have standing on my night table near my bed, wherever I go—since they were first recommended to me by Sir C. Locock[1] when I was so restless before you were born, and I found them very soothing. They are perfectly simple and innocent; he said he found them the answer with ladies—and so have I; taking one in your mouth when you can't sleep does real good, at all times, and I am sure if I went anywhere without them, I should fancy I could not get to sleep; I hope you will try them. I am sure Mrs. Innocent knows them well.

WINDSOR CASTLE, CHRISTMAS DAY, 1858

How can I sufficiently thank you for your dear gifts? That beautiful quilt—your own dear work—which shall go

---

[1] Physician-accoucheur to the Queen.

about with me everywhere, and the lovely bracelet from you both which is on my arm—so like, so pretty, so nicely set and gives me immense pleasure. Dearest child, I missed your dear, warm, affectionate hearty greeting—your busy, anxious endeavours to help and please us and all! No-one showed this more than you, my dearest child!—You are constantly in our thoughts—but your dear letter and your gifts—the kind and touching way in which you thought of all (for which God bless your warm loving heart) brought you very near to us, and our spirits joined at least! I had your picture on my arm (a little photograph in the wedding dress) and Affie's in a locket, and your pretty little locket given me the last evening at dear Babelsberg round my neck—and while I gazed on the happy merry faces—amongst whom you used to be—I thought of the inroad time had made in the "children"! But then I thought also with pleasure, with thankfulness and with security that our dear child was and is surrounded by tender love and affection, is prized and cherished as her loving parents' anxious hearts could wish—by the most devoted of husbands and the kindest of parents-in-law. This is a blessed assurance.

Poor dear Affie is all alone amongst strangers—in the midst of life of no easy kind—but he has a most kind friend[1] near him whom he dearly loves—and he has a Father in Heaven who never leaves us, and to whom we may look up with love and confidence most particularly at this joyful season!

WINDSOR CASTLE, DECEMBER 29, 1858

Sending a photograph of the children the Queen says:

Leopold's is a speaking likeness;—he has still a most strange face sadly out of drawing, and holds himself too awfully; but he is a very clever boy and when he is with the governess and learns good manners—and discipline he will (looks excepted) be a very promising child. He has still

---

[1] Major John Cowell of the Royal Engineers, afterwards Master of the Queen's Household. He was governor to Prince Alfred.

however that unfortunate defect in his throat and speech which are much against him!

By the by, Grandmama is en peine about a commission, she gave Fritz some time ago, about a screen which he was to have made up for you for Xmas. Grandmama sent the work for it (two Highlanders) in October with a letter to Fritz and he has never answered it, or acknowledged the screen or anything. Now Fritz is so punctual, never forgetting anything, that I don't understand it—and wish you to be sure and ask him about it as it distresses Grandmama.

Mrs. Hobbs writes delighted with everything but I am sorry to say she is a decided "hatcher"[1] for she wrote to Mrs. Thurston (who is horrified at the prospect of the little individual speaking Cockney English) "I hear the Princess his getting on very well."

---

[1] The misplacing of "h's" by servants was a constant—though curious—source of merriment to the mid-Victorians.

1859

God has denied me the comfort and joy of welcoming my future grandchild on its appearance in this world of troubles and trials—which is a trial that my good children can not realise, but which is most difficult to bear, but He will grant my prayers and in spirit I shall indeed be near.

Mr. Phillip has brought the picture, but you are not even sketched in and the flowers must be added to your dress which looks quite unbridal and unfinished. Fritz is excellent. I think he had best wait till you come here to finish (or indeed paint) you. It will be a beautiful picture.[1]

I send you a diary for you at least to note down dates— (the Baron could do that for you—) as else your life will pass without any thing to look back to—and when you wish to refer to what you did in such and such a year—you will remember nothing and have nothing to refer to—all will be in one cloud of confusion, so, dear, let the Baron just put down (till you can do so yourself) just as Papa does—what events occur from day to day. Thus "Saw so and so, gave a dinner"! "Heard of such and such an event". I will scribble down what I mean in pencil—and if you have leaves open you can always write fully yourself hereafter if you choose. I send you also a "Remembrancer" for you to put down the letters you receive and write, which prevents all confusion, and I add one for Fritz—who will I think find it convenient—I divide the day and then put letters received on one side—and those I write on the other. We had long detailed accounts of Affie from Malta. The impudent *Times* thought fit to disapprove his being properly loyally received.[2]

---

[1] The painting of the wedding.
[2] At the end of 1858 *The Times* had published a leading article on Prince Alfred, which included the following observations:

Mrs. G. Anson (widow of General A.) one of the former beauties whom the Prince Regent[1] also knew and admired —is also added to the list of sudden deaths. She took an overdose of laudanum and died of it!

The Queen lists various small presents for the New Year:

. . . and last my work for the "little individual"; which I have been employed in since September—and which (with the exception of the marking and joining the long stripes) I have done every stitch of myself. You know that Mama has very little time and that I can only work after dinner when we have no visitors, therefore it was longer about than it otherwise would have been, but it gave me such pleasure that I am quite grieved to have finished it. Many doubted I should get it ready in time. I only claim its being used in preference to other peoples' work as the grandmama has a first claim.[2] Your Grandmama is in despair at Fritz's mistake in making up the screen as a cushion and he must write and defend himself. Grandmama says he never gave her any answer.

You are rather unfair, dear, and a little quick in your judgment about the Duchess of Manchester; since we have known her well—we (Papa is of the same opinion) have

---

"We want him to learn his profession—not in a vapid, half and half, Royal Highness, kind of a way. He was sent out to be trained to salt water, and it is upon rose water that his first lesson in navigation is taking place. What has a Middy to do with royal receptions, and royal salutes and royal fiddle-faddles of every description?"

After describing the official arrangements for his reception at Malta the leader-writer went on:

"Prince Alfred might just as well be tempting the perils of Virginia Water. He was greeted by the slogan 'Viva Alfredo'. But why not 'Viva Midshipman Easy'?"

[1] Of Prussia.

[2] It was a quilt. In a later letter the Queen writes again of her enjoyment in doing it and adds "but I am greatly mortified at your having done the same! However mine is *marked*."

found her very amiable, anxious to improve herself—fond
of reading, very kind to the poor (she even teaches in the
schools in Ireland) and very domestic, and not foolish. As
for her beauty, I admire the profile very much; the front
face much less—and I fear it will not last. The waist and
throat are too short for me to admire her figure. The brother
is gentlemanlike but I thought (when in England) pré-
tentieux.

Pray tell me if it is true that Prince George of P.[1] is
going to make a morganatic marriage. I should be sorry,
because I thought he was too maladif to marry even. If he
could do so, he might do for poor Mary C. Indeed the
Princess of P—— some years ago—mentioned him as a good
choice if he had good health. I am constantly asked about it,
so pray tell me. I must also mention what I quite forgot,
viz: that the swing cot which I sent you was entirely made
in the Isle of Wight, under Butcher's[2] superintendence who
is not a little proud of this fact. I think you will like it the
better, my dearest, for knowing this. We had a few people
staying here all this week—the Wellingtons, Palmerstons,
Hardinges, Mr. F. Bruce,[3] Sir C. Eastlake (who inquired
particularly for you), Sir William Codrington, Mr. C. Gore,[4]
and Mr. Fitzgerald (Under-Secretary for Foreign Affairs).

Tonight and tomorrow we dine quietly alone—as we
take the sacrament with Bertie tomorrow; and on Monday
he starts on his long journey. Nothing can go on better than
he does with Colonel Bruce and Bertie is very fond of him,
looks up to him and seems proud of him, which is a great
blessing! Affie is amongst the Moors and Arabs!

By the by, let me caution you not to make too much of
Mrs. Innocent or see more of her before you are confined
than is necessary because (as Sir J.[5] will tell you) these
nurses are dreadfully spoilt by the ladies and full of pre-
tensions; and even my dear, old Mrs. Lilley had to be put

---

[1] Younger son of Prince Frederick, first cousin of the King.
[2] No doubt one of the outdoor staff at Osborne.
[3] Afterwards Sir Frederick, at this time envoy to China.
[4] Charles Gore, Commissioner of Woods and Forests.
[5] Sir James Clark.

down and put into her proper place before Alfred was born, by the Baron. Since that she has never given a moment's trouble—but I do know that Mrs. I. herself is a little spoilt.

WINDSOR CASTLE, JANUARY 19, 1859

I think it quite right that the dear Princess should write to the Empress as she really is so fond of you and always so kind to you.[1] Lady Clarendon told me a great deal about Compiègne and the Empress. Every thing was very properly conducted while they were there and certainly one could not detect any thing from appearances as to the devotion of the E. for Madame W.[2] The child,[3] they say is a very fine, engaging one—and so like the Empress—quite the same look and the English nurse takes great care of him.

WINDSOR CASTLE, JANUARY 25, 1859

Thousands of good wishes to you both. My thoughts are literally entirely taken up with you and with last year's very eventful, and very touching day. I see it all before me and your dear, quiet face and manner. Your dear letter of the 23d has just reached me, and most warmly do I thank you for it. Also for yesterday's, of the 22d, but that I will answer tomorrow. Today I only write about this day! Yes, dearest child, my thoughts are very mixed, joyful, grateful and yet sad; for "the happiest day of your life" as you call it, and as we are truly thankful to have you call it—tore the bud from the parent tree. If it were not for the distance this would not be felt, but I never hear or see parents in this country having their married daughters so often with them and going so often to see them, without a feeling of envy and without having a turn which makes me loathe my difficult, isolated and trying position which is the cause of this separation!

---

[1] The Queen means that the Princess should write to the Empress to announce the baby's arrival.
[2] Madame Walewski, the second wife of Walewski, Napoleon III's foreign minister. Walewski was the son of the great Napoleon.
[3] The Prince Imperial.

However I am not going to speak today of my trials, but of your happiness, and I do hope that you will be able to spend your wedding-day in undisturbed happiness! I was more fortunate than you, on the first anniversary of my wedding day, I had shaken my burden off 6 weeks before, was as strong and well as if nothing had happened, and your christening took place in the evening for which also dear kind Uncle Leopold, who says he considers you as his grandchild, came over. How well I can see all before me! You, dear child, do understand now that a daughter's wedding must be a very trying day for the mother, far, far more so, than for the young, unknowing, confiding bride.

WINDSOR CASTLE, JANUARY 29, 1859

God be praised for all his mercies, and for bringing you safely though this awful time![1] Our joy, our gratitude knows no bounds.

My precious darling, you suffered much more than I ever did—and how I wish I could have lightened them for you! Poor dear Fritz—how he will have suffered for you! I think and feel much for him; the dear little boy if I could but see him for one minute, give you one kiss. It is hard, very hard. But we are so happy, so grateful! And people here are all in ecstasies—such pleasure, such delight—as if it was their own prince and so it is too! All the children so delighted! You will and must feel so thankful all is over! But don't be alarmed for the future, it never can be so bad again! Your's and baby's healths were drunk on Thursday evening and the Sydneys were here!

We are starting for Wellington College and so I must stop. God bless and protect you.

Dear Papa is so happy too.

---

[1] The Princess Royal's eldest child, the future German Kaiser, was born on January 27. It was a dangerous birth, and there was great anxiety for the baby and some anxiety for the mother.

The delightful accounts of you give us the intensest pleasure and fill our hearts with gratitude and thankfulness!

Today is the anniversary of that dreadful parting, the most dreadful day for us and for you,—but which thank God! is past. Its bitter recollection is wiped out by the joyful feelings of having seen you, and seen you happy and contented; knowing you now in the possession of a child; with all those heavy trials, those cruel sufferings behind you and we poor absent parents looking forward to the prospect of meeting you again, and meeting and seeing you well and strong and happy, and without that load of anxiety and of uncertainty which we have carried about with us since last May! Don't you feel such a weight off your mind, such a sense of returning freedom and thankfulness? I always felt that intense happiness on first waking, so different to the mornings of anxious expectation, of dread and anxiety. It is not a pleasant affair God knows, for any one, but you, my own darling, have had the very worst beginning possible from suffering so much! How I do wish I could go to you now and read to you and beguile the dull hours—but you are now rapidly approaching the great day and I see you already before me on your sofa.

How I do long to see my little grandson! I own it seems very funny to me to be a grandmama, and so many people tell me they can't believe it! That dear, dear locket gives me such pleasure! Not only because it was the dear little darling's hair, but because it shows me that you thought directly of poor absent Mama, who quite pines at times to be with you.

I send you today a little cushion for your back when you are on your sofa, every stitch of which I have worked myself with the English colours which I trust you will like.

WINDSOR CASTLE, FEBRUARY 5, 1859

Countess Blücher says you are very good and tractable—which I am delighted to hear.

I think you and your child must look like two babies

together, as you have such a child's face still. There were
such quantities of people out on Thursday when we went
to open Parliament: and so enthusiastic,—all to see Grandpapa and Grandmama.

BUCKINGHAM PALACE, FEBRUARY 16, 1859

I send you here a copy of Dr. Robertson's account of the
ball on the 9th at dear Balmoral. In Countess Blücher's
letter of today she asks in your name if Lehzen and Späth
have taken notice of "the happy event". Lehzen has written
twice in great delight since,—and poor old Späth[1] understood it and was much pleased, when she heard it, but she
is only sensible for a few minutes now! She is painfully
childish, and often very wilful and unmanageable, refusing
to eat and being obliged to be fed! Is not this sad? I am sure
she would know me though. We went to the English Opera,
—to Covent Garden, last night to see Balfe's[2] new opera of
"Satanella"—the music is very poor, but the story is interesting, and then we saw a very good and droll pantomime.
How well I can understand your delight at seeing dear
Uncle Ernest! It must have felt like seeing a bit of dearest
Papa. The last time you saw them together! I am reading
to Papa Putlitz's[3] play of the "Elector's Will", which is very
fine. Do you like it?

ABERGELDIE, FEBRUARY 10, 1859

My dear Sir Charles,[4]
    The Ball and Supper in honour of the birth of a Prince
of Prussia came off last night with all the mirth and jollity
of a Highland Gathering. Every man, woman and bairn
upon the three estates were invited, and I believe all came.

---

[1] Baroness Späth: Lady-in-waiting to the Duchess of Kent: she had been
with the Duchess before her marriage to the Duke.
[2] Michael William Balfe (1808–70), the Irish composer.
[3] Gustav zu Putlitz, afterwards Chamberlain to the Princess Royal.
Das Testament des Grossen Kurfursten was published in 1859.
[4] Sir Charles Phipps—the Prince Consort's private secretary.

The Minister, the doctor, Mr. McLagan and the Invercauld keepers were the only aliens.

The wives and daughters to the number of 105 had tea, with an abundant supply of bread and butter, biscuits etc. served to them in the servants hall at 7 o'clock—Mrs. D. Albertanson, Mrs. Grant, and Mrs. Paterson doing the honours of the tea table. The husbands and sons met in the iron ball-room. The proceedings of the evening commenced by a proposal, that an address of congratulation, from them as tenants of His Royal Highness The Prince Consort, should be presented to H.R.H. the Princess Frederick William of Prussia, on the birth of a prince of her Royal House. This was received with acclamation—and I undertook to carry out their wishes. This business over, and a little drop of Begg's best administered, the Ball opened with spirit. At 10 o'clock, the assembled party, had served to them an abundant supply of roast beef and bread, with ale ad libitum after which whisky toddy, usque ad nauseam toasts songs etc. etc. The dancing was resumed, and two-o'clock this morning when I left they were going on at it "fast and furious". I hear at 5 it knew no stop or diminution.

Believe me, ever yours faithfully

ANDREW ROBERTSON

BUCKINGHAM PALACE, FEBRUARY 23, 1859

These two last days, telegrams have cheered and delighted me more than words can say. I see a decided progress, and hope each day you will feel stronger and better. Occasional lowness and tendency to cry you must expect. You of all people would be inclined to this; and I am quite agreeably surprised to hear from Sir James how little you suffered with this; for it is what every lady suffers with more or less and what I, during my two first confinements, suffered dreadfully with.

We are so pleased with the names,[1] four like your two younger brothers and ending with Albert like all your brothers.

---

[1] Frederick William Victor Albert.

42 sponsors is somewhat alarming but never mind; I am sure you will look upon us and the Prince and Princess and Grandmama as peculiar sponsors, more really so, than most of the others. I am glad that the christening is put off till the 5th, as, backward as you are, you would have been much shaken and agitated by the pleasure and emotion of such an interesting scene. What it is to us not to be there, and to be unable on account of this dreadful Parliament which we always find a cause of worry, to go and be present at this most interesting and gratifying event for grandparents I cannot say. I tell you both that it goes very near my heart, and I dare not think of it. Everywhere almost the relations assemble for such an event! I deserve indeed every species of dédommagement and of praise for bearing so great and painful privation, so philosophically. But please God the next one I shall see at its christening though I hope there won't be one for a good long time.

I shall give the photographs as you direct but not so largely, as it is difficult to get a sufficient number the right strength.[1]

BUCKINGHAM PALACE, MARCH 2, 1859

Your dear little letter of the 26th—delighted me but still more the quite unexpected delight and surprise of the one of the 28th written quite like your own dear self! It seems does it not—darling—like a sort of resurrection? You poor dear child, have suffered and gone through so much more than I ever did, that you will I fear be some time before you can dispel the recollection of it. But believe my words it will never be so again.

How I envy Lord Raglan and Captain De Ros I cannot say![2] I wish I could go as their servant.

It is very nice of you, dear, to try and console me by saying perhaps if I was there I could not talk to you as much

---

[1] In her letter of February 5 the Queen thanked the Princess for a sketch of the infant Prince "exactly and ludicrously like what all you were at that age". She adds that the sketch was being photographed.
[2] They had gone to represent the Queen at the christening on March 5.

as we should like; but that's nonsense, dearest, because if we came now—we could talk as much as we liked, and if I had been with you all through—we would have seen enough of each other and I known everything so well, that we should not have required to talk. And I should certainly have been most severe as to your talking as I know better than any one, having had 9, (think of that, dear) how very bad and fatiguing it is for the nerves and head to talk much.

Why did you not put on a dress sooner? I always put mine on, as you must remember, some 3 days before I got up from the sofa. I fear if Baby is so lively already he will give you plenty to do hereafter. If you remember what Leopold was! I hope, dear, he won't be like the ugliest and least pleasing of the whole family. Leopold was not an ugly little baby, only as he grew older he grew plainer, and so excessively quizzical; that is so vexatious.

I have not read Barchester Towers all through, but I am told it is not meant to be so ill-natured. But I didn't like reading it aloud to Papa as there was not enough romance in it. The people I could not interest myself in.[1]

BUCKINGHAM PALACE, MARCH 5, 1859

Though we can not be present at this most interesting ceremony, we shall please God! often see our dear grand-child. Poor Grandmama fears she shall never see it, which I told her is nonsense, as please God hereafter it will often come here.[2]

Now I must ask you (what I forgot in my Wednesday letter) how it is that you should have wished so very much for a boy, when you told me so positively at Babelsberg that you wished for a girl, and Countess Blücher told me the same?

As it is—it is a great happiness it should be a boy for the country and for you all, but I own I much wished for a

---

[1] The Queen was unsympathetic to those in Holy Orders.
[2] The Duchess of Kent doubtless meant that she would die before the child came to England. This was the case.

girl, as boys cause so much more suffering, and sometimes one buys the experience with one's first child and therefore a girl is sometimes better. (Though we had no more difficulties with our boys, than with our girls, rather the contrary, while they were babies, excepting Affie with his rash.) But I know that after Bertie was born with whom I suffered far the most severely, the doctors said it was a mercy it had not been the first child as it would have been a very serious affair. But as it is, and as your darling child is so healthy and strong it is much better it should be a boy.

Tonight we give a large dinner in honour of the dear day, and we have asked the Cambridges, Bernstorffs, Count Brandenburg[1] and Count Blücher—and the Van de Weyers (I annexe the list for you to show Fritz and the Prince and Princess) and "Prince William's" health will be drunk, God bless him.

From the Princess Royal

You asked me in your letter why I wished all of sudden for a boy; I only said I did not wish for one, as the fox did not wish for the grapes. I did not wish to be disappointed so I thought best to prepare for a girl, but it was all along my ardent wish and prayer to have a son! Dear Fritz always said he did not care which it was.

Your dear affectionate letter of the 6th reached me today and I thank you and with all my heart for it. It is quite like your own dear self again and it is a pleasure to see how you feel like me even on all those distressing subjects so painful to a woman's feelings and especially to a young child as you are! Poor dear darling! I pitied you so! It is indeed too hard and dreadful what we have to go through and men ought to have an adoration for one, and indeed to do every thing to

---

[1] Secretary of Prussian Legation in London. Descended from a morganatic marriage of King Frederick William II.

make up, for what after all they alone are the cause of! I must say it is a bad arrangement, but we must calmly, patiently bear it, and feel that we can't help it and therefore we must forget it, and the more we retain our pure, modest feelings, the easier it is to get over it all afterwards. I am very much like a girl in all these feelings, but since I have had a grown-up married daughter, and young married relations I have been obliged to hear and talk of things and details which I hate—but which are unavoidable.

I am glad Wegner was pleasant to you, and that Mrs. Innocent has been a real comfort. But I am sorry that she and Wegner did not love each other; how is that and why? That she and your maids did not get on well I perceived, and that is not unusual, but we will talk all that over when we meet again as well as so many other things. I hope however Fritz liked her? He praised her to me very much. I know Papa who has a horror of anything un-nice, said, that the English of that class were so much more nice, quiet, and discreet than the Germans—instancing the house-maids and nurses—and therefore remembering Fritz's feelings about Georgina[1] at first and afterwards—I felt sure that Mrs. I. would not be so repulsive and disagreeable to him as perhaps one of the Germans would be. I shall be most anxious to see her. Mrs. Hobbs is I am sure a second Thurston.

His health was drunk on Saturday evening as "H.R.H. Prince Frederic William Victor Albert of Prussia". The Dessauer March followed! Bernstorff was sitting to my left. You don't tell me, dear, how you like my bracelets for the

---

[1] Georgina Hobbs. She had been housemaid in the Royal Household before going to Germany with the Princess Royal. Writing to her mother on November 15, 1858 the Princess says "Georgina is the most excellent Housemaid one can see and always so punctual at her work, never complaining never dis-satisfied and a general favourite. I wish poor Anne was." "Poor Anne" is presumably Mary Ann Glover who left the Princess's service with a pension of £20 per annum, until she found other employment, at the end of 1858 and was succeeded by Bennett (see page 143). Georgina Hobbs was made the Princess's house-keeper at the end of 1859, and she was presumably related to the children's nurse, Mrs. Hobbs.

No. 13.
The Queen's Pavilion Aldershott   July 9. 1857

Dearest Child,

Here we are since
yesterday Eve: & I feel
the heat so much that
I can hardly find my-
self.— I suffer terribly
from it, and yet it
is not as hot if the thermometer as 3 years

Even during an official visit the Queen found time to write to the
Princess Royal

The Queen and Prince Consort at the Camp at Aldershot, July 1859. (from a painting by C. H. Thuma.)

two ladies and what they said of them. From our dear Countess Blücher I have had a letter of thanks today.

We have been going out a great deal to the play and been seeing that admirable actress Miss A. Sedgwick[1] and last night the Wigans reappeared after 3 years in "Still Waters Run Deep"[2] and acted better than ever. Papa will have no doubt told you that political matters really look better and that please God! the horrors of war, and of the most iniquitous and unjust war ever undertaken (if it had taken place) may and will yet be averted. But I fear our Emperor will never recover his position to regain the confidence he once enjoyed—which I am very sorry for. I fear I must end here without entering into some parts of your dear letter but I will only add that I suspect "baby worship" is going on on a great scale on the part of yourself and Fritz but that it is very pardonable after all you have gone through.

I can imagine Augusta M.'s questions; I hope and suppose you told her very little, for all is written back here.

OSBORNE, MARCH 16, 1859

For two very dear letters of the 8th and 12th have I to thank you, as well as for the dear little bracelet of baby. That he must be a great resource and a great pleasure I can fully understand. In so many ways and things your case and mine are so different; and though I hated the thought of having children and have no adoration for very little babies, (particularly not in their baths till they are past 3 or 4 months, when they really become very lovely) still I know what a fuss and piece of work was made with you; far too much I think, for it was not good to dress you as often as you were, and to have you up so late. I used to have you in my dressing room—while I dressed for dinner, dancing

---

[1] The play was almost certainly *The World and The Stage* especially written for her by Palgrave Simpson.
[2] The farce by Tom Taylor. It was based on a French novel, *Le Gendre*, though some of the starkness in the play was avoided in the novel. The leading parts were played by Alfred and Leonora Wigan.

on Mrs. Pegley's[1] knees—till you got so lively that you did not sleep at night. All that was very foolish, and I warn you against it—but one is very foolish with one's first child. Still I have been much more tender[2] with the younger ones, though they are much less seen and much less fuss is made about them.

Never fear to tire me in writing about the darling, it gives me the very greatest pleasure and I shall be ready to spoil him as much as all grandmamas. It is a proud feeling no doubt to be the mother of a living being!

And you who dote on this little child, will understand now what a pang it is to the poor mother's heart to give that child entirely up to another, whose property she becomes—as I have done you, whom I bore with far less suffering God knows, but whom we watched over with such anxiety.

Papa has told you about Lord Cowley.[3] But I must tell you what he told us of the dear Empress:—how she loves you and what a state of anxiety and agitation she was in about you, before you were confined. If you have not already done so, be sure and write to thank her for it—as she fully deserves it; she is a dear, noble hearted being, very severely tried and much attached to us.

Augusta wrote me rather a foolish letter—and calls herself "your nearest relation abroad" when you have your own uncle and aunt!! C'est un peu trop!

OSBORNE, MARCH 19, 1859

I have had a long talk with Mrs. Innocent, and will tell you all about her in my next letter. Air, air is what you want, and bracing and not hot stuffy rooms and theatres, or you will become sickly and old before you are 20!

---

[1] Nurse to the royal children.
[2] Used in the sense of cautious or circumspect.
[3] Lord Cowley was British Ambassador at Paris. He had just been asked by the Emperor Napoleon to go to the Emperor of Austria on a confidential mission about the disagreement of the two Emperors on the Italian question.

Anniversary of your Confirmation.

This day two years ago was a very eventful day for us and for you! as well as yesterday.[1] If only the dear Archbishop had not made that wonderful charge.[2] I live in dread, he will make a very bad one at Alice's Confirmation.

How shocking is the death of that poor Princess Louise Windisch-Grätz![3] I believe she was rather frivolous, poor thing!

Well do I understand what a pleasure it was for you to see so much of dear Uncle Ernest—who is so kind and warm-hearted.

Really for Augusta to call herself "your nearest relation" when he and Aunt Alexandrine were there! I am rather offended at it!

Mrs. Innocent had come back and, after talking to her the Queen says:

. . . air, air is what you must have; she also says that though your rooms are well regulated, the heat of the house is fearsome, and very unwholesome and relaxing for you now and at all times, and very pernicious for every one and for your nerves and for the baby. In spite of the very mild weather, which she says you had the whole time, the stoves were heated awfully—just as if it had been freezing; and what was still worse—the windows never opened enough.

You say you have to watch that Fritz's rooms are well aired. Now dear, you should positively get someone to be answerable that the rooms and still more the passages, (which ought to be cooler than the rooms), are never above a certain and given temperature, having (as we have everywhere) thermometers hanging up in them and the rooms,

---

[1] On the day before her Confirmation the Princess Royal was examined by the Dean of Windsor in front of her parents and the Archbishop of Canterbury.

[2] "The Archbishop read what seemed a dull address; luckily it was inaudible." Lord Granville.

[3] Daughter of the Grand Duchess of Mecklenburg-Schwerin, and niece of the King of Prussia.

and by keeping to that—the stoves ought to be kept up or let out, according to whether it is warm out, or freezing. And then the windows should be opened regularly 3 times a day, or oftener, if it is warmer. Now if you would get someone of the servants to attend to this, your nerves would rapidly improve—and there would be no colds and for Fritz too it would be much better.

Mrs. Innocent is very anxious about this and quite in despair about it—and I must say, I am too. Do show this to the Baron; perhaps he could devise some method of regulating it.

I now leave this to Colonel Biddulph according to certain rules and the hot air (or water) is much better managed ever since.

She (Mrs. Innocent) speaks with the greatest devotion of you, and of Fritz whom she can not find words to praise sufficiently, for his kindness, goodness and devotion. I knew and expected this, but still it is very gratifying and comforting to us to hear from all sides, and from one who like her witnessed every trifle and saw all in its natural light.

I rather dread your going to the theatre, intense hot rooms are the thing of all others to be avoided. But I envy your seeing Lohengrin for I delight in the music, at least in many parts of it, and am constantly playing it.

The daguerreotypes of you have photographed charmingly and I hope to send you some impressions on Wednesday. What a blessed invention photography is! It is as if we saw you and the dear little baby before us! It is quite touching.

I feel as if I could clasp you both to that poor heart of mine which yearns for you!

BUCKINGHAM PALACE, APRIL 2, 1859

Before I go to another subject let me mention one, which I already spoke of to you last year, for your own home, though that has been fortunately arranged without it. It is on the subject of very necessary conveniences, which are totally wanting in Germany and really make one's life very uncomfortable and very unwholesome; with a nursery this is ten times worse. Now I told you last year that my aunt the Landgravine,[1] sent for a person from here to make a number of these really necessary affairs in the Palace at Homburg and I asked you whether I should not send somebody for your house; you were much inclined for it—but as your house had been so well arranged—it was no longer necessary.

However as I hear Babelsberg is to have a new kitchen, and apartments in the Neue Palais are being arranged for you, I think that such a person might be very useful in engineering one or two—at least of these affairs. In Scotland there was and still is in many old houses the same deficiency and is so now at Holyrood—but one was engineered in Holyrood in the room next to our bedroom; one was made for us at Claremont, at Kensington Palace, also very old, and Louis Philippe had them made in all his palaces, and I am sure you would be benefiting all Germany if they could be generally introduced. Will you mention it perhaps to the Princess, and ask her whether she does not think this might be done? I am sure it would be a real blessing. There was a long story about a very horrid subject—but I thought it best to write it directly to you.

Lane[2] will be delighted to make a lithograph of you and the dear baby after the photograph you mention and Mitchell[3] will publish it. So I hope it will be done very soon —and will sell immensely.

I am glad to say Alice has arrived at her 16th birthday (in 3 weeks) without any engagement, or even thought of one, and the longer we can keep this off—the better. But what will be her lot and those of the others? It is an anxious thought!

Here we are in the midst of internal troubles but I hope we shall be able to retain the Government. On Monday Lord

---

[1] Elizabeth of Hesse-Homburg, third daughter of King George III.
[2] Richard Lane, the line engraver and lithographer. His drawing of the Queen, when she was 10, is well-known.
[3] Probably Robert Mitchell (1820–73), etcher and engraver.

Derby will state the course he intends to pursue. A dissolution will follow. Bad enough but sure to be resorted to, by any government. It is however troublesome and wearing and comes attendant the Ionique troubles.[1] I still think war will be averted.

I am sure the rencontre with the Empress Dowager[2] will go off well. She has always been very kind about you, I know, for I heard it from several people—I wish you could have been with us to see Henry Vth[3] which is quite as fine as your beloved Richard II. I hope you will enjoy it with us.

F. MacDonald[4] wrote you an account and I sent some further ones. I am rather ashamed Phelps[5] should be heard at Berlin, but his company I believe is fair enough.

You will be shocked to see in the papers the accounts of the death of poor Lord Waterford, out hunting! How fearful for her to have her husband brought back dead

---

[1] The Ionian Islands had been under British protection since 1815. Their inhabitants were agitating for union with Greece, and Gladstone had gone out in 1858, as High Commissioner, to investigate the facts.

[2] Of Russia. Prince Frederick William's aunt.

[3] Played by Charles Kean at the Princess's.

[4] Flora MacDonald—one of the Queen's Maids of Honour. She was the daughter of MacDonald of Clanranald and a kinswoman of the Jacobite heroine.

[5] Samuel Phelps, the actor. He was a successful actor-manager at Sadler's Wells from 1844, where he made Shakespeare pay. He was perhaps regarded as rather an old-fashioned tragedian which explains the Queen's comment. His visit to Germany was not a success and he played King Lear to empty benches. In commenting on this to her mother, the Princess Royal wrote:

> "I went yesterday to hear King Lear and enjoyed myself more than I can say although Mr. Phelps is not a favourite actor of mine, yet to hear Shakespeare's sublime words in my own dear, native tongue is a great, great pleasure. The applause was immense, so loud that I think it must have come from some of our countrymen who are never behindhand in making a noise."

In a later letter she says

> "Mr. Phelps did Hamlet beautifully the other night: I was quite astonished, but his King Lear was very bad. Perhaps it was my intense delight at hearing Shakespeare in English again, and my appreciating English acting after the very bad German acting here that made me enjoy Hamlet so much."

in the evening having left her in the morning in full strength.

She has no children to cheer her dreariness, all passes away from her!—They were much devoted to each other, and to Lady Canning[1] it will be such a blow and shock!

I send you today a number of photographs which I hope you will like. I think those of you with the baby too charming and not the least like a negress; the one of you alone is perhaps not very favourable and it is that I conclude which Fritz (who with due respect be it said, is not quite worthy of a photograph)[2] does not like.

I send a book of Henry Vth and lastly a box of (uninteresting to me) Windsor primroses etc. However I hope they will arrive all sweet and fresh as at any rate they are home flowers. You will also get a pair of screens from old Prince Gholam Mohammed[3] who has brought them for you. He and his son and grandson have just arrived—were at the levée and dine with us tonight.

Poor Lady Waterford is wonderfully calm and resigned! I have written to her myself.

There is so much to do, both public and private, such anxieties of all natures that I feel sometimes ready to sink under the burden of it. It will be a great, great comfort to have you with us—to be able to talk openly and quietly over so many things which weigh upon us!

Bertie continues such an anxiety, I tremble at the thought of only three years and a half being before us—

---

[1] Lady Waterford and Lady Canning were sisters, the daughters of Lord Stuart de Rothesay. *The Story of Two Noble Lives*, by Augustus Hare, is about them.
[2] This reference is a joke—to mark the Queen's disapproval of his having raised difficulties about her grandson being brought to see her in England.
[3] The son of Tippoo Sahib—"the once dreaded" as the Queen had called him earlier.

when he will be of age and we can't hold him except by moral power! I try to shut my eyes to that terrible moment! He is improving very decidedly—but oh! it is the improvement of such a poor or still more idle intellect.

Oh! dear, what would happen if I were to die next winter! One shudders to think of it: it is too awful a contemplation. His journal is worse a great deal than Affie's letters. And all from laziness! Still we must hope for improvement in essentials. But the greatest improvement I fear, will never make him fit for his position. His only safety and the country's—is in his implicit reliance in every thing, on dearest Papa, that perfection of human beings!

My greatest of all anxieties is that dearest Papa works too hard, wears himself quite out by all he does. It makes me often miserable. If it were not for Osborne and Balmoral and then again Windsor at Easter—I don't know what we should do, though really London when it is warm, disagrees more with me, even more than with dearest Papa!

These attempts to preserve peace, these endless telegrams coming in every hour and contradicting one another —and raising and destroying one's hopes continually, are very trying to one's nerves! I fear this is rather a melancholy letter, but, dearest child, when one works and plods, and sees such difficulties and looks into the future one does get rather gloomy, though God knows, that is not my nature. I generally keep up other's spirits and won't allow them to flag. For it only enables one to meet the difficulties when they do come!

Well to turn to cheery subjects; I sent you yesterday an account of C. Cavendish[1]—of the Ball; it was very pretty. It was in the large supper-room, which was spacious and cool, in spite of this dreadfully hot weather. One great contretemps was the non arrival of the coiffeur to powder Philippe, Gusty, Amélie and Condé![2] We waited $\frac{1}{2}$ an hour

---

[1] Miss Caroline Cavendish, great grand-daughter of 4th Duke of Devonshire, Maid of Honour to the Queen.

[2] The first three were the sons and daughter of Prince Augustus of Saxe-Coburg, first cousin to the Queen. He married a daughter of

—and then had to go in without them. At last, $\frac{1}{4}$ of an hour after, they arrived.

Clothilde[1] and Amélie looked very pretty; those 2 fat boys—looked well enough—but really they are monstrous in size—poor Philippe's thighs and legs looked as if they were stuffed! Your sisters and little brothers looked very pretty, particularly Arthur and Louise. Lenchen's features are again now so very large and long that it spoils her looks.

By the by, Fritz's poor little godson—Fritz Wilhelm Bernstorff looked too extraordinary as a sort of Cupid—in white satin with gold, a wreath of roses, (he has an old, long, thin face) with Cupid's bow, and, as Lord Clarendon very mischievously observed to me—"fowls' wings". But pray don't let this go beyond you and Fritz.

BUCKINGHAM PALACE, APRIL 13, 1859

Here we live between hope and fear—peace and war— telegrams coming in every hour—crossing and contradicting one another till on ne sait plus où on est! It is an anxious wearing moment!

How well do I understand the heartache and melancholy, which spring, with all its sweet flowers, its fresh leaves, and fresh mown grass gives you; it always makes one rather filled with longing, languid and tired! I wish you would begin riding, dear, again, it is nearer three than two months since you were confined and you recollect how much good, riding exercise always did you.

I am glad baby is installed (not enstalled as you wrote it) in his new rooms. Sir James is delighted; indeed he said you could not have left him in summer in those small, hot rooms.

Poor dear Louise, I am grieved to hear the account you give of her. But she was never well managed, overfatigued and excited. How different to your education! These German princesses never do get enough air or quiet.

Louis Philippe. Their youngest son, the future King Ferdinand of Bulgaria, was born in 1861. Condé was son of the Duc d'Aumale, who was son of Louis Philippe.
[1] A daughter of Prince Augustus of Saxe-Coburg.

I have not yet thanked you for your little letter of the 6th which only reached me on the 11th. Indeed Austria is not very tractable but she suspects (alas! with right) the good faith of France. We do all we can to make them feel the importance, the vital importance of not letting them be the cause of breaking off the Congress.

Cavour[1] is, we hear, much more content and we expect Massino d'Azeglio[2] here which I think may bring matters straight; it must be got right—for there is nothing to fight about!

Poor Lady Waterford has written me this letter which I send you. It is a wrong and unhappy view of misfortunes. It makes God so cruel and selfish which surely He cannot be![3]

We went to the Crystal Palace yesterday morning and yesterday evening to see part of Henry Vth which is so fine. Today we have a dinner—tomorrow my first Drawing-Room, and in the evening Albert Smith[4] is coming.

Matters don't mend yet. It gets more embrouillé and still I hope and trust it will come right.

Thank God! the news are much better this afternoon from Vienna—and altogether I think I see daylight. Tell this the dear Princess.

---

[1] Count Cavour, the Prime Minister of Piedmont, was aiming, with the help of the French, to establish a north Italian kingdom driving out the Austrians who were in possession of Venetia and much of Lombardy.
[2] The Sardinian Minister in London. Sardinia was one of the territories of Victor Emmanuel II, who also reigned over Piedmont.
[3] This letter has not survived. Lady Waterford was pious, and in a letter written at this time and published in her biography she no doubt used the same sentiments of which the Queen disapproved. She suggested that God had taken her husband because his family loved him too much, and were unable to give their whole heart to God. Such sentiments would not have appealed to the Queen.
[4] The lecturer and entertainer.

For two dear delightful letters of the 12th and 14th I have to thank you—they were great pleasure and surprises for I have had 4 from you this week. Papa really scolded me for them, as he always is afraid you write too much, but I said you knew I never wished you to write long letters or indeed at all, when you had no time, but that I knew you liked writing to me whenever you could. It was very hard to grudge me one of my greatest pleasures.

We are so worried and worked to death that I long to get out of Town—even to Windsor—which never is cheerful, but still it is country and the trees will be green and the flowers coming out. The terrible ups and downs in this most miserable state of affairs is most distressing. France behaves too shamefully. Really I can't say how shocked and grieved I am at it!

The Archduke Albrecht[1] is an excellent worthy man whom Papa remembers very well; you know that Papa and he are both called Albert after the same person, viz. the Duke of Saxe-Teschen, but the Archduke inherited all his money and Papa none. We are all shocked at Uncle Ernest not bringing dear Aunt Alexandrine, it was settled last year, she has longed for it—wishes it so much, poor Marie L.[2] wishes it so much, we have invited her again and again, and Uncle never answers even, but comes alone. It is too bad and will not be understood: she constantly travels without him, therefore if he had had to hurry home—she could have followed by herself—but she is always left alone at home and Uncle E. only thinks of himself; it provokes me more than I can say, and poor Alice feels it very much.

What a pity you could not be here for this event![3] All

---

[1] A distinguished soldier, afterwards Commander-in-chief of the Austrian Army.
[2] Marie—the wife of the Queen's nephew—the Prince of Leiningen. She was the younger sister of Alexandrine.
[3] Princess Alice's confirmation. The Duke of Saxe-Coburg-Gotha was Princess Alice's god-father, and she no doubt hoped that both the Duke and Duchess would come for it. The Duke was a notoriously unfaithful husband.

you say about Bertie is true dear, and the accounts of him show a decided improvement, though very slow. Certainly the wife will be of immense importance! I trust he may find somebody at last but it is very difficult.

Affairs look very gloomy, and I fear that (though I do still not think yet, it will come to war) the Congress will not come off! We must take a firm and decided line and I think that the explanations in both Houses on Monday may do decided good.

I hear you model and even paint in oils; this last I am sorry for; you remember what Papa always told you on the subject. Amateurs never can paint in oils like artists and what can one do with all one's productions? Whereas water colours always are nice and pleasant to keep in books or portfolios. I hope, dear, you will not take to the one and neglect the other!

I am shocked to hear baby leaves off his caps so soon; I hope however only in the nursery, for they look so frightful to be seen without caps. In the nursery it is wholesome but it is not pretty.

The babies' party was very successful. They could of course not speak to each other but were very droll. Mrs. Gordon's second (Frederica), Lady Somerton's darling little girl, your god-child Victoria Bernstorff and Victoria Sayer were the company. In the evening we had Albert Smith. Yesterday morning we went to the New Watercolour Exhibition, where there are some beautiful things; amongst others one by Mr. Corbould, called "The Dream of Fair Women" in which there are two female figures which are the finest he has yet painted.

By the by you went to see the "Merry Wives"; you must have found it very coarse; even I have never had courage to go to see it—having always been told how very coarse it was—for your adored Shakespeare is dreadful in that respect and many things have to be left out in many of his plays.

I have seen a fine photograph of the family picture the younger Kaulbach has painted of the King and Queen of Hanover and children; it must be a very fine picture; have you seen it? He is here now painting the Duchess of Manchester. Our dear Winterhalter will be here by the end of this month. He is to paint a full length of me en grand costume and I want baby to be introduced into it; you know he painted one of the Queen of Spain with her little girl, and I think something fine might be done.

I see my letter is getting long but I always feel I have so much to say to you that I have to write volumes—were I not to check myself.

From the Princess Royal

BERLIN, APRIL 16, 1859

I can comprehend your anxiety at the perpetual telegrams which come in. We live in the same agreable suspense, our position is a very critical one.

It is now in Prussia's hand to repair in some degree the mischief she has done to herself and her German position by her indecision, and to win back the sympathies of the other German states which are, at this moment, violently against her. Austria, false as she is, is now to some degree showing "Bonne volonté". Now is the moment to hasten the congress and in the congress to promise co-operation with Austria, if this is not done, we risk everything; first all the rest of Germany will go with Austria, and Prussia's position is lost irretrievably, secondly the Austrians if they gain even a small victory only over the French gain an immense advantage, and do the reputation of our army here an immense deal of harm; then the Austrians may conclude a truce of arms and the French may fall upon us, a pretty position we would then be in.

Then we ought to say to Austria, have patience, we cannot do without England; at this moment England cannot promise to be our ally, England cannot with safety to herself or to us break with France, therefore we cannot urge her; but one thing we can demand of her is that if she remains neutral, she demands of France to remain neutral in the Baltic and German Ocean, and that England send ships to protect our ports, or else our commerce ceases and we are lost—this could not be an unpopular measure in England, as it would be for England's own advantage. It is very unfair to blame England as they do here, it has enough to do with its own affairs at present. The great mistake we made here, was sending Count Pourtalès¹ to Paris with such instructions. We ought to have said to the Emperor of the French: we know you are putting a large force under arms against the Italians; but every man more you arm, we must do the same, because we must suppose that it is against us. The Emperor could not have taken that amiss. I am aware this is a most confused explanation of my ideas, but perhaps you will be able to understand it.

WINDSOR CASTLE (UNDATED, PROBABLY APRIL 18, 1859)

As I send you herewith the ceremonial for dear Alice's Confirmation which alas! comes at a most troubled time, I write you two words (leaving any lengthened letter for tomorrow's messenger) to say that I thank you much for your long letter of the 16th (the anniversary of different days—of the Emperor's and Empress's arrival here!!). Things look very bad; still for that very reason they may mend.

My agony which haunts me day and night, is your being unable to come. Pray don't wait till it comes to that. Come at once, let the Prince give Fritz earlier leave (if matters look more threatening) if it were but for ever so short a time. Only don't wait (if you can) and then say you can't come. Rather come for a very few days only and if all was straight come to Scotland or to Windsor in late autumn for longer; in short think of anything but not coming now—if it be possible. Think how I yearn to see you but for a moment! How much you want your native air! I write in the anxiety and pressure of the moment, knowing that you will do what you can! I am sick of all this horrid business— of politics and Europe in general, and think you will hear some day of my going with the children to live in Australia, and to think of Europe as of the moon.

---

¹ The Prussian Minister in Paris. His sympathies were hostile to Austria. Prussian policy was that provided the war was localised, she would not interfere if the French attacked the Austrians in Italy.

Really to have one's children as you, married so far off is dreadful!

But more tomorrow.

Read the debates in the two Houses. We came here yesterday afternoon.

From the Princess Royal

BERLIN, APRIL 18, 1859

Indeed it is as you suppose my greatest delight to write to you which I do whenever I have a spare moment and you are so easy to please, dear Mama, you allow me to write short or long ones just as I like. I never had a correspondence that I enjoyed so much because it is so natural and like thinking aloud.[1]

I did go to see part of "The Merry Wives of Windsor"; everything improper was left out, but still I hate the subject, and have never read the play; I went because it was English but did not stay the whole time. It was very well acted. I own I think some expressions in some of my beloved Shakespeare's plays very coarse, and not at all suited to our times or to ladies here. But if one tries to "approfondir" the thing he gives the worst names to the worst things, and makes every improper thing revolting. While the French make improper things interesting and gloss wickedness over, that is a thousand times worse in my opinion. I go as seldom as I can to the French play here, as Fritz does not like it. One thing I have never had courage to see is Faust. Fritz read it aloud to me— I think it magnificent but I should feel rather ashamed to see it.

---

[1] The Princess also wrote "It seems to me as if we have never understood each other so well and never enjoyed exchanging every passing feeling and thought so much and with so little restraint; it is indeed a blessed feeling that of knowing that next to one's husband those that one gives one's whole confidence, respect and love to, understand one so well as you do me, dearest parents. It overcomes distance, it lessens the pain of separation, it is always with us."

I have this very moment received your dear letter of the 18th and thank you much for it. I am glad you bear out what I said about our dear correspondence. It is an immense pleasure and comfort to me, for it is dreadful to live so far off and always separated. I really think I shall never let your sisters marry—certainly not to be so constantly away and see so little of their parents—as till now, you have done, contrary to all that I was originally promised and told. I am so glad to see that you so entirely enter into all my feelings as a mother. Yes, dearest, it is an awful moment to have to give one's innocent child up to a man, be he ever so kind and good—and to think of all that she must go through! I can't say what I suffered, what I felt—what struggles I had to go through—(indeed I have not quite got over it yet) and that last night when we took you to your room, and you cried so much, I said to Papa as we came back "after all, it is like taking a poor lamb to be sacrificed". You now know— what I meant, dear. I know that God has willed it so and that these are the trials which we poor women must go through; no father, no man can feel this! Papa never would enter into it all! As in fact he seldom can in my very violent feelings. It really makes me shudder when I look around at all your sweet, happy, unconscious sisters—and think that I must give them up too—one by one!! Our dear Alice, has seen and heard more (of course not what no one ever can know before they marry and before they have had children) than you did, from your marriage—and quite enough to give her a horror rather of marrying.

The marble cross and locket shall be given to dear Alice tomorrow. Papa is much pleased and satisfied with her and so is the Dean. She is a dear, amiable, sensible child,—quite grown-up; very pretty and with perfect manners in society, quite ladylike and cercléing[1] extremely well.

---

[1] Used to describe a royal person moving round and speaking to an assembled company of guests. The Princess of Prussia, in her youth at Weimar, had been trained to "cerclé" by walking round the garden with a few polite words to each tree and bush. The Queen uses a curious blend of French and English.

If matters go on smoothly in Italy Bertie will not go to Germany till August—spending June and July in Switzerland. I don't know when Affie will return. Possibly in July —but only of course for a very short time. Should there be war—he must remain—and do his duty like every other officer. I should not wish him to do otherwise.

About politics dear Papa has I have no doubt written to you fully. Since yesterday evening we are again full of hope! In that case all my fears and anxieties of yesterday would vanish. God grant it! If only Austria is reasonable!

All you say about Prussia is I am sure very true. But we could never help you with ships; we have not near enough for ourselves!

Painting in oils, for a little while, certainly does help one's painting in water colours—and with that object you are quite right to do so; only don't let it exclude the other.

Today is dear Alice's examination. I will telegraph as soon as it is over. Tomorrow at 12—the Confirmation. She feels very much that you cannot be there. She thanks you much for your message.

With regard to what you say about Shakespeare, I quite agree. You need not be afraid of seeing Faust; I am as bad and shy as anyone, matron as I am, about these things and it is so beautiful that really one does not feel put out by it. I advise you to see it, dear. Also as regards the French plays—you should go; there are many—indeed quantities of charming little plays—and dear Papa—who you know is any thing but favourable to the French—used to delight in going to the French play—more than to any other, and we used for many years—when we had a good company (we have had none since 54) to go continually and enjoyed it excessively. It is such good practice for the language. So, I hope, dear, you will go. One's dislike to a nation need not prevent one's admiring and being amused by what is good, clever and amusing in it.

What happiness it will be when we meet again. I am sure, dear, that we shall agree in many things much more than we used to do. Indeed ever since you married I found this to be the case. There is no longer any thing between us which I cannot touch with you—and a married daughter, be she ever so young, is at once, on a par with her mother. We take the communion on Good Friday at 9.

WINDSOR CASTLE, APRIL 21, 1859

After describing Princess Alice's examination before her confirmation the Queen writes:

Then just after, while we were still talking with the company, arrived the sad and alarming news from Vienna.[1] What will happen! However God will help.

WINDSOR CASTLE, APRIL 23, 1859

I have but very few minutes to write; we are all in great anxiety. Rash and unwise as this last act of Austria's is, it is all owing to the Emperor N.'s unjustifiable conduct! What a terrible responsibility to conjure up recklessly a war without a particle of reason! If it comes to it—what will he have to answer for here and hereafter! I am so sorry, for we can't forget the years 55 and 56—and April 55 and August 56! He has so much to make one like him, and that he should do such things! and let wild dreams and fancies urge him on to such acts!

Well, enough of this, though one can talk and think of nothing else! Dear Alice writes to you herself. She shows such deep feeling on this occasion and is altogether so dear, and good and charming. You will find a grown up, dear, and sensible sister able to enter into everything—where you left a child! She will tell you of her presents; such fine ones; from us the Order,[2] and a diamond necklace and earrings

---

[1] It had been urged that the disputing Powers should disarm in Italy before meeting in a European Congress. On April 20 Austria sent a refusal.

[2] In her diary the Queen writes: "From us the family order (our Cameo with diamonds)." This is possibly the earliest example of the gift of the Queen's private, family order (cf. G. P. R. James, *The Royal Family Orders*).

like your's (of her own money except £1000 which I added as she had not as much money as you).[1] She remained in her own room that evening and yesterday morning. Yesterday morning[2] we took the sacrament together as well as Uncle Ernest who does not like our form and our service for it.

This evening Bach's Grosse Passions Musik is to be performed. This morning we had a Council for the Dissolution.

From the Princess Royal

APRIL 23, 1859

The 21st of April[3] will live long in my memory, I do not know when I spent such a happy day! We had felt so sad during this whole time, the thought of all these horrid political complications, of war etc. had weighed so on both our spirits, we felt like carrying a load about with us. I saw the moment when Fritz would go to the war, and altogether was out of my mind. Never did I feel to want the support of the Holy Communion so much before. We went at 10 o'clock with the whole family and almost the whole of our household, footmen, grooms, servants, maids, cooks in short almost everybody, there were forty-two of our servants; it was so solemn, so affecting, I felt what real good it did me. One feels like a different person after one has made firm resolution to try and lead a new life, and after one hears those blessed comforting words, which come like balm to our heart, and give one courage to go on again and bear what is sent us, joy or sorrow!

WINDSOR CASTLE, APRIL 27, 1859

I have so much to do and to think of—that I fear I shall be obliged to write a hurried, short letter when I should have wished to write a long and full letter to you in answer

---

[1] Meaning that the jewels were bought with her own money except for £1000 of the Queen's.
[2] Good Friday. The Queen was writing on Easter Eve.
[3] Maundy Thursday.

to your dear, long one of the 23rd—many, many thanks too, for the one of the 25th just received. The dear 25th[1] was spent as happily as anything can be now in the midst of such anxiety—such extraordinary suspense. Here we still are waiting for the decision! And when one expects hourly to hear the war has broken out—one gets telegrams to give a sort of very faint glimmer of hope! I am quite prepared for the worst and try to steel myself to every thing—to the worst! To me, I own the worst would be not to see you both, dear children, whom I long so intensely to see—as soon as we still will hope! But let us not give this up yet; and I am sure we shall be able some how or other to meet later, if not now. I have answered Stockmar's letter so won't repeat anything here. But never could I ask or wish you to do what was not right or proper towards your new country.

I have always heard from Papa that the German Communion Service was so very much more impressive and touching than ours. I regret to own I never could or can feel émue or strengthened by our's. It is so cold—such a repetition of the same prayers again and again, that it quite takes off the effect—added to which the mumbling of the clergyman to himself each time—has a very unpleasant effect. Uncle Ernest, who had never taken it here before, did not like it at all. One of those fine sermons like we hear in Scotland occasionally, do one real good. But God knows the state of affairs of the present time, coming in at all hours, prevent one's being calm and quiet and recueilli—yet I generally feel calmer and more resigned the greater the danger and alarm is!

Dear child, how happy I am to hear of your enjoying your liberty so much and being like a child again. It is a great happiness and comfort to me God knows.

I don't know what makes you speak of the English not being as good to their wives as the Germans, when England is the country of family life and good ménages! What makes you say that, dear? In the higher classes amongst the

---

[1] Princess Alice's 16th birthday.

fashionable, slang, disreputable young people—there are certainly some selfish, careless husbands, but they are the exception to the rule, and you must retract that assertion. Those separate ménages which you see in the happiest families in Germany are unknown here.

This afternoon we shall probably drive over to Clifden to show it Uncle Ernest. That Alice should be 16—so tall and grown good-looking and wearing the order, makes me think it must be you and not her.

By the by you tell Papa you had begun Afraja[1] and gave it up as it was so tiresome. I know the beginning is dull—but it does become so intensely interesting, is so poetical, romantic and unlike any thing else, that I know you would like it, so promise me you will go on by yourself reading it. Eleanor Stanley,[2] was so delighted with it, that she has entirely translated it! You are however so learned and so fond of deep, philosophical books, that you are quite beyond me, and certainly have not inherited that taste from me; for, to say the honest truth, the sight of a professor or learned man alarms me, and is not sympathique to me. Still I like them and particularly their books much better than I did formerly; but you can see why Bertie dislikes them. He is my caricature, that is the misfortune, and in a man—this is so much worse. You are quite your dear, beloved Papa's child!

I must ask you a 1000 pardons. I have just read over your dear letter of today again (I generally read them 3 or 4 times) and find that I misread what you said about the German and English ménages! And that it was just the contrary. You must think Mama as bad in this respect, as poor dear Grandmama, which really is not the case, for I am very particular about my letters but I devour yours and with such eagerness—that I always read them slowly again the second time, and had not yet had time to do so.

---

[1] *Afraja*, the novel by Theodor Mügge published in 1854. It was translated into English in the same year.
[2] Maid of Honour to the Queen. She was the daughter of Edward Stanley of Cross Hall, Lancashire, and married Lt.-Col. Samuel Long.

I think as a rule—you are right not to go generally to the theatre on a Sunday, and that it even is better for you that you should not do so;—still to do so sometimes is equally right, if Fritz wishes it. You know I am not at all an admirer or approver of our very dull Sundays, for I think the absence of innocent amusement for the poor people, a misfortune and an encouragment of vice.

I think you would much like our service as it is now. It is so much more reverent.[1]

The weather is so dull and windy and we are so busy that we are not going to Clifden today. At this very moment we hear the sad news of the Austrians having crossed the Sardinian frontier! But no details! What will happen, I do wonder! It is most miserable and senseless—but France is the cause of all! It has put every thing else out of my head and I don't know what else to write about! God bless you all! May He however visit the sins of those who have risked— and will be the cause of the loss of—thousands of lives, on them!

I send you a very nice print of dear Affie (poor dear boy he may see fire before long!).

Let us pray to our Heavenly Father to end all this complication soon and to the good of all, and to support us under the weight of this dreadful moment—which threatens the whole of Europe! We must put our faith in God. Let us cling to that, and He will help us! He never has deserted us—and He will support and protect us still!

I tear open my letter to say it is a false alarm!! The Austrians have not crossed! How long may we be spared this calamity?

---

[1] This presumably means the ordinary Sunday service in the private chapel.

(Anniversary of Aunt Gloster's[1] death, and not the 27th)

We were so shocked to hear by your dear letter of the 27th received yesterday morning of the shocking accident the poor dear Princess has met with! How frightened you all must have been! A fall in a room, is always a very bad thing for a grown up person—and when one is as tall and strongly made as she is and passed 40—and unable to help oneself with one's hands—it is very serious—for one must fall with such violence and with such weight. I once fell over Papa's feet—in the passage and hurt myself very much —but then I eased myself with my hands and hurt them. I long to hear how she is going on. I hope, dearest, you have not been falling lately? Little birds have told me of sundry falls last summer which ought not to have been!

Every day and hour brings fresh news. But really as it is—it is better the Austrians should have marched as any longer (wished for at Paris—where the conduct has no name I grieve to say) would only make the French stronger and more ready!! Well we must wait: and be patient and trustful and watchful and of good cheer, dear. We must be stout of heart.

We have a Council again today—for a Proclamation relative to a considerable increase of our Navy. The elections are going on well—which is very important.[2]

Dear Uncle Ernest's stay is alas! drawing to a close. On Tuesday he leaves us. On Monday poor dear Papa (who is very much fagged and has had toothache into the bargain) goes at 6 in the morning to Plymouth to open that great large bridge at Saltash over the Tamar and returns the same night at one!

---

[1] Mary, Duchess of Gloucester. The Queen's aunt and last surviving child of George III. She died in 1857.

[2] The election results came in gradually over several days, but Derby's Conservative Government was in fact narrowly defeated.

From the Princess Royal

Your anxiety must be dreadful but think of what I feel when I hear Fritz talking of the arrangements to be made for a campaign, of what people and horses he will take, etc. It breaks my heart, and he cannot or rather will not understand my distress. It is all very fine of the men talking of defending their country, of a soldier's life being the only one that becomes a man, that death on the field of battle is the thing they wish for; they don't think of their poor unhappy wives whom they have taken from their homes and whom they leave at home alone.

WINDSOR CASTLE, MAY 2, 1859

Though not my day I write one little word to say I have received your dear affectionate letter of the 30th and that I do feel for you, my poor darling, more than words can express! Your position is infinitely more trying than mine, and it is this difference of positions and interests which adds to my anxiety and worry. Our duties lie differently! Formerly they were just the same! But God will support and help us— and don't give up to the last, hopes of a meeting in May.

I am happy you and dear baby are well. Poor, dear little unconscious innocent, it knows not the agonies and passions that are endured and rage around!

Yesterday was the saddest first of May I ever spent. So different to '51[1]—only—dear, darling little Arthur cheered one by his happy, bright and equally unconscious face and feelings! Sweet child! May God ever bless one who is a gleam of sunshine in the house. Children are a great comfort to me at such times, for their happy innocent unconsciousness is refreshing and cheering to one's heart.

Your letter received today of the 30th ought to be numbered 84 instead of 78!! So that the next would be 85— or—if you have written since—the one you write after this, would be 86. If you numbered them down in your remembrancer as I do, and looked before you wrote, you would not make mistakes.

---

[1] Opening of Great Exhibition.

Here we live in the same anxiety as before, and most desirous of learning that the Austrians have given our former Allies a good licking! How times have changed!

I know well that one is always so annoyed if one's children are called small, though I'm sure I don't know why, for the smallest babies are often the largest children; Leopold was the smallest when born—of any of you, and he is the tallest (certainly of the boys) of his age of any of you, and the ugliest. But I know that your little darling is considered a large child. I always thought the Princess was so fond of babies, and much more so than I am; I like them better than I did, if they are nice and pretty, and my grandchild, I should delight in. Abstractedly, I have no tendre for them till they have become a little human; an ugly baby is a very nasty object—and the prettiest is frightful when undressed—till about four months; in short as long as they have their big body and little limbs and that terrible froglike action. But from four months, they become prettier and prettier. And I repeat it—your child would delight me at any age.

I fear you would not find Papa avoir tant d'entrailles for it. He cannot quite enter into Fritz's ecstasy about him; he never has felt that himself. After a certain age if they are nice (and not like Bertie and Leopold were) he is very fond of playing with them.

I send you four copies of Affie's letters. By the by you never thank us for sending them to you, or your sisters for copying them, dear—which shocks us somewhat!

Now goodbye and God bless you, my dearest, and as Papa says (the policeman says it to Hawkesley in "Still Waters Run Deep") "Keep up your pecker; that's right" meaning keep up your spirits and don't be downhearted. Yes that we must all do, or else we could not get through all. I understand Fritz's feelings, but I understand yours also and so ought—and will he—I am sure.[1]

---

[1] This refers to Prince Frederick William's warlike enthusiasm.

How could you my darling—think or dream that we should not let you come? We are dying to see you—and Papa can tell you that I was at one time almost driven to desperation at the thought of your not coming! Then I became calmer and resigned—and even now I tremble at the 12 days still between the time of your arrival. But God will I pray and hope as a reward for so many disappointments— so many trials—so much anxiety past, present and future, grant us this short (far too short) meeting.

Humboldt's death has deeply, deeply grieved us! Pray say everything kind to Madame Bulow on this sad occasion.[1] I wish you or Fritz could manage to get our deep concern on the irreparable loss of this great man to be publicly known! He, like the old Duke of Wellington—was one of those people, who one thought never could die! Prussia has lost much in him!

The movements or rather mere inaction of the Austrians drive one crazy! It is distracting. And those horrid Russians who can be depended on by no-one!

BUCKINGHAM PALACE, MAY 14, 1859

Your darling little note of the 12th reached me this morning; a thousand thanks for the welcome intelligence;[2] E. Stockmar's two telegrams yesterday made me feel ready to jump over the moon. Oh! my beloved child, it really is as if you were our only child, such is our joy—our ecstasy at seeing you. D.V. and unberufen a thousand times!! I felt so very anxious that you should gratify the numbers who long to see you; indeed it would have had a bad effect if you had not come for one day at least, to London. The feeling of affection towards you, and interest in you is so very, very touching and gratifying.

---

[1] Baron Alexander von Humboldt. Traveller, diplomat and scientist. His letters published after his death contained some unfriendly allusions to the Prussian Royal Family and the Prince Consort. His niece married the Foreign Minister, Von Bulow, who had been Prussian minister in London. He was great-uncle of the twentieth-century statesman.
[2] Saying that the Princess would come—though without Prince Frederick William.

Well, very well, my beloved child, do I feel for you the separation from dear Fritz—and I shall think so much of you and feel for you on Thursday. It is a great trial, poor darling. For us it is a great, great disappointment not to see him and people here are so much disappointed at not seeing him; everyone is quite grieved; only do tell him how the good people here regret not to see him, as they quite look upon him as belonging to them!

16 MAY. [The Queen had been to Aldershot.] Yesterday morning, we went to church, to that large wooden church in the South Camp where there were 500 soldiers—many officers, and officers and men's wives. Only morning prayers without litany and communion; I thought it very impressive. Mr. Sabin[1] has a good voice and preaches well. They sang well—accompanied by wind instruments. There are no fittings and seats in the church—and Catholic and Presbyterian services are performed in the same building one after the other. It blew so much that I did not ride yesterday afternoon nor at the field day—Papa thinking I should be so blown about, but I regret it much now—especially yesterday.

I am sorry George of M.[2] is not pleasant to you. Feo is however very very happy and they lead a very rational life. I'm glad you feel about betrothed couples as I do. This sort of liberty is quite new and shocks many people. Both should know one another well—but there should be restraint for many reasons. I never cared for you near as much as you seem to do about baby; I care much more for the younger ones (poor Leopold perhaps excepted) but one makes much more fuss with the first than when one has many more. We used constantly to see you and Bertie in bed and bathed —and we only see the younger ones—once in three months perhaps.[3] There is no time—and everything comes more naturally with the younger ones which is a great blessing for them.

---

[1] J. E. Sabin, M.A., later Chaplain to the Forces (1st class) at Dover.
[2] George of Saxe-Meiningen, heir to the Dukedom, married in 1858 Princess Feodore, daughter of the Queen's half-sister.
[3] Meaning in bath or bed.

I love to look back on that happy time, and on the delightful intercourse between us—so soothing and satisfactory to our hearts and so very much to my heart which requires sympathy, and the possibility of pouring out its feelings quite openly to one who will feel for and understand me! And this I have found in you, my dearest child! It has done my heart more good than words can express— and I thank you for all your love and affection and confidence.

We went to the Adelphi last night and saw a very pretty new play called "The House or The Home"[1] in which the Wigans acted extremely well, but the heat was dreadful.

I can only write you a very few lines as we are very busy trying to form a Government, a pleasant task at the present moment. All I can tell you today is that (after a Drawing Room and an Address on the Throne and a Council) we have just seen Lord Granville and hope he may be able to form a Government. But this you must keep to yourself, though by tomorrow or tonight we shall know. Lord Clarendon—of course at the Foreign Office.

These lines are not an answer to your dear letter of the 10th, but merely to give you some notion of the Government. Alas! Lord Clarendon is not in it! Lord Granville failed as Lord John would not join him unless he had what he calls the second place! Never till that moment did I think that the F.O. was meant by that! Lord Granville would not after that undertake a Government without Lord John; so on Sunday afternoon I sent for Lord Palmerston (who has behaved very handsomely) and he said, much as he wished for Lord Clarendon and felt how I must desire to have him, he could not insist on Lord John's not having the F.O. if he

---

[1] Written by Tom Taylor (1817–80), dramatist and editor of *Punch*, and based on Octave Fenillet's play *Peril dans la Demeure*.

insisted on having it! Which accordingly with his usual selfishness and bad taste he did.

This Government being avowedly one uniting the two rivals, I could not have insisted on this without appearing to have some personal dislike to Lord John. However he will not be violent and the Government intend adhering to the strict neutrality.[1] Lord John will I am sure not keep the Office long. Lord Clarendon, whom I saw yesterday, said it would only be injuring himself and doing no good if he joined in any other Office—so he would at any time be ready to take the F.O. if vacant. But you may imagine what a loss he is to us! It is a great trouble and worry, added to the sad anxiety about the war.

WINDSOR CASTLE, JUNE 15, 1859

Now I must scold you a wee bit for an observation which really seems at variance with your own expressions. You say "how glad" Ada[2] "must be" at being again in that most charming situation, which you yourself very frequently told me last year was so wretched. How can anyone, who has not been married above two years and three quarters, (like Ada) rejoice at being a third time in that condition? I positively think those ladies who are always enceinte quite disgusting; it is more like a rabbit or guinea-pig than anything else and really it is not very nice. There is Lady Kildare who has two a year one in January and one in December—and always is so, whenever one sees her! And there is no end to the jokes about her![3] I know Papa is shocked at that sort of thing. To be truly thankful for the blessing, when one has a child and to be glad to have them leisurely (without which I can assure you, life is wretched I know this from the experience of the first four years of my marriage) and one becomes so worn out and one's nerves so miserable—I can understand—(though I did not when I was younger). Let

---

[1] In the Franco-Austrian war.
[2] Daughter of Princess Hohenlohe, and niece of the Queen. She was married to Prince Frederick of Schleswig-Holstein.
[3] She was the daughter of the Queen's close friend, the Duchess of Sutherland. The Queen is somewhat exaggerating.

me repeat once more, dear, that it is very bad for any person to have them very fast—and that the poor children suffer for it, even more, not to speak of the ruin it is to the looks of a young woman—which she must not neglect for her husband's sake, particularly when she is a Princess and obliged to appear.

Now after this little sermon let me revert to your own dear affectionate self being so well and strong and being out so much, which I am delighted to hear. Your hours seem so sensible; I wish our life admitted of it but I fear it would be difficult—yet perhaps we might be able at dear Osborne where we shall try to go as early in July as we can.

I am glad to hear what you told Papa about the Princes of Hesse.[1] Beauty I don't want though I should be glad of it when it's there; but nice, manly, sensible, healthy, gentlemanlike appearance is essential. As you've sent me so many photographs of people of different kinds and I have got all the Princes,[2] and William of Baden, and these young Princes are often with you I wish you could get a photograph of them for me, and of the young Hohenzollerns—and in short anyone else to prevent it appearing too personal. But pray say everything civil to the young Princes of Hesse and that I remember so well having seen them as fine boys at Mayence,[3] and had a print of them and their sister which their mother sent me.

From the Princess Royal

JUNE 16, 1859

I am getting up all my courage, and hope that we shall soon be engaged—and pass the Rhine—the sooner the better— and by a successful war obtain for us a lasting and honourable peace, secure our position as the first in Germany and help the Austrians by helping ourselves and make for ourselves a great political position, God grant that all may go well. I wish

---

[1] Prince Louis and Prince Henry of Hesse-Darmstadt. The former married the Queen's second daughter—Princess Alice.
[2] Of Prussia.
[3] On her visit to Saxe-Coburg in 1845.

for once I was a man, and baby too to fight the French. I cannot help being savage. When I think that it is their fault that so many poor, innocent people are being made wretched and that so much German blood is being shed and will be shed, and my happy peaceful life is at an end for who knows how long, perhaps for ever.

WINDSOR CASTLE, JUNE 18, 1859

Since I began this I received your letter of the 16th full of enthusiasm;[1] I fear we shall diverge more and more—and to feel that your feelings or rather more interests are so different to ours is a sad trial!

In short I am sick of all—and wish to go and rest away from the world and all its troubles.

BUCKINGHAM PALACE, JUNE 22, 1859

We expect dear Uncle Leopold this afternoon, and have our last concert (an ordinary one) this evening—I long for rest. My turn is not frivolous excitement and bustle and above all not to have to work with some tools who don't quite suit one![2] But when I feel lowest I always find that that All Merciful Power sends some blessed relief. And if those I love are well, and I cling with confidence to Him, I shall find comfort and support; and at this very moment I receive a very cheering account of dearest Grandmama, for which I cannot be thankful enough. It seems she will soon be much better! I know my own darling child will enter into all my feelings—as you did when you saw my anguish.[3]

I am very glad you get on so well with the Queen. I certainly did also in '45.

As for all your military ardour I fear, dear, it will all be of little avail—and I grieve over all the painful separations and all the discomforts of so many families.

---

[1] The Queen is using the word in an unfavourable sense.
[2] Lord John Russell.
[3] The Duchess of Kent had been seriously ill when the Princess Royal was visiting England.

I am truly grieved at this sad misfortune for the poor Princess[1] and am sure good Fritz with his kind heart and dutiful feelings must be much grieved. It was not the intimate relationship of everyday as yours to dear Grandmama is—of course, but a grandmother must ever be loved and venerated particularly one's mother's mother I always think. However that depends—for if the grandmother is kind and affectionate she is equally dear whether maternal or paternal. I never had but Mama's mother, and my dear kind grandmother-in-law.

BUCKINGHAM PALACE, JUNE 29, 1859

Bertie is improved—I see it more now than I did at first—but still he does nothing, and they mean to make him work very hard at Holyrood—where he will go very soon. I think he will stop with us—a little more than a fortnight from the time he arrived. He is a little grown and is as tall as Louis[2] now but his nose and mouth are much grown also; the nose is becoming the true Coburg nose and begins to hang a little, but there remains unfortunately the want of chin which with that large nose and very large lips is not so well in profile.

Winterhalter is making a sketch of him which will be very like.

I do not speak of those hateful politics and that miserable war—the misery of so many thousands and the frightful loss of life for which those are answerable who brought on this strife.

How I pity you about all those grand-duchesses and Russians! Really one ought not to do so much for them, for they are wolves in sheeps' clothings.[3] How did you like "Adam Bede"? People think it so very clever.[4]

---

[1] The Princess's mother had died on June 23. The Princess Royal said that she was one of the last princesses who remembered the year 6 (i.e. 1806) and who was a great friend of Queen Louise.

[2] Dom Louis of Portugal—afterwards King.

[3] In her letter of June 21 the Princess Royal had complained of what she called "a flood of grand-duchesses". They were the Russian relatives

Princess Mary of Cambridge, 1861

Princess Alice and Prince Louis of Hesse, 1860

I want to mention a subject about which I wish to consult you. It is the following. Papa dislikes the lithograph of Alice (after the pretty picture) though it is generally liked very much, and says that it is not like the picture being coarse in the face, and that it will do Alice harm if it is seen by those who don't know her. Now what is your opinion of it? Of course it is important that her likeness should be favourable. Now if you agree with Papa—I have a notion of sending the original to you, to Berlin, to get it lithographed there by that man who lithographed the small full length of you, and added a background to it—and which I think is very like and so pretty, and so much better than the one of the same done here. The man is called Sussnapf. If you agree in Papa's view of the present lithograph and if you think this man would do it well—I should like you to find out by the Baron— how long he would be doing it—and what he would ask for it? Please let the man answer me about it as soon as possible.

After referring to the death of the Princess's mother:

The Grand-duchess, though cold and formal, was a distinguished and excellent woman, who was most deservedly beloved—and what can ever replace a mother's loss?

To wear black woollen and high-up gowns always and long veils is dreadful. But I suppose you wear barège, for that is as neat and I wore it for poor Grandpapa with crêpe. The heat of even that, high-up must be fearful. I think it quite wrong that the nursery are not in mourning, at any rate I should make them wear grey or white or drab—and baby wear white and lilac, but not colours. That I think shocking. Well of course with your German relations you must I suppose do what is custom—but you must promise

of the Prussian Royal Family, and the Princess was nervous of their influence on her father-in-law—"the Prince Regent will be tormented and teased, and who knows whether he may not give way?" Russia had unmistakably sided with Napoleon III.
⁴ In her reply the Princess says "I think it very well written and very interesting but prefer 'Two Years Ago' and 'Westward Ho!' "

me that if I should die your child or children and those around you should mourn; this really must be, for I have such strong feeling on this subject, which certainly is, to say the least, more reasonable than leaving the rooms of dear relatives left for years as mausoleums particularly in the midst of other people's rooms.[1] You will I know understand these feelings fully my own, affectionate, warm-hearted child.

Dear Papa has written a long letter[2] to the Prince and told you all about it, only do take care that the Prince don't show it anyone or mention Papa's name, else if it got to Lord Bloomfield's ears it might come back here and get us into a great scrape. So be sure and don't forget that.

I am wretched about the affairs abroad; that splendid Austrian army, which I have loved from my birth, as so many dear relations have been and are in it, has fought so nobly and must be so mortified and hurt![3]

From the Princess Royal

DAS NEUE PALAIS, JULY 6, 1859

The Empress[4] leaves on Saturday. Today she showed me all her magnificent jewels. Yours are finer. Hers are huge things and really in such profusion that it seems almost magic —sapphires, emeralds, pearls, rubies etc. but the quality is not very fine—her diamonds excepted which are magnificent.

I hear the Queen of Hanover wears the jewels. It makes me so furious that anything which you have worn should be worn by anyone else.[5]

---

[1] The Queen is evidently referring to the room in the Schloss, see page 22.

[2] He wrote on June 15, "We have got a Ministry which exactly suits Louis Napoleon." He deplored the absence of Clarendon from the Cabinet. This is presumably the letter to which the Queen refers. See *Letters of The Prince Consort*, edited by Dr. Kurt Jagow, John Murray, 1938.

[3] The bloody battle of Solferino had been fought on June 24.

[4] Of Russia. The Dowager Empress, sister to the King of Prussia.

[5] Queen Victoria had had to resign Queen Charlotte's jewels to that Queen's male heir—the Duke of Cumberland and King of Hanover.

You will have heard of the surprise of the Armistice, which was proposed by the Emperor N., who we know is anxious for peace. There is something at work. That we know. May it lead to good—to peace and harmony and better Government!

Last night we had a dinner and listened for long out of doors to the band and the distant drums and fifes and bugles! The noise and excitement around me makes writing difficult—now the Stirlingshire militia are coming along marching to the dear bagpipes! Oh! while we are here in peace watching the military array—our poor fellow-creatures in Italy are suffering the reality of a most bloody war! We shall not see today half the number of those who were killed and wounded at Solferino alone.

OSBORNE, JULY 13, 1859

Peace! and concluded between the two Emperors without anyone! I of course am glad that this horrid blood-shed is over—and that we have had nothing to do with it! But you Prussians of course are in an unpleasant position. Your policy has however not been wise; neither one thing or the other! However there is no help for it now, and I am only glad that there is no prospect of general war for the present. Both Emperors have shown wisdom and moderation.

Respecting the mourning, I quite understand your following the German or Prussian customs for your own German relations, but I understand equally that you understood my wishes—strong feelings respecting "dreadful things" as you call it.

By all means send the Empress Dowager a kind message in return from me and tell her I have had much pleasure in making the acquaintance of her two grandsons—the young Princes of Leuchtenberg,[1] who seem nice, intelligent boys.

---

[1] This family linked the Empire of Napoleon I with nineteenth century European royalty. The founder of the house was Eugène de Beauharnais—son of the Vicomte Alexandre de Beauharnais and the Empress

All you say about Abbat is very nice; if only he was not what he is! Mother etc. etc. I feel rather disappointed at hearing nothing about the two P.'s of Hesse. Surely in six or seven weeks' time something might have been said! It often makes me very anxious and pensive and I fear occupies her—very much. She[1] is getting quite fat again, and is very well and strong and growing fast. Bertie left us très à regret on Thursday. He is very fond of his home his parents and his brothers and sisters I am happy to say.

OSBORNE, JULY 16, 1859

In a previous letter the Queen had urged the Princess Royal to write
to her cousin Princess Charlotte, daughter of King Leopold.

I never expect or does Charlotte either that you should keep up a regular correspondence but merely not to ignore her altogether, the more so as she has written three times to you—and has taken so warm an interest in your happy unclouded life—which is a contrast to hers[2]—excepting in her excellent and amiable husband.

I will not touch here in today's letter upon politics—beyond saying that if you hear much that is not complimentary to us (which I am not the least surprised at) I could return the compliment. I saw your letter to dear Papa received yesterday and quite understand yours and others' feelings—but would suggest no too great violence of feeling against the great man,[3] for he has shown great moderation, and generosity towards the prisoners—returning them without exchange—and great violence would only be unpolitic. To be united and well-prepared is the right thing.

Living here—and sitting out writing under the trees, as I am doing the whole morning—is most luxurious and enjoyable and I feel it is quite paradise.

Josephine. His son married the daughter of the Emperor Nicholas I and the Empress Dowager. Their attractive children were a source of some matrimonial anxieties to the Queen.

[1] Princess Alice.

[2] She had no children.

[3] Napoleon III.

My first impression on hearing these dreadful news is to write to you![1] God has taken a pure, lovely angel to him! She was too good for this world, poor dear Pedro! He had found an angel to cheer his hard, trying life—his melancholy character—and now in a moment snatched from him! It is too dreadful! And the poor parents! Dear excellent Prince Hohenzollern! whom I do so honour and the poor, delicate Princess—to think of their agony! To feel that his patriotism and devotion to his country prevented his going as he had intended in March to see her! What will his feelings be! Oh! I can't tell you what I feel! I know what you will both feel—what your warm heart will feel! We who had brought about in a great manner this marriage, who had rejoiced at the happiness of both dear young people—married at the same age as ourselves—the same difference between their ages as between ours—married the year you did! And now all gone—crushed, shipwrecked! It is too, too dreadful! It makes my heart bleed! And we know nothing, heard nothing but that wretched telegram from good Louis![2]

I will not enter into the subject of hateful politics—but you make a mistake in speaking of our policy (before the change of Government). We are in a totally different position to Prussia; do not belong to the Confederation and have no duties. As for the "two old Italian Masters" the one twaddling and theoretical, the other vindictive, shortsighted and obstinate, they are a sad misfortune.[3]

---

[1] Queen Stephanie of Portugal died on this day.
[2] King Pedro's next brother. He became King of Portugal on his brother's death in 1861.
[3] The Queen is distinguishing between the neutral or pacific policy of the Conservative Government (which fell in June) and the pro-Italian and pro-French policy of Palmerston's Government which succeeded it. Palmerston and Lord John Russell are the Italian Masters. She is making the point that England could pursue an independent policy whereas Prussia could only do so by ignoring her obligations as a member, with Austria, of the Germanic Confederation.

Your letter by the post of the 20th grieved me, for it
spoke with such bitterness of Austria! But Papa has written
to you and has again; and your letter to him explains much
—wherefore I shall say no more now—beyond repeating
the immense importance to Europe and Germany—of
Austria and Prussia keeping well together, and the more
you love Prussia, as you truly ought, the more you should
strive not to fan the flame of irritation and annoyance but
to urge and encourage "unity".[1]

As for the old Baron[2] he never writes any more, and
might really be dead to all intents and purposes for he never
takes any notice of anything when one writes to him. It
really is too bad!

Pray, dearest child, always have your letters (sent by
post) pasted as heretofore; it is not safe otherwise I can assure
you.

I am writing in the lower alcove—with the deep blue
sea as a background and the pleasant sound of the fountains
soothing one's ears.

From the Princess Royal

JULY 29, 1859

*I am sorry you quite misunderstand me and say I have so
much bitterness against Austria—as I am the only one here
that has not any. This morning I have written a long letter
to the Princess to try and calm her as she carries her antipathy beyond bounds. Please dear Mama don't think that
I either have exaggerated feelings or try to spread them.*

OSBORNE, AUGUST 3, 1859

I am sorry, my darling, that my few words—merely
meant as caution—should have distressed you. I have asked
Mr. Becker to answer the young Baron and to set your mind

---

[1] The Prince always maintained that if Prussia was to lead Germany
she must not drag Germany down to her own level but by self-sacrifice
and magnanimity show herself worthy of leadership.
[2] Baron Stockmar, father of Baron Ernest.

quite at rest. I only wish (though God knows I know how much reason you have often had to distrust her) that Prussia and Austria should try to keep well together—as it is of such importance for Germany and Europe at large, that there should be no real enmity. In the same way, I think (though there must be distrust and ought to be a great state of preparation) useless abuse of France and the Emperor Napoleon and irritation against them is better avoided—as not doing any good. I don't mean you, but Prussia generally.

From the Princess Royal

Writing about Prince Fritz Carl and his wife Marianne:

He despises women, and will not lose that feeling until he finds one that is his match and tells him the truth. I think he, as most gentlemen do here, considers ladies as un chiffon to be well-dressed, and look pretty. To have stupid compliments and flattery paid them and to have children is all they are made for. I wish some day you would invite them it would do him so much good to see the sort of position women have in England. But still sometimes I think he puts on this opinion on purpose, and thinks differently for he said once that he thought Mary Cambridge so charming: that was the sort of person he would have liked.

OSBORNE, AUGUST 10, 1859

That despising our poor degraded sex—(for what else is it as we poor creatures are born for man's pleasure and amusement, and destined to go through endless sufferings and trials?) is a little in all clever men's natures; dear Papa even is not quite exempt though he would not admit it—but he laughs and sneers constantly at many of them and at our unavoidable inconveniences, etc. though he hates the want of affection, of due attention to and protection of them, says that the men who leave all home affairs—and the education of their children to their wives—forget their first duties. But understandably in your new country, there is a

— 205 —

terrible want of feeling for family life, and I should be very happy if Fritz Carl could profit a little by a sejour with us. I like him extremely—and I am sure I should like her.

The great heat has returned and is very trying. Monday and yesterday at Aldershot and here were really fearful. Poor dear Papa had one of his stomach attacks on Monday, which made him look fearfully ill, but he remained in the field in that broiling sun the whole time and said he was all the better for it. He is however not quite right yet. He is so fagged and worked and our 2 Italian Masters almost drive us crazy. Really I never saw two such obdurate . . . I won't use any expression because I can't trust what it would be.

You will be delighted to hear that Tiny Hamilton is going to marry Lord Dalkeith—a very great parti and a charming one, which I have long wished for.

From the Princess Royal

DAS NEUE PALAIS, AUGUST 26, 1859

I am so delighted at Tiny Hamilton's engagement. Lord Dalkeith is such a nice pleasing young man, one of the few young men in London that are really nice and I do not think there is any chance of Tiny's ever becoming Catholic.[1]

With respect to our going to England Fritz wishes me to say how pleased and flattered he was at your inviting us in so very kind a way—that we cannot give up Baden but that he sees no valid reason against our coming in October late, or beginning of November, for a short time, as far as we can make plans at present. Of course this gives me boundless delight, although he says he does not wish it to be made a rule of—for me to go home twice a year. (I say I know although in your great kindness you might like it as much as I should, yet I am sure you will not expect it.) And that it

---

[1] Lord Dalkeith's mother had recently joined the Church of Rome with some *éclat*.

would make a bad effect here where I was as yet but little known. And he wished me to travel more than his mother who has been but little in the Provinces and is not known much in the country. But this year is really an exception I think. I was there for so short a time and without him, and I cannot see what on earth he can have of very urgent business here in November, which month moreover is dreadful in Berlin, (where we must stay from the end of October till May—a long time)—not a soul comes to town till January and the walks and drives without variety the greatest bores imaginable (this I only say by the way being nothing to the question). We should have to move there after Fritz's birthday[1] on account of Baby for whom it would be too cold and damp here, and who is to be weaned when we go to Berlin. I must say I think Fritz is quite right. As a principle, it would not look well for me to go too often. We princes and princesses are often forced to give up what appears to others easy and what we would most like to have on account of our position; it is hard but one must get accustomed to it. But then I have also a home to which I belong a little bit. And I think it would make a good effect in England if we come again as our time allows it and there is nothing really against it except leaving Baby which will be a distress to me. Notwithstanding Fritz's great wish to go to England and particularly to see you he still hesitates giving his consent to the journey because he thinks twice in one year is too much. You wished me always to tell you openly all we think on the subject, therefore I do. Our stay could not be a very long one, dearest Mama, but not a hurried scramble like the last.

Before finally deciding it must be nearer the time as it is rather early to make plans, and we must ask the Regent's consent. Should anything happen to prevent our carrying out this plan and of course we should let you know. Will you please let Papa know all this?

[1] October 18.

Lady Cecilia Lennox (one of your bridesmaids) is also going to be married—to Lord Bingham a very nice person who has been long attached to her; but the Duchess did not wish it. Perhaps you would send her something—for her marriage; something pretty in china perhaps with views of Berlin or in short anything Prussian.

We drove to the Euston Square Station whence we started at nine p.m. Matresses were arranged on the floor and we came down quite comfortably here arriving at eight this morning.

BALMORAL CASTLE, SEPTEMBER 2, 1859

We arrived here at six on Wednesday after a very rapid journey, and I have never been less tired than this time—taking the journey at night was a great relief. It seemed to get over the length of it so easily.

The Queen then explains why Prince Leopold had not come with the family to Balmoral:

Leopold still has such constant bad accidents that it would be very troublesome indeed to have him here. He walks shockingly—and is dreadfully awkward—holds himself as badly as ever and his manners are despairing, as well as his speech—which is quite dreadful. It is so provoking as he learns so well and reads quite fluently; but his French is more like Chinese than anything else; poor child, he is really very unfortunate.

Bertie has been doing better at Edinburgh than he ever did before; he has worked hard and shown a desire to learn, instead of resistance. He is also grown and spread; but not improved in looks; the mouth is becoming so very large and he will cut his hair away behind and divide it nearly in the middle in front, so that it makes him appear to have no head and all face. It is a frightful coiffure.

From the Princess Royal

I wish you would get dear Papa to read that book of Kingsley's—"Hypatia", it really is well worth the while, it is so powerfully written and so original. We have been reading a good deal lately, the kind good invaluable Baron reads to me nearly every day, he read to me out of Lord Malmesbury's Memoirs,[1]—and then a life of the Duke of Reichstadt, by Adolf Schmidt—very interesting, Fritz and I have finished together the Empress Catharine's Memoirs and Schlözer's book—"Catharine II and Frederick II".

And now we are reading Princess Dashkowa's Memoirs —which are very amusing; but as she seems to have possessed a good deal of imagination and a small quantity of vanity they sound considerably "brodées". Baby is well and in wild spirits. I never saw such a bit of quicksilver, he is never quiet a minute but seldom cries—he has broth and rusks now which he enjoys very much. Fritz adores the child and certainly the baby returns the affection for he is never happy till Fritz has got him on his arm and he never wishes to come to me.

Many thanks for the photograph of "Addie".[2] She must be very plain. I'm sorry for Feo's sake, that you dislike her husband so much. She is happy—and contented, and that is enough. Dearest, a poor girl has not much free choice; a good parti presents itself; if she does not dislike the man— and if her parents like it, why if she refuses him she runs the risk of getting no husband at all, and we see by poor cousin Mary, what the consequence of that is! For a Princess—a very sad, bad look out!

Papa will I am sure read Hypatia, and I shall do so too. Alas! we have both so little time for reading! I finished "Two

---

[1] The first Lord Malmesbury. He has much information about the Russian and Prussian Courts in the eighteenth century.

[2] Probably Princess Augusta Adelaide of Saxe-Meiningen, sister of Feo's husband.

Years Ago" last week and do think it so beautiful! Such knowledge of human nature of our poor, ill-used sex—such truths, so much imagination and a power of description and beauty of language which equals Walter Scott. I never felt so impressed by any book almost, I think. Have you read "Alton Lock" and "Yeast" by Kingsley? They are said to be rather strange and show his (supposed) chartist and socialist views.[1]

By the by, dearest, you say, you are always so happy to do anything for me I like; now I do so very much wish to have that little view out of the glass door at Babelsberg— looking on the fountain. Could you not make a scribble of it yourself for me, or else get someone to do it?

I have excellent accounts of dear Grandmama and the little ones—but I miss Grandmama sadly and the family[2] now at Abergeldie are not at all pleasant remplacements, at least my lady is not.[3] And we have such awful trouble with the "Italian Masters", really you can't think how we are plagued.

Sir G. Grey is a great help and so amiable.

Of course I saw Massow[4] and can see his ugly large, red face before me. He will be no loss.

BALMORAL CASTLE, SEPTEMBER 13, 1859

About writing to the dear Empress Eugénie, whenever you have a good opportunity, we think you should certainly do so—but you should try and seize a good one;

---

[1] In her reply the Princess Royal says "I have not read the two books of Kingsley's you mention. I am so glad you liked 'Two Years Ago' and hope you will read 'Westward Ho!' and 'Hypatia' which are sure to delight you."

[2] Lord John Russell's.

[3] According to her grandson, the present Lord Russell, she was a lady of very advanced political opinions, with the conviction that virtue is to be found only in minorities. She was daughter of the 2nd Lord Minto.

[4] In her letter of September 3 the Princess Royal writes "Minister Massow is dying. I don't know whether you recollect him." He was a member of the Prussian Government.

merely writing for writing's sake would perhaps seem odd,
—but there might easily be an occasion for so doing.

What an odd custom that you have to attend so many
funerals (Massow's etc!). The Princess's doing so is so
strange.

THE SHIEL OF ALT-NA-GUITHASACH, SEPTEMBER 26, 1859

From this pretty "housie" do I write to anticipate your
dear letter by the messenger, which I cannot answer, as my
letter must be sent to Balmoral tonight.

I did not tell you, that the other day when we were
going down Craig na-Ban—which is very steep, and rough,
Jane Churchill fell and could not get up again, (having got
her feet caught in her dress) and Johnny Brown (who is our
factotum and really the perfection of a servant for he thinks
of everything) picked her up like une scène de tragédie and
when she thanked him, he said "Your Ladyship is not so
heavy as Her Majesty"! which made us laugh very much.
I said "Am I grown heavier do you think?" "Well, I think
you are", was the plain spoken reply. So I mean to be
weighed as I always thought I was light.

BALMORAL CASTLE, OCTOBER 4, 1859

I am grieved to hear of your cough and of your travelling
so very fast and always at night. Tell dear Fritz that he
must not whisk you about as he has done himself and as his
father and uncles have done, as that is really not good, and
will do you harm.

I am much pleased with the account of Princess Anna
(minus the twitching). She is, I believe, dark. What you
tell me about the Prince of Orange[1] grieves us, though I
own I always feared it. I wish Fritz would ascertain through
Fritz of B. or any friend of his—the real truth. Unfortunately—at a place like Baden—everything is but too
well known.

---

[1] Prince William, eldest son of King William III. "The Orange boy"—
a possible husband for Princess Alice. The Princess Royal had written
to her mother from Baden when staying with Prince Frederick William's

Now, dearest child, many thanks for your dear letter of the 5th—received on Sunday. You still don't say a word of your movements, which is quite inconceivable! However by the Duchess of Hamilton's[1] letter to Mama, I hear that you only leave Baden on the 14th. I have always heard that the Grand Duchess Sophie[2] is extremely agreeable and distinguée. As for Fritz of B. he is quite charming—Il a un charme indicible, and Louise is fortunate indeed. I can well imagine how well you must be with them both;—and the little boy must be very intelligent, though not pretty and I fear delicate from what our dear Countess has told me.

Poor William of Baden[3] is not in your favour, I see; but dear child, I think you are sometimes a little unjust in your dislikes (you know that always was so)—for Fritz (I mean your husband) told me frequently that he was an excellent person, and very active and painstaking. As clever as Fritz B. he no doubt is not. Fortunately Alice is not at all anxious to marry; only the day before yesterday she said to me she could not dream or think of going away from us—or from here! Of course if she finds a person she really likes and loves—she will go through that trial as you have done. She is wonderfully strong and well since she has been here; has been out almost every day with me on these long expeditions and rides and walks any distance, and is grown quite fat since she has been here, and weighs a good deal. I never saw her better. She is a very dear companion.

sister—"I am shocked at hearing that the Prince of Orange has been leading a bad life here, gambling and drinking and what not, but I hope and trust that it is not so bad as people say—that would be too sad, poor young man."

[1] She was aunt to the Grand-Duke of Baden.

[2] Sophie Grand-Duchess of Baden, daughter of King Gustavus IV of Sweden.

[3] Brother of the Grand-Duke and evidently canvassed by the Queen as a possible son-in-law.

WINDSOR CASTLE, OCTOBER 19, 1859

I am so glad you like the little hat which it gave me such pleasure to plait (not "plat" as you wrote it,) for your darling baby.[1]

WINDSOR CASTLE, OCTOBER 22, 1859

I must say that (though I know the feeling for "home" prompts you to say it) the appellation of "dear, dear Windsor", coming at this moment, when I am struggling with my homesickness for my beloved Highlands, the air— the life, the liberty—cut off for so long—almost could make me angry. I cannot ever feel the slightest affection or tendre for this fine, old dull place, which please God shall never hold my bones! I think I dislike it more and more though I am quite aware of its splendour. I feel the change (as you know you always did) much, though I am well now and in good spirits and won't give way in the slightest degree. You don't say a word about all the affectionate speeches of those dear people at Balmoral, which I wrote to you about, but I am sure you were touched by them all the same.

I miss these people so much. It is so soothing and refreshing when one is in such an isolated position as we are, to be able to talk freely with those below you, and to find such open independence, such sense and such affection for you.

From the Princess Royal

OCTOBER 27, 1859

In this letter the Princess Royal refers to the two younger ladies of her household—Marie Lynar[2] and Walburga Hohenthal.[3] Of Marie Lynar she says:

She is such a dear, sweet, amiable, clever and distinguished person from whom one can learn an immense deal—

---

[1] One of the Queen's pastimes was plaiting paper bonnets—see *Reminiscences of Court and Diplomatic Life*, by Lady Bloomfield, Chapter IV.
[2, 3] See page 38.

they both are so very nice really the more I see of them the more I love them, they are so full of tact, and always so respectful and nice to me, they are more like sisters than anything else. Wally Hohenthal is the cleverest, and having gone through so much sorrow in her life, and living now in very difficult family circumstances she has sense and judgement much beyond her years. Her sweet temper, and merriment remind me much of Alice sometimes, so that I call her Alice now and then when I am absent. They are both so enthusiastically English in all their thoughts and sentiments they talk and write English to each other. They are so enchanted at the thoughts of seeing you again, as they feel your kindness to them very much and they quite rave about Windsor.

WINDSOR CASTLE, OCTOBER 26, 1859

My heart beats and I can scarcely trust my hopes and fears and joys when I think that please God! in less than a fortnight I shall clasp my own darling child in my arms and see you with dear Fritz—see you happy together which I longed for so much! Dear Fritz has written me a most kind and affectionate letter for which pray thank him very warmly—and his announcement to Papa of staying on beyond your birthday is unspeakable pleasure for we have not, really since you married, been able to see each other quietly, peaceably and undisturbedly. God grant nothing may come to cloud over this too happy prospect.

Dear Grandmama is so delighted. I have been delayed in beginning this letter by our dearest Countess Blücher, who has just gone away and who had been here since Monday afternoon. I know no lady I like and love as I do her! She is too charming and there is such cheerfulness, cleverness and such calm, quiet, sound, good sense, such straightforwardness and courage. I envy your having her much with you, though God knows, you, young as you are and away from us—want such a friend still more. She will come here again when you are here.

Pedro V, King of Portugal

Stephanie of Hohenzollern-Sigmaringen, wife of Pedro V of Portugal

Many thanks for your kind letter of the 24th. I will not be angry with you for your feeling for Windsor in consequence of your short honeymoon, still I cannot share it, though my happiness began here too. Early impressions— the unpleasant and unhealthy climate, the restriction of the walks—the Court life and the impossibility of doing what one wishes here—without Court officials etc. all this makes it to me an undesirable and unenjoyable residence.

Much shall we indeed have to talk of; Alice's and Bertie's future of course occupy us much and anxiously. Alice is not however to marry for the next two years certainly; she must be quite strong and set up; but it is wonderful what the dear Highlands did for her; she is grown 4 inches in width across her chest and shoulders and is quite plump! You must not tell her anything about the Prince of Orange's proceedings (of which I hear sad confirmation) or speak of William of Baden in a derogatory tone. We may else do harm and find ourselves in a serious difficulty. Your letter delighted her. I hope you will bring E. Stockmar; it would delight us both and dear Papa in particular as he has so seldom clever and congenial people to talk to. Dear Papa was a little indisposed with his old enemy, but it was not a very bad attack without sickness or shivering. Today he has gone to Oxford to see how Bertie is going on in that old monkish place, which I have a horror of. You will not be able to see much of Bertie, for he is only just gone to Oxford and the vacation begins before Christmas so that he will be able only to come over occasionally for a day—of course for his birthday and for yours.

Please God we shall have all our children assembled on the 9th and 21st November—except poor dear Affie! That is sad! When shall we ever see you altogether again? When once a large family grows up and separates—it is very difficult to bring them altogether again.

We are much pleased that you have got a little property

of your own,[1] which will be a great comfort and interest to you, and in such a pretty country.

From the Princess Royal

I am so glad that my dear Countess has been with you, I feel as if it was a part of myself as she knows what I think and feel upon almost every subject as well as I do myself, and she is so fond of Fritz that she will be able to stand up for him on all occasions. She is indeed a treasure, a sort of "Baron in petticoats".

Louise of Baden and I, we quarrel about her. Louise says she belongs to her because she lives at Baden, and I say she belongs to me because she is a Prussian and an English-woman, in fact all her friends are ready to devour her— Mrs. Hobbs looks upon her as specially belonging to the baby and her. Countess Blooker or "Bleeker" as they call her.

I write today again in order to say that dearest Papa is much better today, and I hope by tomorrow or next day he will be nearly his dear self again. Though of no real consequence whatever, it was the severest and most obstinate attack I ever saw him have, the more annoying as it was accompanied by violent spasms of pain; which he had both on Saturday and yesterday for two hours; he had to go to bed at three on Saturday, remained in bed all day yesterday till 10 o'clock when he got up for an hour and a half and thank God today (unberufen, unberufen)—there has been no return of pain—he is in every way much better and is up. But it has been such an unusual thing to see him in bed (never except for the measles) and naturally cast such a gloom over us all, but it seems as if everything were turned upside down when dear Papa is not able to go about. He I fear made it so bad by going to Oxford on Wednesday

---

[1] Bornstedt in the country where Prince Frederick William had a farm.

last (having been unwell since Monday last) and out shooting on Friday. I am glad there is still a week before your arrival, so that he will be quite well by that time.

I am delighted to see both your dear young ladies. Here you will find in waiting Lady Desart (till the 15th when the good Duchess of Atholl comes) Lord De Tabley or Lord Rivers—Flora Macdonald and C. Cavendish—Colonel Hardinge and I think Lord Alfred;[1] General Grey and Sir C. Phipps also here. Lady Caroline is gone to be with Mary West until after her confinement, which may happen any day almost.

Dear Grandmama has returned looking so well it is quite delightful to see her rajeunie and in excellent spirits. Queen Amelie[2] came on Saturday to see me—she is wonderfully well. Dear Lady Augusta[3] is with Grandmama.

I fear that the reports about the young O. are not at all exaggerated as I have heard them from people who saw and knew the proceedings at B.—and I fear he is in bad hands and has no example before him. As regards dear A.[4] you must promise not to say anything to her (or even answer her) until you have had a long and full conversation with dear Papa on the whole subject.

Dear Papa was much amused and interested by Adam Bede, which I am delighted to read a second time. There is such knowledge of human nature, such truth in the characters. I like to trace a likeness to the dear Highlanders in Adam—and also in Lisbeth and Mrs. Poyser. I'm sure it is only a true picture of what constantly (and very naturally) happens.

We shall ask (of course) your particular friends to come here while you are here. We shall order a packet to be at Calais for you.

---

[1] Paget.
[2] The wife of Louis Philippe.
[3] Lady Augusta Bruce: she afterwards married Arthur Stanley, Dean of Westminster.
[4] The Queen is writing by post hence the abbreviations. A. is Princess Alice.

From the Princess Royal

After speaking of the Prince of Orange's escapades, the Princess goes on:

He is shy but not more so than any other young man, and it is not his fault that he is plain. Besides he has got nice blue eyes—and white teeth, good hair and complexion and I think something frank about him. I cannot help thinking that his bad, loose habits come from bad company and from never having associated with people of his own rank, and then when one has such a father[1] and is left to get on alone in the world at eighteen I think it must want a very rare character and unusual qualities to keep in the straight path of duty and virtue.

You know, dear Mama, I am not the one to excuse such wickedness, if you remember we talked in your room at Babelsberg on that subject and you thought I even went too far in my judgement against such things. Therefore you know that I am not excusing the behaviour of the P. of O. only think him rather hardly judged.

Fritz has said to Adalbert exactly what you wished, there was a good opportunity for it and he seized it immediately— so you see I hope that it was neither forgetfulness on my part or indifference on Fritz's that nothing was said before, but really there was no opportunity and if it had been clumsily done or dragged out by force it would have done more harm than good.

Fritz asked Adalbert whether it was true that his nephew had wanted to marry "Maroussy" and that the Grand Duke of Hesse had not given his consent as he considered it a "mesalliance". Adalbert said he never could have married her as she was not of equal rank being a descendant of a Beauharnais. And then Fritz went on to speak of Alexandrine, and Adalbert did not seem to think that his nephew ever thought of her. Then Fritz said: "I hope he will not marry before having looked at different Princesses my four

---

[1] King William III. His private life was irregular, and he lived apart from his wife, Queen Sophie. By a later marriage he was the father of Queen Wilhelmina.

sisters-in-law for instance, they are none of them engaged".
Adalbert said "that would be grist to Elizabeth's mill as he
knew his sister wished it very much." Fritz said that he spoke
this only coming from himself as an idea of his that he was
not authorised to say anything. He knew your principle was
to let your children choose for themselves out of those you
thought fit for them, he could not imagine that you would be
against Louis and Heinrich coming over to England one day
—but that he thought that you did not intend Alice to marry
for two years.

Adalbert said he would tell his sister of the conversation
as it was sure to please her. I shall send this letter in one of
the Baron's then it will be as safe as the messenger. Please
show it to Countess Blücher.[1]

I don't know that it may be your intention to tell Alice or
no—as I do not know whether you speak to her about her
future or not at any rate you can tell her that Fritz and I
will always be happy to do anything for her and that our
only wish is to see her one day as happy as I am.

NOVEMBER 6, 1859

Many, many thanks for your kind long and confidential
letter of the 2nd, which reached me quite safely on Friday
morning—dear Fritz said quite the right thing, and what
Adalbert answered is very satisfactory so far. The idea of the
mésalliance with Maroussy is absurd, for the Queen of
Portugal married the elder Duke of Leuchtenberg, the
Emperor of Brazil married one of the sisters and the Prince
of Hohenzollern-Hechingen another; moreover our own
dear Prince Hohenzollern's mother was a Murat, and his
wife's mother a Tascher.[2]

---

[1] Prince Adalbert was cousin to the King of Prussia and brother to
Princess Charles of Hesse, the mother of Prince Louis. Her christian
name was Elizabeth. "Maroussy" is the pet-name for Princess Marie of
Leuchtenberg (see also under letter of July 13). Prince Frederick
William had probably told the Queen that Prince Louis and Maroussy
had been attracted to one another. She married Prince William of
Baden in 1863, and was the mother of Prince Max.
[2] Princess Hohenzollern's mother was Napoleon's adopted daughter. She
was in fact a Beauharnais and not a Tascher. The Prussian Royal

With respect to the young Prince of Orange, as I shall see you soon, I won't enter into his character and conduct, but my good Lady Ely's[1] opinion I consider of very little value; the Queen tells her to say all the good of her son she can, in order that she should hear it—and good Janie always excuses everyone from her great kindness. Lastly he is 20 and not 18—and the "white teeth" I fear cannot be his own, as he had bad ones when we saw him three years ago. Poor boy, great allowances must of course be made for him.

WINDSOR CASTLE, UNDATED

I have been speaking to dear Papa and he says that understanding that Fritz meant to stay till the first week in December, he had settled the second theatrical performance for Wednesday the 30 and a Duchy council for first (Thursday)—therefore we could not go to Osborne before the 2nd (Friday). Either—if Fritz cannot possibly stay a day or two longer—you must give up Osborne or you would go with us on the 2nd to Osborne and leave on Monday 5th. I can't but think that dear Fritz could easily ask for two days prolongation of his leave, considering how much you wish to see Osborne, where your last stay was so spoiled, and how uncertain it is when you can do so, with so much ease again. Even then you would only have been absent a month.

I can't think, if you said we and you wished him much to stay two days longer (for you would certainly be back by the 8th) there would be any great difficulty or any objection; if, however there is that difficulty you must then give up Osborne for this time and hope to see it the next time. You can show this to Fritz.[2]

Family had rather an exaggerated idea of rank and the Queen is here combating the idea that these Napoleonic connexions amounted to a mésalliance. (See note to July 13, 1859, also.)

[1] Jane, Lady Ely. Lady of the Bedchamber to the Queen, and a devoted friend of the Queen of Holland.

[2] The Queen, trained by the Prince Consort in this respect, was careful to put things of this kind on paper, thereby saving time and the risk of wrangling.

Dear Papa means to go over to you presently to talk with you and Fritz upon those subjects[1] which you are so anxious about and which we discussed out walking last Monday so I hope Fritz won't have gone out. There is unfortunately so little time left before you leave us.

WINDSOR CASTLE, DECEMBER 5, 1859

I write again today as I don't like you should wait till Friday at Berlin without hearing a word. Here we are instead of being at Osborne! It began to blow and rain yesterday afternoon and we decided in consequence to go in the afternoon to be able to cross at high tide to avoid going round the Spit; but it came on to blow a gale, and I naturally declared I would not go, and indeed the Admiral telegraphed to say it would not do, it blew so hard. So we have now decided to go quite early tomorrow morning— and be able to go the shortest way; and if it should blow hard to wait at Portsmouth till it moderates—even to sleep at the Admiral's, if it came to the worst. Thus provided I go with a quieter mind than I should otherwise have done.

I think much, much of you, dearest child, and of the happy days we spent together, which have flown like everything else in this world—but which also like everything which is pleasant for the heart and soul remain engraved in our hearts!

We both forgot at the very last telling Fritz, that upon no account supposing the poor King were to die before a certain event[2]—must you see him after death. It might do a great deal of harm. Tell this Wegner who I am sure would agree.

OSBORNE, DECEMBER 7, 1859

It is best to struggle against these sad wrenches which unfortunately are our lot, and to look back with pleasure

---

[1] Prussian politics.
[2] The Princess Royal was expecting her second child.

and gratitude to what is past—and with confidence to the future! This dear visit was one of totally unalloyed pleasure; we, for the first time since your marriage could see and enjoy you both à notre aise, and can see how truly happy you are—and what a dear, excellent husband you have! That kind, warm heart and those very high principles, that strict sense of honour and of duty—and that great moral worth, which we know how to value and which dear Fritz possesses in so great a degree are what we value far, far above his position! I perhaps undervalue position too much; but to me the person, the character is everything! I flatter myself that Fritz will not complain of me as a mother-in-law, and does not think me indiscreet? I have so strong a feeling on that subject. On the other hand nothing could be kinder or more full of confidence than dear Fritz's conduct towards us. (Of your affection and confidence I do not speak, but you know how I feel it.) At first it is very trying to a mother to give up her child entirely to another, you will feel this much some day should you have a daughter and I suffered greatly in this struggle, but now this is quite, quite passed and I feel contented and happy—though I could wish we lived nearer and could oftener meet, were it but for a day. I own that the thought of Alice also liking and loving another and leaving us gives me a turn, but I trust that experience will enable me to take it much more calmly and philosophically. We had an excellent passage yesterday—and are very happy to be here, the air is delicious and really the contrast between here and "dear" Windsor—like night and day!

OSBORNE, DECEMBER 10, 1859

The report you sent me through the young Baron of the visit from Wied [1] naturally disappointed us though it would not be right to be guided by one hour's acquaintance with a young lady not quite sixteen. Girls alter so. Two years

[1] Princess Elizabeth of Wied. She was much canvassed as a possible wife for the Prince of Wales. She eventually married the King of Roumania and achieved some fame under the pen-name of Carmen Silva.

ago, she was thought charming; another two years may make a great change. Mariechen Hohenzollern[1] did not strike us last year particularly favourably—Fritz's impression of L. of H.[2] at St. Petersburg in '56 was not favourable at all; in '59 it is. God knows! where the young lady we want is to be found! Good looks, health, education, character, intellect and a good disposition we want; great rank and riches we do not.

I will now copy for you what Sir James says of his long conversation with Sir B. Brodie about baby's arm.[3] "He is of opinion, as it has been gradually improving that it will ultimately get to the natural strength. He made a suggestion which Sir James thinks likely to do good, although it will require to be carried out with tact, and by very slow degrees, it is—to tie up the right arm for a short time occasionally, so that the Prince may be obliged to use the left arm." As Sir James said, it will require some management not to irritate the child and perhaps it is rather too soon to begin the experiment. It might perhaps be deferred till after the teething is completed or at least the early teeth through. "Sir James will write to Dr. Wegner on this subject and perhaps your Majesty will write to the Princess".

This sounds reasonable and sensible, for I know that with any parts which seem weak from want of exertion—with eyes etc.—the way is to tie up the strong eye—to make the weaker one more active.

From the Princess Royal

BERLIN, DECEMBER 10, 1859

Writing of Princess Elizabeth of Wied, she says:

I do not think her at all distinguée looking—certainly the opposite to Bertie's usual taste. She is not tall and has an underset figure not graceful, very fresh complexion and nice white teeth, a great many freckles and a mark of a leaf on

[1] Daughter of Prince Hohenzollern.
[2] Louis of Hesse.
[3] The future Kaiser's left arm was damaged by the use of intruments at his birth. This was first noticed by Countess Blücher, but when it was too late to put matters right.

one cheek but which does not show much. She has not a pretty nose and rather a long chin. She is what you would call a strong, healthy looking girl—nothing more—she does not look very ladylike and head not well dressed—whether she is clever or not I cannot say—I could not speak enough to her. The mother is a charming person as you know though not at all natural, and exaltée.[1]

From the Princess Royal

BERLIN, DECEMBER 12, 1859

Sir Benjamin Brodie's suggestion for Baby's arm is nothing new. For more than six months past his right arm has been tied down to his side and his leg for an hour a day. He does not mind it in the least but lies on his back on the floor or the sofa kicking his legs about, and laughing and crowing to the ceiling as happy and contented as possible, but does not try to use the other one instead as he does not mind the restraint. I do not think he knows as yet that he has another arm as he has not much feeling in it. Wegner pricks his hand with a pin and pinches his arm to see whether he feels it, I think he feels just a little but not much, like a part that is gone to sleep. I suppose when he gets older he will be wanting to hold and grasp things, but not till then I think. He of course cannot crawl and never will as he cannot use his arm but Mrs. Hobbs thinks he will walk all the sooner for never being able to crawl. I am so pleased at the improvement of the muscle of the shoulder blade and neck which were so weak that they did not support the bones in the right place as Wegner says "the whole structure of the shoulder hung down" that is all right again now thank God, though he holds his arm quite tight to his side owing to the leading muscles underneath his arm being stronger than the outside ones and that produces a little crease in his fat little neck between his chest and his arms. We measured the arms, the left one is about a third of an inch shorter than the other, really not more although it may appear more as he keeps the left hand always tightly clenched when he is awake not when he sleeps.

---

[1] Born a princess of Nassau.

From the Princess Royal

BERLIN, DECEMBER 17, 1859

I have finished reading "Jane Eyre". How awfully interesting it is—before I had finished the second volume, I could hardly sleep—that horrid, mad creature with her strange laugh haunts one. Do tell Miss Hildyard I have read it, she said it would interest me so much.

OSBORNE, DECEMBER 14, 1859

After a number of directions about the Princess's second confinement the Queen goes on:

By the by, speaking of activity, only think that Lady McDonald[1] (who came into waiting yesterday) who is to be confined in two months' time (middle of February) travelled in deep snow and frost from the Isle of Skye here! She was from Wednesday morning till Friday morning travelling without stopping, in a carriage (part of the time in an open cart) the great Highland road being almost impassable with snow—then on to York—sleeping there three hours—then on to London—and yesterday here—and is not the least the worse!! Yet she'd been very ill of cholerine[2] a fortnight ago—and is not a strong person. Tell this Fritz—with my love, and that that this is what English ladies do and what they are none the worse for. This will be the 9th child she has had! but only four are alive!

Your account of Princess E. of Wied—is much less disappointing than from E. Stockmar's note, I feared it might be. I can only repeat what I wrote on Saturday. But the more you can ascertain of her character, her intellect, and her acquirements, the better. I am longing to hear what Adalbert says in answer to Fritz's letter. The young Baron sent me the photos of the two brothers[3] but did not put the names underneath; however we think the one with folded arms must be Louis.

---

[1] Wife of the 4th Lord Macdonald and daughter of George Wyndham of Cromer Hall. Lady of the Bedchamber to the Queen. She is not to be confused with Miss Flora MacDonald, see note on page 172.
[2] British or summer cholera.
[3] Of Hesse.

Only think to our great annoyance the Prince of Orange has announced himself for the middle of next month! Papa found it necessary to speak to Alice and without saying too much, just to tell her, that he had not had very favourable reports of him, and that we feared that he was in bad hands. It is very provoking he should come just now, though I conclude he can have no matrimonial projects at present, leading the life he does at present.

You will I know be shocked to hear that poor Lord Macaulay died suddenly on Wednesday evening of disease of the heart. The Princess will be much shocked I am sure! He is a great national loss—though his writings were perhaps rather partial, but so fine and so powerful.

1860

Dear good Leopold Hohenzollern[1] arrived safely on the 4th after a stormy and almost dangerous passage and came down here the day before yesterday and leaves us after luncheon today. I feel as if he quite belonged to us; Bertie is very fond of him and he could not have a better friend. Oh! if only he were not a R.C.!! It is sad when one sees what one would wish to have, one can't get it.

I had much talk with our dear, dear Countess—about many things. You will soon see her. She warned me never to leave Bertie a moment alone with the Prince of Orange; —fortunately (for many reasons) he will be gone back to Oxford before the Prince comes which will not be till after the 24th.

Continuing about Princess Alice the Queen says:

She is much admired for her really beautiful figure and extreme gracefulness and ladylikeness. I feel so anxious about her future. Do tell me anything you may observe or hear, or any indications even, about Abbat also—for it is well to hear and be aware of all. What I meant about the P. of O.'s not thinking of Alice, was, that he could not think of marrying for some time—three or four years—therefore Alice was too old for him. I can think therefore only of two or at the utmost three candidates. I hope the P. of O.'s coming here won't produce false reports and make people think Alice is engaged to him and thus deter others? That would be dreadful.

---

[1] Son of Prince Hohenzollern-Sigmaringen.

Our play on Wednesday went off extremely well and Miss Sedgwick acted beautifully in "The Hunchback".[1] Her voice is too beautiful. The Clarendons and their two really charming girls were with us for two nights—leaving today. It is such a pleasure to talk with him. Our visitor arrives on the 26th—and comes to us from the 28th to the 1st. We have seen a letter from a person standing in near relation to him,[2] who says; "he does not think of marriage; he is too young, and it would be a misfortune for himself and the wife he might choose"—so there is an end for A. I wish this should be known as it may encourage others.

WINDSOR CASTLE, JANUARY 18, 1860

You never answered me about the three following things:

1. If Immensee[3] would do for Alice to read.

2. About Lady McDonald's having twins, whom I thought you would perhaps send a message to.

And last but certainly not least about dear Alice's prospects, which occupy me very much. Have you heard nothing more about Louis of H.—or Abbat's views? Now you see we know that she has only these to choose from. Only be sure to tell people that the Prince of Orange's visit is entirely unconnected with marriage. I could not by the post make myself clear but it is the Queen herself who wrote what I quoted, to two different people here. Alice is quite satisfied (for we told her) and has given up all thoughts of him.

Of politics I don't speak, as I hear only far too much of them, as it is, and as Papa is quite absorbé by them.

How can people be so absurd as to say your hair is fair.[4]

---

[1] A play by Sheridan Knowles, which was first produced at Drury Lane in 1832.

[2] The Queen of Holland—his mother.

[3] By Theodor Storm, Prussian lawyer and writer. It was published in 1852.

[4] The painter of a miniature of the Princess Royal had said that her hair was "quite fair". This was not incorrect but her hair was darker

MEMORANDUM

I think as you will have soon a new Grande Maîtresse Fritz ought to know what position my ladies are in when I am confined. The Ladies-in-waiting merely attend every day, to ask if there are any orders—and Papa sees them, telling them to answer letters of enquiry and perform all those social duties; but they never interfere with me or the child, and I never see them till a week or so after, just as I feel inclined. Now, as Countess Dohna[1] has had no children and is quite a stranger to you, would it not be wiser not to mix her up with the personal details concerning yourself?

Countess Perponcher's case was quite different—she was almost like a mother to you and a dear friend from the day you left your country and had herself had children: but that is over and I think it is better not to mix up the ladies in these things.

But I hope that dear Countess Blücher will be in the house, and take my place; as I can alas! again not be there. I am more than ever anxious about this—as poor dear Sir J. Clarke, though much better, will I think not be able to be there, which is a great sorrow to me, and will I am sure be so to you both; but he said to me "If Countess Blücher is there then you may be perfectly easy." I therefore hope Fritz will settle with her, that she is to be there and to aid him in seeing everything kept right and straight. I shall then be quite easy.

From the Princess Royal

JANUARY 21, 1860

Many thanks for your memorandum, which Fritz has seen. It is impossible to draw a parallel between your ladies and my Grande Maîtresse in any way. The position is

---

than that of her brothers and sisters. Queen Victoria and the Prince Consort always thought the Royal Family would be improved by the introduction of a darker strain.

[1] A most difficult lady. She was appointed Grande Maîtresse to the Princess Royal.

totally a different one. All that Papa is able to do for you and to settle—is the business of my Grande Maîtresse, as it is that of all the other Grande Maîtresses of the other princesses. What is her duty, she must do. How far she is drawn into my "confidence" on that particular occasion as on every other will entirely depend on her character and on the circumstances. As I do not know Countess Dohna—and it is so very early, I cannot decide upon her position.

Countess Blücher is my friend—is your friend, a sort of mother to me—and as such she must have the first voice in my council—but I cannot put Countess Dohna in a false position by taking the management which belongs to her out of her hands; the consequence would only be jealousy, ill-will and discomfort on all sides. Countess Blücher's position with regard to Countess D. will be the result of the most natural causes and therefore offend no one—Countess Dohna not being able to speak or understand one word of English and my attendants at that time being mostly all English. Will you be so kind as to show what I have written here to dear Papa, he will be sure to understand what I mean and should I not have explained myself intelligibly tell you what I mean. Besides you can so completely trust to the tact and discretion of our dear Countess B.

Countess Dohna is old enough to be my grandmother, and whenever anyone was ill of her very numerous family—or any children to take care of she either always went of her own accord or was sent for—as she possesses the love and confidence of all those connected with her. I know that she has repeatedly attended her relations on similar occasions and is considered to be so very sensible and experienced. Voilà all that I have heard of her on this point.[1]

---

[1] The Queen replied to this somewhat severe letter "I quite understand what you mean about Countess Dohna, and the different position of your Grande Maîtresse to my Ladies. I have however no doubt that with Fritz and such a person as dear Countess Blücher all will go right."

Now let me talk of our young visitor.[1] He came on Saturday and stayed till after luncheon today—when he returns to Town. He remains in England for a month to travel about etc. Well I must say, that the impression he has made on us, is not unfavourable. He is very shy and does not talk readily of his own accord—but he pays great attention to what is said (I mean when Papa talks at breakfast etc. about politics and military matters etc.) which a nameless youth never does;[2] and is decidedly clever and intelligent. He is thoroughly done up and exhausted by his fatiguing journeys which M. de Rylandt[3] and Baron Bentinck[4] think have been too much and too fatiguing. He speaks all languages well; his forehead, eyes and nose are very good indeed. The teeth are well kept. But his great shortsightedness gives him a frightened and heavy look. He looks melancholy and said to me himself he had never known a home—and never has had since his poor brother Maurice died, a relation near him, I mean to live with. He is pleased and amused with Beatrice and would willingly romp with the little boys. We have not seen or heard anything which was wrong, and we are told that since Warsaw his conduct has been good. Poor young man he is much to be pitied and we would wish to be of use to him. He asked after you both.

From the Princess Royal

Our soirée went off very well, but I still feel the effects of it—it was very tiring. This week we shall most likely give another—but it is not settled yet. I hope you approve the programme of the music which I made. At all the other concerts they sing such rubbish when there is a concert—that I was determined that we should have some real good music.

---

[1] The Prince of Orange.
[2] Prince of Wales.
[3] Count Rylandt—the Dutchman who was bearleading the Prince.
[4] Adolph Bentinck—the Dutch Minister in London.

*They are all mad about Rigoletto and the Traviata, and will
hear of nothing else—Abbat, Marianne, George and I excepted. Princess Charles is frightened at the very name of
Mendelssohn—and the dear Princess said to Fritz Karl
while they were singing something of Mozart "You are looking soulful": the Prince is the only one of them that will
listen to the German music as well as to the Italian. Here is the
best of operas—and the largest and best of repertoires—it is
really a great delight—but the family those that I have
named excepted, the Corps Diplomatique, and the cream of
the society—think everything tiresome that is not Verdi!
Count Redern[1] says they only like it because of the improper
sujets. I do believe there's some truth in it. Tell Alice and
Papa about the difference of taste. Princess Charles thinks
Meyerbeer's music "si serieuse" and Weber "si ennuyeuse".
Meyerbeer wishes to send you his splendid "Schiller March"
arranged for the pianoforte.*

BUCKINGHAM PALACE, FEBRUARY 11, 1860

I was much amused to see your account of the musical
tastes of the family. I can't understand their not admiring
Meyerbeer, and Mendelssohn and Weber; Mozart I am
not always quite so fond of, as I think the instrumentation
so poor (it was so in those days). You shouldn't set yourself
too much against all Italian music considering the Princess's love for it and even Fritz's liking it. Some of Bellini's
are lovely—(Papa even likes many of them). Rigoletto too,
has some very pretty things, but not the Traviata or
Ernani.

BUCKINGHAM PALACE, FEBRUARY 22, 1860

On Tuesday we saw "Alfred the Great"[2] an extravaganza at the Olympic in which Robson[3] was charming; and
last night we saw at the opera where a very good English

---

[1] Chamberlain of the Court.
[2] *Alfred the Great or The Minstrel King*, an historical extravaganza
by Robert Brough.
[3] See letter of February 7, 1858.

company are performing—Meyerbeer's new opera "Dinorah" very well performed. It is interesting and full of poetry and originality—and dreadfully difficult in its accompaniment and time—but there are most beautiful things in it—though few equal to his great operas. Still it is very charming. Pray say something civil to him about it and about his Schiller March which I shall be delighted to have.

BUCKINGHAM PALACE, FEBRUARY 25, 1860

We have been four times to the play this week. On Thursday we saw a horrid piece of which I send the bill. The last scene is the guillotine with poor Robert Landry standing on the scaffold in his shirt. Unfortunately none of the actors were well suited to their parts.[1]

From the Princess Royal

FEBRUARY 25, 1860

Writing of the time which she spent with Prince Fritz she says:

I see him at breakfast and then usually not again till five —our dinner hour. I go out at one always—and his business is never over till two, except sometimes, then he goes out with me, usually however we take a ride every day, and then a good walk so I see very little of him. The evenings when we do not go to the theatre or to parties are very happy hours but they have been very rare lately. I think Fritz looks thin and rather yellow—he cannot stand hot rooms, as he loses his voice from them and keeps catching colds which are not of long duration however.

---

[1] Undoubtedly *The Dead Heart* by Watts Phillips, which was produced at the Adelphi in November 1859. The plot had some resemblance to that of *The Tale of Two Cities* which was published in the same year. In spite of what the Queen says the play was a complete success. Robert Landry was played by Benjamin Webster. The *Athenaeum* wrote: "As an artistic delineation his Robert Landry stands in the present day alone. There is no London actor who can compete with it in its rough strength and its intense feeling."

From the Princess Royal

We are all in a state of excitement about a most infamous book.[1] *It put me into such a state of rage I could throw it at the head of the editor, anything so mean, wicked, mischievous and abominable never was seen—and A. Humboldt is seen in a I fear a true light. Anything so mean, conceited, wicked and ungrateful never was seen; it is like Voltaire's nastiness, only more raffiné—no one is spared, all his friends and benefactors are turned into ridicule, dear Papa is not spared.*[2] *When one knows as I do that Varnhagen was a man that Humboldt looked down upon, and that he knew that whatever was written or said to him was published immediately, one sees how false a friend he was—how worldly and conceited. It is a good warning to princes to take care what they write. "De Mortuis— . . . " but it is hard to keep one's patience. The Princess is so pained about that book she can hardly speak about it; in short everybody is shocked and enraged.*

You will I know think very much of us now and have a very real longing to be with us here, now that darling Affie is back again. If possible the joy is greater than usual this time, as I was very anxious about him all Monday when it blew a perfect hurricane and knowing the ship was not in a good state, it kept me in a fever till in the evening the happy news of his safe arrival came to relieve our anxiety and gladden our hearts. Papa will have told you of his brilliant examination etc. etc. He looks well, though rather tired from his broken nights. Dear child, I feel so proud of

---

[1] The letters of Alexander von Humboldt to Varnhagen von Ense, the historian, published by the latter's niece.
[2] The Prince Consort was supposed to have told him that the Poles and the Irish deserved to be thrown overboard together—an observation which was naturally badly received in this country. To his daughter the Prince Consort wrote: "The matter is really of no moment, for what does not one write or say to his intimate friends under the impulse of the moment?"

the hardship he has endured—the way he has worked and when I think of ——! The very best there is wretched mediocrity. The joy of having Affie in the house is so great and alas! with —— it is such a contrary feeling! I dare not look forward! There is a dark cloud there—in spite of much good! Affie is writing to you himself and sends you a burnouse. There is that one great blessing in boys—they always still belong to their country and their home—they come back to it but the girls go away, their home and country is another's—and their old home can only be visited for a short time comparatively. Of course this is much worse in your position—if only one could see one another often were it but for a day—or if we lived in the same country so that there could be frequent short visits etc.—then it would be so different—as it is with people of my acquaintance here; that is so nice. If one of you girls were to be able to settle here—it would be very nice, but I dare say so pleasant a dream will never be realised, though I hope the dream will not be so far away or tied down as you are at present. However this can't be helped and, till now I have no reason to complain, nor do I—God knows!

I told Bertie the other day about your prospects, and this is his answer "I am glad to hear such good accounts of dear Vicky, and I trust that the event will pass off quite happily and not give you any anxiety as last time. She has not written to me since her return to Berlin from here (!!!)[1] so I am always glad to hear news of her." I think, dear child, he may more easily think you have forgotten him than he you. He is very affectionate and warmly attached to his brothers and sisters and home. He is showing the Prince of Orange about at Oxford today.

BUCKINGHAM PALACE, MARCH 3, 1860

I feel truly happy and grateful to have this darling boy —always so great a favourite, with his dear handsome, good face—and so like dear Papa—back again for a time! He is much improved and very clever and intelligent—and talks

---

[1] The Queen's exclamation marks.

so sensibly and pleasantly about all he has seen. To see him at the great dinner table, amuses me so much; he cerclés extremely well and everybody is pleased with my dear darling. May God bless him. Faults he still has, but with God's blessing and the care of our invaluable Major Cowell (who I am sorry to say is not well just now) I trust they will be got rid of and his excellent qualities—affection and great intelligence and cleverness will make him very distinguished some day I hope. He is very like dearest Papa—in so many things; his figure too is so like his. Papa has him now every evening—for an hour as he has had you each in turn and seems much pleased with him. His hands are very clean, a great improvement, but so rough and hard from work.

I am sorry to hear of this annoying book which one is grieved at as it shows poor old Humboldt in a bad light; and people often say and write at moments ill-natured things, which ought not to be recorded. Uncle Leopold speaks of it in his letter to me today and says "the letters are extremely ill-natured particularly against the poor King. I have known Humboldt ever since I was at Paris in 1807. I had always been struck with his extreme ill-nature against everybody." Tell this to the Princess. Still those things make one so angry as even if people do say ill-natured things of one, I think one would rather not know it.

We had a large dinner for the Prince of Orange last night—who was very dull—and positively rude to Alice, which is really very wrong; she feels it just as she ought, and it has settled her feelings about him—which never were favourable, I think. I fear that nothing good will come out of him, which I am very sorry for.[1]

Of politics I don't speak but I will just say that the Reform Bill has been taken very quietly. Alice was there;

---

[1] On the other hand the Duchess of Cambridge said that she was sure reports about him must be false because she took him to the play where there was an immense number of ballet-dancers. She told Lord Clarendon that the Prince remained "quite quiet" and Lord Clarendon retailing the anecdote added "as if she had expected him to jump out of the box". (*My dear Duchess*, edited by A. L. Kennedy, John Murray.)

Lady Clarendon kindly taking her, which flattered Johnny and my Lady vastly.[1]

My letter I fear will be confused and short—as we have a great deal to do, go to Osborne tomorrow (it blows today again which always makes me nervous) and have this enormous reception of Volunteers which I fear will last two hours. There are 2,300 officers coming—they don't kiss hands but are merely named.[2] It will be a curious sight. The best spirit prevails among them and there is immense excitement in the country and town about it. This is very useful. We have been a good deal plagued lately with tiresome and annoying business,[3] which unfortunately dear Papa will take too much to heart, and then it makes him unwell always—and affects his sleep. He really ought not to do so, because it makes one's life so difficult if one minds things so much as to make oneself ill.

Dear Affie is our great delight so full of fun and conversation and so full of anxiety to learn—always at something, never an instant idle—such steam power, such energy it is such a great pleasure to see this—but the contrast with some one else is sad. Affie delights in his lessons with dear Papa and Papa is much pleased with him and he is so handsome. Bertie has just come in for this reception and with such a scratched face from a fall he had out hunting yesterday.

The reception went off extremely well—it lasted from a quarter past two to a quarter past four without interruption, the people going by as fast as they could but all bowing

---

[1] On March 1, Lord John Russell introduced his Reform Bill, twenty-nine years after he had introduced the famous original bill to the day. As the Queen hints it stirred no particular interest.
[2] The Volunteer Movement, encouraged by Napoleon III's aggressive behaviour, started in the previous year. Tennyson's "Riflemen, form" caught the mood of the nation. The Queen and Prince Consort were enthusiastic supporters of the movement, and were criticised by John Bright for associating themselves too closely with it.
[3] The imminent annexation of Savoy by Napoleon III.

very properly. Lord Sydney reading out every name—
2,300! There were many curious—some pretty—uniforms.

OSBORNE, MARCH 10, 1860

Dear Papa lost his remains of cold as soon as he got here
and has I think forgotten his annoyances in looking at his
plants and listening to the birds, etc.

From the Princess Royal

BERLIN, MARCH 14, 1860

*Fritz is a little feverish again as he takes matters here
very much to heart which are so complicated, so disagreeable
that we are standing on a volcano. The P.R.[1] is not at all
well, very irritable and excited—I assure you one hardly
knows where one is the whole world seems to go round with
one. I have another annoyance—the accident about baby's
arm has got into all the papers here—and I never hear the
last of it. Of course exaggerations have no end—I must say
it vexes one—and Mrs. Hobbs cries and sobs—and takes it
personally. I have begged the Baron to write to dear Papa by
messenger and explain to him better than I can, the causes of
our uneasiness as to public affairs.*

Although this letter from Ernest Stockmar is here and there difficult
to follow—partly because it is translated—it gives an admirable
picture of the problems (as they began to emerge) by which
Prince Frederick William was faced.

MARCH 17, 1860

We are now living in the midst of a very serious internal
crisis, produced by the propositions of the Government concerning the organisation of the army. These propositions
intend to abolish the Landwehr in its essential character, to
extend the time of service in the reserve, to raise the yearly
recruitment from 40 to 60,000 men,[2] to augment the bud-

---

[1] Prince Regent.
[2] At this time the standing army was 200,000 and the Landwehr about
twice as large. The Prince Regent, who had a lifetime's experience of
service with the Prussian Army, wished to raise the yearly intake to the
Army to 63,000 men. The proposals disturbed liberal opinion.

get ostensibly by 10, probably by 13 or 14 millions; that is to diminish the rights, to do away with institutions to which great recollections are attached, to augment the obligations and charges. The sacrifices which are asked for, are so great, that even in a country like Prussia, which is so much animated by a military spirit and in general so well disposed towards the Government, a considerable opposition necessarily must have arisen. People asked, if these sacrifices are possible, and great financial authorities deny it. In fact the Minister of Finance cannot prove that the means will be permanently secured, and depends upon the hope, that the revenue of the state will naturally increase.

People ask secondly, if these sacrifices are necessary, and receive the answer, that a triennial service is not necessary, because the difference of 3 years compared to two with regard to the efficiency of the army, could not be so great as to compensate for the sacrifices connected with the triennial service. People ask 3dly: What for these sacrifices if we have no guarantees for a liberal policy within and a strong policy towards our neighbours without? If the army shall only be ready for mobilisation and keeping the sword in the scabbard. People ask fourthly: What is the tendency, the secret reason for making these propositions? And many voices answer? These propositions are the triumph of the military caste and of the feudal nobility, which desire to get a complete hold of the army and to eliminate the middle class element entirely from amongst the officers where it is treated with unfairness already now. At the same time these propositions are the lever which the reactionary party is going to apply to strong inclinations of the Prince Regent, in order to overthrow the present ministry and even the Constitution itself. And thus the question, difficult enough by technical, military and financial complications, becomes still more difficult and more complicated by the opposition of political factions of different classes. Triennial and biennial service seems to be the point upon which the whole question turns; and this question again is disappearing compared with the other: how many "cadres" for Regiments must we have and how strong must they be, for even all military men do not agree, upon that point, whether one year more would be of so great and overwhelming importance with regard to the individual and tactical efficiency of the army. What is now the position of the Government and of the Chambers towards these questions?

The Prince Regent has made the military propositions a vital question, by declaring freely to anyone who chooses to hear it, that, should they not pass, he would abdicate, and expressions like those have even found their way into the press. The public opinion does not believe that the Prince will execute his words. But the reactionary party seems to wish this, speculating upon the possibility of the Prince, his son, being carried away by his military ardour and bearing down every opposition if necessary Constitution, and Chambers and all. Happily the majority of the public does not believe in the possibility of a breach of the Constitution.

The ministry has shown great weakness by entering into the military propositions out of deference to the Prince Regent much more than from its own conviction. The greatest part of the blame is falling upon the financial department. But the ministry has also proved very clumsy by doing nothing at all to prepare the country and by gilding the pill in an awkward way. Before the propositions were published, they spoke of 5 millions, and now they say, that the new organisation will make the Landwehr what it was to be according to the ideas of its founders, Scharnhorst and others. Everybody feels the great weakness and inconsistency of the ministry, the want of leading ideas and of one leading will.

As to the Chambers, the house of Peers will support the military propositions and it has made a dexterous attempt to throw off its own shoulders the principal odium, and thus to remove one of the main obstacles to the propositions. The propositions for increasing the tax on landed property and doing away with the exceptions have not pleased the House. But the calculation of the Government is based on their acceptance and the sanction of the military propositions by the Lower House could hardly be expected, if the nobility in its selfish interest refused for its part the means for the execution. Therefore the Government have laid before the Peers a proposition which pretends to take from other parts the means to be raised upon landed property according to the former propositions.

In the House of Commons things are not so clear. The weak, reactionary faction is for the military propositions. But the liberal faction in general is for the biennial service. A conciliatory proposition is to grant to the Government what they request for one year, and to leave the rest to future times. At any rate the decision of this House cannot be expected before Easter, the members will come back from the vacations with increased desire of opposition for the excitement in the provinces is of course still greater than here. This is the situation. Its issue is uncertain, but it would be much to be regretted, if a question so difficult in itself, were decided by Coups de tête and Coups d'état. Reason seems to advise a compromise.

OSBORNE, MARCH 17, 1860

That iniquitous proceeding about Savoy shocks everyone and must take away all confidence.

BUCKINGHAM PALACE, MARCH 29, 1860

Only think how dreadful we forgot the Prince Regent's birthday!! It is the more provoking as I had been thinking of it all the time before, and then came our leaving Osborne and all these worries about politics; I am going to write and make some sort of explanation to the Princess so don't betray us. I am so grieved at all what passed on the birthday;[1] it is very distressing and unfortunate. I feel how painful for you all this must have been!

I send you today also a whole box full of dear Osborne primroses, as I see they gave you so much pleasure, and you shall have spring flowers regularly every messenger—from there or from Windsor. It is strange but even in the south of Germany—primroses are unknown. There is nothing prettier or fresher.

---

[1] Disputes about the Landwehr and the length of service.

We have a levée today. It will be very full I fear. Lord John's speech on Monday has had an excellent effect. It was immensely cheered—and I think that the exclusive alliance is broken.[1] The poor Swiss made a very bold, good stand. There is a Professor de la Rive[2] here—who has brought over their protest; I shall see him at the levée today.

From the Princess Royal

MARCH 30, 1860

Lord John's speech made me very happy; to feel proud of anything that happens nowadays is a rare occurence and one values it accordingly. One feels so downcast, sad and ashamed when one thinks of things here! We are behind the scenes and know why the right things are not done, and it is hard work to keep one's intellect clear enough to understand this net of petty intrigues and considerations in which we are caught and well nigh smothered. It is too long and too intricate to explain and so petty that I should be still more ashamed if you knew all about it still it is the only excuse for our conduct, of which you only see the miserable result. Sometimes I do wish I could be a man just for a few days! The Prince is much calmer and less irritated, and is kind and amiable as usual, I think whenever the Princess goes to Coblentz all will go better, you will think it wrong of me perhaps to say so—and you know how I love her—but for her own peace and that of Prince Hohenzollern and the Prince Regent the sooner she goes the better. Upon the whole the aspects of things in general is more cheering certainly than it was a week ago, and that is a comfort. Easter will do some good I hope and calm down ruffled spirits.

---

[1] On March 26 in the House of Commons Lord John used the phrase: "therefore I do feel that however we may wish to live on the most friendly terms with the French Government we ought not to keep ourselves apart from the other nations of Europe".

[2] A distinguished Swiss physicist. His countrymen were concerned by the French annexation of Savoy especially as Napoleon was believed to be intriguing with the Swiss Roman Catholics, and the claim of the Swiss to Savoy was not without foundation.

BUCKINGHAM PALACE, MARCH 31, 1860

Bertie came yesterday evening and has passed his examination very well—the Dean of Christ Church finding a decided improvement since last December. He is likewise grown, but not handsomer I think. Affie is, I really think beautiful (excepting Papa who is much more so)—but it is such a darling, handsome, round face. Bless him, he is such a dear, dear boy, and I must say we have not had a single fault to find with him since he has been here. How can you ask, dear, which day he is to be confirmed? You know it can only be on Maundy Thursday—(5th of April) if it is at Easter; you have all been confirmed on that day, and I can't think why you should be uncertain about it.

BUCKINGHAM PALACE, APRIL 2, 1860

Papa wishes you to tell the P.R. that his letter came by post, consequently we can guess whence the E.[1] got the letter. Papa says there is nothing which could do any harm, and if people keep spies to open and to read letters, they must expect to see what they may not like.[2]

WINDSOR CASTLE, APRIL 5, 1860

Two words on this eventful day. Your dear letter of the 3rd arrived just after the ceremony. It went off extremely well; Affie was much impressed—looked very much impressed and cried and was much moved when I kissed his dear, handsome face. To see the young sailor, inured to life, its trials, and hardships—its dangers and temptations, who has been in foreign lands and to the Holy Sepulchre itself— standing there before the altar was very moving to a fond

---

[1] The Emperor of the French.
[2] On March 30 the Princess Royal wrote to her father: "We have just received a piece of news which I communicate to you straight away, that the confidential letter which the Prince Regent wrote to you the week before last has been copied and in the hands of the Emperor Napoleon who sent the copy to the Prince de la Tour d'Auvergne here." The last named was the French Minister in Berlin.

mother's heart! The examination went off very well—though he was very nervous and spoke very low, and good Mr. Onslow,[1] who is one of the kindest and best of men—was dreadfully nervous.

He walked out alone with him in the afternoon—and remained in his room in the afternoon also this morning he remained in his room and merely came to wish us good morning before breakfast. The others looked for eggs. This afternoon we walked out with him; we dine alone—both today and tomorrow; tomorrow[2] at half past nine we take the Sacrament. The Archbishop's charge was a very good one—and quite to the purpose.

From the Princess Royal

APRIL 5, 1860

My cough is better but most obstinate. Fritz has a great deal to do now out of doors, and indoors I seldom see him before the afternoon now as he goes away at seven in the morning and does not breakfast with me. I do not think him looking well—so pale—and fagged and of an evening he complains so much of being tired. He says it is being out in the air so much and on horseback tires him, but I think he is not quite right again yet he must take care of himself—only it is difficult because if he puts a paletot or a cloak on in the carriage the others tease him so much, and, particularly the Prince Regent laughs at him, who never takes any care of himself and is always catching cold. Some gentlemen are really as conceited as ladies—in this family it is considered a sin to put on a cloak or drive in a closed carriage—and the worst of all is—is driving with one's wife. If you only knew how we and particularly Fritz get teased because we drive and walk, and go out of an evening together, particularly the Prince cannot bear it, and says it never was done here. All the princes drive in a carriage with two horses with their gentlemen and the princesses drive with their ladies and four

---

[1] William Lake Onslow, a naval chaplain, and afterwards Rector of Sandringham.
[2] i.e. Good Friday.

*horses. We are the only ones that drive and walk together;
even to church and to the railway station the others drive
separately.*

We took the Sacrament yesterday morning with dear
Affie, Alice, Bertie and dear Marie (Ernest is absent with the
yacht which is on a cruise) and several others. Mr. Onslow
(he is such an excellent man, so kind and devoted to Affie)
helped the Dean and read the greater part of the service,
and most beautifully; I don't think I ever was so impressed
with it before. Affie seems to feel his confirmation as we
could wish, and Major Cowell thinks that these three days
will have made a lasting and deep impression on him. He is
already so much improved since last August that I am sure
in another six months we shall find a much greater one
still.

Bertie is delighted to see you which I am very jealous of;
he is not at all in good looks; his nose and mouth are too
enormous and as he pastes his hair down to his head,[1] and
wears his clothes frightfully—he really is anything but good
looking. That coiffure is really too hideous with his small
head and enormous features. He is grown however.

This evening Haydn's Passion or The Seven Last Words
are to be given, which are so beautiful.

I am very grieved dear Fritz is still not quite well; but
what a shame to laugh at him for wearing a paletot; I hope
he don't listen to that, and really how can people blame him
for doing his duty in going out with you!!! If he did not it
would be very blameable.

---

[1] The Queen presumably means exposing the parting. The wilder,
more Byronic style of men's hair, fashionable in her youth, was disappearing.

THE QUEEN'S PAVILION, ALDERSHOT, APRIL 11, 1860

From this dear place I write to you today, and thank you much again for your dear letter of the 7th. It was a beautiful, quite warm day; we took a nice long ride in the afternoon, and in the evening had Haydn's Passion— very beautiful (though all oratorios even the very finest— (and I am particularly fond of them) affect my nerves if they last above three quarters of an hour and make me sleepy (I think from the slow time and the attention one naturally pays)) and it was extremely well done. By the by in your letter to Papa you speak of Bach's Passion, asking him if he ever plays it; we have no four handed or even two handed arrangement—if it is arranged as pianoforte duets— do send it us—for we should be very glad to have it, for our collection of sacred music is very limited.

BUCKINGHAM PALACE, APRIL 14, 1860

The sad news[1] came quite suddenly upon us—for up to the 10th he had been going on quite satisfactorily, his own Langenburg doctor having even gone away on the 8th. Imagine therefore how startled we were to receive this dreadful news without previous preparation (having more-over received a letter from Victor just while I was dressing with very good accounts) at dinner at Aldershot—a large dinner party!

We received telegrams announcing Bertie's arrival at Gotha, and there was a second to Papa; I saw his face change and he said to me "Poor Uncle Hohenlohe was much worse again", and I had better not see the telegram at dinner. I felt it must be the truth or very near it—and we asked no questions and tried to get through the dinner as well as we could. When Papa came in after dinner he called me into my room—and showed me Victor's sad and short telegram. Of course we sent everyone away and came back here yesterday morning when we at once went to poor

---

[1] Prince Ernest of Hohenlohe-Langenburg, husband of the Queen's half-sister, had died on April 12.

Queen Elisabeth, wife of King Frederick William IV of Prussia

King William I of Prussia and Queen Augusta, later Emperor and Empress of Germany

Grandmama—to whom we had telegraphed that the news were again much worse—and broke the sad truth to her.

We are out of mourning today on account of darling baby's birthday, but we shall wear it three months; six months (which we wore for poor Uncle Charles[1]) is the longest mourning here for a brother or sister and three months the shortest—brothers and sisters-in-law are here treated like a real brother or sister. The usual mourning here for an uncle is six weeks (I always wore it three months, which was unusually long) and I hope you will wear it that time (I mean six weeks), or at the least four weeks. You have but one other own uncle, and as all the fêtes are over, and you can have no difficulty surely in showing that respect to your poor uncle; for your own relations, you can I am sure do what is right; you could always take it off—for any occasions which the Prince might dislike to see you in mourning, but I should feel it much if you did not wear it for four or five weeks if six is too long for an uncle-in-law.

We enjoyed ourselves very much at dear Aldershot though it was dreadfully cold. The field day was very pretty on Thursday—in the afternoon we visited the camp, on Friday morning again going into the hospitals etc.—in the women's there was a poor woman in trouble, whose groaning made me feel knowingly for her—and two hours afterwards she got a little girl and was doing well!!

Sir John Crampton's marriage has astonished everyone, but many peers here have done the same and they were received and treated like anyone else if their character before had been good. Miss Victoria Balfe was made a great deal of by the Imperial family and people expected she would marry a Russian prince, but I am sure she has done much better. He is not young nor handsome and has quite white hair.[2]

---

[1] Prince Charles of Leiningen—the Queen's half-brother.
[2] Sir John Crampton (1805–86) was at this time the British Minister at St. Petersburg. He married the singer, Victoria Balfe, on March 31. This marriage was annulled on her petition in 1863.

From the Princess Royal

I should like to know about your mourning, although I cannot wear the same as you here I am sorry to say. We were only allowed to wear six weeks for our grandmother of Weimar, for the King we should only wear two months, for cousins one week. Therefore in this case the utmost I could wear would be four weeks which according to the curious customs here about mourning is considered a very long time. I should only wear silk—as crepe is the very deepest one can wear here. It distresses me much not to be able to wear the same as you, it is very painful in such cases not to be able to do as one likes. And the Prince and the whole family hate mourning as you know. You will understand all this is not my fault.

WINDSOR CASTLE, APRIL 18, 1860

I think, dearest, you should not judge George of M.[1] so harshly; he hastened at once with Feo to Baden, and he makes her as happy as possible, people have very different ways of taking and receiving bad news—particularly men, and one must not for that be too severe towards them. Take care how you speak of him to others—or Feo may hear it and be much distressed and hurt.

Dear Countess Blücher came yesterday—still with a very heavy cold. She sat with us in our sitting room for an hour after dinner (we dine alone until after the funeral—probably longer even) and I saw her for an hour before. She will be able to tell you much, and I trust quiet you on every subject. You don't once enter into any of my observations upon Bertie? It is such a proof of my confidence in you when I speak to you so openly about your brothers—that your silence seems strange to me. Poor Bertie, I pity him; but I blame him too, for that idleness is really sinful.

---

[1] Saxe-Meiningen. He was son-in-law to Prince Ernest of Hohenlohe-Langenburg.

Our letters about the mourning have crossed each other. That dislike of it I think positively wrong. Darling Beatrice looks lovely in her black silk and crepe dress.[1]

You remember poor King who used to be the nursery servant—and then Papa's garderobier etc.—and had to be put down lower and lower for drinking? He died this morning of delirium tremens! So shocking. Papa appointed Archie McDonald, his garderobier—Bray getting another place; he also tipples.

BUCKINGHAM PALACE, APRIL 25, 1860

Only think Lady Susan P. Clinton has gone and married Lord Adolphus Vane,[2] who drinks and has twice been shut up for delirium tremens. She told her father[3] she would, as soon as she was of age! So she did and he would not allow his carriage to take her to church even; and she was given away by her brother Lord Lincoln who is very worthless I fear. It is most sad, for I fear Susan will pay dearly for it and her poor father is heartbroken about it. Lord Adolphus is a good creature and not the one who did all those dreadful things,[4] but between drink and his natural tendency to madness there is a sad prospect for poor Susan. It took place on Thursday.

From the Princess Royal

BERLIN, APRIL 27, 1860

After a discussion of the shortcomings of her Grande Maîtresse, Countess Dohna, the Princess goes on:

. . . but where to find anybody else I cannot tell. I know plenty of charming ladies, but they are all married and have their husbands and children, homes and occupations, which they

---

[1] She was just three.
[2] Vane-Tempest, the second son of the 3rd Lord Londonderry.
[3] The Duke of Newcastle—a friend of the Royal Family.
[4] Lord Ernest Vane-Tempest. Perhaps the worst of those "dreadful things" was his attack on the actress's dressing-rooms in the theatre at Windsor. When the Manager objected, Lord Ernest threw him down a flight of stairs.

cannot leave. I know several widows, but they again do not possess the qualities I wish for—and are not sympathique. To have one that is not, is really not agreeable as I see daily with Countess Dohna, I am always more comfortable when she or I have gone out. An unmarried Grande Maîtresse will not do—one who leaves her family because she is unhappy at home still less—it is really very difficult.

The position of a Grande Maîtresse here is such that no one will take it who has a home—it is really a troublesome burden more than anything else. When a Prince marries here, it is considered a good opportunity of pensioning a quantity of people, that have neither homes or money—one is made Mistress of the Robes or Ladies-in-waiting, others Bedchamber women etc. The unfortunate princess about whom all these people are put is the one least thought of—if she be young, inexperienced and much alone and without her husband she is completely in the hands of these people whom she has no chance of ever getting rid of unless they choose to die or get married. Hence the gossip[1] about princesses in this town! Everybody else thinks themselves too good for a position of this kind in Court. It is the same thing with the gentlemen, the clever, able and agreeable one cannot get because they have all their occupations.

BUCKINGHAM PALACE, APRIL 28, 1860

Poor dear baby's little curl is charming—but why should it be cut off? They ought to be most carefully encouraged, for I suppose he is not yet to be clipped as a soldier?

Susan Clinton walked to church with her governess—no one but her brother there; no settlements, no trousseau, nothing and they say that at any moment he may go quite mad! What a dreadful prospect. The poor Duke cannot hold up his head, he is so distressed! I am so sorry one of your bridesmaids and really a clever, agreeable, handsome girl should do such a thing.

I had a nice ride yesterday. And we went first to the Old Watercolour Exhibition where there are some very pretty

---

[1] i.e. The sources of gossip.

things—also on Thursday to an amateur exhibition and the French one where there are some very fine and dreadfully expensive little pictures.

BUCKINGHAM PALACE, MAY 2, 1860

We are much distressed about Countess Dohna; I and the Countess[1] think a leave of absence when you are confined and there will be nothing going on, would be very advisable for else I fear she will be running in and out of your room etc. and making you ill and nervous and everyone else uncomfortable. As for a successor, the Countess is as much at a loss as you are, but you had surely better, after Countess Dohna's year is over—leave the place open till you find the right person rather than have another failure. What you say about needy gentlemen and ladies wanting to be about the Court, is the case everywhere. The nice ones are always more difficult to get.

There is a dreadful bon-mot about Lady Susan Vane (Clinton) "that there is a bet which of the two will be confined first!!"

I have begun reading Hypatia[2] to Papa—but I think it will read slowly aloud. I have so little time for reading which I much regret.

From the Princess Royal

BERLIN, MAY 2, 1860

Last Sunday we were at Potsdam for church and then a parade. We stayed the whole day there, and drove and walked about and enjoyed ourselves very much, the only place to which I have a real feeling of attachment here (besides this house) is the Neue Palais. I am always pleased even to see it— dear Fritz was born there, and we spent such a happy summer last year—I enjoy even the recollection of it. I have not one tender feeling for Babelsberg—and none for the Schloss here, although I was very happy there—but in some places

---

[1] i.e. Blücher.
[2] The novel by Charles Kingsley published in 1853. "Not a fit book to be read by our mothers and sisters", Dr. Pusey.

one feels at home and in others may they be ever so pretty and may one spend ever so happy a time there one has not a feeling of home. I saw the King again for the first time at Sanssouci last Sunday—he was being wheeled about in a bath chair on the terrace, and I stood at the window of the Queen's sitting room. I could only see him in profile, he seemed bent double, he had his cap very much in his face so I could not see much of him, but he did not appear to look ill or altered only very red in the face. When I saw him last (in August last year) he was very pale. The gentlemen say his face is always much flushed and heated in the afternoon. Poor man I could not look at him without emotion, to live on always on the brink of the grave, and to be such a miserable wreck is a hard fate.

My poor Countess Dohna gives a good deal of trouble, she is so indiscreet, takes offence so easily although she will not take hints. It is really very difficult for me sometimes and I heartily wish she did not live in the house.

I am sure you would be vexed about Countess Dohna— she really is a serious inconvenience, not to say more, to me, and her being in the house makes her still more so. There is something in her manner and in the very tone of her voice "que m'agace les nerfs" more than I can say—the worst of all is that she is completely under the thumb of all her relations here (Countess Amelie Dönhoff, the Queen's Lady-in-Waiting and confidante, and her brother Count Dönhoff, the Queen's Master of the Household who wanted formerly to marry Countess Dohna). They keep pushing her and asking her questions—and the Queen takes her part warmly. I know that Countess Dönhoff cannot bear me and she prejudices the Queen. It is very trying and very disagreeable.

BUCKINGHAM PALACE, MAY 5, 1860

Think how horrid—they say that Lord Adolphus Vane is already gone mad and shut up—and poor Susan had to take refuge with Lady Vane![1] Also that her brother Lord Lincoln urged her to do this awful act because (it is added)

---

[1] Wife of Lord Vane, afterwards 5th Lord Londonderry.

he had bills with Lord Adolphus! Can anything be more monstrous!

Since Thursday we have begun to go out again of an evening. Tonight we shall go to the Italian Opera. The Royal Academy is very good; there are many fine pictures but the gem of the whole Exhibition is your marriage-picture which quite lights the room up.

Really Countess Dohna is a calamity! No lady would be infinitely better. I would certainly give her six weeks leave of absence; you must not be afraid of doing this. You are the mistress—and it is positively bad for you to have such a woman worrying you. Certainly when our dearest Countess is with you she can prevent her coming in (during your confinement)—and you can give her plenty of letters to write—and let her answer all questions just as mine did. She seems to me to be a sort of vulgar Lady Charlemont![1]

Last night we saw at the Princess's (no longer the Keans)[2] a dreadful piece called "The Fool's Revenge"[3] adapted from Victor Hugo's "Le roi s'amuse" and "Rigoletto". It was extremely well acted by Phelps and Miss Heath, who was quite charming, so innocent and gentle. But they have changed the dénoucment and made it worse in point of moral. Your 3 sisters were at the opera last night. Tonight we give our first party (a Concert) of which I send you the programme—which, I think, you will like, and I am going over for a moment now—to hear part of the rehearsal. We have been quiet for so long that I feel terribly lazy about tonight's party.

You observed in your last letter but one very truly "in some places one feels at home and in others may they be

---

[1] An Irish lady who had been Lady of the Bedchamber to the Queen.
[2] Charles Kean had ended his successful term of management at the Princess's in the previous September.
[3] It was written by Tom Taylor. Bertuccio, the Jester, was played by Phelps and Fiordelisa by Caroline Heath, afterwards Mrs. Wilson Barrett. She sustained the part "with all maidenly grace and delicacy" wrote the *Daily News*.

ever so pretty and may one have had ever so happy a time there, one has no feeling of home." Now that is exactly what we feel about Windsor. No pleasure, no affection for anything there. Papa only last time told me how it bored him to go out there—how devoid of enjoyment everything was there.

Mr. Corbould bought today his picture in progress of "Dinah Preaching" which will be extremely pretty. He is more confused than ever poor dear, good man.

BUCKINGHAM PALACE, MAY 16, 1860

After a reference to various matrimonial projects in the Prussian family the Queen adds:

I think decidedly you are all better without any fresh Russian blood or Russian elements for which you and the country have suffered enough already.

After a reference to Princess Alice's marriage the Queen says:

. . . all marriage is such a lottery—the happiness is always an exchange—though it may be a very happy one—still the poor woman is bodily and morally the husband's slave. That always sticks in my throat. When I think of a merry, happy, free young girl—and look at the ailing, aching state a young wife generally is doomed to—which you can't deny is the penalty of marriage. All you say of Louis of H. is however very favourable, but what are his prospects? I hear no good reports of the young Prince of Orange. He shuts himself up and does not go out in society.

Today we have our first, great Ball which I dread. It is such a bore. I and Alice and my ladies will be in deep white crepe. Friday is "the Birthday"—a still greater bore.

BUCKINGHAM PALACE, MAY 19, 1860

Princess Waldeck[1] is pleasing and clever and has a very pretty figure—but such a plain, flat face. She brought me her four little girls the day before yesterday—the eldest

---

[1] The wife of Prince Waldeck and Pyrmont, the ruler of a small principality near Cassel.

five, the youngest twenty months—enormous, fine children but with cheeks like Eliza Löhlein's[1] children and literally no noses! That is a real misfortune.

From the Princess Royal

BERLIN, MAY 21, 1860

Princess Peter of Oldenburg[2] is here with her whole caravan. She has become such a bore, because she can talk of nothing else than the details of the interior of her nursery, or of Russia which is worse because she goes into ecstasies about everything that is Russian. She begs to be remembered to you. The cockchafers are on the increase; yesterday evening one was crawling in my hair and on my face—they scratch with their claws and are very tiresome.

OSBORNE, MAY 23, 1860

Now many, many thanks for your dear letter of the 19th and for Fritz's little memorandum. I must say the latter is very unsatisfactory and I much wish L. & H. of H.[3] were not coming for if he is épris of Maroussy it is most unfortunate that he should come here.[4] I trust that their journey at any rate will attract no attention, else it might do great harm. Altogether we must all be perfectly passive in these affairs—for one never can tell what may in the end be advisable and one incurs such responsibility if one is active in such affairs.

Now, dearest, I want to tell you something which I had only meant as a surprise, but I think confusions and delay might arise from it, so I rather tell it you myself. It is that I have got a beautiful little pony, quiet and steady and strong for your dear baby, and I wish to know when I should send him? Beatrice rides him and he also goes in the little carriage. Now I think he would be so useful for you now, to go

---

[1] Wife of the Prince Consort's valet.

[2] Her husband was a general in the Russian Army.

[3] Louis of Hesse and his brother Henry. See note on pages 201 and 219 (July 13 and Nov. 6, 1859).

[4] Prince Frederick William's reservations about Prince Louis are clear from this letter of the Queen.

in a little carriage, just as I used before the children's births, and also after you recover and can't walk a great deal. Now tell me have you got such a little carriage if not I can send you one just like mine, when the pony goes with his little saddle. In a fortnight or three weeks he could go. I can send somebody to Cologne with the pony and chair if you would send a groom to take them on from there? Lord Charles Fitzroy[1] looked out for the pony which is nine years old and we were anxious that nothing that went to Berlin should go which did not do honour to England. I have called him Tommy. He is very like the one I sent to the Prince Imperial. Faithful Jones is taking the greatest care of him and said he would do so well for "panniers" too—which foresight for the future amused me. I think you will like to have one which has carried Beatrice and been all about here. You know you generally began at 13 or 14 months to ride, and the exercise was thought peculiarly good for the children. I can send panniers later.

It is really too absurd and too great a mockery with that room; cela me révolte.[2] But you must not go yourself. Fritz told me in the winter that he would not let you go, and in your present condition it would be very wrong. I am sorry that you have got the photograph of Princess Charlotte's monument just now, for I fear you will be looking at it—and hipping[3] yourself about it which is very wrong just now.

---

[1] Afterwards 7th Duke of Grafton; equerry to the Queen.
[2] The Prussian Royal Family indulged themselves in somewhat morbid celebrations on the anniversary of the deaths of prominent members of the family—especially Queen Louise. The occasion to which the Queen is referring was the anniversary of the death of King Frederick William III. The family assembled in a room, converted into a mausoleum, for a religious ceremony, and then went to the vaults to lay wreaths on the coffin of the deceased majesty. On this occasion (June 7) a room in the part of the Neue Palais inhabited by Prince Frederick William and the Princess Royal was used for this purpose. One of the dead King's daughters—the Grand-Duchess of Mecklenburg-Schwerin—had amiably said that she would never set foot in the Neue Palais while the Princess Royal was in it. For that and other reasons the Princess Royal did not attend the ceremony.
[3] A rather unusual use of slang by the Queen—meaning "make yourself melancholy".

You won't of course go to see your room turned into the mockery of a mausoleum.

BUCKINGHAM PALACE, JUNE 2, 1860

Well yesterday morning Louis and Henry of Hesse (who arrived it seems on Monday but did not manage to get to Bernstorff's[1] till Thursday evening) were presented to us, and they came in the evening to a party we had to hear the Yorkshire Choral Union. They are gentlemanlike, natural and pleasing, not handsome, but have very nice, manly figures—and Louis has a very nice, good, open face, very like his mother. Heinrich looks delicate and is very like his father. They are shy but not put out. They dine with us tomorrow and come to Windsor from Tuesday to Friday. We also saw yesterday the young (sovereign) Prince of Liechtenstein, very handsome, very tall and dark, only twenty and with quite a smooth face; quiet, and very shy. He dines here tonight.[2]

Doctor Combe's book is, I believe, extremely good, and I shall read it—but it contains, as all medical books, "theories", which, though excellent cannot always be put into practice but Wegner ought certainly to translate it.[3] I have just been reading Tennyson's "Idylls of the King" which I think you would delight in. They are so very peculiar, quaint and poetic. "Enid" I think quite beautiful, and the latter part of "Elaine" very touching. "Guinevere" very fine—the early part quite sublime. You would make such beautiful sketches for them.

---

[1] The Prussian minister.

[2] His territory had close affinities with Austria; he did not marry.

[3] Dr. Andrew Combe, an Edinburgh doctor who was much admired by the Royal Family. The book is probably *Physiological and Moral Management of Infancy.*

Louis and Heinrich of Hesse dined with us on Sunday and again here yesterday, and stop till Friday. I like them extremely, so nice, natural, sensible, quiet and so unblasé—or foppish, and taking interest in everything. I think them the nicest young men I have seen for very long. You will imagine my agitation, not to do too much and yet not to neglect anything. Louis gets on extremely well with Alice, who is wonderfully composed and quite à son aise. I am quite proud of her. The difference between these young men and the Prince of Orange is very striking.

BUCKINGHAM PALACE, JUNE 13, 1860

Dear Papa has written you fully about Louis and Heinrich so that I have but little to add; in my two previous letters, I merely said how much I liked them and how much I hoped for a good result. Papa has given you his impression of their mutual feelings which it struck him that there were on Louis's and Alice's side which I can entirely corroborate, and of which I could give many little instances. One thing Papa however did not mention which I think you should know—viz. that in the course of conversation Alice and Louis came to talk of the Grand Duchess Marie and Maroussy. Driving home from Ascot with the Duchess of Cambridge, Philip and Louis we equally came to this subject and the Duchess who seems to know nothing whatever about it said to Louis "Is the young Leuchtenberg princess really so lovely?" upon which he quietly answered "Yes, she is lovely" and I said she was "ravishing". I feel with dear Papa the necessity and wisdom of being patient and passive, but I own with the best intentions it is quite impossible for me to help thinking of it constantly, first thing of a morning and the last at night. You, who have a very lively imagination, and strong feelings, will understand this, and feel with me. I put my trust in Providence to order all for the best but the uncertainty is trying. Alice is as amiable and quiet and cheerful as possible. The man who marries her will indeed have an enviable lot too, for she is so gentle and so very unselfish.

From the Princess Royal

The last trick the Countess Dohna has played us is the worst. Only think she actually went and wrote of her own accord to the Hausministerium to say the prayers were to begin for me without saying a syllable to Fritz or to me about it—either that she had written or was going to write or what she was to say and what day, we wished. What was our surprise when the Prince Regent told us last Friday (the 8th) that he had signed the order for the prayers in all the churches to begin for me on Sunday 10th (which they did accordingly) in consequence of Countess Dohna's "announce" which he supposed had been sent by our desire. Really I think I have never been so angry—the Countess Dohna is heaven-knows-where now—but she shall hear of it all the same. I really don't know what she will do next and all so silently and underhand, she never said a word to Countess Perponcher or to the young ladies or anyone. They would have prevented her writing.

BUCKINGHAM PALACE, JUNE 16, 1860

I think often (as I told you) of the important subject which engrossed me so much then—which we both wrote to you about in our last letters—and feel impatient, though I know I ought to be patient. Prince Frederick and Marie[1] came to the concert here on Wednesday and certain three nameless fat ladies[2] were rude and pushed before her; the second,[3] just arrived ne m'est pas du tout sympathique. Poor M.[4] I am very fond of.

---

[1] Probably Prince Frederick of the Netherlands and his daughter Marie.
[2] The Duchess of Cambridge and her two daughters.
[3] Augusta.
[4] Mary.

23rd Anniversary of my Accession

I yesterday paid dear Mary Biddulph[1] a visit, and she is so embellié and rayonné as to look like a young girl. The baby is a very dark—and small, thin (and entre nous) extremely ugly little thing—but I have no doubt it will become as nice as any other baby at 2 months.

I see by Wally's letters received today that Louis and Heinrich dined with you. How fidgety and nervous I feel about that I can't say. I am surprised Princess Charles of Hesse has not written to me, for I sent her a plaid shawl which she wished for by her sons and she has so frequently written on occasions! I suppose she will later.

We all think that this much dreaded meeting at Baden will end to be a great blessing in bringing all the German sovereigns together![2] I am to have 474 presentations at this my fifth and last levée today—and tonight we go to a concert at Apsley House. And it is so close today!

If you have anything to say about L. of Hesse—at any time—and are tired—don't scruple to use the pen of the excellent Baron—for he you know—knows everything.

BUCKINGHAM PALACE, JUNE 22, 1860

I am glad Louis and Heinrich were pleased with England and showed you the photographs. Louis asked (as she afterwards told me) Alice for hers, and she told him she had none, for that I had them all, and upon that he asked me for all; I think this is not unfavourable.

We heard last night at the Ball, to our great astonishment from Marie Leiningen, that her brother William[3] was coming over with Uncle Ernest (who is to arrive on Monday)—on a visit to her and Ernest! Uncle Ernest never

---

[1] Daughter of Mr. Frederick Seymour and wife of Colonel Thomas (afterwards Sir Thomas) Biddulph, Keeper of the Privy Purse from 1867. The baby was Victor Alexander Frederick Myddelton, to whom the Queen was sponsor.

[2] The meeting between the Prince Regent and Napoleon III to discuss "natural frontiers" for France. In Napoleon's eyes this, of course, meant the Rhine.

[3] i.e. Prince William of Baden, see letter of October 11, 1859.

mentioned a word of this to us. You will easily understand how awkward and embarrassing this is for us!

Every thing, thank God seems to have gone off so well at Baden.

We received yesterday the 2 Moorish Ambassadors and they also came to our Ball. You would be charmed with their appearance. They are entirely wrapped up in their white burnouses—and nothing can be more picturesque. The one, the 1st, who is not tall—is very handsome, the 2nd—the spokesman is also handsome—with a fair complexion and fine features, and a white beard. They are so like Horace Vernet's pictures and make one think of what the patriarchs of old must have been. I shall get their photographs.

Our Ball was fine but very hot, Rotkehlchen[1] was wonderful; he admired the reel, and then alluding again to the old customs said "Your Majesty also wears the Scottish dress in Scotland". Then he added, "It is such a noble and distinguished company, it is so magnificent." Little Hans[2] had the hay fever and did nothing but wipe his streaming eyes—and look in the glass to see how he looked. They are so wonderfully absurd—that really one can't help laughing at almost everything they say. Papa takes them off so well.

Today is the great review of volunteers and we live in trembling lest it should pour, but I think the wind is so high that it will hold up.

On Monday we go for 1 night to Aldershot.

From the Princess Royal

DAS NEUE PALAIS, JUNE 27, 1860

Perhaps the baron will have told you also that we saw the King the other day. I never saw so lamentable an object— Fritz and I were quite overcome, a human ruin—he is nothing else now—he was lying in his bath chair his left hand and arm which he has quite lost the use of as well as both his legs tied up in cloths—he did not recognise Fritz and me I think, at least

---

[1] Robin Redbreast. Prince Fritz Carl—the Red Prince.
[2] Not identified. Probably one of the Prussians in attendance on the Red Prince.

he showed no sign of having done so, he can neither speak nor look at anyone as he has lost the power of directing his eyes—he can only look up—and towards the right—he held my hand for a long while but without seeming to know it—you never saw anything so sad.

Your little letters of the 22nd arrived on Monday shortly before we left for dear Aldershot where we spent a very pleasant time and were most fortunate in our weather. It poured the greater part of Monday morning and was quite fine in the afternoon so that we rode about and saw the different regiments under canvas—who were well soused—but none the worse. But the ground is very damp. Yesterday morning we had a beautiful field day and the troops never looked better or marched more admirably, and it was poor dear General Knollys'[1] last day—I can't believe it, and it makes me quite melancholy! Aldershot without General Knollys, seems to me impossible. We shan't go there again this year. Philip went with us—Uncle Leopold went to Frogmore,[2] and Uncle Ernest joined us in the morning for breakfast. We came back in the afternoon.

The review of the volunteers was one of the most gratifying and striking sights, imaginable—and one which would have made your heart proud to see, and would have delighted and surprised Fritz. 18,000 there were and really splendid they looked and marched past like the finest troops! And held themselves so well, had such a proud bearing and were such fine men. Many of the best educated people, peers, gentry, artists in the ranks!

Sergeant Edwards[3] is adjutant to one of the regiments and rode past!! Immense crowds and immense enthusiasm, you should read the account in Monday's *Times*.

---

[1] The camp at Aldershot was the Prince Consort's idea, and started in 1855. Sir William Knollys was the first commander. He was later chosen by the Queen as Comptroller of the Household to the Prince of Wales, and Governor in succession to General Bruce.
[2] The Duchess of Kent's home at Windsor.
[3] Not identified.

The Princess Royal in the robes she wore at the Coronation of William I in 1861

The Coronation of William I at Königsberg, 1861 (after a painting by Thomas)

We were just in the same place as when the Guards came back— Rotkehlchen rode near the carriage and can tell you all about it. It must have made a great impression upon all foreigners and will do so on somebody on the other side of the water.

Dear Papa has written to you about Louis.

I can only echo what he says and can't overrate the great difficulty and embarrassment we may be placed in.

William of Baden is arrived but went straight to his sister;[1] I live in dread of some allusion or some attempt being made, which under the present circumstance would be very awkward.[2]

Your bas reliefs are safely arrived and are quite beautiful. You are a wonderfully clever child![3]

BUCKINGHAM PALACE, JUNE 30, 1860

I can't say how I admire your bas reliefs! I hope you will go on with those historical ones—they are charming. You should have them done in a galvanoplastic.[4] Won't you do your dear Henry 8th? or is he not romantic enough? Or Richard the 2nd? Your sketch of the nurse is masterly.

Dear Uncle alas! left us with good Philip at 10 this morning. They are so delightful to have in the house and such dear, kind visitors, so little gênant that we shall miss them much. Dearest Uncle too—is so interesting to talk to at the present moment, and so wise, that it was quite a comfort to have him here.

On Monday is that celebrated target-shooting and I am by some machinery to fire off the first rifle. On Wednesday we go to dear Osborne. Tonight we are going to see Gluck's Orfeo which is beautifully given, they say—at the Opera. Last Wednesday we heard Mr. Leopold Meyer,[5] who has

---

[1] Duchess of Hamilton.
[2] Meaning that this Prince would come, hoping for an engagement with Princess Alice.
[3] Her father also wrote and said "they are complete successes".
[4] The process of covering them with metal by galvanism.
[5] Leopold Meyer (1816–83). An Austrian pianist who gave many concerts in Germany.

played before you and I don't think I ever heard anything more beautiful than his playing and his touch. Papa says he never heard anything finer.

OSBORNE, JULY 7, 1860

Now let me give a piece of news which will interest and please you both. Alice Villiers[1] is engaged to be married since Thursday to Lord Skelmersdale,[2] a good-looking young man, 22 years old, well off and of very good character, nephew to Lady Derby by his father, and to Mr. Brook (of Corriemulzie recollection)[3] by his mother. The good Clarendons are much pleased. Constance[4] refused a very good offer, the other day because she did not know the person well enough and because she is so happy at home she is in no hurry to marry; Alice V. herself—for the same reason, wished rather to wait, Lady Caledon told me; she thinks Constance will, in the end, accept this same person who is much devoted to her. The account you give me of Louis and above all the little telegram from Fritz yesterday—are very significant. I leave to you to think how my mind and heart are occupied with it.

OSBORNE, JULY 11, 1860

Many thanks for your dear and affectionate letter of the 7th. This very interesting subject of your and Fritz's letters —is fully answered by dearest Papa and so I won't say anything more beyond telling you how much they interest and engross me, how much my heart must be agitated and filled with their very important contents—and how much touched we are by the anxiety you both show in this.

All you say about dear Princess Charles of Hesse is what I felt when I made her acquaintance now 15 years ago, and I have ever retained the same feelings for her and long to

---

[1] Lord Clarendon's second daughter.
[2] Afterwards first Earl of Lathom.
[3] This was the scene of a torch-light ball in the open air to which the Royal Family went on September 10, 1852.
[4] Lord Clarendon's eldest daughter.

see her again. The dear young Queen of Bavaria I also have always heard so much of—as Mariechen.[1]

The arrangements, you mention are indeed too horrid—and quite like an execution.[2] Oh! if those selfish men—who are the cause of all one's misery, only knew what their poor slaves go through! What suffering—what humiliation to the delicate feelings of a poor woman, above all a young one—especially with those nasty doctors. Do you know, I think some of the chapters of Dr. Coombe's book so horridly disgusting upon all those subjects, that I closed it with indignation and shut it up in the press! Especially the horrors about that peculiarly indelicate nursing (which is far worse than all the other parts).

I am very fond of Orpheus, and "Che faro" which is the song, you mention—is an old acquaintance and favourite of mine.

Countess Dohna's return is deplorable. But the next serious indiscretion (like about the prayers) she commits you should take advantage of and get rid of her. I was pleased to get a letter from Countess Brühl.[3] I hope she will write to me sometimes in English for I have seen how well she can write in it.

From the Princess Royal

DAS NEUE PALAIS, JULY 7, 1860

I am quite done up with the fatigues of these last few days[4] driving to railway stations to wait—and waiting at home for

---

[1] Queen Marie of Bavaria. She and Princess Charles of Hesse were daughters of Prince Frederick William of Prussia and sisters of Prince Adalbert. Princess Charles was Prince Louis' mother, Queen Marie was the mother of King Ludwig II.

[2] The Princess Royal had written: "I shall arrange my rooms and make all final preparations the same as a person does that is going to have her head cut off".

[3] Countess Hedwig Brühl, a member of the Prussian Court, who remained with the Princess Royal for many years. She was cousin to Walburga, Lady Paget, and her mother was a daughter of Field Marshal Gneisenau. In *Embassies of Other Days* Lady Paget tells us that the Princess had first seen her in deep mourning in church and chose to think her handsome.

[4] A family gathering of the Prussian Royal Family.

visits—driving backwards and forwards to Sanssouci for dinner, tea and visits—dressing and undressing which is the worst of all—as the result is so distressing to look in the glass and behold oneself a monster.

OSBORNE, JULY 21, 1860

Meriel Lyttelton was married on the 19th.[1] That Major Baring[2] who lost his arm at Alma, is, I hear, to marry Sir J. Graham's youngest daughter. We give our rural fête on the 27 inst this year.

Lord Clyde is arrived and we hope to see him very soon. Poor Fritz Strelitz[3] is coming here to W. Cowes to bathe again!

The Crown Princess of Württemberg—to Ryde next month, but we shall be gone I hope.[4]

William of Baden left last night. He was wonderfully discreet. I am, naturally very impatient for an answer from Fischbach.[5]

Mr. Leitch has been here for 10 days and more giving us all lessons and making lovely sketches.

OSBORNE, JULY 25, 1860

Thousand, thousand good wishes, blessings and congratulations![6] Everything seems to have passed off as easily (indeed more so) as I could have expected though I always thought it would be very easy, and totally different to the last time, and the darling baby—such a fine child. I am delighted it is a little girl, for they are such much more amusing children. This will be another Beatrice. How I

---

[1] To Mr. J. G. Talbot, a distinguished member of the Bar and one of the burgesses for Oxford.
[2] Charles Baring, afterwards a general in the Army.
[3] Prince Frederick of Mecklenburg-Strelitz, the husband of Princess Augusta of Cambridge. He was virtually blind.
[4] Daughter of Czar Nicholas I—a relationship which explains the Queen's comment.
[5] A large property in Silesia which belonged to Prince Louis's mother.
[6] The Princess Royal gave birth to a daughter on July 24.

long to hear who she is like and what she is to be called! Here the joy was so great, dear Grandmama, and good Sir James being still here too! The children had a half holiday and cooked at the Swiss Cottage. To dear Alice it was a very eventful day, as Papa told her all, and by Fritz you will hear how joyfully these news were received by the dear child.[1] We took off our mourning (which we should have done only today)—and all drank the new baby's health. I am very glad that you escaped all the visits of the family; they will probably be gone before you could see them. Our fête takes place on Friday, and your's and baby's healths will be specially drunk.

I send you a photograph of a face you will have missed much all this time and who is much occupied with you.

OSBORNE, AUGUST 1, 1860

How delightful the accounts are of you and baby! Many, many thanks for that charming, tasteful locket and the dear hair. The dear little nameless lady seems to have a great quantity of it! How I long to see her! I assure you I am not at all offended at hearing her called like me, for though I am no admirer of babies generally—there are exceptions (besides all of you were always thought like me when born) —for instance Alice, and Beatrice were very pretty from the very first—yourself also—rather so—Arthur too—though not so much so as the 2 first named. Bertie and Leopold— too frightful. Little girls are always prettier and nicer (Arthur alone making an exception).

I send a most interesting description of the confirmation of Princess Elizabeth of Wied, they say it was most striking. Only think that Maroussy arrived in England on Friday! What does that mean?

---

[1] Presumably the Prince explained to her about the birth of children. The reference to her receiving the news "joyfully" no doubt means that she was pleased to know that on this occasion her sister's labour had been easy.

BUCKINGHAM PALACE, AUGUST 6, 1860

You are right in supposing I don't admire the name of Charlotte,[1] but I expected from what you had once told me, —she would be called so, and it is dear Cousin Charlotte's and poor Princess Charlotte's names—and I shall love it for my dear little granddaughter's sake. We quite understand your not asking us to be sponsors, which moreover is not the custom here each time. Grandmama has only been twice to our children. I regret baby has not got Louise amongst her names—on account of Queen Louise.

HOLYROOD, AUGUST 7, 1860

Speaking of your little darling's names—let me only say that I do hope one of your daughters, if you have any more, will be called Victoria, so that there may be the 4 generations of Victoria.[2]

I have got on nicely with the bracelet of great grandchildren for dear Grandmama.

6 O'CLOCK—Just returned from the review which was a most splendid sight—far exceeding London for naturally with such scenery as Arthur's Seat, it must be so; and while I am writing there is the din of endless bands passing by— as at Aldershot (and as we had it in London). Imagine Arthur's Seat one mass of human beings to the very top and immense enthusiasm—which the Scotch have in a much more violent way than the English.

Dear Lord Breadalbane came by at the head of his splendid Highlanders and was much cheered. Dearest Grandmama was with us the whole time in the carriage from $\frac{1}{2}$ p. 3 till near 6—and enjoyed it so much. She had not been with me to anything of that kind (the Victoria Cross excepted) and she was so delighted.

[1] The child's full names were Victoria Elizabeth Augusta Charlotte and she was called by the last.
[2] The Queen means not only christened but called by the name— Victoria.

I write to you from this dearly loved spot where we should be so happy to see you all and where please God! we shall see you next year—to thank you for your dear little note of the 6th—which I received yesterday morning. We had a good and short journey on Wednesday—the railway going to Aboyne so that we had only 2 hours posting in sociables. They have here also had very wet cold weather—so that the snow of the whole winter is still lying on Lochnager and Ben-na-Bhourd and though the air out is mild and pleasant the house is unusually cold, but open windows and fires will I hope set all right. The heather is not yet out —but the bell heather and french heather of which I send you 2 little bits are most beautiful, in brilliant patches, as well as every sort of wild flower you can imagine! Truly beautiful. The ground in front of this house has been levelled and the effect is charming. Papa must explain all this to you.

I must not omit telling you of Lady Emma Stanley's[1] intended marriage, to Col. P. Talbot,[2] a charming person— a long attachment, but they will be poor. He must be 18 or 19 years older than her.

BALMORAL CASTLE, AUGUST 14, 1860

Many thanks for your dear letter of the 10th which I got this morning. I am so delighted that my gifts to baby and yourself have given satisfaction and pleasure. We are very sad and anxious about poor dear Aunt Julie.[3] I was terribly low yesterday, for though I have only seen her twice—and not for 15 years—she is dear Grandmama's only sister—was up to this illness as active as a girl, and though she is within 6 weeks of her 79th birthday—we looked upon

---

[1] Daughter of Lord Derby, the Prime Minister.
[2] Sir W. P. M. Chetwynd Talbot, Serjeant-at-Arms, House of Lords.
[3] The Duchess of Kent's elder sister; she had married the Grand-Duke Constantine of Russia in 1796, and separated from him in 1802. According to King Leopold the Grand-Duke was dreadfully *taquin*— "given to teasing". Her private life is believed to have been somewhat disreputable.

her as strong and still full of life. She had a sort of paralytic stroke, I think on the 5th—which we only heard of from Uncle Leopold on Thursday 9th. Then she seemed to be out of all danger; but yesterday we heard by telegraph that the speech was affected indeed "perte de parole" and difficulty of swallowing though not loss of consciousness. This is very bad. To have to send these sad news to poor Grandmama and to be unable to be with her—and near her, has distressed me dreadfully and thrown such a gloom over every thing here! If only nothing happens before poor Grandmama's birthday! It would be so sad! Victor is with her and Ernest and Marie will arrive there the day after tomorrow.

I was not either so much surprised at dear Wally's marriage, but very sad for you. I am delighted she should marry an Englishman and one in so important a position and sure to get on in the world.[1]

From the Princess Royal

AUGUST 10, 1860

I am so relieved you are not vexed at the baby's being called "Charlotte". I feared you and Papa would not like it—but I wished it on account of cousin Charlotte; and in remembrance of Princess Charlotte—Fritz wished it on account of Charlotte of Meiningen[2] and the Prince Regent wished it also. The Queen was so much displeased at the name that it made her still more cross and ungracious the two times she has been to see me. Altogether I just wish you could have heard the exclamations of all my relations when they have come to see me. I wish you could have stood behind a screen—and heard all the senseless remarks and seen the upturned eyes and shrugging of shoulders at everything I did and had on—they were not satisfied with anything—it is a hard trial to one's patience sometimes; when we meet I will make you laugh with all the things that have been said to me.

---

[1] Sir Augustus Paget—a successful diplomat.
[2] The daughter of Prince Albrecht and wife of the Duke of Saxe-Meiningen.

BALMORAL, AUGUST 17, 1860

We got the news of the christening being well over at 3 here! It was the finest day we had had, warm and beautiful, and bright—with splendid lights. In the evening we drank little Charlotte's health (a name which astonishes people here very much—) and prayed that every blessing might rest on her little head!

Victor and Ernest and Marie are with dearest Grandmama. All her prints and photographs are decorated with wreaths of flowers.[1]

BALMORAL CASTLE, AUGUST 21, 1860

Poor Marianne, I pity her much! I prefer the name of her baby to your's.[2] Cousin Mary writes: "I cannot at all reconcile myself to the name Fritz and Victoria have chosen for their baby and only trust they will never suffer Charlotte to degenerate into Lotte, and worse than all Lottchen."

BALMORAL CASTLE, SEPTEMBER 8, 1860

We had a very gay Ball last night, and I, old woman, danced a great deal and I do so enjoy reels.

From the Princess Royal

PUTBUS, SEPTEMBER 16, 1860

I am going to an evening party to the old Fürstin Putbus this evening, I don't admire (sic) having anything to do with her.[3] She has such a shocking reputation but this place belongs to her and she has been most civil and kind all the time I have been here so it can't be helped. She is one of the handsomest old ladies I have ever seen, and was quite beautiful, her daughters are very handsome and all but one, as bad as herself, but her grand-daughters I am very fond of; they[4] are almost the only ladies at Berlin that I know really well and

---

[1] It was her birthday.
[2] Louise, afterwards Duchess of Connaught.
[3] Louise, Princess de Putbus. She was born in 1784.
[4] i.e. The grand-daughters.

see much of, they are both here now and go out with me
every day, one is the lovely Countess Pourtalès of whom
Winterhalter painted a beautiful picture (two indeed) and the
other, her cousin and sister-in-law Countess Lottum, whom
Winterhalter has also painted a lovely picture of—the
photograph of which you know I think. These two ladies are
extremely pretty I don't know which I admire most. I can
hardly take my eyes off them, how delightful it must be to be
pretty—I should look in the glass all day long if I had that
blessing!

PALAIS AT BRUSSELS, OCTOBER 15, 1860

The Queen and Prince Consort had been to visit the Princess Royal
in Germany.

I am happy to be able to write to you again today, but I
am still very weak and shaky.

I arrived so unwell here on Saturday as to make me fear
I was going to be very ill; I could not leave my room—and
remained in my apartment (a charming one belonging to
Leopold and Marie) all day yesterday. I was very unwell all
Friday at Coblentz and could hardly hold up my head. But
now let us not think of that—but of the blessed, happy time,
we all spent together at dear old Coburg—that delightful
fortnight, except the dreadful episode of Papa's accident,
which we could enjoy so peaceably and which was so
gemütlich and quiet.[1] It is indeed our second home, and a
beloved and happy one to which I wish you all to cling with
love and affection.

Dearest child, it was great happiness to see you and be
with you, to see you both so happy—and to see that dear,
darling, little love, that sweet little boy—whom I do so
dearly love—the parting from whom gave me quite a pang.
I do assure you we are both so fond of that little cherub,
who is such a very charming, engaging little thing. God
bless him! I am sure I shall be quite as foolish about him

---

[1] The Queen was returning from Coburg and her first meeting with her
grandson. The horses in the Prince's carriage had run away, and he
only escaped serious injury by jumping into the road.

and "little Ulizabeth"—as all grandmamas are supposed to be. What a pleasure it will be d.v. to have them with us next year!

Was it not very cold on Friday night travelling?

The poor dear Princess looked so poorly and unhappy—I was grieved to see. Do both be all kindness and affection to her. She is in great need of it, for believe me, she is very unhappy. There where she ought to meet with most affection and in the quarter whence is it most valued, she does not find it! Both, she and the dear Regent were all kindness to us and do pray say everything most kind and affectionate from us to him and how much I trust all will go off satisfactorily at Warsaw.[1]

Here dear uncle and the cousins are all kindness and attention and we are very comfortable. The little children[2] are very pretty particularly the dear little girl who is very like her mama. The poor little boy looks pale from teething.

WINDSOR CASTLE, OCTOBER 20, 1860

From this dull old prison, which however I was not sorry—once we had left Coburg and parted from you—to arrive at—do I thank you for your two dear letters of the 14th and 17th. Alice has I think told you all about our voyage—which was not pleasant—but which—all things considered was better than might have been, and most fortunate we did come over when we did—for I don't think we could have crossed since!

But I own I was not in a sentimental mood about the yacht, considering how much motion there was. The parting from you was indeed very sad! I saw how upset you were to see us go—and felt much so myself! Here we have found all well, Beatrice is my darling, but she is fast, alas! growing out of the baby—is becoming long-legged and thin. She is however still most amusing and very dear.

---

[1] The meeting between the Prince Regent and the Emperors of Austria and Russia following Napoleon's claim for a revision of frontiers on the Rhine.

[2] Of Leopold and Marie, Duke and Duchess of Brabant.

Darling William, I feel indeed, as if he quite belonged to us—as much as our own children. He is such a little love, and such a darling, so pretty and so intelligent.

I am glad you have begun riding—as I am sure it will do you good.

Dear little baby—it is really too stupid and foolish of Wegner not to allow her to travel.[1] So many German people have told me that they always travel about with their babies. It seems really as if he had done it on purpose to disappoint me. You must not ask him again.

Today is Wally's marriage. I hope it went off well.

WINDSOR CASTLE, OCTOBER 24, 1860

Many, many thanks for your dear letter of the 20th written just after the marriage when you must have been so busy. I thought much of the wedding and hope they will be happy. I am all impatience to see them, and receive my new subject. Hedwig Brühl[2] has given us a very nice account of the event and Lord Bloomfield writes quite pleased. There is a chance of your losing him—but not of getting Mr. Paget.[3] I can't say more now and beg you not to mention it.

Now I must tell you about the Grand Duke Michael[4] and Cécile. They came for luncheon on Monday and stayed till yesterday, after luncheon. Dear Marie L. came with them. They were both most amiable and friendly. Cécile is as unlike her sister as possible—but Marie says her features are like their brother Carl. The features are fine but the figure is not good and she stoops and bends which spoils her very much; she is very good humoured, merry and agreeable and clever, and the sisters were so happy together. But I think our dear Marie both prettier and more distinguée looking.

---

[1] She had not been allowed to go to Coburg with her parents.
[2] Countess Hedwig Brühl, who succeeded the bride as one of the ladies to the Princess Royal.
[3] Lord Bloomfield was Minister at Berlin, and was appointed Ambassador to Vienna on November 22, 1860.
[4] Fifth son of the Emperor Nicholas I. He married Princess Cécile of Baden, sister to the Princess of Leiningen.

The Grand Duke is really quite charming—so mild and gentle and gemütlich—always speaking German, and so unlike his brother Constantine and his sisters. We were charmed with him, and I hear wherever he goes—high and low, love him. He is not handsome, but very pleasing looking—but looks very delicate, and so I think does she. Strange and sad to say it is—that all these poor princesses abroad (Ada is another instance for she looks so thin and drawn) never recover the treatment they receive in their confinements and wither away! Cécile looks also very delicate. It really is a crying evil, and shows how right I was in insisting on your not being treated in that way. I am sure you are a contrast to these delicate, coddled ladies! They say that the little boy of Cécile's is lovely. Unfortunately I could not see him.

I have inquired and Miss Dickson[1] will be charmed to go to Berlin. When should she arrive? She can't well leave before next month which to be sure is near at hand. She does paint young children quite beautifully—and you could superintend it. She could do two—a full length, and merely a head, and then by that time "little Elizabeth" could also be done.

I want very much another photograph of you—without a bonnet and the head please, not larger than those of Alice and me by Mayall.[2] I am having two bracelets arranged with the photographs of you all and the one of you with the bonnet is too large. I want it as soon as you can get it done—and wish to buy the plate. Pray don't forget it, dear. It is for your dear Aunt Alexandrine's birthday (6th Dec.) and for Alice for Xmas. Let the Baron answer about Miss Dickson by next messenger as she is waiting to know and about the photo.

---

[1] Annie Dickson, who painted miniatures of the royal children.
[2] J. E. Mayall, a leading London photographer.

Your dear letters of the 23rd from the Hubertus Stock[1] reached me yesterday and I thank you much for it, as well as for the little view. The house is just like a pretty one Uncle Ernest has near Rheinhardtsbrunn called die Jägersruhe.[2] I can well imagine how you must have enjoyed it. Why did you not stay longer, and could you not go there again? Change of air and scene is so good for you both and the quiet and real country life still more so.

From the Princess Royal

DAS NEUE PALAIS, OCTOBER 27, 1860

"The Woman in White"[3] *is fearfully interesting. I am reading it on General Grey's recommendation. Do tell him I can hardly get away from it.*

From the Princess Royal

DAS NEUE PALAIS, OCTOBER 31, 1860

We shall not stay here longer than a day or two, but I cling to my rides and walks with Fritz as when we are at Berlin he has hardly ever leisure to go with me, and walking round and round the horrid old Tiergarten[4] with one of my ladies—two footmen at my heels to keep off a troop of dirty little boys is no great amusement, and this will be my lot till May or June next year. I shudder at the thought.

From the Princess Royal

BERLIN, NOVEMBER 2, 1860

I never saw the Prince in such a state,[5] he does not complain or give any outward sign of his grief—but he looks

---

[1] A hunting lodge close to Berlin.
[2] The hunter's rest. This was near Gotha.
[3] By Wilkie Collins and published in this year.
[4] The large public park separating Unter den Linden from Charlottenburg.
[5] His sister the Empress Dowager of Russia had died on November 1. He had always been devoted to her. She was his confidante in youth when he wished to marry Princess Elizabeth Radziwill. The marriage was eventually forbidden by his father on the grounds of inequality of birth.

*broken down and aged by several years—Fritz said he never
saw his father so before—and of course it grieves him dreadfully. I knew it would be so because the Prince Regent loves
no one as he loved his sister—and he was saying yesterday
that since he could remember he had never been separated
from her longer than a year and a half—either she came
here or went there or they met somewhere, she had been his
friend, his companion, almost a mother to him although she
was not much older and to know her gone is a severe shock to
him. I am sure it would have quite touched you to have seen
how he felt your kind sympathy expressed in your telegram
to Fritz last night which I translated for him, he has such a
feeling heart you know and any mark of friendship at such a
time he values much. Prince Albrecht is quite prostrate, does
nothing but sob and cry like a child, poor man. Prince
Charles as if nothing had happened joking as usual. I do not
believe that horrid man has a heart at all—laughing and
joking when he heard of his sister's death, whom he professed
to be so fond of.*

WINDSOR CASTLE, NOVEMBER 3, 1860

We feel much for all the family (the older generation)
this death of the poor Empress Dowager for it will be the
first link of the chain which is broken, and that must be a
great shock to all. Besides they adored her! You all know
what an influence unfortunately she had over them all—
and how they considered her smallest wish law! The
world was made subservient to all she wished; every
earthly object she possessed, which could render life (in a
worldly point of view) agreeable, and now all is gone! Still
she was a kindhearted woman, a devoted wife and loving
mother and I am sure the young ménages at St. Petersburg
will feel her loss greatly.

I can well understand your dislike to go to Berlin; but
could you not drive out further and walk sometimes on the
Chaussées outside the town? If we had not that despised
garden at Buckingham Palace we should be just as badly in
fact worse off than you—for we can't walk anywhere in
London without being mobbed.

We drove over with Marie and Ada (we like Fritz Holstein[1] very much, he is so sensible and clever and you can talk to him about anything) to Clifden which unfortunately was en papillotte; the Duchess[2] came down from London on hearing from her housekeeper we were going over; and today we have been with dear Marie to New Lodge,[3] (the Van de Weyers) which is quite charming.

I shall certainly read "The Woman in White".

I hope Louis will brush up his English as much as he can before coming; nothing pleases here—more than speaking English with people—be it ever so little.

WINDSOR CASTLE, NOVEMBER 7, 1860

As regards Abbat we should be very happy to see him in England and the same with the Weimars but do you think they expect all to be invited to the Palace? This never used to be the case except in some exceptional cases; and we have so much to do (as you can tell everyone from your own experience) that to have all one's leisure time taken up by visitors is really more than we can undertake. The Prince R.[4] himself did not come to the Palace in 44 (he came for a few days to Windsor) nor in 48; Nemours did not (nearly connected as he was) before his marriage nor the heirs to thrones or any of the Russian princes. Neither the Duke of Genoa[5] etc. In short very few except crowned heads or people we specially asked. But if they came of their own accord—and lived in an hotel—they would be much more independent, and we should all the same see them very often, and horses and equipages would be at their disposal.

---

[1] Heir to the Duke of Holstein who had married Ada—Princess Adelaide of Hohenlohe-Langenburg—the Queen's niece.
[2] Of Sutherland.
[3] At Windsor. M. Silvain van de Weyer was the Belgian Minister in London.
[4] Prince Regent of Prussia.
[5] Ferdinand, brother of Victor Emmanuel II. He visited England in 1853.

We hear today Louis is to arrive on the 24th. Now that it is settled, I must own, I am a little alarmed and wish it was deferred for some time! It seems so lately that I went through the same with you, and to begin all over again alarms and agitates me! We are so quiet and peaceful now—that to take a stranger into the family anew is a great undertaking! I hope you will tell him to look to Papa for everything, for advice and guidance etc. I am anxious to be as much hors de l'affaire as I can.

WINDSOR CASTLE, NOVEMBER 10, 1860

Dear Wally looking like a rose and her amiable and sensible husband came here yesterday—and stay till Monday. She is in great, good looks. Poor Lord Cawdor[1] died on the 17th to our great regret. He was such a good, amiable man—and such an excellent husband and father.

We are somewhat shocked at your speaking of "those horrid Yankees"—when Bertie was received in the United States as no one has ever been received anywhere, principally from the (to me incredible) liking they have for my unworthy self; the Duke of Newcastle's[2] words were "No sovereign or prince in any country or at any time ever received such an ovation" and that the order and good behaviour throughout was wonderful. He and all anticipate the most wonderful results from this visit. Don't therefore abuse the "Yankees" for their natural defects—on this occasion at least; for their reception of Bertie has been something so marvellous and naturally so uncalled for and unexpected.

From the Princess Royal

NOVEMBER 10, 1860

I think so much of Alice now and of myself in past times, and when I reflect on it I own I am very glad those two years of our engagement are over—I never wish for them back. It

---

[1] The first Earl; lord-lieutenant of Carmarthen.
[2] The fifth Duke: he was Colonial Secretary at this time, and accompanied the Prince of Wales on his trans-Atlantic tour.

is the most awkward, trying and uncomfortable position in the world. By showing one loves one's "future" with all one's heart and longs (as one must do if one loves him) that the day of the wedding were nearer, one is afraid of showing ingratitude to one's parents and one's home, and one feels so shy and wretched and always between two fires. And for you I can feel and understand with all my heart for it is very trying. Papa had the patience of an angel with us both, and I used always to feel that I must be provoking both yours and his very often. But with Alice it will be different. She is older than I was, you were used to the whole thing already and she has always been able to give you more pleasure and satisfaction than I did. Please don't be angry at all this.

WINDSOR CASTLE, NOVEMBER 14, 1860

I am grieved to be unable to give you any news of Bertie, but the wind has been so very contrary that I fear from all we hear—he may yet be kept out some days longer; the "Hero" carried barely eight days' coal, and has only an auxiliary screw—so that they say she can literally not make any way at all—or something like six miles a day. It is however most annoying for he, and everyone else are losing most precious time and are—very likely—very uncomfortable besides. We have therefore ordered out two very powerful steamers to go and look for the Hero—and help to bring them in.

You must not be discouraged about darling William's arm; it will be long—and slow, but you must not worry yourself too much about it. I saw Dr. Baly[1] yesterday who had been consulting two of the most eminent London surgeons, Mr. Cesar Hawkins and Mr. Paget who have given their opinion in writing and which he described to me as favourable. Sir James will send them to you.

I can well imagine how tiresome and tiring the life at Berlin must be—but I hope you do go out in all weathers?

---

[1] The Queen's regular doctor under Sir James Clark. A few weeks later he was crushed to death in a railway accident at Wimbledon.

Try and force yourself to do it, dear, tiresome as it must be —and pray don't let your house be overheated as long as you can;[1] the hot air above all, I warn against. It enervates and weakens and predisposes to catch cold.

I am not the least angry, dear child, for your observations respecting Alice and the relationship generally. But I think yours was peculiarly difficult from the great length of the engagement, and your being still in fact quite a child. I trust that everything will be easier with Alice and Louis, from being more natural. I often wonder how well and sensibly you behaved. Dear Papa is writing to you about it so I will say no more.

We are very much obliged for the very interesting and sad yet peaceful account of the blessed end of the poor Empress—for to die so peacefully surrounded by all one's children is indeed a great blessing and an enviable end.

WINDSOR CASTLE, NOVEMBER 17, 1860

My beloved child, these lines are to wish you heartily and warmly joy of your 20th birthday—an important age—though married nearly three years and with two children it seems but of little consequence. Still to bid adieu to one's "teens" is a serious thing! May every earthly blessing and happiness be in store for you for many and many years—and your beloved husband and dear children be spared to you through a long and happy life! Our gifts will I trust please you.

Last year we had the happiness of having you here; how I wish it could be so now again! But as we cannot embrace you, and celebrate the day in person—we must and shall do so in thought.

Far or near, my love and affection and my solicitude will ever be the same, my beloved child. God bless you. Ever your devoted Mama.[2]

---

[1] i.e. Until the weather in Berlin got really cold.
[2] This is a special letter of birthday wishes, written without mourning margins and not numbered as part of the correspondence. The Queen had been in mourning since September 24 for the Prince Consort's step-mother.

Bertie is then at last arrived—well—grown, and decidedly improved; he tells us a great deal of what he has seen. He looks a little yellow and sallow—and his hair so fair near Affie. Affie is very dark and very handsome I must say. Bertie arrived at a quarter to seven on Thursday evening with his whole party; the Duke of Newcastle (who has done everything so well) Lord St. Germans, the dear General (Bruce), Major Teesdale, Captain Grey, Dr. Acland[1] and Lord Hinchingbrooke (whom they picked up in Canada and who the General says is a very good companion for Bertie). All except the Duke and Lord St. Germans (and of course the General) left yesterday—and the Duke today. Tonight Mr. and Mrs. Dallas,[2] the Palmerstons and John Russells come.

The voyage of Bertie was very tedious. Last Thursday they were actually further from England than the Tuesday before!! and a very rolling sea all the time. But Bertie was only ill at first. He stays here till the 21st and then goes to Oxford for four or five weeks to finish his term there.

You will have heard how ill the poor, young Empress of Austria is so that she is obliged to go to Madeira. We have given her the Victoria and Albert to take her there, as being the only really fast and comfortable vessel and she goes over tomorrow to Antwerp to carry the beautiful, fragile young Empress alone without husband and children to a distant land! May it not be too late.

Then imagine, (or fancy as you always used to say) your favourite Empress has arrived suddenly in England quite incognito and goes on today to Scotland to Hamilton Palace! She has written to me herself and we hear the same from Paris—that her health and nerves are so shaken by the death of her sister[3] that a journey was absolutely necessary

---

[1] At this time he was Regius Professor of Medicine at Oxford. The Prince of Wales had a great admiration for him.
[2] George Mifflin Dallas, the American Minister in London.
[3] Duchess of Berwick and Alba. She had died in September aged 34.

but that on her return she hoped to see me! It seems that she has been much impressionée with her poor sister's death, and some say wished to consult Dr. Simpson.[1] Others say that there has been a quarrel at home; whatever it is is very extraordinary.

Dear Charlotte is coming to Brussels in December; I have a hope she may possibly come over here before she returns south.

I have finished "The Mill on the Floss" and I must say it made a deep impression upon me. The writing and description of feelings is wonderful and painful! Poor Maggie! Why must they be drowned, but poor Philip Wakem I pity the most of all! Stephen did behave very ill,'Tom had much good, but was very hard.[2]

From the Princess Royal

NOVEMBER 17, 1860

The newest feat of Countess Dohna is that she has gone off to Dresden to pay an aunt of hers a visit, in whose house she is going to live where her two cousins died last week of smallpox! Wegner forbid her going there, but she would do it, and he has been obliged to write her that he cannot allow her to come back here directly from there and bring the infection of the smallpox into this house with her and that she must go somewhere else before she comes here.[3]

---

[1] Afterwards Sir James Simpson, the renowned authority on obstetrics at Edinburgh.

[2] George Eliot knew of the Queen's enjoyment of her books. "It is interesting that Royalty can be touched by that sort of writing" she wrote. See *Life of George Eliot* by J. W. Cross.

[3] This feat of Countess Dohna ended her connexion with the Princess. The latter writing a few days later to Walburga, Lady Paget, said: "Countess Dohna is now really gone over the hills and far away—that is to Dresden—never to return. God bless the goody."

BERLIN, NOVEMBER 20, 1860

How kind you are to give the Empress Elizabeth the yacht, the Queen who, when she can, says something sharp and unkind about England or anything English to me told me yesterday the yacht would be much too small for the Empress and it was a pity she could not have her own Austrian vessel.

And now before I end let me thank you with all my heart for all the love and kindness you have showered upon me in my 20th year. God bless you and dear Papa for all—and grant me power to repay it in deeds as I do daily, hourly in thoughts and feelings.

WINDSOR CASTLE, NOVEMBER 21, 1860

The poor Empress Eugenie is said to be very ill and in a morbid state of mind. She is going about in Edinburgh and no one knows where she is going to next! The poor young Empress of Austria embarks at Antwerp this morning and will stop to coal at Plymouth. I feel so for her, and I am glad to have been able to give her at least the most comfortable ship that exists. I had a very kind letter from the Emperor Franz Joseph thanking me for the facility I afforded her for her sad journey yesterday. I wonder that none of her brothers or sisters went with her.

WINDSOR CASTLE, NOVEMBER 24, 1860

We are delighted that your presents gave you pleasure and fully believe that the happy recollections of a happy childhood in a happy and peaceful home must have crowded on your mind and made you long to be with us! On such days one feels separation from those one loves dearly—very much.

But the dear children must make up in a great extent for the younger brothers and sisters particularly darling William. I have long since ceased caring for our children being thought smaller than other people's and hope you won't give it a thought for they really are not the stronger or the prettier for it.[1]

Our guests[2] arrived safely for luncheon, and Colonel Hardinge[3] must have slept through their arrival at Dover—for there he was waiting for them while they arrived early in the morning and went on to London whence they came on here.

After repeating what she said in a previous letter about the Empress of Austria the Queen goes on that she had had:

. . . a most affectionate letter from the Empress herself written from the yacht; she expresses herself as delighted with everything and hoping to visit me on her way back. What a shame for the Queen to make that evil speech about the yacht. Something to the same effect is in the Allgemeine Zeitung.

WINDSOR CASTLE, NOVEMBER 28, 1860

Dear Leopold Hohenzollern,[4] who is so charming and clever—left us early yesterday morning. He had a cold, and hoarseness—but I trust he will lose it as soon as he reaches Lisbon. I doctored him on Sunday night with a poultice and cold draught, which did him a great deal of good. What a charming young man he is, and how fortunate Antonia will be if she marries him, of which I trust and think there can be no doubt.[5]

Our dear good Louis gets on extremely well, though I see that he is nervous and agitated; but he takes great pains to speak English to the people who are presented to him. nothing has passed yet between any of us—but every day seems to bring him and Alice nearer. It is a little trying

---

[1] Meaning that the larger children, with whom her own were compared, were not the stronger for being large.
[2] Prince Louis and Henry of Hesse.
[3] Son of the 1st Lord Hardinge, Governor-General of India. He was at this time equerry to Queen Victoria.
[4] Eldest son of Prince Hohenzollern.
[5] Donna Antonia of Portugal: they were married on September 12, 1861. King Ferdinand of Roumania was their second son.

for them to be looked at by everybody—but it is well and right that everybody should see his marked attentions to her, and her bright and happy face when speaking to him. Alice behaves admirably; perfectly quiet and behaving just as usual and satisfied with everything that is done.

I send you (*to look at only*) a wonderful photo: of the Queen of Naples,[1] which Countess Bernstorff gave me. It must be in her hunting costume—for she is a great sportswoman and an excellent shot. Pity she didn't shoot Garibaldi —Papa says. She certainly smokes, but I don't know about the Empress of Austria. Uncle Leopold is charmed with her[2] beauty and her manner; and Lord Valletort, who saw her at Mount Edgcumbe, says she is the loveliest person he ever saw! We must see her on her way back. The Empress Eugenie has been as far as Blair! She met the Duke of Atholl on the road and when she heard who he was she took him into the open hack vehicle (they are terrible rough things) and they went to Blair—arriving there in the dark— the house covered up and shut up—and the Duke showed her over it with six tallow candles!! They only got back at 11 o'clock at night! She is to go by Loch Katrine and Glasgow, and on Tuesday she comes here in private—merely to luncheon.

WINDSOR CASTLE, DECEMBER 1, 1860

I had meant to write you a long letter—but I am so agitated and delighted by the happy "dénouement" of last night and have besides many letters to write so that I must scurry this letter very much. Matters came nearer and nearer to the climax since Wednesday—so yesterday dear Papa, whom I pressed at last, on our return from Aldershot, where we had been for a few hours—went over to Louis to break the ice and found him dreadfully nervous and agitated. Papa told him however he would tell me of his wishes and would take care he should have an early opportunity of expressing his hopes to Alice.

---

[1] This is clearly the Queen Dowager. She was Thérèsa, daughter of an Austrian archduke and widow of King "Bomba" of Naples.
[2] The Empress.

I saw how very much agitated Louis was at dinner, and after it—while I was talking to some of the gentlemen and Alice happened to be standing alone at the chimney piece with Louis—he seized the opportunity (which dear Papa in his very quiet way thought he might wait for till today or tomorrow—as if people violently in love could wait for a stated time) and when I passed to go to the other room Alice and Louis whispered it to me. We had to sit quiet and crochet, till the evening was over and then Alice came to our room, much agitated and we told Papa. We then sent for dear Louis to Papa's room, where we went in with Alice and here the confirmation of what occurred took place, and which was very moving, as poor Louis was so completely overcome with his feelings as to be unable to say a word; he seemed quite overpowered. Dear Alice was a good deal upset too—but very quiet and so sensible and reasonable.

Dearest child—it makes me think of Balmoral and the 20th and 29th of September '55 though it is very different.[1] I do love dear Louis much, and am sure our good child will have a very happy, peaceful life with this dear, good, excellent young man. He is so natural and unaffected—so quick-witted and taking interest in everything, and I think him so good looking.

I am so agitated that I write nonsense, besides not sleeping hardly at all, and being somewhat off my food.

You have both been so kind about all this (which I will now confess I have so very ardently wished for sometime) that I know you will be very happy and feel everything with us.

From the Princess Royal

BERLIN, DECEMBER 3, 1860

What a blessing that dear Alice's happiness is now secured! We were very anxious as all we had written and done and said this summer gave us a responsibility which

---

[1] Prince Frederick William on September 20 asked the Queen and Prince Consort if he might propose to the Princess Royal which he did on September 29.

often I own made me nervous. But now I am so happy and thankful all has gone off so well, I think of myself, five years ago—and can perfectly understand dear Alice's feelings, may she have drawn the same golden lot as I have and only be as happy, she will be more free and independent than ever I shall be and more mistress of her time and actions, and not such a difficult "terrain" to work upon as God knows I have here; on the other hand my position is a finer one—in the main point I feel sure they will be the same—domestic happiness.

WINDSOR CASTLE, DECEMBER 5, 1860

Everything goes on here with our dear young lovers as one's heart could wish—and it is a perfect delight and quite touching to see their intense happiness. Alice is radiant and only too delighted to be wished joy by everyone. We like darling Louis (I call him so—because though very manly and bright there is something so very young and child-like in him—daily more). He is very shy—and so blushing and bashful when one speaks to him alone about Alice. He speaks with everyone and gets on very nicely though it is a great trial for him. We think him all that you said he was and you have of course not seen him in the very intimate relations of life which we do. He is quite one of the family already—but excessively shy and modest. It delights all our people to see her great happiness and how they love one another. He appeared yesterday evening for the first time in the Windsor uniform which gave him such particular pleasure.

The poor Empress came yesterday—such a contrast to '55! A wet dark day—no demonstrations beyond Papa's going down to the station to bring her up and our being all at the door to receive her.[1] She was in deep mourning—lovely and charming—but so sad! She cried in speaking of her shattered nerves—(she could neither sleep nor eat till

---

[1] As a mark of respect the Queen met rulers or their consorts at the entrance whether they were on a state visit or not. This was the French Empress, and the Queen is contrasting the visit with her own to Paris in 1855.

she came here). She never mentioned the Emperor but once and that once de presenter ses compliments and never went near politics. I fear there is some great sorrow preying upon her. She asked most kindly after you and her manner was as kind and charming as ever—but it gave one a sad impression. By the by the dear Princess has never said one kind word about Alice's prospects? Why? I wrote on Monday to announce it—but had written about it on Wednesday.

From the Princess Royal

DECEMBER 7, 1860

You asked me why the Princess said no more to you about Alice's engagement. The trouble is (but this is only between us) that she takes no interest in anything that has to do with love, as she cannot understand it, and besides Louis is no favourite of hers and she has never taken any notice of him whatever and she does not like his mother! This please, dear Mama, is only for your ears and Papa's. When I spoke to the Princess about Alice she answered me impatiently "I am not excited like you and your mother are over this young man." Who talks of excitement? No one. I only told her how happy I was to see Alice happy—but you know with the Princess outward circumstances are only those that weigh—and the heart goes for nothing. She could not understand how Louise could be fond of Fritz of Baden, and she cannot understand my adoring Fritz.

I send you now a photograph of Prince Christian of Denmark's lovely daughter.[1] I have seen several people who have seen her of late—and who give such accounts of her beauty, her charms, her amiability, her frank natural manner and many excellent qualities. I thought it right to tell you all this in Bertie's interest, though I as Prussian cannot wish Bertie should ever marry her. I know her nurse who tells me that she is strong in health and has never ailed anything and I can find out anything else by Wally Paget. I must say on the photograph I think her lovely and just the style Bertie

_____

[1] Princess Alexandra.

admires, but I repeat again that an alliance with Denmark would be a misfortune for us here. Elizabeth of Wied is coming to spend the winter here with the Princess. I cannot reconcile myself to the idea of your thinking of her for Bertie. She does not look well-bred enough for him.

WINDSOR CASTLE, DECEMBER 8, 1860

Everything is on the same footing as with you and Fritz —only I think perhaps they are more together than you were. Then during this horrible weather they have been sitting in my room—when they could not go out; I wish you could see what a pretty picture it is—to see those two dear, young, happy faces, as they sit looking at picture books on the sofa in my room! God bless them dear children! Dear Papa is very happy now, and unselfish as he always is—his heart is gladdened at the sight of such perfect happiness— and to see what an excellent, dear young man we have got for our darling Alice (how much we owe you both, dearest children, and how do I thank God for it!). You are quite right in saying "he has fascinated Alice"—but he has fascinated me too, and quite entwined himself round my heart. They are not at all sentimental but like two very happy children—adoring one another and full of fun and play. He is so intelligent and clever. Papa has begun talking a little upon German politics with him—which will I am sure be very useful—but from Papa's having last week had a great deal to do—and these last days been unwell and unable to go out, he has been much more with me than dearest Papa.

Alice has had such quantities of kind letters. We have had (and so has Louis) such very kind nice letters from Prince and Princess Charles[1] who seem to be as happy together as we are (Papa and I). What a comfort! I feel as if Alice had been safely brought into port and would be landed in safety—after the storms of uncertainty. Oh if only our darling Lenchen is as lucky!

[1] Prince Louis's mother and father.

Many, many thanks for your dear letter of the 8th which I received in the railway carriage on our way back from London whither we had gone with Louis, Alice and Affie to see the Cattle Show after which to visit the Empress at Claridge's Hotel. She said she did not wish us to put ourselves to the trouble but as we were in town—(and even if we had not been) we felt we should not be civil if we didn't go—besides that, people would very probably have said we had been uncivil to her. She looked very pretty yesterday with her hair in a net and a black lace handkerchief thrown over her head. She was in very good spirits, is going to stay here some little time longer, but never mentioned the Emperor or politics though she was very lively and conversable about all she saw! I fear she dreads returning sadly. She shops a great deal and goes about everywhere seeing things which she delights in, but always without any ceremony.

Referring to Princess Alice's engagement:

I am sorry the dear Princess does not feel as we could wish, on this subject, but never mind it. It will come right by and by. I can't understand a mother not loving the man (if she once consents to give him up her daughter) to whom she confides the future (soul and body) of her own daughter. It is a trying, anxious moment, and if you cannot have confidence and cannot love the son-in-law as I could and did and do—your dear excellent husband, and as I can dear Louis—it must be torture to one's feelings. All the difficulties and trials of such a step are only in my opinion to be got over by a certain amount of "exaltation".

I am glad that Elizabeth of Wied is coming to the Princess to Berlin as that will do her a great deal of good, by giving her a knowledge of the world and of society.

In a reference to some photographs which the Princess sent her mother the Queen writes:

. . . the one of Princess Alexandra is indeed lovely! All what you have had I have had also! What a pity she is who she is! Who is her nurse?

WINDSOR CASTLE, DECEMBER 15, 1860

I will let you know what you can give Grandmama for Christmas; but there may not be time to get it. I know that she is passionately fond of cloaks and shawls, etc. Therefore a good large, new-fashioned warm cloak would please her particularly—either black, or black and white or violet. She is always wanting me to give her cloaks.

We had our second performance yesterday—a pretty new piece—very well cast and acted by Tom Taylor called "The Babes in the Wood". The Cambridges—mother and daughter—Churchills, the Duke of Atholl, C. Lewis's, General and Lady Alice Peel were there. The Duchess was very kind to Louis and Mary very kind to Alice, but the Duchess with wonderful good taste told Alice "It is a very insignificant match, you will agree" as if that signified and as if that had anything to do with one's happiness!

WINDSOR CASTLE, DECEMBER 18, 1860

We are anxious to know as much about Princess Elizabeth of Wied and Anna of Hesse as possible, I think future choice of Bertie must lie much between them. You gave a very favourable report of Anna after you saw her at Darmstadt last year (which I have lately read over). Did you find her improved this year or not? Has she a good complexion and figure—is she quick and intelligent as dear Louis is? You know, dearest, we must feel very anxious about this choice and the beauty of Denmark is much against our wishes. I do wish somebody would go and marry her off— at once. If Bertie could see and like one of the others first then I am sure we should be safe.

I hear very unfavourable reports of the Prince of Orange. His mother wrote to Lord Clarendon saying that Alice's engagement had filled her with regret and hope.[1]

Papa is much pleased with your memorandum—which I shall certainly read. Papa paid you the compliment by

[1] Regret that her son was not to be the bridegroom, and hope that Princess Alice would be happy.

quietly telling me (which I am sure is quite true) that I could not have written such a thing. What do you say to this?[1]

From the Princess Royal

In answer to your question about Anna of Hesse. I do not think her pretty—she has not a fine figure but a passable one. She has a very flat, narrow and upright forehead, which may to be sure look so from the way in which she is coiffée, but still a fine forehead is a great thing. She has an incipient twitching in her eyes, like Heinrich—and her teeth are nearly all spoilt. I think when she is a little older she will improve greatly but she will never have anything graceful in her deportment, but one must not be too hard on her—girls of her age never appear to advantage when they are shy and she was too awfully dressed. She has a very deep voice, and rather a gruff, abrupt way of speaking, frowning when she speaks, partly to conceal her shyness and partly to conceal her eyes which are perpetually twitching while she is talking. Her nose is very pretty and has a bent shape and finely cut nostrils. Her eyes are small and insignificant and she has not much expression in her face. Whether she is clever or not, I have not the slightest idea, for although for a week I saw her several times every day yet I had no opportunity of judging on this point. On the whole I should say she was nice-looking but nothing particular—still beauty is rare—and not

---

[1] The memorandum was on the subject of the Prussian Constitution and the propriety of appointing a minister with a particular responsibility for safeguarding it. Both the Prince Regent and Prince Frederick William were opposed to such an appointment, but the Princess Royal strongly favoured it, writing a memorandum in German in support of her view for Prince Frederick William. She sent this to her father telling him that Prince Frederick William's ideas came from Professor Perthes (Professor of Law at Bonn University)—"a most pernicious influence". She added "This is quite between you and me, dearest Papa, and please do not answer me on the subject". In a later letter she wrote, she said that her father-in-law was terribly afraid of being influenced by anyone, consequently saw Prince Hohenzollern and the Ministers as little as he could but listened to people with "stained names and characters".

a necessity only a pleasant additional gift. Whether Bertie thinks it a necessity or no you must know best. I fear you will be very angry with me for picking poor Anna to pieces but you asked my opinion! Elizabeth of Wied I shall soon have an opportunity of seeing—there is a great dearth of nice princesses at present. The Weimars are very nice girls but delicate and not pretty. The little Princess of Sweden is a dear little girl, pretty and nice but of course much too young for Bertie. The Queen was very cross and ungracious and said one sharp and cutting thing after another about England and I don't know what more, but it was very difficult to sit by and make a civil and indifferent face when one's blood was boiling. It would have been the greatest satisfaction to have given it back.

WINDSOR CASTLE, DECEMBER 22, 1860

I have been (like you) so busy with my enormous range of Christmas presents including Papa's, our children, and Grandmama etc., the Court, servants, Claremont inmates— etc. that I have but little time to write.

Many, many thanks for your dear letter of the 17th and the two lovely photos which I return. I think the Empress is very lovely—Princess Alexandra less so than in the other. Bertie shall not see one of them. That must not be.

Referring to Louis the Queen writes:

What a dear good young man he is! Papa finds him very young and shy still, in talking to him alone, and not having as yet thought at all seriously about his arrangement for life, etc. but that is quite natural, and now everything will take a new form and have a new interest for him. But he is very unselfish—so unprejudiced and pleased with every-thing and very wide awake. Good Sir James as well as Saunders have taken his poor teeth in hand; they require much care.

WINDSOR CASTLE, DECEMBER 26, 1860

Now many, many thanks for your dear letter of the 21st in which certainly you do pull poor Anna much to pieces;

Das Neue Palais at Potsdam

The Kronprinzenpalais at Berlin

time will show whether she will do—or not. But the account of Elizabeth of Wied's qualities are excellent. Do give a little advice about her dressing.

Now before I turn to the dear happy Christmas let me say one word about our darling Affie. You will find him much improved, in every way and a great darling—but he must be looked after and is never allowed to go out alone. Besides I wish to add that he has not permission to smoke, and therefore beg you will not allow him to do it. Bertie has only now received permission to do so, and only on condition he does not do so in public or in the house.

1861

WINDSOR CASTLE, JANUARY 2, 1861

What a dreadful New Year's day you must have spent![1] While we were surrounded by all the children and received your dear letter and wishes—and all was gaiety—you were watching the flickering lamp of life gradually going out of the poor dear King whose memory will ever be remembered with gratitude and affection by us!

I trust, dearest child, this sad and to you so novel scene, (I have never even yet witnessed a death bed) will not be too much for your warm and feeling heart! My thoughts are constantly with you and I feel so much for the present dear King, the poor Queens, Dowager and present—and for our dearest Fritz for whom I feel so deeply. He will be so anxious for his dear father.

From the Princess Royal

POTSDAM, JANUARY 2, 1861

At last I can find a moment for myself to sit down and collect my thoughts and to write to you an account of these two last dreadful days! My head is in such a state, I do not know where I am hardly—whether I am in a dream or awake, what is yesterday and what today! What we have so long expected has come at last! All the confusion, bustle, excitement, noise, etc., is all swallowed up in that one thought for me.

I have seen death for the first time! It has made an impression upon me that I shall never, never forget as long as I live—and I feel so ill, so confused and upset by all that I have gone through in the last forty-eight hours, that you must forgive me if I write incoherently and unclearly. But to go back to Monday evening (it seems to me a year now). At a quarter to eight in the evening of Monday the 31st, I took dear darling Affie to the railway station, and took leave of him with a heavy heart. You know I love that dear boy

---

[1] The King of Prussia died on January 2.

distractedly, and that nothing could have given me more pleasure than his dear long-wished-for visit. At 9 o'clock Fritz and I went to tea at the Prince Regent's; we four were alone together. The Princess was rather low and unwell, the Prince low spirited and I thinking of nothing but Affie and of how dear he is. While we were sitting at tea we received bad news from Sanssouci, but nothing to make us particularly uneasy. Fritz and I went home and to bed—not being in a humour to sit up till 12.

About half past one we heard a knock at the door and my wardrobe maid brought in a telegram saying the King was given up, and a note from the Prince Regent, saying he was going up immediately. We got up in the greatest hurry and dressed—I hardly know how; I put on just what I found, and had no time to do my hair or anything. After we had hurried on our clothes we went downstairs and out—for there was no time to get a carriage, or a footman or anything—it was a splendid night, but 12 degrees of cold (Réaumur). I thought I was in a dream, finding myself alone in the street with Fritz at 2 o'clock at night. We went to the Prince Regent's, and then with them in their carriages to the railway station—we four all alone in the train.[1] We arrived at Sanssouci and went directly into the room where the King lay— the stillness of death was in the room—only the light of the fire and of a dim lamp. We approached the bed and stood there at the foot of it, not daring to look at one another, or to say a word. The Queen was sitting in an arm chair at the head of the bed, her arm underneath the King's head, and her head on the same pillow on which he lay—with her other hand she continually wiped the perspiration from his forehead. You might have heard a pin drop—no sound was heard, but the crackling of the fire and the death rattle—that dreadful sound which goes to one's heart and which tells plainly that life is ebbing. This rattling in the throat lasted about an hour longer and then the King lay motionless. The Doctors bent their heads low to hear whether he still breathed and we stood, not even daring to sit down, watching the death struggle,

[1] From Berlin to Potsdam.

every now and then the King breathed very fast and loud, but never unclosed his eyes—he was very red in the face, and the cold perspiration pouring from his forehead. I never spent such an awful time, and to see the poor Queen sitting there quite rent my heart—3, 4, 5, 6, 7 struck and we were still standing there—one member of the Royal Family came in after the other and remained motionless in the room, sobs only breaking the stillness. Oh it is dreadful to see a person die! All the thoughts and feelings that crowded on my mind in those hours I cannot describe; they impressed me more than anything in my whole past lifetime! The light of the morning dawned and the lamps were taken away. Oh how sad for the first morning in the year! We all went into the next room, for I assure you, anxiety, watching, standing and crying had quite worn us out. The Princess fell asleep on a chair, I on a sofa, and the rest walked up and down the room, asking one another "How long will it last?" Towards the middle of the day Marianne and I went into the room alone, as we wished to stay there, we came up and kissed the Queen's hand and knelt down and kissed the King's—it was quite warm still. We stood about and waited till 5 o'clock and then had some dinner, and I felt so sick and faint and unwell, that Fritz sent me here to bed.[1] At 1 o'clock this morning I got up and dressed and heard that the King had not many minutes more to live, but by the time I had got the carriage I heard all was over. I drove to Sanssouci and saw the King and Queen. May God bless and preserve them and may theirs be a long and happy and blessed reign. Then I went into the room where the King lay, and I could hardly bring myself to go away again. There was so much of comfort in looking there at that quiet peaceful form at rest at last after all he had suffered—gone home at last from this world of suffering—so peaceful and quiet he looked—like a sleeping child—every moment I expected to see him move or breathe—his mouth and eyes closed and such a sweet and happy expression— both his hands were on the coverlid. I kissed them both for the last time; they were quite cold then. Fritz and I stood

---

[1] The Cabinettshaus in Potsdam, a small building belonging to the royal household.

looking at him for some time. I could hardly bring myself to believe that this was really death, that which I had so often shuddered at and felt afraid of; there was nothing there dreadful or appalling—only a heavenly calm and peace. I felt it did me so much good and was such a comfort. "Death where is thy sting, grave where is thy Victory?" He was a just and good man and had a heart overflowing with love and kindness, and he has gone to his rest after a long trial which he bore with so much patience! I am not afraid of death now, and when I feel inclined to be so, I shall think of that solemn and comforting sight, and that death is only a change for the better. We went home and to bed and this morning went there at 10. I sat some time with the poor Queen, who is so calm and resigned and touching in her grief. She does not cry, but she looks heartbroken. She said to me, "I am no longer of any use in this world. I have no longer any vocation, any duties to perform. I only lived for him." Then she was so kind to me, kinder than she has ever been yet, and said I was like her own child and a comfort to her. I saw the corpse again this morning, he is unaltered, only changed in colour and the hands are stiffened. The funeral will be on Saturday, the King will lie in State till then, his wish was to be buried in the Friedenskirche before the altar—and his heart at Charlottenburg in the Mausoleum.

OSBORNE, JANUARY 5, 1861

This very quick funeral astonishes us much, for Fritz told me that though they have that fearfully dangerous habit of burying people so early—that for a sovereign or Prince—it always lasted some time and this is only six days after! Our gentlemen will I trust be in time but only just. Colonel Ponsonby (now in waiting) goes—as Colonel Seymour is ill and could not—and will take this letter. To see him will remind you of dear Coburg.[1]

---

[1] He had been with the Queen and Prince Consort on their visit to Coburg in September.

From the Princess Royal

POTSDAM, JANUARY 4, 1861

Yesterday the body of the poor King was removed from his room and after all the sad duties doctors have to perform —he was dressed in his uniform and laid in his coffin. He now lies in state in the room in which Frederick the Great died. The room is hung with black and the coffin is in a large niche of two steps which are covered with a mantle of violet velvet and ermine—and under the same dais as William and baby were christened under—surrounded by candelabras and wreaths of bay leaves. The whole is extremely simple as there was so short a time to prepare everything in but it is very well arranged and looks most dignified. I saw the poor King three times on the 2nd, the last time in the evening. He did not make a pleasant impression upon me—the alteration was not great it is true—but it looked like death and no longer like sleep— the Grand Duchess of M.[1] pushed me so close up to the pillow and stood behind me I own it gave me a great shudder—and today when I went up to the coffin I kept my eyes cast down— I had not courage to look at the King's face. I only looked at it when I was a little further off—he still looks peaceful as before but the mouth is much changed and I own it costs me a great struggle to overcome my feelings now whenever we are obliged to go.

Is the King[2] going to receive the Order of the Garter? I suppose that is an indiscreet question, if so I beg pardon.

OSBORNE, JANUARY 8, 1861

I cannot wait till tomorrow to thank you for that most beautiful and touching letter of the 2nd received on Saturday. It shows what deep and right feelings my own darling child has! God bless you for them, and go on to be an element of peace and conciliation in that family. Everyone praises you, and the Queen (your mama-in-law) writes in the highest terms of you. But you have had much to try you.

[1] Mecklenburg-Schwerin—the King's sister.
[2] Her father-in-law.

— *300* —

OSBORNE, JANUARY 8, 1861

Many thanks for the brooch of the poor King—and for
all the sad and painfully interesting details about the poor
King's last hours. I cannot say how beautiful I think your
letter of the 2nd. I agree in every word you say. You know
all I felt when I saw my beloved friend Victoire at Claremont! I have had it copied (leaving out a few personal
observations) and shown to a few worthy ones, and it has
been so much admired.

I am sorry you were obliged to see the poor King's body
so often. I think that is a bad custom, and must leave distressing impressions. If it had happened last winter you
could not have gone! I had a written promise from Wegner
to that effect.

I am so glad I have seen all the places and know where
everything took place. That beautiful Friedenskirche is a
fine resting place, but I don't like the idea of being pulled
to pieces and having one's heart put elsewhere.

OSBORNE, JANUARY 12, 1861

I can easily imagine what dreadful chaos and confusion
you must be living in. That is more or less always the case
with the Berlin Potsdam life—and now must be fearful!

Only think that in spite of all remonstrance and to the
extreme annoyance of both families, that foolish Victor will
marry Miss Seymour[1]—and it is to take place on the 29th
instant! It is the height of folly and very reckless! Of course
I shall ignore it. Aunt Feodore is much provoked and
annoyed, but some years ago she could have prevented it—
now it is too late.

From the Princess Royal

BERLIN, JANUARY 11, 1861

*What do you say to Gerlach's[2] death? Is it not extra-
ordinary? He caught cold at the poor King's funeral, and*

---

[1] She was daughter of Admiral of the Fleet Sir George Seymour,
brother of Lord Hertford. The marriage was a morganatic one.
[2] Leopold von Gerlach, Adjutant-General, a very strong Conservative.
It was to him that Bismarck wrote his celebrated comment on the

died yesterday, it will be a great blow to the Queen Dowager, but he is a good riddance, poor man. The King and Queen's new Court is not formed yet and at present there are two, and no one knows who's who which is not at all pleasant and it gives rise to all sorts of quarrels, scenes and misunderstandings, which deplorable as they are, are really very ludicrous sometimes.

From the Princess Royal

BERLIN, JANUARY 15, 1861

Here is a letter from our poor Queen. Your letter gave her so much pleasure, she wrote to me today saying how she envied Gerlach being allowed to die!

WINDSOR CASTLE, JANUARY 16, 1861

Many thanks for your dear letter of the 11th. I am not the least angry with you for not writing, dearest child, and only must insist on your not worrying and fidgetting yourself about that, for I know well from experience what confusion and excitement an accession produces! Like yesterday do I recollect mine, and think of a young girl only just 18 placed in such a position without a single relative to support and sustain her—no husband to lean on and pour out all one's anxieties and to receive peace and comfort in his love and affection—and worse than that—brouillée with my poor mother—so as to be almost at that time at enmity with her—my own brother[1] acting against me. You may think what it was.

Our gentlemen came back delighted with your and Fritz's and the King's and Queen's kindness[2]—much interested with all they saw and charmed with the children. Lord de Tabley could not cease speaking of your happy, domestic life—of how it gladdened their hearts to see how

---

Princess Royal, at the time of the engagement—"If the Princess can leave the Englishwoman at home, and become a Prussian, then she may be a blessing to the country".

[1] Prince Charles of Leiningen.

[2] From now on the Princess Royal's parents-in-law are referred to by Queen Victoria as the King and the Queen.

happy you were and how surrounded in your pretty palaces by reminiscences and recollections of home. You will recollect how people imagined you did not care for Fritz before you married and how ill you were used by him afterwards, and that after such falsehoods as that, one can understand fresh ones being invented about poor Alice and Louis. Though Louise of B. ought indeed to know better, considering my description in two letters to her of the touching love and devotion of the dear young couple, and certainly here people have been delighted to witness it. Louise however wished something different, and that may explain all.[1] Good Marie L. told me herself that she was sure it was much more for Alice's happiness that she should marry Louis than William for that she did not think it would have been comfortable at Carlsruhe for her. I am sorry Louise is not looking well.

How like the poor King that letter or memorandum he left about his burial is![2] Who carried the heart to Charlottenburg? Poor General Gerlach's death is rather shocking, but still no misfortune.

WINDSOR CASTLE, JANUARY 19, 1861

Victor's marriage is a sad affair and distresses poor dear Grandmama sadly. It is to be on the 26th and she is to be called Countess Gleichen.

Papa is too naughty—when he read your letter saying that the poor Queen envied your being able to cry he said "That you must be very happy as you did so so easily! and that Lenchen ought to be sent specially for the purpose." Certainly the whole family (not excluding myself though much less than formerly) are very prone to tears: Affie as much as any. But it is a good sign of a warm heart—though it should be kept within bounds, and the not doing so is no

---

[1] i.e. That her brother-in-law, Prince William of Baden, should have married Princess Alice.
[2] By his will, which he made in 1854, King Frederick William IV instructed that his heart was to be buried at the foot of his mother and father in the Mausoleum at Charlottenburg. His body was to be buried in the Friedenskirche in Potsdam.

sign of the want of feeling. Have you ever read "Scenes of Clerical Life" by George Eliot who wrote "Adam Bede" and "The Mill on the Floss"? They are admirable, particularly "Mr. Gilfil's Love Story" which is most touching.

I have no letter from you to answer and so will give you the news of our doings—to begin with a household marriage which was settled the day before yesterday evening after the play. Mary Bulteel to Colonel Ponsonby! For the last fortnight I saw (what many had seen before) a great and marked attention on his part towards Mary which was quite different to ordinary flirtation. But Mary gave him no encouragement; however on Thursday the day she went out of waiting, she went to the Deanery and he followed her in the cloisters—and proposed. She gave no answer, and was in a great state of distress etc. for she had turned her face against all marriage—said she "had put her foot in it" and in short was quite upset. However, Mrs. Wellesley (as Lady McDonald had likewise done before) urged her strongly not to refuse so amiable and good and nice a person— though he has been a little bit of a flirt, and accordingly after the play that evening she accepted him in the Waterloo Room, and told him it must be in earnest which he assured he was—for he is most devoted to her. I believe she would not have accepted him if her friends had not advised her to do so. The General (Grey) was most anxious for it. I tell all these details—as I know how fond you are of Mary B.—but you won't repeat them to others. I shall be very sorry to lose Mary but am very glad of the marriage as I feel that she will still be in the Household.

The play on Thursday was very interesting L. Bulwer's "Richelieu".[1] The Duchess of Cambridge and Mary in the best of humours and spirits (much wishing for photos of your children) the Westminsters, Tankervilles, Mr. and Mrs. Disraeli (she was the cause of constant mirth and amusement).

---

[1] Given privately at the Castle.

Let me express to you both my warmest wish that every possible blessing may be showered on our precious little William for this and many succeeding birthdays through a long life! May he be a blessing and comfort to you and to his country! He may be born for great deeds and great times—be that as it may, but do you both bring him up to be fitted for his position, to be wise, sensible, courageous— liberal-minded—good and pure. He has a fine head, is full of intelligence, and God will bless the endeavours of his dearest parents if they will but strive to do their very best to fit him for the task! I can't say what love and affection for and what intense interest we take in that very dear little boy. How I do pray that we may see him and little Charlotte here this year—and above all that poor dear Grandmama, whose existence is alas! one of such suffering and privation, and who takes such interest in your children, may have the very great delight of seeing them! It would I am sure do her health more good than medicines.

BUCKINGHAM PALACE, FEBRUARY 6, 1861

The opening of Parliament went off very well yesterday. Lady Ely (acting for the Duchess of Sutherland) and Lord St. Germans (Lord Ailesbury having lost a nephew) were in the State Coach with us. Yesterday evening we went to the Adelphi to see a very interesting play or melodrama called "Colleen Bawn".[1] It is an Irish story taken from a celebrated novel called "The Collegians",[2] and beautifully acted by the principal actors. People are wild about it—and the scene when the poor Colleen is thrown into the water and all but drowned is wonderfully done.

---

[1] *The Colleen Bawn* or *The Brides of Garryowen*, a domestic drama by Dion Boucicault (1822–90), actor and dramatist. He took part in the play, and his wife, Agnes Robertson, was the heroine.
[2] By Gerald Griffin (1803–40), the Irish dramatist and novelist.

BUCKINGHAM PALACE, FEBRUARY 9, 1861

It is strange, but I find Germans never hardly take any opening medicine and of course the result is "fever" always fever with any and every cold.

We saw on Thursday a most melancholy and dreadful play—which we'd seen some twelve years ago in French called "The Isle of St. Tropez" in which Wigan acts beautifully; he dies of poison and thinks till just at the end, that his poor wife—who did not marry him for love has poisoned him! "The Scenes of Clerical Life" are very sad, but don't you think that there are such beautiful and true pieces of writing in it, feelings and thoughts—far more elevating than many sermons and religious books? You should read "The Collegians" from which "Colleen Bawn" is taken; I will send it to you as it is out of print. It was published thirty years ago. You will think of us tomorrow! Our dear wedding day, twenty one years ago! Those have been twenty one blessed years—though not without their trials, and other people made the beginning of our marriage (happy and devoted as we were) very different to what yours was and to what it ought to have been.

From the Princess Royal

BERLIN, FEBRUARY 12, 1861

What you say about people never taking medicine here of the sort you mention is so true. What is more you can not even get the doctors to give it you. At the same time I must allow that it would not do to take the same remedies as you do in England. They are not necessary. The food and drink is not near so strong, so nutritious and so substantial as in England. One eats about half as much as you do there and the air is quite different—hence the different treatment. In England when anything is the matter with you it is either the liver or the bile or the stomach that is at fault, here inflamation is the usual illness. The cure for everything here is to sweat. I never hear anything else recommended.

You must spend that dear day with us sometime or other and anyhow you must promise to be with us for our silver wedding D.V. which will be in four years—if God spares us—as I trust He will.

I wish to tell you that Mr. Corbould has painted (although they are not quite finished yet and he's to make some alterations) for me, two beautiful pictures from "Adam Bede" the one "Dinah Preaching in the Cart"—the other "Hetty in the Dairy". They are to go into the Exhibition. Mr. Lundgren has also just done me some charming sketches from the "Colleen Bawn", which I will send to you to see when I've got them all.

We spent the beloved 10th peaceably and happily, and I lived in thought over every minute of that truly blessed day! Lenchen dined for the first time at a great dinner. We had some really very fine sacred music in the evening (of which I annexe the programme) in the great Ballroom and though there were only sixteen voices—and only my band and the organ it had the effect of a very large orchestra and chorus. We had got together to dinner the few remaining people of our household who were there on that dear day 21 years ago Lady Jocelyn (one of my bridesmaids), Lord Alfred[1] (in waiting then and now—) General Grey, Lady C. Barrington, Lord Torrington and Col. Seymour. Dear Papa gave me a beautiful bracelet which he got at Coburg—from Gotha—a large elastic gold bracelet like a cuff—and so pretty.

Just two words to send you this pretty little photograph of Alice on horseback, and also to say I hear that Princess Elizabeth of Wied, has arrived at Berlin; pray take every means of knowing her thoroughly and of becoming acquainted with her real character and disposition. Also try and get a nice carte de visite made of her.

---

[1] Paget.

— *307* —

BUCKINGHAM PALACE, FEBRUARY 16, 1861

Poor dear Papa has been suffering badly with toothache since three days—which wears and worries him dreadfully, and seems particularly obstinate; it comes from inflammation at the root of the tooth; he had a little of it last autumn on the journey to and at Coburg, and also at Babelsberg in '58, but not near so bad as now; I hope, however, it is a little better today, but dear Papa never allows he is any better or will try to get over it, but makes such a miserable face that people always think he's very ill. It is quite the contrary with me always; I can do anything before others and never show it, so people never believe I am ill or ever suffer. His nervous system is easily excited and irritated, and he's so completely overpowered by everything.

From the Princess Royal

BERLIN, FEBRUARY 19, 1861

After discussing the new appointments to the Queen's Household the Princess explains that it is taking time.

Skirmishes and storms of various dimensions ensued as soon as the subject is named and I am usually 'catspaw'!

Elizabeth Wied is decidedly improving. She is not so noisy and boisterous and does not talk so much, she has the best temper in the world and the Queen does not find her task[1] at all difficult I think. You asked me whether I had anything more about the Danish beauty. I hear almost every week about her but never mentioned it as I thought you did not wish to hear anything more about her and were determined not to give her another thought. Wally, who is very difficile[2] writes such raptures about her, saying in her gentle and lady-like manner and sweet voice and expression she reminded her again and again of Alice—that sounds very inviting does it not? I own to you the other[3] is not my taste, but however she may be of the person in question(B.).[4] Marie Hohenzollern

---

[1] i.e. Of finishing and polishing her.
[2] i.e. To please.
[3] Princess Elizabeth of Wied.   [4] Bertie.

s quite lovely—a thousand times better looking than poor Stephanie was.[1]

I have an audience of 14 ladies today which is such a bore!! Fritz hardly ever breakfasts with me now or takes walks and drives with me as he used. He has so much to do, here at Berlin we see each other so little, and our rooms are so far from each other with the whole house between them that we might just as well not be married at all, I do not even know whether he is in the house or not, but I assure you I can say with a good conscience I never complain about it now, though I long for the time to come when we can be more together as it is the being I care about most in the world—but I know he cannot possibly do otherwise, he is at work all day long, in the morning with his military duties then the councils, and the people to see, the King's papers to arrange and audiences etc.

BUCKINGHAM PALACE, FEBRUARY 20, 1861

Your account of Elizabeth of Wied interested us much. How can you think I shall be angry if you find faults? I only wished you before—not to have a dislike for her as she was not as pretty as you would like her to be. Tell us everything, dear, and aid in correcting the defects if you can. Can't you get her photographed as well as Marie Hohenzollern? Isn't Alexandra old to be taking lessons? Though to be sure there are lessons which one is never too old to take. Bertie was up here yesterday evening to go with us to see the "Colleen Bawn" returning this morning. He is reading with Kingsley who is now Professor of History at Cambridge, and whose lectures he attends, and he has taken to him very much.

I saw our new doctor today; Dr. Jenner, about the same age as, and a great friend of our poor Dr. Baly. He is also extremely clever, and has a pleasing clever manner. Papa told me he was so frightful but I was agreeably surprised to find him not so; he has a very fine high intellectual

---

[1] Prince Hohenzollern's daughter—a Roman Catholic.

forehead; his eyes are small and deep-set, and he has large, long teeth, like poor Mr. Coombe. But I am sure from his manner that we shall like him.

BUCKINGHAM PALACE, FEBRUARY 21, 1861

After a long account of the Prince's gumboil and his pain the Queen goes on:

It has been a most trying, wearing and distressing time for I could not bear to see him suffer so much and to be so despondent and weak and miserable—I would so willingly have borne it all for him; we women are born to suffer and bear it so much more easily, our nerves don't seem so racked, tortured as men's are! Saunders says it is the severest, most obstinate attack he has ever seen.

BUCKINGHAM PALACE, FEBRUARY 23, 1861

I am glad to hear that Elizabeth of Wied is improving. Though I don't think the connection with a certain beauty would ever be desirable—I shall always be thankful to hear what you hear, but I must observe that the excessive gentleness—unless coupled with great cleverness and firmness—would not do in the particular case. Good temper, and cheerfulness—but superiority of mind and a certain determination are very necessary—else invariably advantage is taken and rudeness and an amount of tyrannising people takes place. You will understand me. Those who never knock under, but hold their own, are always those most liked, and who get on best with the nameless individual.

We were much pleased by a very good performance last night at the Princess's (no longer Kean's, but where they give very good things) of a not very moral piece, which we had seen several times in French before "Don Cesar de Bazan?"[1] The great attraction was the principal actor,

---

[1] A drama in 3 acts by G. à Beckett (1837–91), an original member of the staff of *Punch*, and Mark Lemon (1809–70), editor of *Punch*. It was founded on a play by the French dramatists Dumanoir and Dennery. This must have been the last occasion on which Queen Victoria went

The Duchess of Kent in old age

Queen Victoria's private sitting-room, Windsor Castle

M. Fechter,[1] who is a celebrated French actor, the original of the Corsican Brothers, but who acts beautifully in English, with wonderfully little accent, the little there is being agreeable; he is tall, good-looking, and very graceful and quiet; his parents were German—he was born here and remained here until twelve years old, since which age he has been in France! He is to appear as Hamlet which is a bold undertaking!

From the Princess Royal

BERLIN, FEBRUARY 22, 1861

I wish I could say that after very careful observation of Elizabeth I could say more in her favour. She is so odd—the Queen says that owing to the state of health of the Mama and Prince of Wied and poor little Otto[2] are in, she is accustomed to hear details spoken of which are not exactly meant for the ears of young ladies. Be this as it may she keeps me on coals and says such things sometimes that I do not know which way to look—I get so hot—and she talks so much, and so loud and laughs so loud, manners that are really very strange considering she is 17. It is very difficult for me to say anything as she is continually being taken up by the Queen and by other people and I am afraid of saying too much considering she is not a baby and nearly as old as myself. She seeme very learned, not at all stupid but I fear tact, esprit ds conduite and royal bearing are not yet developed. Nothing in the world seems to cure her as she talks just as much when strangers are there as when there are none. I think she seems

---

publicly to the theatre. A few days afterwards she left for Osborne, and the death of the Duchess of Kent on March 16 kept her in retirement till the calamity of the Prince Consort's death. This absence from the theatre was a great sacrifice to the conventions of the day for she loved seeing plays (see *Henry Ponsonby* by Arthur Ponsonby, pages 82–4). Professor J. R. A. Nicoll, in *Early Victorian England*, has pointed out that the Queen's interest in the theatre had a decided influence in civilising theatre audiences, and stimulating more subtle and refined modes of acting.

[1] Charles Albert Fechter. His father was German: his mother English. He was brought up in France. In March 1861 he played Hamlet. "Mr. Fechter does not act: he is Hamlet" said the *Athenaeum*.
[2] Her brother, aged 10.

— *311* —

very healthy and strong and accustomed to a simple mode of
life—her figure is decidedly bad in a low gown, such broad
square shoulders, not refined-looking but dress may do a great
deal for that. It seems so cruel to pick a poor girl to pieces
behind her back but it would be more cruel to overlook all
faults out of a false feeling of good nature. She speaks excel-
lent English, not very refined German, the expressions being
rather too strong for a lady now and then, I tell you all
I know and all I see. I wish I knew more of Anna of Hesse
and of Princess Alix of Holstein—the difficulties are so very,
very great to find the person wanted, and their being so
vividly present to my mind makes me more difficult to satisfy.
I think of our English ladies, their manners and appearance,
and of how much Bertie admires them and of what use would
cleverness be—without some attractions to captivate him, all
the influence of a clever wife would be gone if he did not care
about her and from what I see Elizabeth is far more learned
than clever. At the same time a perfect being is not to be
found in this world—and faults everyone has—it depends
upon finding someone whose faults can be easily cured and
are not of a kind to form a serious barrier to her success.

BUCKINGHAM PALACE, FEBRUARY 25, 1861

Your account which we are very thankful for is not
promising—as the defects are those which in the particular
position could be very serious. Time may make a difference,
but I own I am not very hopeful.[1] This being the case, I must
ask you to do all you can to hear about the 2 others.
Mademoiselle de Shuckman (whom you praise so much) saw
a good deal of Anna I think last year, and ask her pray, what
she thinks of her character, temper, disposition, education
etc. I have heard that she was both clever and well educated.
She wrote a very pretty letter to Alice the other day. Then
as regards Princess Alexandra of D. you could surely for

---

[1] The misgivings of the Princess Royal and Queen Victoria are borne
out by the shrewd picture of Elizabeth of Wied, then Queen of Roumania,
in *The Story of My Life* by Marie, Queen of Roumania.

yourself get Wally to find out everything about her education and general character; whether she is clever, quiet, not frivolous or vain, fond of occupation etc. The looks and manners we know are excellent, and whether she seems very outrée Danish. The mother's family[1] are bad—the father's foolish.[2] Valerie could write to Wally and find it all out. The subject is so important—the choice so circumscribed, that I am sure you will kindly set about at once finding out all these things. It is so very important—with the peculiar character we have to deal with. The Princess of Meiningen, he did not like, and she is not strong; Marie of the Netherlands is clever and ladylike, but too plain and not strong, and poor Addy not clever or pretty.

From the Princess Royal

BERLIN, MARCH 4, 1861

I hope the gentlemen are pleased with their reception.[3] It is so very mortifying when such is not the case. And particularly for me—as I am so anxious that my countrymen should carry away a good impression of this country—and if you knew the ill-nature, the jealousy and the antipathy of the Russian set here at Berlin you would hardly know whether to laugh or to be angry. And all this ill-feeling against the English and everything that is English I am usually made to feel but this is not the general feeling in the town and in the country at large. They have a friendly and kindly feeling towards England in spite of The Times and that always comforts me and I do not care a straw for the good feeling of the Russian reactionary, pietistic[4] set, and I despise their way of thinking with all my heart and hope to goodness their day is over.

---

[1] The Queen must mean here the Danish Royal Family which at that time was conspicuously decadent. The mother's mother was a Danish princess.

[2] Schleswig-Holstein.

[3] The new King of Prussia was invested with the Garter on March 4 by a special mission of which Lord Breadalbane was the head.

[4] A curious word for the Princess to use. She means perhaps formally devout—as distinct from intellectually religious.

All you say about dear Fritz delights and pleases us so much! But he must not over fatigue himself, and you must also get more air. Surely Fritz's military duties ought to be of a different kind now, and he ought to be relieved from them, while he has so many things upon his hands? How very gratifying to you, and what a comfort to the dear Prince, to see your dear husband on the footing you could wish with his mother. I hope you will soon be able to see more of him.

Now before going any further let me return to the very important, difficult topic of the princesses. While we may not entirely give up Elizabeth W.—I own the want of tact is the one thing which we so much fear will not improve. Could she not be a good deal with the Queen—and perhaps with Louise too? If she does not improve in that and in manners etc.—within the next year—there is no hope. What you say about the different candidates is most true. Oh! why can't Marie H.[1] become Protestant? I think you ought to do all you can to hear about Anna of H. not because she is the best of them, but because it seems to me that taking it all together she has the fewest disadvantages— both personally and politically. Madame Bauer, who is perfectly unbiased about her own princes and princesses and very sensible, says Anna is very clever—but very shy and very childish for her age still being kept much back. That Princess of Dessau[2] I have also heard as being very pretty but she is too old—and the parents are very foolish and frivolous people, and the Duchess of Nassau—the eldest sister—at one time a very bad wife. As one must look round everywhere, I want to know if you've ever seen or heard of a young Princess of Altenburg[3] a step-sister to the young hereditary Princess of Dessau who was born in '45? Prince or Princess Hohenzollern ought to know about her. There would certainly be no marriage I should think before three

---

[1] Hohenzollern-Sigmaringen.
[2] Anhalt-Dessau.
[3] Saxe-Altenburg.

years' time. Then I think it would be advisable. You knew I suppose that Charles Hohenzollern[1] is rather in love with that Princess Hilda?[2] At least Louis told me so. I fancy Princess Charles (Elizabeth) is rather strict, for by her letter to Alice I see that Anna still has religious lessons—and that Wilhelm, though fifteen, has never been to a play. The Queen of Bavaria is so also, and their mother was very much so.

I can't say I am quite happy about dearest Grandmama. Her general health thank God! is good, and the attack of feverishness is past, but the poor arm continues so swelled and so inflamed—brought on I think by using it when she ought not. But it is now utterly useless, and a great trial to her. Though she sleeps well—and is not ill otherwise, till the inflammation is gone I shan't feel easy. Her dear health is alas a constant anxiety. Don't delay your visit, don't delay bringing both children—God knows when you could again show them to your beloved grandmother. Both Papa and I feel strongly that it is not merely for your and our great pleasure that we wish so much that you should come in July—it is a duty which you owe her, your only grandmother, who has ever been so kind to you! This the King and Queen will I know feel. Don't speak of the arm though, only generally of her suffering state.

OSBORNE, MARCH 7, 1861

I will still add a few words on the topic of princesses. Papa says that there will be no difficulty in a short time to hear, and see enough of Anna of H. so that enquiries in that quarter are of less importance. I think that as once we have admitted the possibility of one in the position of

---

[1] The second son of Prince Hohenzollern-Sigmaringen.
[2] The Princess of Anhalt-Dessau alluded to by Queen Victoria earlier in this letter.

Elizabeth W. we might look for others in the same[1] and therefore tax your and perhaps the dear Queen's brain and find someone. More than four years younger she should not be; I think even that too much; three or two or one year would be the best and the same age would be no objection.

We are grieved and distressed and alarmed at your account of the state of affairs and of the K.'s great excitement, alarm and depression! It is most distressing. Let us hope it may take a better turn and that dear Papa's letter may do good.[2]

The one thing that weighs upon me now is dear Grandmama's suffering state, not, thank God that there is any immediate cause of alarm—or that she has been very ill—but she is so suffering—so uncomfortable—so utterly helpless that it made my heart bleed to see her so and I was quite overcome when I came back here yesterday evening. Her pulse is quite good, her sleep good (thank God!) the organs all sound—but besides the old original wound, which I hoped—like two years ago—had emptied out the various swellings on Monday, there is the sore hand. And now (which has discouraged her and I must say us very much today) since yesterday morning there is another gathering under the left arm which till now has never been affected and the fear of this breaking, and so many sores at once, is that her strength will not be able to stand it. Still she has such a strong constitution and takes it all with such heavenly patience and gentleness that with God's help we may hope for improvement soon—and for her so precious life being prolonged.

You will understand my anxiety and distress—why I so

---

[1] Meaning that she was not a member of a sovereign family.
[2] The Prince Consort evidently said that the only defence for Germany against her menacing neighbours lay in a German sense of nationality. But he emphasised that it was the duty of statesmen to guide these national ambitions and not indulge them by militarism, and that Prussia need only maintain its constitution to serve as an example to the rest of Germany.

earnestly urge your not delaying your visit beyond the end of June or beginning of July, and bring both your children; let no timid, foolish Wegner be asked again. If the King and Queen allow it—the baby is well and Mrs. Hobbs is satisfied —there can be no difficulty. You shall have the yacht to bring you over—and old Mary in it to assist. I repeat, I think it is a sacred duty you owe your beloved grandmother—who does require to be cheered in the midst of the heavy trials which she has to bear but don't speak of the details of dear Grandmama's health to anyone but Fritz, who is so kind and good.

I am surprised you think Lord Hinchingbrooke[1] charming; I don't think him very attractive or very clever, but I honour him for his high character and sensible tastes. The dress and tournure and style of our young men of the present day are to me perfectly odious though to be sure he has little of that, for he is anything but slang. Constance is not engaged to him nor will Lord Clarendon hear of it being considered so. Lord Sandwich can really I believe not give him enough for them to marry upon; his mother has such a large jointure and his own fortune is not large; old Lady Sandwich might do something and perhaps she will, but she is not a very amiable old woman, now 80 years old.

FROGMORE, MARCH 16, 1861

On this most dreadful day of my life, I must write you one line! Dear Lady Augusta (who has been like her child) will write to you an account which I could not, beyond that the end was peaceful, painless and that her dear hand was in mine to the last. Oh! but the agony of watching the ebbing of the life of one so dear, so precious, is not to be described. I have just been to see her, so peaceful, so beautiful an expression! that when I think that she can never speak to me again, that that dear loving voice is forever still that her love and affection can no longer cast a sunbeam

---

[1] Heir of Lord Sandwich.

over us—then I feel as if my heart would break! You, my darling, have seen a death bed—I never. But then you saw only the death of one you did not know and who had been unconscious for so long! You may imagine what it is—when it is the dearest object (but one) you possess! I never shall forget those dreadful hours of the night and this morning. But God's will be done! What the loss is to me—no one can tell! For forty-one years never parted for more than three months! One of the great sorrows is that she never saw your children. That was her greatest and my greatest wish. Oh! if only you had come last winter! She said when William was born she feared she would never see him! I own that that breaks my heart to think of![1]

On going back to Germany after spending some time with the Queen on the occasion of the Duchess of Kent's death, the Princess Royal writes from Berlin:

APRIL 4, 1861

Only one thing pains me—when I think of it and that is the relation between you and Bertie! In the railway carriage going to Dover I thought so much about it, and wished I could have told you how kindly, nicely, properly and even sensibly he spoke, his heart is very capable of affection, of warmth of feeling and I am sure that it will come out with time and by degrees. He loves his home and feels happy there and those feelings must be nurtured, cultivated for if once lost they will not come again so easily. I admire dear Papa's patience and kindness and gentleness to him so much I can only hope and pray that there may never be an estrangement between him and you—as it would be the source of endless misery to both. I know, dear Mama, you will forgive my saying all this and not be offended.

---

[1] The Queen's grief for her mother, who died after a long life (though her illness was distressing), will strike the twentieth-century reader as selfish and exaggerated. But it will be remembered that indulgence of

I know you will think of your poor sad Mama. It is all the same still, and my head is so very bad—so fearfully sensitive; I can't bear the least noise or talking in the next room even. I feel so stupified—stunned—can't think how I lived through these three weeks which seem like an hour!

Lovely as the spring is here—I hardly can look at anything—I seem as walking in a dream! I still take my meals alone—as I eat but little—and can't bear many faces.

You are right, dear child, I do not wish to feel better. My head has been tiresome and troublesome and I can still bear little or no noise. The relief of tears is great—and though since last Wednesday night I have had no very violent outburst—they come again and again every day, and are soothing to the bruised heart and soul.

Yesterday I went down for the first time to luncheon with Papa and your sisters—but breakfast and dinner I still take upstairs in my room. I find it does me good to be very quiet. The more distant the dreadful event becomes, and the more others recover their spirits—the more trying it becomes to me! Oh! the slightest approach to ordinary habits is so painful to me! Every evening we are occupied with the dear papers. The preliminary sorting is finished—and now remains the arranging of those that are sorted. Such touching relics I have found! Her love for me is beyond everything! Not a scrap of my writing—or of my hair has ever been thrown away—and such touching notes in a book about my babyhood. We found a most precious relic of my poor father, which I had never seen. His little writing desk—with his Garter purse, the drawing of the room he died in—his three last letters to dearest Mama (in French) and such loving, tender letters, and a little book of hers in which she wrote in every week after his death expressive

---

woe was, in those days, the measure of love for the departed. This was the first great sorrow in the Queen's life; it prostrated her.

of such love and tender affection for him—such despair at his death, such longing to be soon re-united to him! It is so touching to see! And now after forty-one years they are re-united, and both surely bless their poor orphan child! Yes, and she trusts one day to be everlastingly with them. That is a blessed thought and one which I love to dwell on—much as I love to remain in this world for the many very precious ones I possess!

But I see I run on about myself—and the object which fills my heart, and I don't speak of you and your dear darling baby. How sorry I am you should find her looking ill; but, dearest, you are only a beginner and will find that babies and little children always are dreadfully pulled down and in a day—and then get up as quickly again, so don't be alarmed about it.

As regards Bertie—I quite agree with you, dear child—that he must be a little more tender and affectionate in his manner—if he is to expect it from me—and take a little more interest in what interests us if he is to be at all pleasant in the house. And now, dearest child, I must say, without I hope making you angry—that you did not quite set about making matters better, for you kept telling me all his most stupid and silly remarks (said as he too often does—without thinking—partly to tease you and partly to give vent to his temper) and enraged me, low and wretched as I was—greatly. If one wishes to pour oil and not to "keep the kettle boiling" one must not repeat everything another who irritates has said—else it of course makes matters much worse. He left on Monday. His voice made me so nervous I could hardly bear it. Altogether I never felt in such a state of nerves for noise or sound.

OSBORNE, APRIL 13, 1861

Don't worry yourself about me. I love to dwell on her, and to be quiet and not to be roused out of my grief! To wish me to shake it off—and to be merry—would be to wish me no good! I could not and would not! Daily do I feel more the blank—the loss I *shall* experience—and the power of enjoying other things is not possible at present. Don't expect or wish it, dear, for it cannot be! Young people with their elastic spirits are different and can hardly understand —the sort of quiet, serious state of mind which I am in and wish to remain in.

OSBORNE, APRIL 17, 1861

Many, many thanks for your dear and affectionate letter of the 13th. But before I say anything else—let me set you right about Bertie. I don't in the least want to convey the meaning that you had made mischief dear by what you had said. Only as you continually reverted to my relations with Bertie (which I assure you are not at all what you suppose— though at that moment he was a trial from his listlessness— in the winter his séjour had gone off very well) I could not help pointing out to you—that at that moment repeating his stupid remarks—irritated and pained me more than usual and that it was better—if you were so very anxious about the relations between me and him not to do so and that you did not quite set about improving matters in the right way. As for Papa's opinion I only remember saying to him I wish Vicky would not repeat these silly stories of Bertie— it only makes me very angry with him. Mischief you never made, dear; it was only momentary annoyance and it was to point out to you—what, in future you had best avoid, that I mentioned it at all. I felt so weak when you were here and so utterly disinclined to talk of anything but one subject—that I never would have stopped you in your observations—much less attempted to argue upon them so don't give what has passed on the subject another thought.

From the Princess Royal

APRIL 17, 1861

I have gathered some more information about Princess A. of Holstein. I got Mrs. Hobbs to question the nurse of Marianne's children who walks with her almost every day and who was ten years with Princess Alix. Her account of her is that she is the sweetest girl who ever lived—and full of life and spirits. She says she has always been as strong and healthy as possible and has a very good constitution. That she has never ailed anything in her life except having the measles. The Queen taxes her brains all day long on this subject and has arrived at the same conclusions as I have—that is that the accounts of Princess Alix sound better than those she could give of any other German princess she knew, but she is of course much against the match for other reasons, political etc. etc., on account of the Holstein relationship but that is one that in my idea can be overcome. The Queen is most afraid of the influence of somebody at Kew,[1] which I own I am not now, though I should have ten years ago. The Queen says if she only had an idea who was to be the one she would take her in hand and initiate her into everything necessary for her to know but she could not do so with the one in question as she was sure all the unmarried princes here would fall in love with her as she is so lovely.

From the Princess Royal

BERLIN, APRIL 20, 1861

I have nothing the least cheering to tell you, we are both most exceedingly out of spirits, and have plenty of cause to be so—for public and private matters go on as badly as possible— I fully expect if this goes on much longer in this way the cart will upset one fine day. I am so sad and so discouraged I cannot tell you. I hear from all sides from people that I can rely on that there is a general feeling of discontent prevailing here at this moment—distrust of the King and dislike of the Queen. I see Fritz much cast down, well-thinking people disheartened nearly despairing, the false and mischievous ones triumphing on every occasion great and small, the Queen thoroughly unhappy and heaven knows not without just cause, though she has to thank herself for it partly. The King confused in his ideas and irritable in his humour, we both with our hands tied seeing all the evils—seeing our future position made more difficult hour by hour—and unable to prevent it.

---

[1] The Duchess of Cambridge, great-aunt to Princess Alexandra.

Is that not enough to make one sad! Anything like the com-
plications and intrigues going on in every corner I cannot
describe to you. And the right road is so straight forward, so
easy, so plain and simple, carrying its rewards along with it
step by step and yet the wrong road is wilfully chosen.

But to talk of something else. I send you here a letter from
Wally which I received yesterday and which speaks for itself.[1]
Alas! the chances become less and less—if we are already to
strike this charming creature off the list of those to be chosen
I really don't know at all what to say because I own Princess
A. of Holstein is the only one of these princesses for whom
I feel portée—it would be dreadful if this pearl went to the
horrid Russians.

After going through various names and striking them off for several
reasons the Princess goes on:

What are we to do? Unfortunately, princesses do not spring
up like mushrooms out of the earth or grow upon trees. I am
quite 'au bout de mon latin',[2] *and neither the Baron nor*
Countess Blücher nor the Queen can help me. I sit continually
with the Gotha Almanack in my hands turning the leaves
over in hopes to discover someone who has not come to light!

OSBORNE, APRIL 24, 1861

Many, many thanks for your dear long and interesting
but—in part—very melancholy letter of the 20th. How
grieved I am for you both, about many things—which
are so easy—and are not done. It makes every thing so
difficult for us too.

Dear Papa has undertaken to answer all about the matrimonial subjects, so I say nothing more.

---

[1] Hinting no doubt that the son of the Emperor Alexander II was being
considered by Princess Alexandra's family.
[2] Means "at my wits' end".

Your dear letter of the 23rd with so many kind wishes
for dear good Alice's birthday reached me yesterday afternoon and I thank you much for it as well as for the charming
little cross which I received 3 days ago and which looked so
pretty, full of primroses and violet flowers! Yesterday was
a very sad birthday[1]—the saddest I ever remember, which
grieved me so for her, poor dear child, but she was as sad
herself. I cried constantly yesterday and the grief and yearn-
ing and almost despair which at times comes over me are
dreadful! I find even that that gets worse than better, and
when we all entered the breakfast room, I felt as if my
heart must break! Not one day these weary 6 weeks have
I passed without tears—and very often cry bitterly still! It
seems very long since I saw her—and heard from her—and
so it must go on for the rest of my life! It seems a fearful
thought. My nerves are still very bad, I suffer very much
from my head and from that dreadful sensitiveness. I think
I am no better than I was 3 weeks ago—only I am less weak.
But the power of enjoyment of any thing seems (for the
time) entirely gone!

It was a very fine day—very hot sun—everything so
green—the trees nearly out—profusion of primroses and
violets, king-cups—anemonies—oxlips etc.—and the night-
ingales singing beautifully. In the afternoon we drove in
the small char à banc but the noise of the wheels on the
road hurts me very much; Alice has driven me every morning in the little Sardinian pony carriage which with india
rubber wheels makes no noise.

Now I must defend myself about dear Fritz's accusation
about Louis being more favoured than him. In the 1st place
as regards the calling me "Mama" (which is only "Mama
in the future")—that is because he does not know what else
to call me; Fritz must remember that since 51 he always
called me and Papa "Aunt and Uncle" which made everything quite easy—whereas Louis really could not call me

[1] Princess Alice was 18.

anything but "Majestät" or "Mama". I had never called
his mother Cousin as I did the Queen. Then another and
very strong reason was, that Fritz was so much older (he is
only 13 years younger than we are)—whereas Louis could
perfectly well be my child and I look upon him as a child in
many ways. These are the true reasons. If Louis has more
easy work of it—it must be remembered, dear—that you
were quite a child—and in fact ought not to have been
engaged so soon—you were only 15 and that Alice was
nearer 18 than 17 when she was engaged, so that everything must be very different. And lastly I was younger and
certainly had to learn that one must put one's maternal
feelings aside altogether if one is not to be very jealous;
when Princess Charlotte's[1] time comes—I shall like to hear
what you both say and feel. But if I was severer than I ought
to have been perhaps, the first time, I am determined not
to err in that respect again—though I never could allow
the free and constant intercourse between "promis" which
is the fashion of the present day. Now here is a long explanation—but it will be satisfactory.

   We go to Town tomorrow. I dread it much. On Tuesday
(quite privately) there will be a Council for Alice's marriage
to be declared, which I equally dread very much. Every
thing is so changed since that fearful blow! Goodbye and
God bless you.

From the Princess Royal

                                    BERLIN, APRIL 30, 1861
   What I said about Fritz, dear Mama, was only in joke,
I never complained of anything as I thought you were always
right and even if you had allowed Fritz and me to be a great
deal more together it would not have been either my desire or
for my good. And I do not think you ever heard me complain,
although every minute I spent with him was inexpressively
precious to me, yet I always felt wretchedly uncomfortable,
shy and miserable when with him in your presence or alone.

---

[1] The Princess Royal's daughter.

I know you thought me too young and were provoked at seeing us together and at my going away and altogether were not satisfied with me (and I remember how often I gave you cause for dissatisfaction!). I understood your feelings all along and thought to myself often and often how very trying it must be for you to see one of your children being stolen away from you, and thought it very natural for you to think so—this only made me the more ill at ease when I was with Fritz and you as I was afraid of showing my affection to him for fear of offending or distressing or irritating you—and yet dared not beg him to be less demonstrative which I wished from the bottom of my heart for fear of hurting him who was so dear and kind and so unaccustomed to kindness at home. But everybody's feelings are not alike—I think the free and continual intercourse of promis neither becoming nor suitable nor judicious in any way and the younger one is the less advisable I think it, so I am quite on your side—but as I said before opinions and feelings differ on that subject. I have said over and over again to Fritz that I thought you were right and I should have been very sorry if you had been different. But he will not be convinced and thinks himself ill-used and says he was so much older than me that you should have trusted me all the more to him. But you know how he adores you, Papa and our home and how grateful he always is for kindness and affection and confidence, therefore you must not be angry with him or attach more importance to his complaints. And all the reasoning in the world will not convince a person who views a matter from a totally different point. For instance he will not believe that I was shy with him—he says that you had forbidden me to speak to him when I sat beside him at dinner or take his arm out walking etc., and I tell him over and over again that you had not forbidden anything of the kind but my own (perhaps too delicate) feelings prevented my doing so—he cannot understand a young lady's feelings. I cannot explain them so there the matter ends. This I feel to be a very unnecessary and déplacé explanation of things that are bygones and on which you and I understand each other so perfectly but as I was once upon the subject I let my pen run on hoping that you will not be displeased with me and as, thank God, my intercourse with you is so natural, easy and open I never feel any difficulty in pouring out my heart and mind to you—as I should wish my daughter to do to me when she is my age. If Fritz knew I had written all this he would be dreadfully frightened as he has no idea of what a confiding and fearless love of a child to a parent is—he has never been accustomed to look on his parents as an oracle—as his best friends as I have. He has much more that feeling towards you and Papa than towards his own parents. With Alice all is so different! She is older than I was and (luckily for her) a different person to me, Louis is different to Fritz. You are older—the whole thing is not new to you and Alice has so much more natural ease and aplomb and savoir faire than I have and not the crushing feeling that I had, that of being in a false position namely in being in fact a baby with the feelings of a woman and always of offending somebody either her Mama or her promis. Please let her read this, she will understand all I mean.

BUCKINGHAM PALACE, MAY 1, 1861

I can't write to you as I wished to do unfortunately as I have got a very weak head—the remains of a violent sick headache yesterday. My poor head is in a wretched state—and the little exertions I made since I came up to town have thrown me back. The passage made me uncomfortable as there was rolling at Spithead—then the first going to the Chapel made me nervous, and then on Monday and yesterday I spent the whole morning at Clarence House looking out things which was both very painful and dreadfully fatiguing and trying to one's head. That was followed by the Council yesterday, though only half were present—and no-one in uniform—for the declaration of dear, good Alice's marriage and though I did not break down it agitated me dreadfully—and I finally knocked completely up and had to leave the dinner. This was an unnecessary addition to my poor weak nerves.

I write to you from here. I think I am deriving benefit from the complete change and the great quiet. It is a small, old fashioned but comfortable house, and stands in the middle of the fine park—which we are able to walk in without being molested. There are endless drives too. Dear Papa has gone to Town each morning returning about 5. Today is the first levée (his). I have been this morning with your 3 sisters quite privately to Kew Gardens (which are closed till 1—and where Mary met us). All would be so pleasant, were it not for the dreadful reality which constantly breaks upon my mind of my fearful loss—and damps the possibility of any enjoyment.

Many thanks for your dear and amusing letter of the 30th—pouring out your feelings on byegone subjects. I won't here enter into it—but I could tell you many reasons for my feeling annoyed which might have been avoided—when we meet I shall. I must however say that I am surprised and somewhat shocked that Fritz could think I forbad your speaking to him. You talked incessantly. As for taking his arm—I never dreamt of allowing or forbidding it—as I never say anything approaching to it. You view things quite rightly. Your and Alice's cases are quite different. Pray read to Fritz my explanation of the other day, for it is the case and the exact truth.

What you mentioned about Princess A.'s[1] letters to her nurse—I think very nice. It speaks so much for her.

I got the young Baron's letter about your fear lest your visit in July might be spoiled. But, dear child—don't fear that; the worst I really think that could happen would be your visit being curtailed at one end or the other, and though that would be very unfortunate, still 3 weeks or even less are better than nothing and between the last week in June and the 1st in August you have plenty of room if the Ceremony of the Oath of Allegiance was in June—the latter part of it—why you could come about the 2d week in July—or if in August come about the 25th of June. Please

---

[1] Alexandra.

speak openly to the Queen about it and tell her how anxious we are to know something. If the King knew that we also waited to arrange our plans—perhaps he might decide. You may make ample use of my name. But 3 weeks sea-bathing Fritz and you ought at least to have.

Good-bye and God bless you, my own dearest child. Kindest love to dear Fritz.

From the Princess Royal

I have many other worries in the house as a certain name-less person at the head of the establishment is the most difficult person to deal with under the sun—just at present I have not an easy life of it I can assure you. But please do not take any notice of what I say here or answer it as I do not wish to appear as if I complained to you about M. de H.[1] or threw a bad light upon him but it is a sort of safety valve letting out a little steam now and then when one is boiling under the surface. I feel that I am getting more savage against people every day which is very wrong I know and I don't observe that all the difficulties I have to encounter great and small do me any good whatever! The Queen is extremely kind to me and I do whatever I possibly can in a small way to make her burthen lighter and take away from the bitterness which she herself in a great measure adds to a life of few pleasures and many hard trials. She knows that I am sincerely and devotedly attached to her, and that she need not fear to be misunderstood by me, she knows that I know how much she has to bear and go through—and that I value and admire her many so truly noble and great qualities and that I am ever grateful for her kindness and confidence and return it from my heart. From her peculiar constitution of body and spirit and the peculiar circumstances in which she is situated she is doomed to suffer much—and

---

[1] This is Monsieur von Heinz, Chamberlain of Prince Frederick William's household. From a letter to the Prince Consort in the previous year, it would seem that the Princess Royal did not greatly like him. See also note on page 43.

only those who can appreciate her and who know her as well as I do, know how much! And yet nature has endowed her with—I may say lavished upon her—her choicest and noblest gifts and this is what I strive always to put before her when she complains so bitterly of her unhappiness—that God has given her unusual gifts and appointed her to a great and unusual vocation—and the sense of that privilege must make up for the absence of so much that makes the life of other women, less highly gifted and in humbler spheres, so much more tranquil and happy. I know no one I pity more. She stands so alone—she has and makes so many enemies and there are so few who bear with her foibles and know what she really is. And yet you do not know how difficult it is to be her friend for she always is her own enemy! I am sure there are few mothers-in-law on so good and warm a footing with their sons' wives as she is with me—and she spoils me a great deal. It is my greatest endeavour to do all I can to keep up this good feeling but I must acknowledge that I make many sacrifices for I am at her beck and call all day long—whenever she wants me whether it be morning or evening I go but I look forward with dread to some future day when, as last year, being faint and sick and unwell I really could not be there at all hours and as the Queen is rather tyrannical, she did not like that and if ever I am in the same predicament again, I know that it will be the old story over again.

WHITE LODGE, RICHMOND, MAY 8, 1861

I begin my letter today to you, in much distressing anxiety as we heard last night that our dear old Sir James is again very seriously ill with a similar attack to the one he had 15 or 16 months ago—and that yesterday they were in considerable anxiety about him. This morning we have not heard—but you will easily imagine how little fit I am to bear such trouble just now! I pray God mercifully to spare our dear old friend yet some time longer—though I fear we can only hope for a very few years for he is 75. Dearest child, life is sad—and since our dreadful misfortune in March I look on all that I love best with such trembling lest it should be taken from me! Till the loss of beloved Grandmama—I never realised the possibility of losing any out of my own family circle—now I do!

Upon the whole I am better: I care more to go out, and the pretty country about here, much of which I have known from my earliest years, does me good; but my head is terribly weak and tender still. Noise still affects it painfully and I can't occupy myself for long at a time without getting pain in it—and getting bewildered and confused, which is tiresome and trying.

Many many thanks for your dear long letter of the 3d which we only got on Monday night as the messenger was delayed.

Really, dear child, though no one approves more than I do, your devotion and dutifulness to the dear Queen, I would not mind telling her that "for the children and my own health I must go before the end of the month into the country". You could go in to Town frequently, and that ought to suffice.

Just this moment arrives a better account of dear Sir James, thank God! I really felt as if I couldn't bear to hear any worse news! It would have been too much.

To return to your letter, dear. I fear you can't have explained properly to Mrs. Hobbs what position the new governess would have. Else she ought not to be in that foolish state. I never allow the Lady Superintendent to put herself between me and the governesses or nurse, but merely to superintend and to do what I can not do—to revise the accounts—and see that what I wish and order is carried out. If you keep strictly to this and let Mrs. Hobbs see this in writing—I feel sure there can be no mistake, I can speak to you from connaissance de cause and from the experience of 19 years (Lady Lyttelton[1] came in '42).

Poor Queen, with so much that is great, noble, and good to be so unhappy and enabled to do so little. Still the time will come when her great qualities are recognised. Our dear Countess says that you have been of the greatest use to her

---

[1] Governess to the Royal Family.

(the Queen), which is a great thing and which gives me the greatest pleasure. She is much and warmly attached to you.

What do you hear of the young Weimar? Clever he is, I know. He was to spend the winter at Geneva; the girls you told me, were particularly well brought up.

We expect Louis on the 19th or 20th; I, a little dread it, dearly as I love him, for any new face makes me nervous and I am so little fit for being a chaperon but we shall manage it, dear Papa will help and Louis is so little in the way.

WHITE LODGE, RICHMOND, MAY 15, 1861

I write to you for the last time from here, and since yesterday we have summer weather which is not very beneficial for my poor, weak head. Many, many thanks for your dear long letter of the 10th.

All you say about beloved Grandmama knowing every thing better than she did before—and our being not really separated from her—is what I feel. I feel as if she lived on with us—(though alas! I get sudden shocks when I feel I can't write to her). And we must look upon it as a temporary separation. At times the thought of the impossibility of all my present sorrow and suffering ever bringing her back to me (as suffering often is rewarded by a happy result) makes the misery and hopelessness of it very dreadful, and little trifles often, don't you think, upset one even more than great things?

How touched I am by old Wrangel's[1] kind and touching thought of me! By all means send me the little cross— though I have your's (I can place this at Frogmore) and say that I am deeply touched by his thinking of me in my sorrow, and give him this photograph of dearest Grandmama with dear Affie which I am sure he will like. I would have sent one of Papa and me besides but have no good

---

[1] The Prussian Field-Marshal known as "Papa" Wrangel. He had carried his regimental colours at the Battle of Leipzig. He was largely responsible for putting down the disturbances in Berlin in 1848.

one—by me. The universal sympathy shown me, the kind letters from so many friends and acquaintances which I have received have been most gratifying and soothing to my feelings—for they seem all so truly to understand what I must have been suffering.

I am grieved to hear that dear Mrs. Hobbs's temper is not of the best, but however with a little management—I dare say you will be able to avoid any very distressing scenes. So many good servants have that defect.

I am sorry that you are forced to stop in Town—for if you have the warm weather we now have Berlin will be very hot. For this year—nothing can be done, but for another you must get the doctors to say positively what is necessary for the children. If good Wegner was not so very timid, he ought to say positively what was right and then there would be no difficulty.

We went on Monday to the old Kew Palace where you once were years ago, and yesterday morning to Syon (the Duke of Northumberland's) which is a beautiful place and such fine grounds and such a magnificent house; I had not been there since I was a child. No one was there. We have besides taken many pretty, long drives in the neighbourhood.

I am dreadfully nervous just now—as I am expecting the good old Queen[1] every minute and have not yet seen her since my misfortune. Every new person I see—makes me so fearfully nervous.

Dear Papa was at Cambridge yesterday.

The dear Queen has just left; she was most kind and I am glad the first painful meeting is over—for I shall now not be so nervous again. She was much overcome and so was I. She is dreadfully thin and fragile but wonderfully recovered again. Uncle Nemours, Françoise[2] and Paris[3] came.

The young Weimar should travel and get in contact with other young men and then, his learnedness would wear off. I always think that would be a very good match

---

[1] Queen Amélie of the French.
[2] Wife of the Prince de Joinville, third son of the Queen.
[3] Comte de Paris, grandson of the Queen and Louis Philippe's heir.

for one of your sisters—with the position of the Grand Duke and his liberal, patriotic views—and the vicinity of Coburg and Gotha—I think it would be a good and useful position for one of them. The girls must be nice children; one might do for Affie—but this is only amongst ourselves and still one must look about; in Affie's case the thing is not near so difficult; there is a greater choice and his wife need not unite so many qualities as Bertie's must, for many reasons public and private. Philip saw Princess Alix and the whole family last summer and will be able to tell us all about them.

I am sorry to hear my poor Jane Ely has been taken ill again. She really is very unfortunate.

BUCKINGHAM PALACE, MAY 18, 1861

Many thanks for your dear little letter of the 14th with such amusing accounts of darling William. He seems to take after his mama as sons are supposed always to do. (And baby after her papa!)

The Queen writes to me today—that though she can't say when the oath-taking ceremony will be that she is sure it will be over before the end of June—and that she is sure nothing will prevent your coming for the month of July. This is a great satisfaction.

We leave at $\frac{1}{4}$ to 3 for Osborne. Tomorrow we expect dear good Louis—whose visit I had looked forward to—with such pleasure—but now—I must own I rather dread it as I am quite unfit and unable to be cheerful. Dearest Uncle Leopold will arrive D.V. on the 22d. His visit will be a great comfort to me, for his whole manner is so soothing and kind.

I must end. Aumale has been so successful in an admirable speech he made at the Literary Fund dinner on Wednesday. You should read it. In Thursday's papers the speeches are.

My poor birthday is fast approaching. How I dread it! We shall make it as little like one as possible. No music (that would kill me)—no change of mourning—and dine merely en famille.

I was much vexed to hear of this violent lumbago—which according to German fashion kept you two days in bed. I have no doubt that you caught it in that cold ride which you describe to me. There is nothing so wretchedly cold as being on horseback in a cold wind. I am distressed and alarmed at so much scarlet fever and measles being about—especially the former. You should all take Bella Donna—you know we always did, and it saved us all. You and Fritz and the grown-up people 20 drops in water, baby 1 drop and William 2 drops, in water every morning the first thing. Never mind Wegner's laughing at it; none of us who took it got the scarlet fever.

OSBORNE, MAY 25, 1861

My beloved child

You wrote me a dear, beautiful letter which touched me very deeply. You are a dear, warm-hearted affectionate child, and knew what I should feel. One's birthday above all others is the day when one loves to have one's mother who gave it one—with pain and suffering—near one. And to miss her—to miss even a sign from her—was dreadful. But I felt it even more the night before—when I looked out of my dressing-room window on the terrace—lit up by splendid moonlight! Fast and many were the tears which fell. But she was and ever is near me, and thank God I got better through the poor day than I expected. But the great contretemps which really quite bouleverséed one—was poor dear Louis being ill and in bed with measles.

OSBORNE, MAY 31, 1861

Good dear Louis is extremely well; since the day before yesterday he is able to go about in the house—which is great happiness to him and to dear Alice (who has borne this trial with her usual sweet temper and patience—which will enable her to bear all the trials which we poor doomed women are born to bear—easily).

Tomorrow Papa insists on our going to Town for no

earthly reason but that tiresome horticultural garden—
which I curse for more reasons than one—and have to leave
poor little, sick Leopold behind here—in his bed which
makes me sadly anxious, and adds to my low spirits! They
say there is no danger whatever at present, but I own I
think it both cruel and wrong to leave a sick child behind,
when I have nothing earthly to do till the 19th. I am very
much annoyed and distressed at being forced to leave him
by the very person who ought to wish me to stay. But men
have not the sympathy and anxiety of women. Oh! no!

Respecting your ladies—dear, two in all is what we can
lodge here and no more. Therefore either the Governess
and one Lady—or the 2 Ladies and no Governess. You
know the house and that a number of single ladies with
maids is the very thing we can not put up. And pray not
too many gentlemen either. In London or at Windsor there
may be loads of them but not here.

I am very curious to hear about your visit[1]—but I should
be almost glad if there was not great beauty; nice looks—
and good sense, but no dazzling beauty.

From the Princess Royal

BERLIN, JUNE 1, 1861

*I suppose you had heard of the duel between General
Manteuffel and M. Twesten[2] which took place last Tuesday
and causes immense sensation here! An anonymous pamphlet
appeared which I send you here which is very clever and
contains indisputable truths; you must know that General
Manteuffel is all-powerful, has the King completely in his
pocket and though he is said to be an honourable man which
I venture to doubt, has the most pernicious influence; he is the
head of the King's Maison Militaire, and is with him at all
hours of the day. He is of the Zeitung[3] persuasion and you*

---

[1] She was about to go to Strelitz to stay with the Grand Duchess where
Princess Alexandra was also staying.
[2] General Manteuffel was first cousin to the Prime Minister: he was a
reactionary with some influence over the Regent. Karl Twesten was
one of the founders of the National Liberal Party in Prussia.
[3] Kreuz-Zeitung, the extreme reactionary political party.

may imagine how dangerous he is. I dislike him du fond de mon âme and distrust him equally—Fritz knows exactly what he is and how far his influence goes but does not dislike him as much as I do. However this pamphlet attacks him as you will see—I have marked the passage which caused the challenge. Twesten is the son of the Rector of the University and a clever, distinguished man. Manteuffel sent two Generals to ask him whether he had written the pamphlet and whether the opinions it contained were his—Twesten answered "Yes". Manteuffel demanded satisfaction, Twesten said he was ready to give it—so early on the next morning they went to Tegel— the seconds tried to make it up on the ground and Manteuffel asked Twesten to take back his offensive words. Twesten said conscience would not allow him to do so. Twesten had the first shot and missed (what a pity). Manteuffel then fired and shattered Twesten's right arm. Twesten said "I give you my left hand as you've shattered my right one. I have no rancune against you but I stick to my opinion." They both behaved as well and as chivalrously as possible people say. I think it is a deplorable sign of how far back our civilisation is if a man must fight another because he's attacked in an anonymous pamphlet. Rubbish offers no rewards. What a blessing if we had been rid of Manteuffel! And now he will only rise in the King's estimation.

From the Princess Royal

STRELITZ, JUNE 4, 1861

It is very difficult to be impartial when one is captivated, and I own I never was more so—I never set eyes on a sweeter creature than Princess Alix. She is lovely! Not a dazzling, striking beauty but an indescribable charming.[1] She is a good deal taller than I am, has a lovely figure but very thin, a complexion as beautiful as possible. Very fine white regular teeth and very fine large eyes—with extremely prettily marked eyebrows. A very fine well-shaped nose, very narrow but a little long—her whole face is very narrow, her forehead too but well shaped and not at all flat. Her voice, her walk,

---

[1] So written.

carriage and manner are perfect, she is one of the most lady-like and aristocratic looking people I ever saw! She is as simple and natural and unaffected as possible—and seems exceedingly well brought up. She speaks English and German without the slightest accent. I hear she speaks Swedish and French as well, usually she speaks Danish. She is not at all shy, and such a childlike, maiden-like manner without being the least childish. The expression is very sweet when she laughs or smiles but rather severe when quiet. She takes a good deal of part in the conversation and all she says is very natural. Whether she is clever or not I cannot say but I paid the greatest attention and could not perceive the slightest thing to make me think the contrary. She seems quite at her ease with me and we get on very well together. She told me she still took lessons which she liked very much—and she did not like writing essays much, as she found it difficult but she liked history immensely. She does not seem the least aware of her beauty and is very unassuming. The meeting seems to be as natural as possible and neither the mother[1] nor Augusta or anyone here seemed to think that it's anything else than the merest accident. Princess Christian seems very amiable but is very deaf. You may go far before you find another princess like Princess Alix—I know you and Papa would be charmed with her. She is so bewitching. She says she likes being in Germany very much indeed and longs to go to England. She seems very lively and merry—but as she's so very graceful it suits her very well.

She's got a mark upon her neck, but it comes from an accident or neglected cold. Augusta told me that she is very healthy and I am sure she looks so. She is very well dressed indeed and her manner in society is very posée and dignified. Oh if she only was not a Dane and not related to the Hesses I should say yes—she is the one a thousand times over.

At first sight she did not captivate me as much as she does now, the more I see of her the more charming and attractive I think her. I am very careful in all I do or say—and feel rather nervous. I was all in a tremble and almost ready to

---

[1] Princess Christian.

cry—when I first saw this sweet young creature! If she is to be the one she must be made to live in Germany a little, perhaps with the Queen or with me, but not until it is decided whether she is to be the one or not but if she is seen at Berlin she will be snapped up by some unmarried prince immediately as to see her without falling in love with her is impossible. But she must be initiated as Stephanie was if you mean to think of her for Bertie! I don't know what impression this description will make upon you I only hope that it will be the right one. If you can imagine a mixture of Louise of Baden, Stephanie, Alice and all Lord Abercorn's daughters particularly of Georgie[1] you could picture Princess Alix to yourself. I don't feel the slightest doubt as to Bertie's admiring her as she is just what he likes. We arrived here yesterday at two. I with a coup de soleil on my forehead and right cheek so that I look an unearthly object; when I look at myself in the glass I am quite frightened—my face is quite swollen and red on one side and hurts me so much as if I had had a bad bruise. It is so odious arriving at a strange place looking such a figure, and everybody asking what had happened. Augusta and Fritz[2] are most kind—the Grand-Duchess Mother[3] too odious, she is the most vulgar, common, disagreeable woman I ever saw, and leads poor Augusta a dreadful life as I have plenty of opportunity of seeing. The décousu, unpunctuality and want of order in this house is something extraordinary— no one knows who gives orders or what is going to be done etc. In short all seems to go topsy-turvy I never saw such a badly managed household. Adolphus[4] is a dear boy. The little Princess Dagmar of Denmark[5] a dear little thing with a pretty figure and a very plain face—all excepting her eyes which are very pretty.

I shall try and talk a little more with Princess Alix and find out what her disposition is. She tells me she's very fond

---

[1] The eldest daughter who married Lord Lichfield.
[2] The Grand-Duke of Mecklenburg-Strelitz.
[3] Sister to the Duchess of Cambridge.
[4] The Grand-Duke's only child.
[5] Princess Alexandra's sister who later married the Emperor Alexander III of Russia.

of music and plays—and very fond of pictures. But I don't like talking so much to her before others, for fear of attracting attention and with Hessian eyes in every direction one must mind what one is about. I prefer sending this letter by the messenger, beloved Mama, so you will have to wait some time before you get it.

When the Royal Family got to London, the measles spread rapidly among the children.

BUCKINGHAM PALACE, JUNE 8, 1861

It is plenty to keep me in a fidget with 3 sick children, nervous and low as I am—running up and down stairs continually and one[1] alas! far off! But it is a great comfort to have had them, and to be able to nurse them. Dearest child! that Wednesday evening when the bad news of poor darling Leopold arrived was a terrible moment for me! I thought we should have another dreadful journey down![2] But God was very merciful! And I trust He will continue to protect the little fellow. Surely he must be meant for some great things to have been spared in the midst of such frequent illness! Poor little boy, he was alarmed himself that evening, when he was so exhausted, so restless and cold—but said when Lady Caroline said we must be telegraphed to "Don't alarm dear Mama, lest it should distress her" which showed such thought and affection for so young a child!

I forgot in my last letter to answer your observations about your photograph in that peculiar bathing-dress.[3] Whatever dear Fritz likes you to wear, you are right to wear, dear, for it is a pleasure and happiness to wear what one's husband likes and to feel that he cares for such things. Speaking of books, dear, have you ever read any of Alfred

---

[1] Prince Leopold.

[2] As they had had from London to Windsor when the Duchess of Kent died.

[3] The Princess Royal had written on June 1, 1861: "I was sure you would not like the photograph of me without a bonnet but Fritz wished to have it so—and I did it to please him, as he likes me best with my hair so, and that gown, and I would put on a Chinese costume if he liked to see me in it. I myself do not much like the photograph—but the coiffure is not much different from what I usually wear."

Monod's sermons. He was a very eminent and most excellent French Protestant clergyman at Paris, well known to poor Hélène and to Augusta B. There are two published separately called 1^{ière} La Femme (La Mission de la Femme) 2ième La Femme (La vie de la Femme) which are most beautiful. The Vie de la Femme is quite admirable and would I am sure please you extremely. Shall I send them to you?

BUCKINGHAM PALACE, JUNE 12, 1861

Now, dearest, let me thank you most warmly for your kind, affectionate and most interesting letter of the 4th from Strelitz as well as for dear Fritz's kind and affectionate note —and yours of the 8th. You are, I know—perhaps a little inclined to be carried away if you are pleased with a person— like you were with the Empress E. but Fritz is not and as he so entirely coincides with what you say about Princess Alix (why is she called so?) I feel quite sure she really must be charming in every sense of the word—and really a pearl not to be lost. The thought of having in Bertie's wife so charming a daughter—would be a great comfort for me and there is nothing I should not do to be quite a real mother to her; I shall else be dreadfully alone—when your sisters marry—one after the other—though I hope and think some at least, will be much more with me than you ever can be. But, dearest, we only look at one side of the question—have you at all thought if she will take him? I am sure I think it is not so certain. Alice (who is the only one consulted) declared she would strongly object to be selected without knowing for whom. But what we both feel so deeply is your and dear Fritz's great kindness in going to Strelitz to make this girl's acquaintance and taking so much pains about it. I am so glad that Augusta suspects nothing. I only hope that you cautioned the mother to be discreet—so that the Cambridges don't get wind of it? They always made more of the second, Dagmar, who you say is plain but who they thought so very pretty. Is the mother still good looking? I suppose the father did not come. Dear Papa has written fully to you—and I entirely agree in what he says.

— 341 —

You must not expect to find me at all myself yet! My spirits are very bad, my nerves terribly weak—and there is a heavy weight which weighs upon me and makes everything seem weary work!

So, dear, you and dear Fritz must be patient with poor, old Mama, who feels old, and much shattered, for I am not an amusing companion—though I rejoice in the happiness of others—but I am so dull and listless still, and London air and noise don't improve one. It is to you and dear Fritz that we owe our dear Alice's happiness also! Louis is a most dear, amiable creature with such a very charming disposition.

BUCKINGHAM PALACE, JUNE 19, 1861

I begin my letter before my first Drawing Room which will be awfully hot—long and trying; I feel very nervous and dread this my first appearance in public—greatly but I feel I am doing my duty and that she would have approved that—and that helps me over it. So far I got when I had to go to luncheon—and now I am half melted by the fearful heat of the Drawing Room which lasted two hours. It is a dull, thick very foggy day—71° out of doors and not a breath of air! I leave you to judge what this was in the crowded Drawing Room. However I am thankful to say I got quite well through it—and am not more tired than usual.[1]

Dear Papa and I are both so grateful to you about all the trouble you have taken about Princess Alix. May he only be worthy of such a jewel! There is the rub! When I look at Louis and —— at the charming—sweet, bright, lively expression of the one—and at the sallow—dull, blasé —and heavy look of the other I own I feel very sad . . . but enough of that. The contrast pains me very deeply. Let us hope that certain prospects may make a great change.

How people can be so worldly! I am sure the pleasures of the world seems too dreadful, too inconceivable to me now. People seem quite mad to one! Augusta always was fearfully pleasure-seeking—more than her mother and Mary even.

---

[1] This was the last Drawing Room attended by the Prince Consort.

Princess Alexandra of Denmark, afterwards Princess of Wales

Princess Elisabeth of Wied, afterwards Queen of Roumania

Poor Alice Skelmersdale has been waiting for 3 weeks for her confinement which has not yet taken place—terrible in this hot weather. Let me caution you, dear child, again, to say as little as you can on these subjects before Alice (who has already heard much more than you ever did) for she has the greatest horror of having children, and would rather have none—just as I was as a girl and when I first married—so I am very anxious she should know as little about the inevitable miseries as possible; so don't forget, dear.

From the Princess Royal

DAS NEUE PALAIS, JUNE 21, 1861

I have been to the races today which is the greatest bore imaginable, too dull, stupid and such a collection of silly people which one sees there!

The Princess with Prince Fritz and their children had visited England for several weeks.

FROGMORE,[1] AUGUST 17, 1861

My thoughts are much with you though they are so much engrossed with this dear, sad day! But your loving heart will rejoice when you hear that this morning's visit to the dear mausoleum has been most soothing and comforting to my poor bleeding heart—and that I feel the better in every way for it and so relieved and soothed and comforted. The day is most splendid—and the stillness and beauty of the whole spot—its repose and calmness—were most soothing. Beloved Papa is the cause of all this—he planned and designed it all! We walked there after breakfast with Alice and Augusta B.—carrying the four pretty wreaths, and others of myrtle and immortelles; dear Papa opened the gates, and we went into the vault which is so light and airy and nice and here we stood before the noble, granite sarcophagus on which and at the feet of which

---

[1] The Duchess of Kent had lived here, and her mausoleum was here. August 17 was her birthday.

we placed the wreaths—and here we remained some few minutes. Tears flowed—but they were soothing, not those bitter, despairing ones—which I shed yesterday evening before dinner when I sat in those dear rooms full of everything she used and liked. But I got calmer and better—the night was good—and this morning on waking I felt quiet and calm and the impression left upon my mind of living in the dear sweet house is pleasing—not one of desolation. This afternoon we return to Osborne.

Now, dearest child, let me tell you what I could not—for my heart was too full yesterday morning—how sad we were to see you go—how very, very pleasant and satisfactory your dear visit has been, what a happiness to us it is to see you so happy—how dearly we love and honour your beloved and excellent Fritz—and how we doted on the precious little darlings. May we all soon meet again, and may the good precedent of 7 weeks often and often be repeated—when and where you like.

OSBORNE, AUGUST 20, 1861

On arriving here from Frogmore I found your and dearest Fritz's letters, which were a delightful surprise and touched and pleased us both much. That you should love your own old home so much is but right, I think, and it would be hard for the poor parents if that were not to be! It's bad enough to lose one's children, so that if besides they forgot or cared but little for their home it would indeed be very cruel. But I feel each time happier in seeing what an excellent, devoted, loving husband, one so full of everything that is right and good—so honourable and so sweet tempered—you have; I know how you value him and love him (it would be better, dear, to show it a little less demonstratively before others) and I am sure you will ever try to make him happy. Never, dear, in little things show yourself teasing or wilful—don't so often speak of how different everything is here—don't contradict too much, though you do much less—for it lessens the good you can do in great things where your opinion, counsel, and advice is of such use and has done such good. You are indeed (in spite of many trials and difficulties in your position) most fortunate in having such a husband, and I am proud to think of the use you can be to him and to the country! You are blessed with a strong, powerful mind as well as a most loving heart, —you have inherited much from your dear Papa, and it is a great blessing to think of the good you can do—and of the blessing darling little William can be to the country some day. He is a very dear, clever, promising child—who we daily pray God to bless and protect. Your dear visit was one of unmixed satisfaction, though it could not take away the sadness of my heart—which has made me feel twenty years older! The loss of the head of the family places me in her place, and I feel the grandmother, which five months ago I should not! I feel everything so differently since that dreadful sixteenth of March.

VICE-REGAL LODGE, PHOENIX PARK, AUGUST 23, 1861

I feel much for you, dearest, since the separation from dear, excellent Fritz. It is a great trial, and experience does not make one more accustomed to it! But oh, dearest, what is such separation to the one I am enduring and shall have to endure till that blessed reunion in our eternal home! Oh! what it is to miss always her love, her solicitude, her interest, her tenderness! I feel that at times unbearably, and very bitterly like a child who has lost its home! I know that no one, not even dearest Papa, ever loved me as she did! Besides maternal love is a so different love—even if the other may be as great! And then woman's love exceeds what man's, I think, ever can be? That tenderness, that intense devotion, that attention—and delicate attention— in all trifles as beloved Grandmama possessed and showed— no man can have—and I feel that loss of all this—as life goes on—as each season passes—most acutely. On our leaving Osborne (which cost me much) on our voyage—our journey —how I missed and miss her! But then I turn towards the thought of her happiness—and I feel I must be still and thank God! The other vain but natural and dear regrets are selfish—but oh when one loves so dearly one must be a little so!

We landed at eleven—and came on here at once where we are very comfortable. Good Lord Carlisle[1] is all smiles and kindness, Lady Caroline Lascelles[2] is also in Dublin and dined yesterday evening. Bertie came for luncheon yesterday and already holds himself much better.[3]

My next letter will be from Killarney but I fear may be too late for the messenger. I shall however send by him a very pretty flounce just like what Alice has got—and it costs only £4. I hope you will like it. But it is not Carrick Mackross. There was one large flounce of that which is quite different to Alice's which cost £33—so I did not take it.

SEPTEMBER 6, 1861

About the lace, dear, I fully expected you would not take it now—but I will keep it, in case some future time you should like to buy it.

If you could get Edward L. to marry it would be a great thing—for you know if Ernest has no children—the whole property goes away to Catholics and utter strangers which one could not bear to think of. Handsome I don't think Edward.

I have read your long letter to Papa, and do feel for you, dearest, more than I can say! But I think we must be strengthened and comforted by what the old Baron and yours say—for that is the truth. It is a misfortune but it can't be helped—and if we got another Princess (but there are none!) who was infinitely inferior the mischief it might make with Bertie would be incalculable. Uncle E. is wonderful! It is very wrong though![4] Her mother's letter shows

---

[1] The 7th Earl, Viceroy of Ireland at this time.
[2] His eldest sister. Lord Carlisle was unmarried.
[3] He was serving with the Grenadier Guards on the Curragh.
[4] Uncle E. and U.E. in the following letter means Ernest, Duke of Saxe-Coburg. He had come down against the proposed marriage with Princess Alexandra, and in her letter to her father the Princess Royal had evidently voiced the objections in Germany to the marriage.

great discretion and prudence—and this being the case, you must not scruple speaking to her in the sense I wrote, for I have been thinking a great deal about it—and it is the Cambridges we must take precautions against—if matters are not to take a very disagreeable turn for me. Bertie and his wife must be one and the same with us—or else my peace will be at an end.

BALMORAL, SEPTEMBER 6, 1861

Papa has written to Bertie just as matters stand relative to U.E. and ———.[1] I must say I resent his conduct for he has no business to meddle with our affairs. Poor Lord Edgcumbe[2] died on board his yacht in the Thames—on the 3rd from mere exhaustion.

BALMORAL, SEPTEMBER 13, 1861

Your two dear letters of the 4th and 7th both arrived safely on the evening of the 10th—many thanks for them. I gave dear Papa the enclosures. Certainly there are difficulties enough and its having got into the papers is very annoying. However we are doing what is right, and I am sure that more mischief would result from preventing than promoting this affair. The more I reflect on it the more convinced I am of it. B. has written such a very nice letter about U.E.[3] that it quite touched us! So anxious not to appear ungrateful towards him. Now Princess C.'s father is very ill;[4] I hope that won't be another difficulty.

I am sure what you say about Uncle Ernest's shooting is true;[5] Aunt Feodore has heard the same. Dear Papa has been very fortunate. He has only been out four times and got eight stags; the two last times he got three each day.

---

[1] Princess Alexandra.
[2] Third Lord Mount Edgcumbe; he was A.D.C. to the Queen.
[3] Uncle Ernest.
[4] Princess Christian's father, Landgrave of Hesse-Cassel.
[5] The Princess Royal had written "I do not think he shoots half as well as Papa".

From the Princess Royal

Dear Bertie being here is a great pleasure to me, and I cannot say how I rejoice to be able to tell you what a very favourable impression he makes. I think him grown and improved in every way—and much more communicative than he was—we drove a long way together yesterday, and talked the whole time together, and I assure you, all he said was as nice and sensible as you could wish, he has a very good heart, and is very anxious to do right and please you in every way. Everybody is struck here with his speaking such good German. Our number of guests has increased, Prince Oscar of Sweden, the Prince of Orange and the Crown Prince of Saxony are here. The Queen is gone to Coblentz for two days and I am the only lady amongst this multitude of Princes. Dear Hermann[1] is here, I was so delighted to see his good handsome face again, he is so charming and I think everyone likes him, Fritz has a great predilection for him. We look after Bertie as much as we possibly can—as you can imagine that when so many princes are together, and so many of them mauvais sujets the conversation amongst each other is not very choice—and not fit for a young man like Bertie to hear, but he has so much tact, that he avoids it of himself. I spoke to the King about our plans and Bertie's on leaving this[2]—and nothing could be kinder than he was, he said I might do just as I liked, that he would think a certain union a very good thing for this country, in short I was much relieved, and he is really so very kind to Bertie, and to all the English that are here and takes pains to show how fond he is of England and of you, that I am quite touched and I only hope there will be no more rude articles in The Times to spoil the very great, good feeling existing just now.

---

[1] Eldest son of the Queen's half-sister—Prince of Hohenlohe-Langenburg.
[2] The Prince of Wales and Princess Alexandra were going to meet on the Rhine.

From the Princess Royal

The Queen's humour "sauf tout respect" is just at present a very great trial. Nothing pleases, nothing satisfies her. There are quarrels without end. Thank heavens there has only been one with me—and that one is over but I assure you it is not easy to please just now—and I have burnt my fingers very often. And as really the King has the best temper in the world when he is well and away from people whose whole occupation it is to irritate him, he really bears everything with exemplary patience and good humour. I assure you I feel quite worn out with continual useless discussions about things upon which the Queen is of totally different opinion from the King, Fritz and myself—namely respecting certain alterations in the church service. The Queen little by little tries to make it as Catholic as she can—and when finds she cannot succeed with the King she tries to get round other people behind his back—and when I remonstrate upon such proceeding I get into a nice scrape—and am in disgrace for a day. Please, dear Mama, keep this to yourself and dear Papa as I should be forgetting my duty if I complained of the Queen behind her back. Just now my life is no easy one and yet I feel that I am doing my duty—and can never forgive myself if for the sake of peace and quiet I gave up my opinion on subjects of such vital importance. I have got a thick skin and scenes don't take much effect upon me![1]

I can only give Bertie the greatest praise, he behaves as well as possible everywhere and I can see how pleased people are with him.

---

[1] Religion was one of the subjects of disagreement between the Princess Royal and her mother-in-law. Many years later, when Princess Alice died, the Queen (then German Empress) said "Perhaps it is just as well for her children that she has died; because, like all English princesses, she was a complete atheist." *The Empress Frederick*, by Princess Radziwill, page 153.

All you say about the King and Bertie is most kind and gratifying. One hears so much of the difficulties que cela fait peur but we both feel that we can't help ourselves and that there is no one else. Still I own it makes me anxious. One great thing is that we have talked quite openly about it to dear Aunt Feodore, who is most sensible and kind about it—and has herself written to Fritz H.[1] to urge perfect passivity upon the subject. I long to hear what you will have to say about it all. Your arrangements sound very good. Your praise of poor Bertie gives us great pleasure! Poor child, I pity him much and wish so much that she should be happy with us and show us confidence!

From the Princess Royal

BADEN-BADEN, SEPTEMBER 26, 1861

My beloved parents, I have but a short time before dearest Bertie leaves to write and give you an account of the meeting which seemed quite natural but which will now most likely appear in the newspapers and cause much sensation of a disagreeable kind.

I felt very nervous the whole time but Prince and Princess Christian are such charming people so full of tact and quiet that they soon put one at one's ease. I see that Alix has made an impression on Bertie, though in his own funny, undemonstrative way. He said to me that he had never seen a young lady who pleased him so much. At first I think he was disappointed about her beauty and did not think her as pretty as he expected, but as she has nothing striking or aufallend and her beauty consists more in the sweetness of expression, grace of manner, and extreme refinement of appearance, she grows upon one the more one sees her, and in a quarter of an hour he thought her lovely, but said her nose was too long, and her forehead too low. She talked to him first in her pretty, simple unaffected way. She was not shy. I never saw a girl of

---

[1] Fritz Holstein, her son-in-law. There were political difficulties between his family and Princess Alix's family.

sixteen so forward for her age: her manners are more like 24. She always travels without her governess when she is with her mother, and I never saw her mother say a word or give a sign to her about anything. I don't believe it would be possible to find a fault in her behaviour. She is so simple and unaffected and quite unaware of her charms. I think General Bruce must have been struck with her.

The mother and I talked a great deal together and I cannot say how struck I am by her great cleverness and sense, she is so quick and so sharp, nothing escapes her but all she said was so sensible that I only wish Papa had been there; he will have no difficulty with her. I think she "hears the grass grow" and with all is so gentle and amiable and ladylike.

He is handsome in appearance and a perfect gentleman in all he says and does; it is impossible not to like him and he seems such a good husband and father. He is not at all wanting in sense and one is struck with the contrast to Jules and Jean.[1] He was particularly tactful and never made up to Bertie at all and took no more notice of him than Fritz whereas Prince Frederick of Hesse[2] at Buehl[3] hung about and was always at Bertie's side. My conversation with the Princess was just as you wished. I began by saying that Bertie was very glad to make their acquaintance; the Princess said she was so pleased they'd met as it would make everything so much easier. She perceived that Bertie was not indifferent to her daughter but he had seen few young Princesses, she supposed and he might see many others who pleased him better. I asked her whether she would go to England some day and whether if the idea should become more serious on Bertie's side she would ever consent to let her daughter remain with you for a while. She said—Oh yes to be sure. Then she began talking of the possibility of the idea becoming serious and said that if her daughter ever did go to England she did not wish her to have anything to do with the Duchess of Cambridge or Mary or Augusta as they cultivated acquaintances and

---

[1] His brothers who were serving in the Prussian Army.
[2] Elector of Hesse-Cassel, Princess Alexandra's uncle.
[3] Near Baden-Baden.

*frequented society which she would never allow her daughter
to go near; that at Rumpenheim¹ she had had hard work to
keep her children away from them as Mary's conversation
was not fit for young girls; she had seen Mary flirt to that
degree that she had said to Alix who was present "If you ever
become such a coquette as Mary you would get a box on the
ears". Alix answered that she would deserve it. She said that
the Duchess of Cambridge and Augusta had almost teased
her life out about Bertie and her daughter, and that Augusta
had made her a great scene saying she knew all! Princess
Christian merely answered "I'm very glad you do as for
myself I know nothing!" Princess Christian told me Augusta
was not to be trusted at all that she could not possibly depend
on her word, as she had had so many instances of her having
made downright inventions. She says that Augusta is very
much against the thought of Bertie marrying Alix as she is
jealous of everybody—but still she wishes it to appear as if
she Augusta had arranged it and spares no pains to tell
people so. Princess Christian said "If something came of this
marriage it would not be political, thank God, but personal"
so you see all you wish me to say to her she said to me and in
spite of her deafness she is so quick that she understands one
in a minute the whole rencontre was arranged as naturally as
we possibly could. Fritz and I travelled under the name of
Berg and Prince and Princess Christian under the name of
Holk. Dr. Meyer² dined with us at Heidelberg and had not
the least idea who Count and Countess Holk were. He will be
enlightened by the newspapers soon.*

BALMORAL CASTLE, OCTOBER 1, 1861

For two most interesting letters have I to thank you, of
the 21st which I only received on the 29th and of the 25th
which Bertie brought us yesterday. We can never sufficiently thank you and dear Fritz for all your love, affection

---

¹ A castle east of Frankfurt belonging to Landgrave William of Hesse-
Cassel, grandfather to Queen Alexandra. This was a great holiday centre
for the Danish, Hessian and Cambridge families.
² Probably the Prince Consort's librarian and German secretary.

and kindness in this important matter. Bertie is certainly much pleased with her—but as for being in love I don't think he can be, or that he is capable of enthusiasm about anything in the world. But he is shy and I dare say we shall hear more from Alice, to whom he is sure to open his heart. What has relieved us immensely—is the right view Princess Christian takes of the Cambridges—for I own that was my only fear: she must indeed be a very superior woman and the Prince also—an estimable, sensible person! This opinion has opened Bertie's eyes entirely to the Cambridges. This is an immense load off my heart. I am sure the journey must have been of great use to Bertie; it has put new views and ideas into his mind. Poor boy—he does mean well—but he is so different to darling Affie! I am vexed to hear people defend that odious Prince of Orange—for they may try to bring him over—and propose him for Lenchen, and whatever other parents may do and think—we never will give one of our girls to a man who has led a life like that young man has done! You and I know what a blessing it is to have a spotless husband, and Alice thank God! will too; a poor girl does not know what marriage really is—but a mother does—and I for one could not give one of my sweet innocent, loving girls to an immoral man! Papa feels the same. By the by the Grand Duke of Hesse[1] has answered officially our demand of the young couple, having for 2 years the use of the Palace at Darmstadt by flatly refusing it and suggesting they might live with Prince and Princess Charles![2] The rudeness and stupidity of this is too great. Of course now they will live principally with us. It is the only thing fit and proper—and Louis is quite of the same opinion. In 2 or 3 years their house will be fit to receive them and meantime they must save in order to build. Tell Fritz: he will I am sure be shocked. For a few weeks at a time—they can live in the adjoining house, where Louis and Heinrich live—but this will not be fitting for them as a home. The people here would not like it. Poor Louis, I am sorry for him—but I think perhaps—it is as well—it is so.

---

[1] Prince Louis was the nephew and heir of the Grand Duke of Hesse.
[2] Prince Louis's parents.

I am grieved to hear of all the trouble and worry you have to go through; it is very trying. Patience and a sense of duty are the only way of getting through it.

I quite agree in your anxiety about Uncle Ernest. I love him dearly too, but his conduct to Papa has lessened my affection for him[1]—as well as his unkindness about Louis and others. You say no one is perfect but Papa. But he has his faults too. He is very often very trying—in his hastiness and over-love of business—and I think you would find it very trying if Fritz was as hasty and harsh (momentarily and unintentionally as it is) as he is! Today is the anniversary of that awful accident[2]—and we must again thank God for his great mercy and goodness.

BALMORAL, OCTOBER, 1861

What Duncker[3] has written is just what your Baron wrote to Papa. I must say that where political feelings take the form of calumniating personal character—especially that of a woman—it makes me very indignant. I believe that some years ago, 1856, there were some money transactions which reflected on the father; but the ménage was always perfect—and not a word can, I believe, be breathed against the mother; but against her mother and sisters, plenty!! Surely Wally knows all about that well enough. By next messenger Papa will write to you. We must spare you further trouble and annoyance—but I think the mischief and harm it may do is greatly exaggerated—and you have the sanction of the King and Queen.[4]

Bertie is much more occupied with his journey to the

---

[1] He had interfered over the projected marriage of Princess Alexandra and the Prince of Wales. "What annoys me is, that you spoke to a third person about such delicate and secret affairs and that you sent me a memorandum which was written by a secretary." *The Prince Consort to his Brother*, letters edited by Hector Bolitho, 1933.

[2] The carriage accident to the Prince Consort at Coburg.

[3] Professor Max Duncker, a Prussian deputy attached to Prince Fritz to advise on political matters.

[4] The Queen is dealing with various whispers against Princess Alexandra's family, and against the marriage.

Holy Land this winter and with the private affairs of Mr. this and Mr. that—than with the other! This tells volumes —I knew it would be so!

From the Princess Royal

The King starts directly after breakfast for Compiegne.[1] I own that "it closes my throat"—the very thought he goes without a Minister without a Secretary (for he has no one except a former footman like Rath). To me it is quite incomprehensible how they can let him go with only aide de camp and generals! Fritz and I did all we could to persuade him to take Bernstorff or Schleinitz[2] with him and the King was very much inclined to do so, but the Queen would not hear of it and did not rest until it was decided neither B. nor S. should go. The Queen says it is no official visit and everything which attaches importance to it is most undesirable. I cannot share this opinion at all as I do not see what the King of Prussia has to do in France if it is not for some distinct and certain purpose and I think he ought never to go out of his country without one of his Ministers. I cannot understand the Queen at all on this point. The disagreements (in fact quarrels) which have been going on the last few days between the King and Queen you have no idea of. I assure you Fritz and I both felt quite unwell from it—and all for the merest trifles upon which it was not worthwhile to waste two words. It is difficult to say who is in the right and who in the wrong as both are right and both are wrong—but the King never begins. Such scenes are most sad to witness anywhere but when it comes to be one's parents it is really enough to make one quite unhappy. I am only thankful that Louise is not present at these discussions. I pity both parties so much— as apart they are so easy to get on with, particularly the King and all the things which cause tiffs could be settled in one minute with a little goodwill.

---

[1] Where he was to meet Napoleon III. They in fact discussed generalities, and met on October 11 and 12.
[2] The Foreign Minister.

BALMORAL CASTLE, OCTOBER 7, 1861

I send you here what dear Papa has written down and which you are to send to the Princess Christian. Bertie has been and is most incomprehensible about it all! It is in another shape—the same thing which prevented any tears to be seen during those trying scenes in March at Frogmore, which upset me so and made me so unhappy. There is not the head to feel the things. But it really is dreadfully trying.

We heard yesterday such a beautiful sermon from a Mr. Stewart[1]—whom we had heard some years ago, which touched and enchanted us all, and has done one good for a month. The text was from Amos Chap. 4 v. 12. "Prepare to meet thy God, Oh Israel". It was fine! Those things affect me now so much! I feel now to be so acquainted with death —and to be so much nearer that unseen world.

From the Princess Royal

DAS NEUE PALAIS, OCTOBER 12, 1861

What you say about Bertie is true. I was quite sure it would be so, his head will not allow of feelings so warm and deep, or of an imagination which would kindle these feelings which would last for a long time! I own it gives me a feeling of great sadness when I think of that sweet lovely flower— young and beautiful—that even makes my heart beat when I look at her—which would make most men fire and flames— not even producing an impression enough to last from Baden to England.

It is natural that every woman should wish to be loved by some one person to a very great degree—and those who are by heaven's gifts so entitled to produce an impression of this kind cannot help feeling it hard sooner or later that they do not. If I were as lovely as she is I should feel that. Bertie may look far before he finds another like her. If she fails to kindle a flame—none ever will succeed in doing so. Still there

---

[1] On October 6 the Queen wrote in her diary "Mr. Stewart of St. Andrew's Church, Edinburgh, preached a most delightful sermon".

*is this to be said for him—he is young of his age; he is by
nature differently constituted (as regards his head) to many
others. That is not his fault poor boy. I love him with all my
heart and soul but I do not envy his future wife!*

BALMORAL, OCTOBER 10, 1861

Just as we were starting on Tuesday morning for our
most interesting and successful expedition—I received your
dear letter of the 4th. I share entirely your feelings about
the King's visit. Sovereigns should never go without one
of their ministers. I am very anxious to hear how it
passed off.

I must have a Council this morning, and my letter will
therefore be very hurried and confused. As for B——'s
affair it is not very prosperous. A sudden fear of marrying
and above all of having children (which for so young a man
is so strange a fear) seems to have got hold of him—but I
hope he will see this in its right light ere long—indeed he
does now when talked to.

Then follows an account of The Third Great Expedition described in
Leaves from a Journal of Our Life in the Highlands.

My heart sinks within me at the prospect of going back to
Windsor; on the 22nd we leave. Windsor bereft of her
neighbourhood—will be more dreadful than words can express. But God will support and help me—and the dear ones
I have around me will be a comfort and a support—but I
own I tremble at the thought.

BALMORAL CASTLE, OCTOBER 15, 1861

After a reference to the Crown Prince's birthday—" May God ever
protect and bless him and you"—the Queen goes on:

Many thanks for your dear letter of the 12 received this
morning and the enclosure. We are much vexed about Lord
Clarendon; really we do make a mess of every thing and
bungle matters and never do ourselves justice! I trust however you tell all this openly to Lord Clarendon and give him

good advice[1]—It will be a sad day here, for dear Louis leaves us and we love him so much! Altogether since Saturday there are nothing but departures. We are very sad! It is a sad fore-runner of that dreadful return to Windsor where every thing is the same but her alone; she will be missed in a manner which I dare not contemplate! But God will support me then and there as He has done before and I will not mope but try and struggle against it—as I ought—with heart and soul.

What you say about Bertie and that lovely young Princess is so true—so sad and the prospect a melancholy one! Still we must not despair. In his way he is occupied with her, for on Sunday evening he complained to me of not having received the promised photographs, which I think a good sign. The disputes and quarrels you mention are most distressing; I shall never breathe a word, but I fear Bertie has, and he is not discreet; I have constantly to warn him.

BALMORAL CASTLE, OCTOBER 18, 1861

May every possible blessing be poured down on our beloved Fritz—who is so very dear to us—so completely a son of ours—and whose goodness and excellence we know how to appreciate and value! May he be long, long preserved in health and happiness and you both as happy and united as you are now! Do you, my dearest child, try ever to make his life easy and happy and to soften the trials which are inseparable to this life and his station! I write before breakfast and much émue, as dear Louis left us at 8, and we dressed to see him off. Both were much affected; we shall miss him sadly—for he is so good and amiable and cheerful and on all these expeditions he has been such a pleasant dear companion! Though please God! they will very often be here together, it will never be the same again—and there is much melancholy in that word "never" which alas! I have—so

---

[1] The Princess Royal had written that Lord Clarendon, who was representing Queen Victoria at the Prussian Coronation, was "miserably lodged". He was at the Hotel Royal "fit for travellers but not for a special mission".

Princess Marie of Leuchtenberg

The Princess Royal with Prince William and Princess Charlotte of Prussia

cruelly experienced the truth of—this year—and shall yet have to drink that cup of bitterness to the dregs![1] But all does tend and lead to our eternal and everlasting life. If we but live and work for that! That is so great a comfort—so great a blessing!

But I will not speak gloomily—but revert to the great events of today—with which we are all much occupied! May God bless and preserve the beloved King and Queen![2] We have been studying it all very attentively last night. Dear Papa is shocked at Geissel[3] being placed in the position of a foreign Royal Prince. Why is that?

I forgot answering what you told me about E. and M.L.[4] in your letter of the 5th. It is nothing new to me as regards E. He is so awfully indolent that I can fully believe what is said on that score but as regards his not being kind to her—that is not so—further than that if he is bored, he can be cross. As for poor dear Marie, she does cry a great deal—but that is from nervousness and fretting so much about not having children! That is the real misfortune for both! Edward does not do good there I think. They are coming in the middle of Nov. to us—and I shall do my best to set E. right.

BALMORAL CASTLE, OCTOBER 21, 1861

I begin my letter here in this dear place which alas! alas! we leave tomorrow morning—at ½ past 9—and shall finish it at Holyrood—tomorrow evening. Many thanks for your dear letter of the 15th from Königsberg—which interested us much. The speech of the King has alarmed and rather distressed us.[5] Who framed it? We received all the telegrams

[1] i.e. By returning to Windsor without the Duchess of Kent.
[2] Their Coronation at Königsberg, where the first King of Prussia was crowned.
[3] Cardinal and Archbishop of Cologne.
[4] Prince Ernest of Leiningen and his wife.
[5] It amounted to an explicit assertion of the Divine Right of Kings, and was severely attacked by *The Times* which described the scene. " 'I receive this crown from the hand of God.' The King then proudly shook his sword to the four quarters of heaven." This last sentence was exaggerated. In fact he merely raised the sword and sceptre in sight of the congregation.

and do tell the King that his ended with Gott helfe mich which made us laugh so much.[1] Yesterday afternoon the view was glorious—the evening sun making the hills quite pink. Oh! those beloved hills—that pure air—those dear people—all must be left tomorrow. But I am truly grateful for what I have enjoyed. How fine everything at Königsberg must have been, and how glad I am there was such a German feeling!

WINDSOR CASTLE, OCTOBER 26, 1861

I can not sufficiently thank you for your 2 dear letters of the 19th and 24th. Many many thanks too for the beautiful drawings of crosses—so sensible and pretty. Your loving attention to and affection for me in sending them to me now—when you can hardly have time to breathe, has much touched me—and shows what a warm, loving and affectionate heart you have. I do need cheering for the existence here is completely changed—and the blank—the silence as incredible as painful! Our night journey was very successful, and I not the least tired. The return here was bad though I bore up at first.

Your description of the coronation was beautiful[2] and so graphic, and you know how I like those details. The whole must have been so magnificent, but so fatiguing—and I am so distressed to see that you had one of your very bad colds—though it is not surprising. Danzig[3] must also be very interesting and the King's reception—very gratifying. How pleased and happy I am to hear of dear Antoinette's[4] success —and your opinion and description quite tally with Uncle Leopold's. I do not begrudge it the dear Leopold.

How I long to see her! We are also so pleased at Prince Hohenzollern's being made R.H.[5]

---

[1] The German is grammatically incorrect. It should have read "Gott helfe mir". The mistake of "mich" for "mir" is Berlin slang.
[2] This letter is printed in *Letters of Queen Victoria*, III, p. 580.
[3] Two days after the coronation at Königsberg there was a reception by the City of Danzig in honour of the King and Queen.
[4] Sister of the King of Portugal. She had married Leopold, the heir of Prince Hohenzollern.
[5] Royal Highness.

Lord Clarendon writes charming letters—and his admiration of and love for you are most touching. He thinks you perfect! Pray thank him very much for his 3 very kind letters, and tell him how much I enter into what he says—and am sure he will have done much good. I will write to him on Monday—if I can.

WINDSOR CASTLE, OCTOBER 30, 1861

Many thanks for your dear letter of the 26th. Don't worry yourself about writing long letters and I fear mine today cannot be long—for I have just come back from a long ride (I am obliged to ride for my health and nerves—which are much tried here else I should—after Balmoral air and exercise—get quite ill) and must go out again a little after luncheon. I am so sorry for all your troubles of tooth-cutting, ring worm and colds! I hope that the great fatigues will soon be over—for you must all be half dead. Your ladies gave me full accounts but Valérie's hand is so dreadful—that we can hardly read it—and one letter of hers I had to burn without being able to read it! Pray thank them all though.

Those 2 drawings of crosses you sent me are lovely; one shall go into the dear Frogmore album—and the other into my copy of *In Memoriam*. Aunt Feodore will, I hope, be able to stay till the 13th but I don't feel quite sure. She told me of Augusta of Meiningen's intended marriage with Prince Maurice of Altenburg—but then not as certain. Alas! poor Mary. I really am in despair about it! It is all her mother's fault for she should have taught her better manners.

Mary Ponsonby (Bulteel) is here—looking very thin and in bad looks—the usual happy fate of poor brides! It is really such an exhibition; she seems very happy and I hear that their house is charmingly fitted up.

I forgot to tell you—that all our dear people, from Balmoral (that is all the servants, not the gillies) are coming up for the Exhibition next year—and the Grants, J. Brown—and Duncan for Alice's marriage. They are so delighted and one of the chief hopes is to see you. Mrs. Grant who has never been beyond Aberdeen and fears people will "look at her in London" comes up almost entirely to see you, and Grant declares that if you should happen not to come—he thinks "she will go over to Prussia as she says she must see the Princess Royal". This affection is quite touching.

WINDSOR CASTLE, NOVEMBER 2, 1861

We are both sadly grieved to hear of your being quite laid up and according to approved German fashion in bed. I have no doubt that the dreadful fatigue and excitement as well as exposure to great heat and draughts have brought this on. I fear you are very susceptible to cold—which everyone seems to get abroad. Many many thanks for your dear letter of the 19th. I shall be very curious to hear what M.C.'s[1] last chance is. We all wore the ribbon and order at dinner last night. And after dinner the band played for the first time—nothing that was likely to upset me. Still it made me nervous, and I almost dislike the sound of it now.

Poor little Leopold left us at 8 this morning. He cried when I kissed him—and wished him good-bye—but he was in good spirits otherwise. Leopold had a nice dark grey jacket—waistcoat and knickerbockers—which is what little boys wear so much now.[2]

WINDSOR CASTLE, NOVEMBER 4, 1861

I must write a line today to say how utterly in despair I am to hear of this terrible cold. I feared that you would be ill—for everyone said that they were knocked up and that the awful heat of the rooms was enough to kill anyone! But I can not bear to think of your having suffered so much. Show this note to Fritz and Wegner and tell the latter that I rely on his keeping you up—and giving you strengthening and nourishing things—as you belong to our family who are so easily lowered.

---

[1] Mary Cambridge.
[2] He had gone to the south of France for his health.

The good news of these last 2 days have cheered us much and relieved our anxiety. Really I think if they had not been better I should have sent off Dr. Jenner or have started ourselves. I began to get very fidgetty at no improvement—and so many leeches alarmed us all. I trust it was right? Dear Papa has written to you and I will say no more nor bore you with the account of my great depression. Can you imagine I have taken quite a dislike to music! It hurts my head.

Tomorrow evening before dinner we expect the Grand Duke and Grand Duchess Constantine[1] and their little girl —who stay till Saturday 9th.

Were you not dreadfully shocked about poor Ferdinand of Portugal's death?[2] We saw Louis[3] and Joao[4] for an hour yesterday. Poor fat Louis was so sad.

Dear Aunt Feodore I miss much. She left us on Thursday morning early. She read Parker's Life,[5] and herself asked Papa to let her read the book—but she did not like it at all.

We go on Wednesday for three nights to Madingley to Bertie for a change of scene, and to see Cambridge.[6] Today is Bertie's 20th (!) birthday!—we could do nothing—but give him a chasse. The feu de joie I could not have.

---

[1] Son of Nicholas I. He had married a Princess of Saxe-Altenburg.
[2] Brother of the King, born 1846.
[3] Brother of the King, born 1838, afterwards King of Portugal.
[4] Brother of the King, born 1842.
[5] This is possibly Theodore Parker's *Experience as a Minister*. He was a popular though unorthodox American unitarian minister. His *Sermons and Discourses* are still among the Princess's books.
[6] The next letter accounts for the abandonment of this expedition.

What an awful misfortune this is; what a fearful loss to his country and to Europe and to his family dearest Pedro is! We are in great sorrow and quite stunned and bewildered at the awful suddenness of this blow. Some time ago, I saw in the papers that Pedro had an attack of fever but thought it was nothing but one of those frequent little feverish attacks which foreigners so continually have from not attending to their stomach and bowels, and thought no more of it—and heard nothing from any one—till this day week like a thunderbolt arrived the news of poor young Ferdinand's death! This shocked us very much—directly alarmed me for our dearest Pedro, and I then recollected this report of fever which I had not thought of before. I telegraphed at once to Pedro saying that I implored him to be very careful and begged to know how he was. The answer came on Thursday (the last message we ever had from him) thanking us for our sympathy and saying "Je suis bien affaiblé par la fièvre le changement d'air me fera du bien". This relieved us greatly. Then on Friday we saw (as I told you) Louis and Joao and found the former terribly sad and full of anxiety for Pedro—who he said, was so imprudent and ought never to have gone to the Alentejo[1] which was very unwholesome. He promised to let me hear the moment he arrived—and was much moved in taking leave! I am so thankful we saw them and pressed them to come down for an hour. We were easy about dearest Pedro—and thought as we heard nothing —all was well—when on Sunday night we received at dinner (only ourselves)—that dreadful first telegram from Lavradio—saying that Pedro was "en grave danger", which I sent you the next morning. I own, I felt struck as if by lightning and gave up hope!

The next morning came and I remained in a state of dreadful suspense all day (dear Papa away)—but hearing nothing at night and knowing how long people often are in danger with this horrible fever—our hopes revived—when

---

[1] The district south of the Tagus.

on waking yesterday morning unwell all day from it—
with a violent, sick headache and retching! God's ways are
not to be understood, and we are quite sure that they are for
the best, but one can't understand why such a perfect being
—the blessing of his country and family—so gifted—so
excellent—should be carried off—at once and so young! For
him, dearest boy, I cannot repine! He was not happy and
Stephanie's death was a blow—from which he never could
rally—and now he is with his dear angel again—which it is
such a comfort to think of and gives one a feeling of blessed
calmness—and he has been spared the pain of having to
marry again. But poor dear Louis—can you believe him
King? He never I am sure dreamt of it! He was so devoted to
his brother! It is enough to kill him when he arrives today as
we believed he would. But he is not wanting and has seen a
good deal of late. Joao is extremely clever and said to be very
like beloved Pedro in character!

Oh is it not shocking, too incredible that he should be
gone! For the poor father it is too awful—he—who was so
proud of his five sons to have 2 swept away within 6 days! It
shows how uncertain life is! How large a family may be and
yet be half swept away in one day! It strikes me so peculiarly from two circumstances which occurred at Balmoral.
The one was that in speaking and lamenting over our
leaving Balmoral, Brown said to me he hoped we should all
be well through the winter and return all safe, "and above
all, that you may have no deaths in the family". Well—
and then the last day—he spoke of having lost (12 years
ago) in 6 weeks time of typhus fever three grown up
brothers! and one grown up sister. This struck me as so
dreadful that I told it Papa—and several others saying how
dreadful such things were! Now not 4 weeks after we left,
this same fever has entered a royal house nearly allied to us
and swept away two and nearly a third—though thank God
the accounts of little Augustus[1] are good and he has been
removed from the Palace. But here there are 2 "deaths
already". These 2 coincidences struck me so much since,

---

[1] Youngest of the brothers of King Pedro.

that they keep returning to my mind—like as if they had been a sort of strange presentiment.

Now, dearest, let me thank you a thousand times for your dear welcome letter of the 9th, though I am sadly grieved to see you still suffer. You must be very careful, but I grieve to see how sensitive you are to cold; I perceived it already this summer and you are going to begin with rheumatism. It is such a misery to be continually in fear of getting such attacks.

I wrote the other day by Papa's desire to the Queen very earnestly begging her not to expect you to go out so much of an evening and to let you remain at home occasionally as the intense heat of the rooms in which parties are given (which the Clarendons and Lord Granville told me was enough to make any one sick) was so very bad, and with the contrast out of doors was so very bad for you, and besides that your nerves required rest; and here is her kind but very explicit answer so that you must take her at her word and I will say to her I shall write to you. I am certain (and indeed you told me yourself so) that it is the impossibility of getting more out in the day and the foul air of those un-ventilated over heated rooms filled with human air, which gives you these horrid colds and relaxes the whole system, depresses it and predisposes you to catch cold.

I have already told you I liked "Sanny"[1] very much; I think her very sensible, speaking so sensibly about the in-judicious education of the Russian Princes and of the Russian mode of life and the perpetual bustle which she hates—and says kills her. She says she was so happy here. I found her a very pleasant companion and very gemütlich and friendly—and Papa also likes her very much. And the child is a great darling and excessively clever. He was very amiable too.

WINDSOR CASTLE, NOVEMBER 16, 1861

Repeating her grief at the death of the King of Portugal the Queen adds:

---

[1] Shortened name for Alexandra—Grand Duchess Constantine.

It has been a terrible blow to us—and to dearest beloved Papa—who found in him one entirely worthy of himself—which he alas! does not find in those where it was most expected and wanted. We have been much crushed by it and have since Tuesday (the day the fatal news arrived) not dined in society.

I have been much shaken again—but try to bear up as dear Papa (who has many worries) is so dejected and wants cheering. I try and ride out whenever I can as that is the only thing that does my health and spirits good.

From the Princess Royal

NOVEMBER 15, 1861

I hope you will forgive my using the Baron's hand to answer your dear letter just received. I return you here the Queen's letter with many thanks. The letter you wrote her was a little taken en mauvais part as I suppose her conscience smote her a little. The Queen said you did not understand our circumstances that it was so much more necessary to go out here than in England.[1] But how can the Queen[2] say that I am more at liberty to do as I please in that respect than the other princesses. Morning, noon and night she expects me to be at her beck and call, then with the greatest kindness she says I am useful to her that she cannot do without my helping her—it ends in my being a sort of slave. Two winters ago I resisted that a little but the consequence was that I was not in favour. So Fritz always says "never mind how tired you are, if it keeps Mama quiet it is in everybody's interest." But then you cannot be astonished if the late hours, the heat of the rooms and bodily and mental fatigue every night does knock one up now and then. You see this is rather a difficult dilemma. To establish a principle is still more difficult, as the state of things results from the complicated and abnormal state of affairs in the King and Queen's ménage. The Queen lives upon society and representation. She has a sort of morbid restlessness

---

[1] Not in Queen Victoria's sense of getting fresh air, but meaning to go out in society.
[2] Of Prussia.

which increases day by day which adds to destroying her health more and more. How can nerves which are in a perpetual state of excitement become restored to their natural condition? It is a craving which like that for stimulants is always on the increase. The Queen has an immensely strong constitution and does not know what fatigue is when she is amused and unfortunately this perpetual going out is the only thing which does amuse her and keeps her in good humour. The Queen expects everybody to share this and is displeased if I am wanting on any occasion great or small. Then you know that the etiquette here is very stiff and that Fritz likes its being adhered to. Consequently the respect due to the King and Queen demands that wherever they appear I should appear too. This does as much harm to Fritz as it does to me and when he left for Breslau, I thought he looked anything but satisfactory. He had rings round his eyes and looked yellow and fatigued—so different from what he did before we came to Berlin. The King cannot stand this life either. He knocks up now and then which the Queen says is owing to his having a bad doctor because this unfortunate individual remonstrates from time to time against so much fatigue. The Queen has no pity, nothing makes her so angry or impatient as when anyone is unwell, either the King, or one of us—or her ladies—or her maids. They are sure to fall into disgrace for the time, it is really something quite extraordinary this love of going about. How the Queen can find words to say to everybody passes my short horizon, but certainly the stock is inexhaustable. She sometimes makes three circles in one evening when we are all ready to drop. I think it must be a quality inherited from the Weimar family which certainly not everyone can stand. You will think it very wrong of me to criticise my betters but really I cannot help it. It must come out and I assure you it is no exaggeration.

From the Princess Royal

BERLIN, NOVEMBER 19, 1861

I have been reading all the authentic accounts about King Arthur, he really did exist in the 6th century and was buried at Glastonbury. Henry III had his bones dug up and they

— *368* —

were said to be of an enormous size. His Queen was found beside him and also her golden hair quite perfect then I also read the real old tale of King Lear by Holinshed from which Shakespeare made his play—keeping almost exactly to the original story which Holinshed placed in the century before the foundation of Rome and the scene in Gaul half in Britain.

This letter will arrive on my birthday most likely—I wish it was my eighteenth instead of my twenty first which seems a most uninteresting age—and yet I wish I was thirty sometimes perhaps I should be wiser.

WINDSOR CASTLE, NOVEMBER 20, 1861

I am well and dear Papa, too—and the fine and very unusually frosty weather has done me good.

WINDSOR CASTLE, NOVEMBER 23, 1861

With respect to what you say about my letter to the Q.—and your not going out yet, we must repeat that you must not yield to it, but be firm and stout about it. As dear Papa says—your health and strength is of such importance to them—that if you ruin it—they and the country lose the benefit of it. Papa is quite decided about it—and says it is your duty not to do what is bad for your health, and that you ought to have frequent evenings at home.

I was sure you would rave about the "Idylls" and quite agree about Guinevere. How much you must have read about Arthur to know so much about him. It is most curious. Have you read "La Mort d'Arthur"?

WINDSOR CASTLE, NOVEMBER 27, 1861

Many, many thanks for your dear letter of the 23d. As you do not mention yourself—I hope you are all right again and that the rash is past. Dearest Papa has written to you that he is not well—and so he is—but thank God! unberufen not one of his bad, old attacks—but a cold with neuralgia— a great depression which has been worse these last 3 days— but I hope will be much better tomorrow. The sad part is— that this loss of rest at night (worse than he has ever had before) was caused by a great sorrow[1] and worry,[2] which upset us both greatly—but him, especially—and it broke him quite down; I never saw him so low. Please God, this will soon be past and the heavy cloud be dissipated.

WINDSOR CASTLE, NOVEMBER 30, 1861

I can begin by saying that dear Papa is in reality much better—only so much reduced and as usual desponding as men really only are—when unwell. He was never confined to his room—and able to come to dinner and other meals—every day—and yesterday he went out with us to see the Eton Volunteers (200 of the boys). Dr. Jenner said yesterday evening Papa was so much better, he would be quite well in two or three days—but he is not inclined himself ever to admit he is better!

I do hope you will get away somewhere either to Dolzig[3] or elsewhere, for I have always been told that one don't recover well at Berlin.

It is quite true that Lady Londesborough (not Lonsdale) a handsome widow of J. Churchill's uncle[4] has been foolish enough to refuse Lord Granville, for a penniless young mauvais sujet Lord Otho Fitzgerald![5] She also refused Lord Wilton, which one can understand.

The great and all absorbing event of the day is the American outrage![6] The Government have decided (and they could not do any thing else—as the act is quite illegal) to ask reparation and if this is not given—we know what must follow. They are such ruffians!

The Eton boys looked so nice yesterday and had afterwards a breakfast in the Green House—which had a very

---

[1] The sorrow was the death of the King of Portugal.
[2] The worry was the conduct of the Prince of Wales.
[3] Dolzig was a large estate with an eighteenth century castle, in the south-east corner of Brandenburg, due south of Posen. It belonged to the Duke of Schleswig-Holstein-Augustenburg who had married the daughter of Princess Feodore, Queen Victoria's half sister.
[4] Jane Churchill.
[5] Afterwards Treasurer of the Queen's Household.
[6] The celebrated case of the "Trent".

pretty effect.[1] Today is dear Alice's and Louis' betrothal what a happy time that was—so unlike the present. But still the remembrance of it remains unclouded in my mind!

We shall go to Osborne on the 13th and truly thankful shall I be to see other scenery than this most tiresome—and this year to me—most distasteful place. I long so to see something new! I wish so I could travel a little, but that can't be—so I must not complain.

We have good accounts of Leopold; his arm is well again. But poor Sir Edward is sinking![2] It is very sad. Mr. Cavendish will go out shortly to be in readiness to do whatever is wanted.

WINDSOR CASTLE, DECEMBER 4, 1861

You know from last year—what it is—to be keeping company to a beloved invalid—so I can only write a line to say beloved Papa is improving, and I hope now each day will make a decided difference. But he is so depressed and so low—that it is always very distressing and the amount of sleepless nights has lowered him, besides the impossibility to touch food is very vexatious. This time the bowels are perfectly right. He likes being read to constantly. I have had to put our visitors for tomorrow off. The sketch of baby is charming, but why does she wear such extraordinary long gowns?

WINDSOR CASTLE, DECEMBER 6, 1861

Many, many thanks for your dear letters of the 3d and 4th, I am thankful to say beloved Papa is better today, and has had much more sleep—at intervals; he has also been able to eat more (from Monday night to yesterday evening he would touch nothing) and altogether they think now that this abominable feverish attack,[3] the result of worry and colds caught one after the other has unberufen unberufen taken the turn. But they tell me it will be slow—and

---

[1] A review of the Eton Volunteers—the last public appearance of the Prince. The boys were entertained in the Conservatory and the Prince, in a heavy fur coat, looked conspicuously ill.

[2] Sir Edward Bowater, a Waterloo veteran of 74. He had accompanied Prince Leopold to the south of France.

[3] Ominous words implying typhoid fever and not to be interpreted in the modern sense.

that we must not be discouraged by his not getting on more quickly. I will not now enter into details, but I have lived through 3 days of dreadful anxiety—though there was not one alarming or unfavourable symptom. I feel shaken—as for four nights I had not more than two or three hours sleep! And though I slept more last night and for Papa's own sake slept in the next room—I was for two hours in such a state of anxious suspense listening to every sound—that I feel very trembly myself. The doctors and I of course, would not have felt the least anxious had the dear invalid not been that most precious and perfect of human beings. Beloved Papa has never been confined to his bed, and is dressed and walks about his rooms. He is very irritable today. Dr. Jenner has been most attentive, and is excellent, very clever, very kind and very determined.

Good Alice is a very great comfort—she is so devoted to dear Papa and reads to him and does every thing she can to help and cheer me! There is nothing now, my darling child, to be alarmed about—but I own that the trials this year—have made me feel very old! Still no sorrow—no anxiety equals that about one's adored husband!

WINDSOR CASTLE, DECEMBER 7, 1861

Don't be alarmed about adored Papa but it is a sort of feverish attack which will be tedious—and you must not expect his being better for some days. But you will imagine easily that I am much worried. Sir James writes to you himself. Don't alarm others pray. You shall hear daily—and don't now, pray don't fret and worry—there is no reason for it, beyond the distress of knowing dearest Papa—at all unwell. But he doesn't suffer the least pain of any kind.

We shall not be able to get to Osborne when we wished, but that we can't help.

WINDSOR CASTLE, DECEMBER 8, 1861

Dearest Papa is going on as favourably as we could wish—and please God! we shall have no drawbacks and then we shall patiently submit to the tediousness of it. But it is all like a bad dream! To see him prostrate and worn and weak, and unable to do any thing and never smiling hardly—is terrible.

I am well but very tired and nervous for I am so constantly on my legs—in and out and near him. I sleep in my dressing-room, having given up our bedroom to dear Papa. He has changed for the day, according to his own wish, over to the King's room, and likes the change. He is not in bed, and walks from room to room. Nothing can be more attentive or clever than Dr. Jenner.

I know, my darling, how anxious you will feel—but all is favourable and you shall hear daily.[1] God bless you.

WINDSOR CASTLE, DECEMBER 10, 1861

Many, many thanks for your 2 dear letters of the 7th and 8th. Thank God! beloved Papa had another excellent night and is going on quite satisfactorily. There is a decided gain since yesterday and several most satisfactory symptoms. He is now in bed—and only moves on the sofa made like a bed, for some hours. He takes a great deal of nourishment—and is really very patient. But it must be still some days before the fever leaves him, and it is very, very trying to watch and witness. I am constantly in and out—and a great deal with him. It is my greatest pleasure and comfort—but it is a life of intense anxiety and requires courage. I am most kindly supported by Alice, Marie, Sir C. Phipps—and dear Augusta[2] etc. and Dr. Jenner is admirable and so clever. He and Mr. Brown[3] sit up every night with Papa since Thursday. Sir James sleeps here every other night. Lölein is most attentive and devoted and indefatigable, poor little Mayet also does his best.[4]

Dear Papa was much amused at the anecdotes about dear little William which are charming.

---

[1] Though the Queen could not herself write daily, the Princess Royal heard from the Queen's ladies.
[2] Lady Augusta Bruce.
[3] The Windsor doctor.
[4] Gustav Mayet, a Swiss who was appointed valet-de-chambre to the Prince Consort in 1859. He was later valet to Prince Leopold, and was subsequently employed by the Queen as a copyist. He retired in 1873.

I am sorry you have a cold, dear. Take care pray. I am sorry too there are so many troubles.

I can, I am thankful to say, report another good night. I am writing in the room next to where beloved Papa is sleeping. The doctors are satisfied; he holds his ground and contrary to what is generally the case with such fevers—he is not weaker, though he gets sadly thin. It is a dreadful trial to witness this, and requires all my strength of mind and courage not to be overcome—when I look at him—so totally unlike himself. We are very fortunate in the doctors. Jenner is admirable. It was thought necessary to satisfy the public to have another eminent doctor to come and see him, which I own distressed me much, but however I submitted, and Papa did not dislike it or object to it—and so Dr. Watson[1] comes to see him, who is a sensible, good, clever man. My time is entirely taken up with precious Papa— and so engrossed with him—that I can think of little else.

I am sorry the elections have taken such a very liberal turn. That will alarm the King.

---

[1] Afterwards Sir Thomas Watson—a general practitioner, and the author of one of the best text-books on English medicine.

On 13 December the Prince Consort's private secretary sent a telegram to Prince Frederick William advising him to prepare the Princess Royal for the news of her father's death. The Prince died on the following evening, and the news reached Berlin on Sunday, December 15. The Princess Royal, who was expecting her third child, had been forbidden to travel to England. This selection from the letters between the Queen and her daughter may be fittingly closed with a moving but dignified fragment from the letter which each wrote under the impact of overwhelming grief on December 16. The Princess wrote:

"Why has the earth not swallowed me up? To be separated from you at this moment is a torture which I can not describe."

On the same day her mother began her letter:

My darling Angel's child—Our Firstborn. God's will be done.

INDEX

A BECKETT, G. A. (1837–91), comic writer, 310

Abercorn, Lady, daughter of 6th Duke of Bedford, wife of 2nd Marquess and later 1st Duke of Abercorn, 122

Aberdeen, 4th Earl of, Prime Minister (1852–5), 117

Accession Day, the Queen's, 119

Acland, Dr. (1815–1900), afterwards Sir Henry, Regius Professor of Medicine at Oxford, 282

Adalbert, Prince. See Prussia

Adam Bede, 198, 217, 304

Adam Graeme of Mossgay, 67

Adelaide, H.M. Queen (d. 1849), daughter of Duke of Saxe-Meiningen, married the Duke of Clarence, afterwards William IV (1818), 56

Adelaide, Princess. See Hohenlohe-Langenburg

Adelphi Theatre, 194, 233, 305

Afraja by Theodor Mügge, 187

Ailesbury, 2nd Marquess (1804–1878), 305

Albrecht, Archduke. See Austria

Albrecht, Prince. See Prussia

Aldershot, 77, 96, 193, 206, 246, 247, 262

Alexandra, Grand Duchess, wife of Grand Duke Constantine. See Russia

Alexandra, Princess (afterwards Princess of Wales). See Denmark

Alexandrine, Duchess of Coburg. See Saxe-Coburg-Gotha

Alexandrine, Princess. See Prussia

Alfred, Prince (1844–1900), later Duke of Edinburgh and Reigning Duke of Saxe-Coburg-Gotha, 29, 38, 47, 73, 80, 83, 110, 128, 131, 134, 139, 140, 150, 153, 155, 157, 158, 183, 185, 188, 234–5, 236, 237, 243, 244, 245, 282, 291, 295, 334

Alfred the Great, 232

Alice, Princess (1843–78), later Grand-Duchess of Hesse and the Rhine, 29, 37, 73, 78, 79, 83, 85, 97, 98, 123, 142, 148, 171, 177, 180, 182, 183, 184, 187, 199, 202, 212, 214, 215, 217, 226, 227, 228, 236, 245, 254, 258, 267, 279, 280, 281, 285, 286, 287, 288, 290, 291, 303, 307, 324, 327, 335, 341, 342, 343, 346, 353, 371, 372, 373

Alison, Major, A.D.C. to Sir Colin Campbell (1835–72), 90

Altenburg, Prince Maurice of, 361

Alton Lock by Charles Kingsley, 210

Amalie, Queen, wife of Louis Philippe, King of the French, 217, 333

Anhalt-Dessau, Princess Hilda of, 314, 315

Anna, Princess. See Hesse

Anna, Princess. See Hesse-Cassel

Annual Register, 29

Anson, Mrs. G., daughter of 1st Lord Forester, married Major-General Anson, 156

Antonia, Donna, of Portugal, 360

Argyll, Duchess of, daughter of 2nd Duke of Sutherland, wife of 8th Duke of Argyll, 56

Becker, Dr., 71, 126
Beletti, Giovanni Battista (1813–1890), 91
Bellevue. See Prussian Palaces, 21–3
Bennett, Miss, 141, 143, 147, 149
Bentinck, Baron Adolph, 231
Bentinck, Major-General Sir Henry (1796–1878), later General, served with distinction in the Crimea, 99
Bernard, Simon, 98
Bernstorff, Count Albrecht von, 49, 52, 102, 143, 165, 166, 257, 355
Bernstorff, Countess, wife of above, 102, 143, 165, 286
Bernstorff, Fritz William, son of above, 175
Berwick and Alba, Maria Francisco Montijo (1825–60), married 8th Duke of Berwick and Alba, sister of the Empress Eugénie, 282
Biddulph, Colonel Sir Thomas (1809–78), 40, 53, 170, 260
Biddulph, Mary Frederica, wife of the above, 40, 260
Bingham, Lord (1830–1914), afterwards 4th Earl of Lucan, 208
Blankensee, Countess. See Carolath
Bloomfield, Lord, 2nd Baron (1802–79), diplomatist, Minister in Berlin, 106, 152, 200, 274
Bloomfield, Lady, daughter of 1st Lord Ravensworth, wife of above, 106
Blücher, Count, 165
Blücher, Countess, 39, 40, 49, 51, 78, 103, 106, 129, 138, 151, 160, 161, 164, 167, 214, 216, 219, 223, 227, 229, 230, 248, 251, 323
Bolitho, Hector, 354
Boucicault, Dion, 305
Bowater, Sir Edward (1787–1861), General; Groom in Waiting to the Queen, 371
Brabant, Leopold of. See Leopold

Brandenburg, Count, 165
Brandis, Christian August, 80
Brazil, Emperor of, 219
Breadalbane, 2nd Marquis, entertained the Queen on her first visit to Scotland at Taymouth Castle in 1842, 63, 268, 313
Brodie, Sir Benjamin, surgeon (1783–1862), 223
Brough, Robert (1828–60), dramatist, 35, 232
Brown, John, 139, 141, 146, 211, 361, 365
Bruce, Lady Augusta (later married Arthur Stanley, Dean of Westminster), 24, 317, 341, 343, 373
Bruce, Frederick (later Sir Frederick), Envoy to China, 157
Bruce, Colonel Robert (1813–62), afterwards Major-General, Governor to Prince of Wales, 142, 144, 147, 148, 152, 157, 282, 351
Brühl, Countess Hedwig, 265, 272
Brunow, Baron, 90
Brunswick, William, Duke of (1806–84), 36, 132, 148
Buckstone, J. B. (1802–79), 30
Bülow, Gabrielle von, 192
Bulteel, Mary (1832–1916), afterwards Lady Ponsonby, 29, 95, 127, 304, 361
Bulwer, L., 304

CALEDON, Lady, wife of 3rd Earl and daughter of 1st Lord Verulam, 73, 264
Cambridge, Adolphus, 1st Duke of (1774–1850), son of George III, 39
Cambridge, Augusta, Duchess of, wife of above, 10, 39, 69, 105, 108, 165, 236, 258, 259, 271, 292, 304, 322, 342, 351
Cambridge, Princess Augusta of, daughter of above. See Mecklenburg-Strelitz

and her husband to Gravesend, 29; receives farewell letter from the Princess, 31–2; as Chancellor of the University of Cambridge tenders congratulatory Address to the Queen, 33; approves the marriage of Stephanie, daughter of Prince Hohenzollern to King Pedro of Portugal, 34; receives further Addresses, 37; attends lecture by Faraday, 40; is concerned at imprudent remarks made by the Princess Royal in her letters, 46; inspects the White Lodge, Richmond Park, 47–8; holds evening discussions with the Prince of Wales, 49; letter from the Princess Royal on maintaining her position in her new life, 64–5; and another on the unhappy state of affairs existing in Prussia, 74–6; plans to visit Prussia, 91; attends review at Aldershot, 96; arranges Court concert, 100; visit to Coburg, 109; the Queen contrasts the imperfections of her childhood with the perfections of her married life with him, 111–2; visit to Kenilworth, 114; will not permit Princess Alice and Princess Helena to take part in the visit to Germany, 123–4; meeting at Cherbourg with the Emperor Napoleon III, 127–8; arranges for Prince Alfred to go to sea, 134; reproves the Queen for too much letter writing, 135; receives a letter from Baron Stockmar complaining of too much interference from England in the Princess's affairs, 137–8; evening lessons with Princess Alice, 148; visit to Westminster School, 152
1859
described as a hard worker, 174; enjoys French plays, 183; finds the German Communion Service more impressive than the English, 186; opens new bridge at Saltash over the Tamar, 189; field day at Aldershot, 193; dislikes lithograph made from a picture of Princess Alice, 199; letter to Prince-Regent of Prussia on the political situation in England, 200; present at Aldershot though unwell, 206; visits the Prince of Wales at Oxford, 215; ill and confined to bed, 215–6; reads and enjoys *Adam Bede*, 217
1860
evening discussions with Prince Alfred, 236, 237; letter from Baron Stockmar on internal crisis caused by changes in organisation of the Prussian army, 238–41; learns that letter received from the Prince-Regent of Prussia was copied and passed to the Emperor Napoleon, 243; attends the camp at Aldershot (which he started in 1855), 262; explains to Princess Alice the details of childbirth, 267; meets with an accident during visit to Coburg, 272; is pleased at the engagement of Princess Alice to Prince Louis of Hesse, 290; praises a memorandum on the Prussian Constitution prepared by the Princess Royal, 292; has private talks with Prince Louis of Hesse, 294
1861
gift of gold bracelet to the Queen on 21st marriage anniversary, 307; suffers from toothache, 308, 310; letter to the King of Prussia urging Prussia to maintain a non-military constitution, 316; his kindness to the Prince of Wales, 318; holds a Levée, 328; visits Cambridge, 333; attends his last Drawing Room, 342; plans a visit to the Duchess of Kent's mausoleum on her birthday (August 17), 343–4;

Lincoln, Lord (1834–79), afterwards 6th Duke of Newcastle, 249, 252

Lind, Jenny (1820–87), first sang in London in 1847; became a naturalised British subject in 1859, 91

Listowel, Lord, 1833–1924, 3rd Earl, 122

Locock, Sir C., 152

Login, Sir John, surgeon at the British Residency, Lucknow, guardian of Dhuleep Singh, 49

Lölein, 41, 373

Londesborough, Lady, wife of 1st Earl and daughter of Rear-Admiral Charles Bridgeman, 370

Londonderry, 3rd Lord (1778–1854), soldier and diplomatist, 249

Lottum, Countess, 272

Louis, Dom. See Portugal

Louis Philippe (1773–1850), King of the French, 94, 171

Louise, Princess (1848–1939), afterwards Duchess of Argyll, 83, 146, 175

Louise, Princess, of Prussia. See Baden

Louise, Princess, of Hesse-Cassel. See Denmark

Louise, Queen. See Prussia

Louise, Duchess of Saxe-Coburg-Gotha. See Saxe-Coburg-Gotha

Louise, Princess, daughter of Prince Charles. See Prussia

Louise, Princess de Putbus, 271

Louise, Princess of Hesse-Cassel. See von der Decken

Lucknow, relief of, 88, 100, 117

Lundgren, E. S. (1815–75), watercolour painter, born in Sweden, 307

Lynar, Countess Marie, 38, 213–214

Lyttelton, Lady, wife of 3rd Lord Lyttelton and daughter of 2nd Lord Spencer, governess to the royal children, her letters published (1912), 331

Lyttelton, Meriel, eldest daughter of 4th Lord Lyttelton, married John Talbot, 266

MACAULAY, Lord, 226

Macclesfield, Lord, 4th Earl (1811–1896), 115

Macclesfield, Lady, wife of above. Lady-of-the-Bedchamber to the Princess of Wales, 115

McDonald, Lady, 225, 228, 304

Macdonald, Flora, 172, 217

Macleod, Norman, Scottish Divine, editor of *Good Words*, 135

Malmesbury, Lord, 3rd Earl (1807–89), Conservative Foreign Secretary (1852 and 1858–9), 102, 209

Manchester, Duchess of, 58, 62, 156–7, 179

Manteuffel, General, 76, 131, 336–7

Maria II. See Portugal

Maria, Donna. See Portugal

Maria Theresa, Queen. See Naples

Marianne, Princess. See Prussia

Marie, Queen of Roumania, 312

Marie, Archduchess, wife of Leopold of Brabant, 52, 56–7, 117, 120, 128, 272, 273

Marie, Grand Duchess. See Leuchtenberg

Marie, Princess, of Baden. See Leiningen

Marmorpalais. See Prussian Palaces, 21–3

Martha, by Flotow, 121

Martin, Sir Theodore (1816–1909), trained as a solicitor; biographer of the Prince Consort, 2

Mary, Duchess of Gloucester. See Gloucester

Massow, Prussian Minister, 210

Maximilian, Archduke. See Austria

Maximilian I. See Bavaria

Mayall, J. E., 275

Mayet, Gustav, 373

Mecklenburg-Schwerin, Alexandrine, Grand Duchess of, 42, 50, 58, 128, 169, 256, 300

Vane-Tempest, Lord Adolphus (1827–64), 249, 252
Varnhagen von Ense, Charles Augustus (1785–1858), diplomat and writer, 234
Victor, Prince. See Hohenlohe-Langenburg
Victor Emmanuel II (1820–78), King of Sardinia (1849–61), and of Italy (1861–78), 132
Victoria, H.M. Queen—
1858
Satisfaction at the marriage of the Princess Royal to Prince Frederick William of Prussia, 27–8; visit to the British Museum, 30; asks for an exact description of the Princess's apartments, 34; praises her for her dignified behaviour, 36–7; discourages any arrangement for a marriage between Prince Christian of Denmark and one of her younger daughters, 39; her advice to the Princess Royal on her behaviour at court, 44, 47; cautions her against too great intimacy with Augusta, Duchess of Mecklenburg-Strelitz, 46; reports on the fall of the Government arising out of the presentation of the Conspiracy Bill, 53–4, 56; and on the formation of a new Government, 58; sees *Much Ado About Nothing* at the Haymarket Theatre, 59; has audience with out-going Ministers, 62–3; comments on the Prussian Royal Family, 68–9; her despair over the Prince of Wales, 73, 81; visit to Aldershot, 77; entertains Prince George of Saxony, 86–7; rejoices in news of the relief of Lucknow, 88; visit to the Kensington Museum, 90; to horticultural show at St. James's Hall, 93; to Watercolour Exhibition, 94–5; disapproves of the acquittal of Simon Bernard, 98; entertains the Queen of Portu-

gal, 102–5; her plans for the marriage of Princess Mary of Cambridge with the Prince of Württemberg; 105; is upset to hear of the Princess Royal's pregnancy, 108; urges the Princess to continue to wear mourning for family bereavements, 110–1; contrasts her unhappy childhood with life with the Prince Consort, 111–112; visit to Birmingham to open Aston Hall, 114; her views on child-bearing, 115; visit to Deptford to see the *Leviathan*, 118; advice to the Princess Royal on care of her teeth, 119–120; visit to the New Opera House to see *Martha*, 121; disappointment at proposed visit of Princess Alice and Princess Helena to Germany being disallowed, 123; alludes to some of the Princess Royal's faults as a girl, 125; is entertained by Napoleon III at Cherbourg, 127–8; visit to Leeds to open the Town Hall, 129; disapproves of prayers being said for the Princess Royal, 130; reports on improvement in the behaviour of the Prince of Wales, 130; her fears concerning the Regency of Prince William of Prussia, 134; urges that the Princess Royal should retain her English title instead of being called Princess Frederick William, 133; is distressed at Prince Alfred being sent to sea, 134; tries to get the Princess Royal to promise to attend her baby's christening standing, 136; approach by Baron Stockmar to the Prince Consort regarding the Queen's attempt to continue to exercise authority over the Princess Royal, 137–8; appointment of John Brown as her special servant at Balmoral, 139; her regret at leaving Balmoral, and

31136